TRANSFORMATION
of a
RAILROAD COMPANY

This is Burlington Northern

TRANSFORMATION *of a* RAILROAD COMPANY

Burlington Northern 1980–1995

BY EARL J. CURRIE

• RAILS NORTHWEST •

(*hardcover*) ISBN-13: 978-0-9961225-8-0
(*paperback*) ISBN-13: 978-0-9961225-9-7

Library of Congress Control Number: 2019938279

2nd printing, 2023

Manufactured in the U.S.A.
Design by Ariane C. Smith
CAPITAL A PUBLICATIONS, LLC

FRONTISPIECE

Burlington Northern had diverse holdings in both transportation and resources, as shown in a brochure's illustrations of service offered by rail, truck and air freight, and in resources by its holdings in timberlands, oil and gas fields, forest products manufacturing, and real estate. BURLINGTON NORTHERN.

ON THE COVER

(*front*) Two trains on Crawford Hill, Nebraska. TIM ZUKAS. (*back*) Unloading continuous welded rail from a train of rail "ribbons." BURLINGTON NORTHERN. (*front flap, dust jacket*) A drawing of the SD40-2, the most commonly used locomotive type in the 1970s and 1980s. BURLINGTON NORTHERN. (*back flap, dust jacket*) Icons that illustrate BN's varied industries. BURLINGTON NORTHERN.

CONTENTS

Part III • Reducing the Asset Base

Part IV • Innovation and New Directions

ILLUSTRATIONS

UNLESS OTHERWISE CREDITED, MAPS ARE BY MIKE BARTENSTEIN.

PREFACE

Several books have been written in the last twenty-five years or so on Burlington Northern and its predecessor companies, the most recent, being *Leaders Count,* a history of BN written by Lawrence Kaufman. Other books about BN are made up mainly of photographs of trains, freight cars, and locomotives, with a limited amount of text covering its history and legacy. Kaufman's book opened the door for additional writings on BN by qualified researchers and business historians, or in my case, by people who worked for BN who are willing and able to document and interpret their experiences, and also reveal the evaluations they have formed of events and decisions made since the company was formed.

My writings are not intended to be a history or chronology of landmark events in BN's history. An effort has been made to avoid repeating much of what has been covered by others and, instead, to write from the perspective of an operating officer who went "through all the chairs" of the Operating Department at BN and two of its predecessor roads to Senior Vice President–Maintenance and Transportation. My writings cover the series of changes in policies and directives, the challenging cases and conflicts, and the major undertakings that set the course. There is particular emphasis on the roles and contributions made by representative individuals and groups of employees and managers who, from all levels of the organization, came to contribute to the success BN built in its early years.

My first book, *Burlington Northern: A Great Adventure,* concentrates mainly on the years 1970 through 1979, when the foundation was laid for the achievements the company made in those years. My second book, *Transformation of a Railroad Company,* covers the years 1980 through about 1995, years of transformation and innovation in which BN broke away and differentiated itself from the alliances, practices, and norms that had been built up in the railroad industry over many decades. A period of high stress for the people of BN, it was worthy of interpretation and evaluation of the efforts they applied while working under a much different culture, with new objectives, strategies, and directives, while having to cope with a fundamental change in leadership style.

The statements, recollections, and opinions I have expressed are from first-hand knowledge I obtained in the years I was employed with BN, from research material I located or gathered over the years, and from conversations with fellow officers and employees with whom I have maintained contact over the years. Every effort has been made to accurately convey our recollections of events and the spirit of the times. My writings are centered on the work, talents, and commitment applied by the people of BN who moved it into a position of success in its first fifteen years.

It is hoped that those who had an association with BN in those years—whether as an executive, manager, employee, customer, business historian, or resident living on or near one of BN's lines—will find empathy and satisfaction in reading of the progress the company made through periods with mixtures of blessings, opportunities, turbulence, trial, and tension on its way to becoming a leader in the rail industry.

To avoid this manuscript becoming encumbered with footnotes, the bibliography at the end of the book lists the sources that have been consulted for this project. For direct quotes and certain key data, the sources are stated in footnotes. A list of "primary sources," i.e. references used throughout the book and not limited to one chapter, are listed at the end of the book.

Although I am fortunate to have had access to many highly knowledgeable and capable people, and excellent research material for these writings, I assume responsibility for errors or omissions in the text, tables, and drawings, for facts and opinions stated, and for interpretations of facts and events.

The pronouns "he" and "him" are used for clarity, to reduce the number of pronouns needed, and for grammatical convenience. They are not intended to limit the ideas or thoughts in this book to one gender.

ACKNOWLEDGEMENTS

THE POSSIBILITY OF WRITING THIS history of Burlington Northern's first two decades originated with Robert W. (Bob) Downing, who held positions as Executive Vice President, President, and Vice Chairman–Chief Operating Officer from BN's formation in 1970 to his retirement in 1976. He felt it was important that BN's history be reviewed and documented by employees and managers who contributed to the success the company had in merging the properties and organizations of four railroad companies, and then in taking on the challenge of upgrading a large part of the railroad's network to handle the unprecedented tonnages of low-sulfur coal mined in the Powder River Basin. I was privileged to spend many days with Bob Downing while serving as an operating officer on BN, as well as after his retirement as he shared his recollections, insights, and evaluations of many aspects of BN's history.

I was also fortunate that Norman Lorentzsen, who followed L. W. (Lou) Menk as President and CEO, contacted me when he learned I had started to write a history of BN. Norman encouraged me to look over and include some of his writings on specific issues in the late 1970s when he was responsible for leadership and direction of both the Transportation and Resources divisions.

I am grateful to Francis J. (Fran) Coyne, retired Vice President–Human Resources, for putting me in touch with C. Robert (Bob) Binger, who headed BN's Resources Division from 1970 through 1980. Bob gave generously of his time and provided insights to the strategies he employed to generate the ever-increasing level of operating income that was sorely needed to finance the high level of operating expense and capital expenditures to upgrade and expand the capacity of its railroad.

I wish to thank two senior officers in BN's Finance Department, Robert F. (Bob) Garland and Raymond C. (Ray) Burton, who contributed generously to these books, sharing experiences that were highlights in the years they held positions of leadership. Other Vice Presidents who took time to meet with me on one or more occasions to provide information or simply to refresh my memory of certain events and challenges were David Ylkanen (Human Resources), Edward Bauer (Mechanical), Wayne Hatton (Regional Vice President and also Vice President–Transportation), Fran Coyne, Norm Doerr (Purchasing and Material), and Roger Nelson (Safety).

Several officers in the Engineering Department (the function responsible for maintenance and construction of track, bridges, buildings, and signals) have been particularly helpful, among them Mike Armstrong, George Lamphier, Dave Hesterman, Bill Ferryman, Jim Daume, Cliff Inmon, Chuck McCormick, Don Rogers, Eldon Ficke, Mark Sprattler, Carl Peglow, Sam Melonas, Ralph Knutson, and Bill Bergmeier. In the Mechanical function (responsible for maintenance of cars and locomotives), I am especially grateful to Ed Bauer for sharing the strategies and implementation plans for the innovations he developed so successfully in the 1980s. Other Mechanical officers who have been helpful include Bob Seeley, Max Lary, Tom Hackney, and John Hilliard.

A number of operating officers who served as Division or Terminal Superintendents in those years shared a great deal about the challenges to which they applied their leadership skills. Among them were Tom Lynch, Cliff Tye, Mike Martin, Bob Seeley, Mike Holsteen, Dave Burns, Bill Reilly, Dan Watts, Max Steele, Wayne Eisenman, and Don Maze. Other operating officers whose work contributed greatly to the company's success and were very helpful to me were Bob Hanson, Jerry Wick, Jake Greeling, Forrester Dusell, Pat Keim, Cal Evans, Jerry Pinkepank, Al Johnson, and Greg Mangieri.

Jim Hudson, a retired Conductor for the Spokane, Portland and Seattle (SP&S) Railway and BN at Vancouver, Washington, organized a meeting of six former SP&S employees. These men had also served as General Chairmen or held other positions of leadership in the two unions that represented Conductors and Brakemen in the United Transportation Union (UTU), plus Engineers who belonged to the Brotherhood of Locomotive Engineers (BLE). This group of union officers played a major role in developing the unprecedented agreements BN and the unions made for wage guarantees and lifetime job protection. Reaching agreement with the unions was vital in the efforts undertaken by the applicant railroads to get the merger approved upon reconsideration by the Interstate Commerce Commission. Meeting with these union officials provided a unique opportunity for me to learn of the contribution they made in working with the railroad companies' Labor Relations officers to make the proposed merger a reality. Jim Hudson also was helpful in providing insights to the new work environment that employees of the former SP&S Railway had to adjust to in the early years of the consolidated operation.

Merle Geiger, a Locomotive Engineer in Vancouver who advanced to President of the Brotherhood of Locomotive Engineers (BLE) in the 1980s, provided insights on the implementation of merger agreements and on how many new and vital issues were handled several years after the merger was consummated.

Wendell Bell, Assistant Vice President and Attorney in BN's Labor Relations Department, provided excellent assistance to me in working through details of landmark events in the development of new or revised agreements governing the work of the operating crafts from 1980 and into the 1990s. Especially valuable was the opportunity to draw on Wendell's participation in preparing the strategies applied in the effort to reach agreement with the UTU for reducing the number of employees required on train crews on a major part of the BN system.

I am grateful to Robert L. (Bob) Portsche, Operating and Safety Officer for BN, and in later years, for the Federal Railroad Association (FRA), for his assistance in making sure I was drawing upon a consistent set of numbers and facts relative to BN's record in employee safety.

I am fortunate to have had the interest, time, and support of several BN employees in my effort to reveal details about the changes in work environment and other cultural adjustments they had to work through as the merger was implemented. Among the employees who deserve particular recognition are John Langlot (Conductor at Spokane), Gary Nelson (Conductor at Minneapolis), Dale Wright and Joe Donovan (Engineers at Minneapolis), Bob Neumeister (Engineer at La Crosse), Alex Hasson (Engineer at Whitefish), and Maury Godsil (Yardmaster at Galesburg).

I particularly enjoyed putting together the anecdotes of a selected group of Operating and Maintenance employees and officers who worked mainly on the Alliance and Nebraska divisions in the years when BN was going all-out to hire and train the large number of people needed both to upgrade and expand the capacity of its railroad, and to operate the increased number of trains needed to handle the heavy tonnage of coal being mined in the Powder River Basin. I was able to meet with most of these railroaders or talk with them by phone, but for a few of them, I had to rely on information from their fellow workers or reports about their work in company publications. In any event, it was rewarding to prepare brief summaries of work histories and remembrances of this representative group of railroad people in the chapter entitled "How and Why They Came to BN."

I wish to give a great amount of thanks and credit for helping me get these two manuscripts finalized and ready for publishing to Dave Burns, a long-time friend and fellow operating officer. Dave generously applied his fine skills as a leader, teacher, and communicator to these tasks over the five years this manuscript has been under development, review, and reconstruction. Through the entire process, Dave's talents have been very valuable to me.

There are many members of what I would call the "supporting cast" who made it possible to complete my writings on BN history. Amy Jo Stockinger and I have worked together for many hours in assembling the various drafts and making an untold number of revisions to finally get the text in shape. I am fortunate she has been available to do similar work on other books and essays I have written about railroad operations in the past ten years.

Mike Bartenstein, a retired Engineer for Alcoa at Malaga, Washington, drew all of the maps I have used. Having a person with Mike's skills at graphics, together with a good knowledge of railroad history and operations, has been fortunate.

I have been fortunate to have had the service of Ariane C. Smith of Capital A Publications for editing and layout. I am well pleased with the exceptional skills and experience Ariane demonstrated in editing, page layout, design of the dust jackets, and the general advice she provided on creating attractive and professional publications. I became acquainted with the high quality of work done by Ariane in my reading of *The Rusty Dusty*, written by John Langlot and Mac McCulloch about their work as employees on the Great Northern's Wenatchee–Oroville line. I was so favorably impressed that I asked John and Mac for Ariane's e-mail address. I am fortunate that she was willing to edit the two books I had nearly completed on Burlington Northern history.

I am grateful to Don Hofsommer for his willingness to review the entire manuscript when it was still in the early stages of development. With the success Don has had in writing several widely acclaimed books on railroad history, I was fortunate that a person of his standing would take the time needed to advise me on how the manuscript should be constructed and prepared. Don evaluated the content as to the significance it would have to potential readers, and offered advice as to the style of writing that should be applied in reviewing the history of a railroad company.

The personnel at several libraries were very helpful in locating materials of interest in various activities and local issues involving BN. Among those libraries were the John W. Barriger III National Railroad Library in St. Louis, the libraries of the Minnesota and Montana historical societies, public libraries in Alliance, Nebraska; Gillette and Douglas, Wyoming; Spokane, Washington; and Missoula, Montana; and the Galesburg (Illinois) Railroad Museum, the Newberry Library in Chicago, and the libraries of the Great Northern and Northern Pacific historical societies.

In looking back over my career of forty-two years in the rail industry, I reflect on the large number of fine people who had a hand in my development and the progress I made in my career as a railroad operating officer. It has been through that kind of support that I developed the spirit, interest and background needed in later years to undertake the writing of a history of the company and its predecessor railroads that opened opportunities for me to advance and contribute toward their success. These railroaders became part of a network I could rely on when for coaching, advice, or other input at important junctures. For all of the "rails" I worked with who applied professionalism in their work and upheld the standards, values, and traditions that helped make BN and the other freight railroads of North America that are ascribed by many as "the envy of the world," I am most grateful and respectful.

EARL J. CURRIE
December 4, 2016

INTRODUCTION

BACKGROUND AND PURPOSE

In 1980 and '81, BN was hit by three major life-changing events: merging with the Frisco Railroad, the hiring Richard Bressler to replace Norman Lorentzsen as president and CEO, and the advent of deregulation of the rail industry that came with passage of the Staggers Act. Having even one of these three events would have been enough to cause a transformation of the company, but having all three occur within only a short time really set things astir in every department and function in the company.

This book contains considerable detail on the aggressive command-and-control style of leadership and a series of new methods in operations and maintenance that were applied upon merger with the Frisco Railroad. Deregulation of pricing brought the rail industry into a highly competitive environment that required established rates be reduced in order to secure new business, and to be able to make long term contracts with shippers to prevent the loss of business to competitors who had become free to negotiate rates without government review or restriction. To maintain profitability, operating and maintenance costs had to be drastically reduced, by improving productivity, reducing the size of the management staff and the workforce, applying tighter and more challenging standards of performance, and somehow, reducing the enormous cost of the merger protection payments BN was required to make to employees who held jobs at the time of the 1970 merger. The author relates his experiences and evaluations of the methods applied in making these and other fundamental changes in culture, work methods, and the company's system of values in those times.

BN was ahead of most of the rail industry in preparing for deregulation, by starting to aggressively reduce its costs early in 1981 in anticipation of passage of the Staggers Act. BN developed creative marketing programs to attract new business and to offer to negotiate long-term contracts to retain business. BN was ahead of its competition in setting up programs for the sale or lease of marginal branch lines, and even some of the secondary lines, to start-up, low-cost operators. This strategy made it possible to keep hundreds of miles of line in service that otherwise might have been shut down and abandoned in a few years. With upwards of 25 percent of the U.S. railroads' single-car shipments originating or terminating on a short-line railroad, the line sales program has paid off for many shippers, as well as for BN and its short-line partners.

BN may have pushed the line-sale concept beyond limits intended in the Staggers Act when it leased its 530-mile Laurel–Sandpoint main-line corridor and several connecting branch lines to a prominent and successful industrialist in Montana. However, taking that aggressive approach turned out to be a successful venture in meeting the interests of shippers, local communities, and the people who were hired to work for the new company.

With the coming of deregulation, it became possible to turn intermodal service into a market segment with a bright future for BN. On a railroad company, intermodal service is generally defined as the movement of containers and truck trailers between terminals by rail, and in combination with truck service used for delivery and pickup. BN and the rail industry embraced the idea of shifting a large amount of intermodal business away from trailers to double-stack-container equipment and then running much longer and heavier dedicated intermodal trains. With this change, the economies of scale inherent in railroading took hold, making intermodal service a business profitable enough to justify major expansion of intermodal terminals and to acquire the locomotives needed to handle it on a large-scale basis. With competitive pricing and improved service-delivery practices, BN's intermodal business grew rapidly.

To lead the company in this new competitive environment and to increase the return from capital investments made in recent years, the board of directors brought in a new chief executive officer, Richard M. Bressler, from Atlantic Richfield. Bressler immediately set goals to increase revenues and profitability from BN's non-rail assets, primarily by investing heavily in the oil and gas business. By setting up a holding-company structure, each of the company's units was put on a more independent basis, and each charged with generating cash that would be "dividended up" to the holding company where decisions would be made on the investments and capital expenditures needed to bring the net income of the non-rail units up to at least the level the railroad company generated.

The railroad was charged with reducing the amount of maintenance capital it required to maintain the roadway and equipment to the standard and level of utility needed for safety and to be able to provide competitive service. Out of that mandate came innovations in engineering and maintenance that would extend the service life of expensive assets, mainly for rail, ties, locomotives, and freight cars. BN's Engineering and Mechanical departments became industry leaders in developing and applying new technology and maintenance methods that reduced the amount of capital required annually to replace or renew those assets on a normalized basis. At the same time, capital expenditures for equipment or to apply new technology (defined as productivity capital) that would reduce costs enough to generate a high rate of return were encouraged and authorized without delay.

An aggressive, controversial agenda was undertaken to reduce the cost of compensation and benefits of railroad managers and employees to levels more in line with those paid in other basic industries, including over-the-road trucking companies. This approach immediately brought confrontations with the rail unions, which by tradition and past practice were not open to revising any of the agreements they had made over many decades for work rules, the staffing of train crews, and the level of wages and benefits they had negotiated in the past. By increasing the income it was earning from non-rail sources, BN anticipated having the strength it would need to "go it alone," i.e., negotiating independently with the unions for new contracts, instead of simply giving its proxy to a rail industry team of negotiators empowered to represent all of the nation's railroad companies. That effort, together with some unprecedented and creative efforts to reduce labor costs, resulted in considerable unrest between labor and management on BN. The unions challenged some of BN's initiatives through the courts and the process for appeal provided under the Railway Labor Act. In the end, BN had to settle such major issues as the number of employees required on train crews and yard switching crews on nearly the same basis as had been agreed to by the rest of the industry in national negotiations.

There was a strong drive from the early to mid-1980s to reduce the railroad's asset base in order to help improve the rate of return on invested capital. That effort went so far as to sell or abandon some key segments of main line trackage where BN had alternate routes. There were some senior executives who had little faith in the railroad's ability to grow or even to hold the business it had, due to the competition it faced and the difficulty it was having in pricing its service competitively due to its high labor costs. Hence, it was believed the railroad should take aggressive steps to reduce the capacity and extent of its network, including some segments of its main lines.

In that process, some controversial decisions of a permanent nature had to be made. With the growth in coal, grain, and the import of containerized freight that accelerated in the mid-1980s, some line congestion and general inefficiency developed from the loss of line capacity on some parts of the system, or from having to rely on a less efficient route that remained in service. Some important examples of the impact of decisions that reduced line capacity and operating flexibility such as abandonment of the main line of the former SP&S Railway between Pasco and Spokane are covered in the text.

The decision BNI made in 1988 to separate its railroad company and resource-based units by a spin-off of its Burlington Resources unit produced an excellent return for the shareholders, whose interest was first on BNI's agenda. It also was of great benefit to the railroad and its people to be released from restrictions on the amount of capital it could invest in growth opportunities and

THE 1980S: THE DECADE WHEN EVERYTHING CHANGED

THE FOCUS ON MAXIMIZING SHAREHOLDER VALUE AND AN EASY-COME, EASY-GO ATTITUDE TOWARD the workforce started during the 1980s. But there were larger forces at work: major innovations in capital markets, deregulation of financial institutions, and significant increases in the level of debt deemed acceptable for U.S. firms.

Corporations were increasingly seen as bundles of tradable assets that could be reconfigured or restructured to maximize short-term financial returns. Power within corporations shifted from leaders responsible for production, human resources, and labor relations to finance executives, who served as agents of ever-more-demanding financial markets. CEO income rose rapidly as stock options and other incentives linked to share price became core elements of compensation packages. The financial sector attracted more top talent from business schools (and other university majors with strong mathematical training) and absorbed a higher proportion of national income.

These trends built stronger pressure for short-term returns, which in turn prompted firms to cut jobs as a preemptive act rather than a last resort. The net effect was to chip away at the more balanced view of the corporation as an entity with responsibilities to other stakeholder groups, not just shareholders.

Author's note: Burlington Northern was among the many large corporations that established strategies and goals in the 1980s to maximize shareholder value as its highest priority. A strong corps of executives was bought in at the holding-company level and to each business unit to plan and oversee this shift in BN's system of values.

SOURCE: Thomas A. Kochan, "A Jobs Compact for America's Future," *Harvard Business Review*, March 2012, page 70.

for modernizing its roadway and equipment. The price the railroad paid for gaining its independence was the assumption of $2.7 billion of debt that turned it into a highly leveraged company. It took until 1995 to work that debt down to an acceptable debt-to-equity ratio.

Throughout this book there is an emphasis on the evolution of culture and leadership style that impacted all levels of management and in all areas of activity in BN. It is amazing how well the people weathered the ever-changing winds, maintained their work ethic, and continued to work hard in making improvements to BN's maintenance and operating practices. No matter who was in charge or what course or direction was being taken, they did what was expected of them. Most people of the railroad figured that since they would still be around when the new phase of transformation had passed, they had better work hard enough to maintain the basics of railroading. They wanted to insure the railroad would be in the shape they would need to run it successfully.

Overall, BN's franchise was so strong that it could withstand periods of changing, differing, or even unfavorable agendas, as well as whether some officers may have lacked the appreciation, respect, or knowledge of what a treasure of a company BN was, through its heritage, legacy, and because of the quality of the franchise it held.

Through the years of a challenging and sometimes difficult transformation, BN and its people became stronger and better equipped to manage the railroad. The company built a reputation for innovation in pricing and in its systems for service delivery. It became the rail-industry leader in innovation in the design and maintenance of its track structure and for lowering the cost of replacing rail, ties, and ballast. BN also developed a new structure for ownership, maintenance, and utilization of locomotives. By 1984 BN had the lowest operating ratio of the major North American railroad companies. The rather complex, sometimes over-staffed organization structure set up in the 1970s was replaced with a flatter, simplified structure. Reducing the bureaucracy helped speed up decision making and responsiveness to new opportunities.

The safety of employees and in train operations improved considerably in the early 1980s. This book also covers the serious setbacks to safety that occurred in 1984 after those years of improvement, and also the changes in leadership in safety that built an enduring foundation for all of BN's operating and maintenance practices in later years. Employee pride and technical skills were built up in this period of transformation. BN became better positioned to handle the ever-increasing challenge to move higher tonnages of coal and to maintain what had become the highest tonnage lines of railroad anywhere in the world.

The new values and attitudes BN people had developed toward innovation, flexibility, and responsiveness in the new competitive, deregulated environment were helping create new opportunities for expanding intermodal service and such international business as grain, import automobiles, and containerized shipments of consumer goods.

Throughout this book, emphasis is provided on how BNI's shareholders benefited from the years of its transformation from a successful "standard" type of railroad model to that of an aggressive, goal-oriented business that was more typical of how large companies operated in the 1980s. Many of the successful, transformative undertakings made BNI a leader in both its rail and resource-based units. However, it is reasonable to question whether the same or even greater accomplishments could have been made if less stress and upheaval had been imposed on the organization and its people, and if more respect had been given the values, norms, and general business culture that had been instilled in BN's first decade.

LIST OF ACRONYMS, ABBREVIATIONS, AND SHORTENED NAMES

AAR	Association of American Railroads
ABS	Automatic Block System
AREA	American Railway Engineering Association
BLE	Brotherhood of Locomotive Engineers
BRC	Belt Railway Company of Chicago
BN	Burlington Northern
BNI	Burlington Northern, Inc.
BNRR	Burlington Northern Railroad
CB&Q	Chicago, Burlington and Quincy (Burlington Route)
CGW	Chicago Great Western
CSTPM&O	Chicago, St. Paul, Minneapolis and Omaha ("the Omaha")
CMSTP&P	Chicago, Milwaukee, St. Paul and Pacific ("the Milwaukee Road")
CN or CNR	Canadian National Railway
C&NW	Chicago and North Western Railway ("the North Western")
CP or CPR	Canadian Pacific Railway
C&S	Colorado and Southern
CTC	Centralized Traffic Control
DM&IR	Duluth, Missabe and Iron Range ("the Missabe")
DOT	Department of Transportation (may be federal or state)
FRA	Federal Railroad Administration
FW&D	Fort Worth and Denver
GN	Great Northern
GTW	Grand Trunk Western
IC	Illinois Central
ICC	Interstate Commerce Commission
Manitoba Road	St. Paul, Minneapolis and Manitoba
Metra	An operating organization established by the Regional Transportation Authority for the greater Chicago area for rail commuter train service on lines acquired by Metra, or to negotiating purchase of service agreements for service on lines that continued to be in the ownership of privately-owned railroads, among them BNSF and UP.
Milwaukee Road	Chicago, Milwaukee, St. Paul and Pacific
Missabe Road	Duluth, Missabe and Iron Range
MP	Milepost or Missouri Pacific
MRL	Montana Rail Link
MSTP&SSM	Minneapolis, St. Paul and Sault Ste. Marie ("the Soo Line")
M&STL	Minneapolis and St. Louis

North Western	Chicago and North Western
NP	Northern Pacific
NS	Norfolk Southern
OE	Oregon Electric
OT	Oregon Trunk
PC	Penn Central
PCRR	Pacific Coast Railroad
PRR	Pennsylvania Railroad
RRV&W	Red River Valley and Western
RTA	Regional Transportation Authority
SI	Spokane International
Soo Line	Minneapolis, St. Paul and Sault Ste. Marie
SP	Southern Pacific
SP&S	Spokane, Portland and Seattle
SSW	St. Louis Southwestern (also known as the "Cotton Belt")
STB	Surface Transportation Board
UMTA	Urban Mass Transit Authority
UP	Union Pacific
UTU	United Transportation Union
WC	Wisconsin Central
WP	Western Pacific

PART I

DRIVING FORCES IN THE 1980S

CHAPTER 1

THE NEW LEADERSHIP TEAM

THIS CHAPTER CONTAINS A SUMMARY OF the backgrounds of and principle contributions made by the presidents and CEOs who were in office in BNI and its Transportation and Resources divisions in its second decade, from 1980 through 1988, the year when the non-rail units were spun off to the shareholders, and to 1995, the year of merger with the Santa Fe Railway. Attention is given mainly to the leadership styles, goals, and priorities they set; cultural changes they imposed; major accomplishments made under their direction; and the legacy left by each president in his years in office.

• R.M. BRESSLER •

BN Railroad is the crown jewel of our corporate family and we are very proud of it.

R. M. BRESSLER TESTIMONY BEFORE A SENATE SUBCOMMITTEE, MARCH 26, 1982, REPORTED IN *MGR.*, APRIL 1982

Dick judges strictly on results, and he's not slow to replace people—even personal friends—when he's not satisfied.

COMMENT OF AN UNNAMED FORMER EXECUTIVE QUOTED IN JONATHAN B. LEVINE, "WILL A TAKEOVER DERAIL BURLINGTON NORTHERN'S MAKEOVER?" *BUSINESS WEEK*, AUGUST 3, 1987

We intend to make Burlington Northern Railroad one of the most efficient carriers in the industry.... Our second objective... is to achieve a better balance between our transportation and resource businesses.

R.M. BRESSLER, LETTER TO SHAREHOLDERS, *BURLINGTON NORTHERN, INC., ANNUAL REPORT FOR 1981*

You couldn't put such an array of assets together today at any price.

PAUL GIBSON, "A RAILROAD FOR THE LONG HAUL" *FORBES*, APRIL 27, 1981

FOR A LONG TIME, GOING BACK TO PRE-MERGER days on the NP, some board members seemed convinced that the "railroad management" had neither the skills nor the mindset necessary to exploit the vast resources the NP owned. Appointing Robert Binger as president to head up BN's Resources Division was intended to raise the management of the non-rail assets to a level of prominence and expertise equal to that of the railroad. But the

R. M. BRESSLER WORK HISTORY

General Electric Company

1952–1967	Various positions in financial management
1967–1968	Manager of Corporate Finance

American Airlines

1968–1972	Vice President and Treasurer
1972–1973	Senior Vice President–Finance

Atlantic Richfield Company

1973–1975	Vice President–Financial Administration
1975–1977	Senior Vice President–Finance
1977–1978	President of Arco Chemical Company Division
1978–1980	Executive Vice President (responsible for Arco Petroleum Resources Company, Arco Chemical Company, and Arco Transportation Company) and member of Board of Directors

Burlington Northern, Inc.

1980–1981	President
1981–1990	Chairman, President, and CEO

Burlington Resources

1987–1990	Chairman

Plum Creek Management Company

1989–1993	Chairman

El Paso Natural Gas Company

1990–1993	Chairman

results in the ensuing years failed to satisfy some board members. They felt the company still was underperforming in the management of it resources.

When deregulation loomed on the horizon, and because some board members were also dissatisfied with the return on the large capital investments being made in the railroad, they found they had an even stronger argument to support their view that a change in leadership was needed. Their evaluation brought about the decision to hire Richard Bressler, a senior executive at the Atlantic Richfield Company (Arco), as president and CEO of BNI, with responsibility for both the Transportation and Resources divisions.

At the time Bressler took over as president, the application for merger with the Frisco Railroad was thought to be close to approval. Menk had his sights set on Richard Grayson, president of the Frisco, to head the railroad company. In *Leaders Count*, a history of the BNSF, Bressler revealed that he was not impressed by any of the CEOs of other railroad companies he had met since joining BN.[1] Apparently Bressler relied on Menk as to who was the best of the lot. Within a few months of Bressler's arrival at BN, and even before BN received approval from the courts and the ICC to merge with the Frisco, it was announced that Grayson would replace T. J. Lamphier as president.

Before coming to BN, Bressler had held senior management positions at General Electric and American Airlines, in addition to Atlantic Richfield. His experience at each company was concentrated mainly in finance and planning, although he had served as head of two large operating units owned by Arco. However, it does not appear he had ever been directly in charge of either line operations or marketing. Robert (Bob) Downing recalled that some members of the BN board had wanted to hire an executive who had the experience needed to better manage and achieve much higher returns on BN's resources, especially in the production of oil and gas. According to Downing, some board members were later surprised to learn that Bressler's experience at Arco had not made him into what that industry considered "an oil man."

Bressler was an intelligent, soft-spoken person, easy to converse with. When BNI was in the process of establishing its new headquarters in Seattle during the time

1 Kaufman, *Leaders Count*.

I served as vice president–General Manager of the railroad's Seattle Region, I was in position to spend considerable time with him over the next two years. Bressler did everything "first class," as exemplified by the appointments in the office he set up in the new headquarters building, the decorating of a railroad business car set aside for his use, and the type of aircraft BN purchased for company business travel. At the same time, he wanted to have a low profile in Seattle. He made himself available for a limited number of interviews with the news media and was not out to make a major impression on the public by quickly becoming a member of several high-profile nonprofit boards, as some newly appointed senior executives often do when they move into a new location.

At the time the holding company was established, a considerable number of BN's senior executives were transferred from St. Paul to Seattle. It was surprising and quite alarming to observe how many of them left the company or retired within a short time of their moves. They were replaced by people with a variety of backgrounds: in the management of oil and gas, forest products, or minerals; and others in Law, Finance, and Planning. Even some of these newly hired, hand-picked officers did not stay with BNI more than one or two years.

Shortly before Bressler moved into the new office in Seattle, he told me that he did not want to become a "lightning rod" for matters concerning the railroad. He said he had neither the interest in nor the background for dealing with routine railroad matters, and that all inquiries or challenges he or his staff received concerning local matters on the railroad would be directed to me. He said he expected me to handle them to conclusion and that I should not take time to consult with him as to a recommended response or course of action. Bressler made only occasional trips on the business car he had remodeled and upgraded. We kept the car parked at the King Street Station in Seattle, for occasional use by Bressler to receive visitors in the unique setting of an inspection car used by rail-industry executives.

Bressler stated a number of times that he did not have much confidence in the future of the rail industry. He viewed it as mature, at the stage where its cash and nonoperating assets should be "harvested" and used for other kinds of investments. He wanted to shift BNI away from focusing too heavily on railroad transportation and to instead give more attention to the vast holdings in resources that he and the investment community thought BNI had failed to exploit. He made this very clear, right from the start. However, he also said many times that the railroad company was BNI's "crown jewel," that it was an excellent company but that it must start to produce increasingly better returns. In the first year after BN's merger with the Frisco, heavy cost reductions were made, and the railroad's net income soared.

Bressler also said from time to time that he wanted the railroad to have good tools and equipment, to be modernized, and to invest in projects that would have a high return on invested capital and a quick payback. He wanted to reduce the capital invested in the maintenance of the infrastructure, because while it was necessary to keep the track, bridges, and operating facilities in good condition, such projects usually had a low return. He was not interested in pursuing projects that were thought to have a long-term benefit but were likely to produce a low return in the short term.

What Bressler did not like about the rail industry was mainly the bureaucracy in which it was entrenched and the hold that labor had on it through high wages and such restrictions as the size of train crews, as well as in general, because railroads were not earning their cost of capital. It should be noted that the massive program of capital investment and the large amount of operating expense put into expanding capacity, upgrading the roadway, acquiring additional locomotives and cars, and constructing additional maintenance facilities that BN undertook in the mid-1970s was nearly complete by the time Bressler came to BN. As the volume of new coal business grew, the density of traffic increased on the strong, upgraded coal corridors, causing the inherent economies of scale to take hold. As the rates for moving coal could finally be raised to a remunerative level, the $2 billion investment paid off handsomely. As Bob Downing often stated many years later, "I haven't run into anyone in the last twenty years who even suggests that we should have done nothing," to upgrade the railroad and expand its capacity.[2]

2 Panel discussion on Powder River Basin, annual meeting of the Lexington Group, Sheridan, Wyo., September 23, 2009.

When we were forced by the Interstate Commerce Commission (ICC) to allow the Chicago and North Western Railway to acquire a 50 percent ownership in the new 127-mile line we built to serve new mines, Bressler and a few others who had come to BN from outside the rail industry remarked how they preferred having the C&NW's check for $76 million and splitting the business with it, rather than our being able to haul all of the coal from the mines to which the C&NW would now have access. The profit margin on a number of coal movements at the time still was too low to produce an adequate return on the investment we had made.

I made a number of trips with Bressler to meet with civic leaders and the management of the ports in Bellingham, Everett, Astoria, and Portland on the possibility of our moving coal to the Pacific Northwest for export to countries in the Pacific Rim. Bressler supported partnerships between BN and the port authorities to develop such opportunities. His interest in such long-term projects seemed to be in conflict with the negative views he sometimes expressed on the future of the rail industry. His concern was whether the rail industry would be able to overcome the major structural problems it faced even after deregulation.

Bressler took a strong interest in the operations we had in place for handling imported automobiles and containerized shipments and for exporting grain. Although these were growing segments of our business, his enthusiasm for them was dampened by his statements that the railroad's return on its massive capital investment was woefully inadequate. He questioned the wisdom of making the $2 billion investment BN had made to handle the huge tonnages of coal, which all too often were being hauled at noncompensatory rates. In a presentation Bressler made to the Western Coal Transportation Association in 1980, he advised that in 1979 BN earned less than 4 percent on what it had invested in coal-hauling alone.[3] He added that at the same time, U.S. Treasury bills were yielding 6.3 percent.

Bressler and Grayson initiated an all-out effort across departments and functions in the railroad company to drive costs out of the operation, raise the rates on coal transportation that were too low to recoup our investment, and curtail further investments in coal-hauling capacity until we knew with certainty that we could make a reasonable return on such investments.

The inconsistency we sensed at times in Bressler's views on the future of BN's railroad unit was apparent in the strong push he made to establish a Research and Development function in the railroad. Bressler felt the amount spent on R&D by the rail industry was far less than what it should be to identify and develop technology that would increase productivity and help overcome problems we had with the old technologies we were using. He directed Thomas (Tom) Lamphier to recruit someone with the kind of background and attitude suitable to establish such capability on BN. Bressler also challenged us to substantially increase our budget for R&D, since he was convinced there had to be more opportunities to apply modern-day technology than were being developed by the railroad supply industry.

The establishment of a holding-company structure in 1981 provided the foundation BN needed to begin moving ahead on Bressler's plans for expanding the non-rail side of the business. Bressler had the plan for the holding company prepared and announced within a matter of weeks after he took over as president. He made a concerted effort to explain the benefits for BN and its future with such an organization structure in place. Managers and employees of the railroad needed reassurance that it would not be drained of the cash a railroad needed to continue maintaining its plant and equipment at a high standard. Among the reasons Bressler gave for setting up a holding company were:

- A decision for a railroad company to acquire a non-transportation company with BN stock or securities required approval by the ICC, which was reluctant to allow railroad companies that opportunity. Without the right to issue stock, the funds required for such acquisitions had to be taken from cash generated from rail operations.
- It was likely that a holding company could obtain outside financing on more favorable terms than BN's combined transportation and resources company could on the open market.
- By giving considerable independence to each unit,

3 Richard M. Bressler, "Remarks before the Western Coal Transportation Association," September 10, 1980, quoted in "An Assessment of Development and Production Potential of Federal Coal Leases," U.S. Department of Interior, December 1981.

the performance of each would stand out clearly, and not be masked by "subsidies" transferred internally from one "sister" company to another. As a result, the profit-making potential of each company would be revealed more clearly. Plans for improvement of the unit's performance could be defined and developed with greater clarity and efficiency.

- With each unit having to stand on its own, goals and expectations could be set that would form the basis for evaluation of its managers.
- A holding-company structure makes it expedient to transfer funds from one or more units to those units that hold higher potential for growth and earning returns on invested capital.

Initially, eight independent operating companies were put under the holding-company structure. Bressler pushed hard to accelerate the cutting of timber and to expand BNI's interests in oil and gas. He was determined to increase revenue from non-rail activities enough to equal the revenue coming from the railroad company. By doing this, shareholder interests would be better protected in case it was necessary for the railroad to take a lengthy strike in order to get its labor costs reduced. To provide the cash needed for expanding the oil and gas business, pressure was put on the railroad to reduce its capital expenditures and to increase its operating income through aggressive cost-cutting measures.

Expenditures for "maintenance capital," needed mainly for rail and tie renewal and for replacement or rebuilding worn-out locomotives and cars, were to be reduced by finding ways to extend the lives of those expensive assets. These categories of capital expenditures make up the largest part of a railroad's capital budget. Projects defined under "productivity capital" with a high "hard dollar" return on investment were encouraged. The primary goal for the railroad company was to increase cash generation rather than striving for a low operating ratio. Cash generated would be "dividended up" to the holding company and used mainly to expand BNI's holdings in oil and gas.

In 1980, when Bressler came to BN, the market value of the stock was less than $1 billion. As of April 1993, the combined market value of the four publicly held companies[4] formed in the spin-off and restructuring of BNI and BN Resources was $13.3 billion.[5] Clearly, the increase in shareholder value that was achieved under the strategies carried out by Bressler and the team he formed to carry out his agenda was impressive. Bressler met the board's mandate to extract more value from BN's resource holdings. His second major goal, to improve the financial performance of the railroad, was met as well, although at the expense of turmoil and disruption caused by frequent turnover in the executive ranks, and destruction of the culture that had been formed to embrace opportunities for growth that had not existed elsewhere in the rail industry for many years.

A very positive outcome for the railroad was in finally being freed from the concerns of longstanding that BN should be investing more to develop its non-rail holdings and reduce investment in the railroad. The other positive result was the development and application of new technology and maintenance methods that would extend the lives of expensive components in the track structure—mainly rail, ties, and ballast as well as cars and locomotives. The entire rail industry of North America has benefited from the pressure that initiated from Bressler to reduce the amount of maintenance capital that BN was spending under the standards and practices that had been employed prior to that time. Adoption of new technology and standards has improved the quality of track and equipment on the entire rail network and, by extending asset lives, freed up capital for other purposes.

4 Refers to BN Resources and the two companies that were spun off by Resources to shareholders in 1988. The first, Plum Creek Timber, was sold to a master limited partnership in 1989. A tax-free separation of El Paso Natural Gas was completed in 1992. The fourth company, BNI, retained ownership of the Burlington Northern Railroad Company.

5 Gordon Donaldson, *Corporate Restructuring: Managing the Change Process from Within* (Harvard Business School Press, 1994), 114.

• R. C. GRAYSON •

Be the low cost carrier
We're going to look very closely at every possible way to increase productivity that's the name of the game today and I think it is accepted by all of our people as the way railroads stay viable, and that's our primary objective.
BN NEWS, FEBRUARY 1981

We regret having to furlough employees, but in our new deregulated environment, we must improve our overall efficiency so that BN's labor costs are in line with those of our competitors.
BN NEWS, MAY/JUNE 1981

OF THE PEOPLE I HAVE WORKED UNDER WHO were knowledgeable in operations, Richard Grayson was among the best. He was skilled implementing operations that would improve productivity and the use of cars and locomotives. Once the new methods were in place, a more disciplined, consistent operation was established. Grayson showed remarkable skills in revising bureaucratic processes that had impaired decision making in BN. He came to BN in December 1980 and served as president and CEO of the railroad company until April 1, 1982, when he was appointed CEO of BN's transportation group (made up of the BN Railroad, BN Transport, BN Air Freight, and the Colorado and Southern and the Fort Worth and Denver railways) of BN, Inc. In the relatively short period of twenty-six months that Grayson headed the railroad, a great deal was accomplished. By 1984 BN broke through the threshold of 80 in its operating ratio, down to 78.7, which was the lowest ratio of any of the large railroad companies for that year. Grayson was succeeded by Walter Drexel, who had come to BNI from Anaconda Copper Company, a subsidiary of Atlantic Richfield, in 1981, as senior vice president–Strategic Planning.

Grayson came to BN a short time before the courts ruled favorably on the merger of BN and the St. Louis–San Francisco Railroad ("the Frisco"). Grayson's appointment was effective only seven months after Richard Bressler took over as CEO of BNI. Grayson replaced T.J. Lamphier, who was reassigned as senior vice president–Transportation Policy and Analysis. Grayson and Lou Menk had worked together for many years on the Frisco and had kept in close touch in the fifteen years since Menk left the Frisco to go to the Burlington (CB&Q Railroad) as president.

Grayson came up through the ranks at the Frisco Railroad. He worked as a brakeman, conductor, and dispatcher before being promoted to an officer position. He served as president for eleven years. During their years together at Frisco, Menk developed great respect for Grayson's abilities and sought him to take over BNI's railroad company late in 1980. The appointments of Bressler and Grayson signified the start of the transformation of all units in the Transportation and Resources divisions of BNI.

Grayson had little formal education and learned railroading from the ground up. Shrewd and very adept at handling the wide range of issues that the CEO of a large railroad company had to face, he was very knowledgeable on all aspects of railroad operations and maintenance, as well as all of the other major functions that make up the organization of a railroad company. Although he was not particularly charismatic, Grayson had the kind of verbal communication skills needed in dealing with any of the constituents a railroad company has, whether that be employees, customers, public figures, or management personnel in any department. He was able to break complex situations down into brief but very credible messages that people could grasp and retain. He repeated those messages often and with consistency in meetings, speeches, and company publications. As a result, employees in all departments could understand what direction the company was taking, the reasons for the decisions being made, how progress toward meeting our goals was being measured, and what was expected of them—their roles, responsibilities, and accountabilities.

Even when some employees or managers did not like or agree with what was happening in the company under his direction, they had to give Grayson credit for communicating clearly in a way they could understand and relate to. Most of all, people appreciated the fact that Grayson was consistent and stayed the course. With him, there was not a "flavor of the month" approach: there were no new agendas being piled up, one upon the other, and no litany of trite, condescending catch phrases, often called "business-school buzz words" at that time. Underlying all of Grayson's messages and directives was the theme he developed for BN in the new competitive environment: "Be the low-cost carrier." That was our first priority, and every activity or initiative we undertook was to be tied to that goal.

Grayson came to BN at the time that deregulation was about to be implemented in the rail industry. To prepare for the all-encompassing changes that would have to be made under deregulation, Grayson reminded us repeatedly that competition would require rates to be reduced, and that we would have to cut our costs significantly if we were to survive and prosper in that new environment.

Although Grayson was not a particularly great speaker, by careful selection of words to describe the problems and opportunities we faced, he communicated effectively. Perhaps most importantly, it did not take long for results of Grayson's agenda to show up in reports of the company's financial and operating performance. The results spoke for themselves, they were not debatable in terms of what the numbers meant, and no one could reasonably say that favorable results in one area were obtained at the expense of another department or important facet of the company's business. Because of this, Grayson and the management team of the early 1980s developed credibility. Whether one liked the methods employed to get results or the character and management style of some of the leaders, there was no question that management knew what it was doing and was demonstrating its ability to get the job done.

Grayson devoted considerable time to the serious problem of coal rates being far too low on several large coal movements. It was difficult to have to battle

R. C. GRAYSON WORK HISTORY

St. Louis–San Francisco Railroad Company

1941–1945	Brakeman and Conductor
1945–1948	Train Dispatcher
1948–1950	Terminal Trainmaster
1950–1955	Asstant Superintendent
1955–1956	Division Superintendent
1956–1958	Assistant General Manager
1958–1960	Frisco Transportation Company, Vice President and General Manager
1960–1964	General Sales Manager
1964–1969	Vice President–Operations
1969–1973	President and CEO
1973–1980	Chairman, President and CEO

Burlington Northern, Inc.

1980–1981	Vice Chairman and President, Transportation Division

Burlington Northern Railroad Company

1981–1982	President and CEO
1982–1983	Chairman and CEO of Transportation Group of BNI and Chairman and CEO of Burlington Northern Railroad

Burlington Northern, Inc.

1983	Vice Chairman of BNI

customers across the table or confront them before the ICC and in the courts. But it was an effort that was vital to getting the profit on coal high enough to justify the huge investment that had been made in plant and equipment to handle it. Through combined efforts of Grayson, the Law Department, and the coal Operations and Marketing group, progress was made in the early 1980s.

Although Grayson was tough on reducing costs and demanded quantum results, he was equally concerned that good equipment and material be acquired and put into service. In his years as president, capital expenditures were maintained at a level nearly as high as they had been in the mid- to late 1970s. He promoted and taught "smart railroading," a fact that is often overlooked when his work is evaluated. Grayson introduced methods for operations and maintenance that were effective and up to best industry practices. The management structure and many administrative procedures were simplified. As a result, the pace of decision-making was speeded up and counterproductive, bureaucratic management processes were revised or eliminated.

Grayson was a good teacher and a good coach. He spent considerable time out on the railroad to learn the property and to look for additional opportunities for improving the company's performance. I was fortunate to spend considerable time with him on several hi-rail and business car trips.

While much was accomplished in the short time Grayson served as president, it is unfortunate that the corporate values and leadership style that had been developed and applied so successfully in BN's first 10 years were virtually destroyed in the early 1980s. Implementation of the changes that made BN more efficient and increased profitability in those years could have been handled in a more affirmative manner and without compromising results. Grayson himself did not manage by fear and intimidation, but at the same time, it did not appear he put much if any effort to curtail such conduct on the part of some of the officers of the former Frisco Railroad who were placed in key positions on BN.

A statement from Grayson's family provided an interesting description of the character of the Frisco that was developed under his leadership: "On his watch, the Frisco was a much admired model of lean, smart, Midwestern honesty, efficiency and profitability. It was also a model of a warm, close-knit family corporate culture, although they didn't use words like that back then."[6]

As already mentioned, a great deal was accomplished in the twenty-six months Grayson was at the helm of BN. In many ways, it is unfortunate he did not stay on as CEO for another five years or so. If he had, far better decisions might have been made for succession in some senior management positions. The improved operating and maintenance practices he instilled during his brief tenure might have been sustained longer than turned out to be the case not long after he moved up to vice chairman. We missed having the skills and influence Grayson had in reconciling differences that arose at times in the goals and agendas of various departments. Also, we could have used his help in working through the differences in performance expectations that arose in having to work under the holding-company structure. Tension developed in major issues such as having to balance the need to maintain quality in the roadway in the face of pressure to cut capital expenditures enough to reduce the asset base and to generate more cash to fund nonrail investments.

---

6 From a statement on Grayson on www.ancestry.com.

• WALTER A. DREXEL •

Our goal is to earn $1 billion in operating income to be dividended up to the holding company.

OFT-REPEATED STATEMENT MADE IN MEETINGS HELD IN 1985

We won't have one more person working for us than we need.

...

We have come to a turning point in our management style.
Fear, intimidations and militaristic styles do not belong in modern management.
They have no place in our company.

...

When we deal fairly, decently and honestly with all of our people,
we will reap benefits beyond what we imagine is possible in this industry.

EXCERPTS FROM A SPEECH GIVEN AT
A CONFERENCE OF BN EXECUTIVES GIVEN IN
MARCH 1983 AND PRINTED IN *BN NEWS*, MAY/JUNE 1983

WALTER A. DREXEL REPLACED RICHARD Grayson as the president and chief executive officer of the railroad company in 1983. Grayson had done an outstanding job in leading the company through the transformation necessitated by deregulation. The initiatives he established in cost reduction and improved productivity paved the way for Burlington Northern to achieve the lowest operating ratio among the large railroads in 1983. Higher profitability was achieved in the face of the large reductions in rates that had to be made to hold on to the business we had, and to develop new business in the new deregulated environment. Under Grayson, BN began to produce a much higher return on the large investment made in the 1970s and early 1980s to handle the rapidly expanding coal business generated in the Powder River Basin.

Along with Bressler, Drexel came to BN from the Atlantic Richfield Oil Company (Arco). He had worked in Arco's Finance Department as auditor and treasurer. Walter talked often about his role in shutting down the mining operation near Butte, Montana, that Arco had acquired from the Anaconda Corporation in the 1970s. At Anaconda, Drexel served as vice president. His first position at BN was senior vice president–Strategic Planning at the holding-company level.

Drexel fit the stereotypical image of an old-line, tough, no-nonsense Texan, a heritage in which he took great pride. From the outset of his time as president, Drexel established that our goal would be to maximize cash generation. Our efforts would be focused on that number more than the operating ratio, which heretofore had been given the most attention in evaluating the performance of a railroad company. The idea was of course that the cash the railroad generated would be sent up to the holding company as a dividend. Increasing the amount of cash generated would be accomplished by reducing operating costs and by minimizing capital expenditures. Walter led a charge to significantly reduce spending on all types of capital projects, except those that would produce substantial hard-dollar savings in the short run. Having to maintain the level of utility of thousands of miles of roadway, in several maintenance facilities and on a large fleet of locomotives and cars, required a railroad company to fund large capital expenditures every year. Investment made in the form of "maintenance capital" produced a low rate of return, at best. Maintenance capital had to be targeted for major reductions in order to free up the cash generated in operations for investment in non-rail projects and acquisitions.

Walter Drexel may be best remembered for his

WALTER A. DREXEL WORK HISTORY

Atlantic Richfield Company

1957–1977	Treasurer; various positions in financial area

Anaconda Copper Company

1978–1981	Vice President

Burlington Northern, Inc.

1981–1982	Senior Vice President–Strategic Planning
1982–1987	Member, Board of Directors

Burlington Northern Railroad

1982–1983	President and CCO
1983–1985	Chairman, President, and CEO

Burlington Northern, Inc.

1985–1987	Vice Chairman of the Board
1987–	Retired

introduction of a new program generally known as "Corporate Culture." Drexel acquainted the entire company with this program by recording a speech of about twenty minutes on a video tape and employees watch it at virtually every work center on BN. It was well received because Drexel clearly outlined a break in leadership style from the recent past. He made it clear that we had to move out of a mode of management by fear and intimidation, and that all of us were expected to treat others in the company in the way we would want to be treated. He emphasized his belief in the importance of affording everyone the opportunity to increase their skills and use their talents. We were expected to treat each other with respect and thereby improve relations at all levels. Drexel came across as sincere, clearly establishing the leadership style that he would follow and that he expected everyone in the company to embrace.

Drexel's message was a complete break from the leadership of the recent past, from the time we had merged with the Frisco in 1981 and had come under the type of culture its leaders imposed on BN. People throughout the company were relieved and very pleased to know the days of oppression, ridicule, and mean-spirited treatment of others was at an end. The time in which we had endured a lot of unwarranted pain, tension, and bad treatment had produced some good bottom-line results, but a price had been paid. Organizational development had been set back. Morale had suffered at all levels. People were apprehensive as to their future and the quality of work life and the values held dear by many that had been destroyed. But for those who were still around, it appeared those days were behind us. From what Walter was telling us, there was good reason to believe we were onto better times.

Unfortunately, the good spirit that had been raised through the program on corporate culture did not last long. Some of our leaders who had practiced the intimidation leadership style believed his new initiative to change the culture was a slap at them. Since some of them were among the most effective cost cutters we had, and because they had earned their stripes in the first three years following the Frisco merger, Drexel became concerned that the rest of the organization seemed to think those leaders had been "set out." Also, as would be expected, there were some contract employees (and a few managers as well) who began to complain that our continuing to eliminate jobs, and any reprimands or disciplinary action for rules violations, ran contrary to what they thought the new corporate culture was to be. You could always find that someone who did not like a particular business decision or company practice would say, "This violates corporate culture." Drexel took this as a sign that BN people were too immature and otherwise inadequate to work under the new set of values and the kind of leadership style he had espoused.

Drexel decided to put less emphasis into the program and we deferred "work out" sessions that had been set up in the field to help in communicating and understanding the new norms for conduct, developing teamwork, and building better working relationships. The program for corporate culture began to fade away, as will happen with any "flavor of the month" program for which senior management does not stand behind and at least appear to support after rolling it out. Drexel's initiative to change the culture had the potential to make BN a great place to work once again. Nearly all of BN's people were ready for that kind of change. If we had stayed with the program, Drexel might have been rewarded many times over with improved results, by any measure of performance.

I was present when, shortly after it was decided to give less emphasis and direction to the program, a junior-level manager in the field asked Drexel what was going to happen to corporate culture. Drexel replied in two words: "practice it." The people of BN remained ready to embrace the new program. All that was needed was to get the two top levels of management on board, including those who had sounded off that corporate culture was tantamount to "giving the keys to the inmates." However, changing the culture of the company would have to wait for another day. To this day, I still am not sure exactly what else caused Drexel to get cold feet on this one. In watching how he worked through other new initiatives, he always moved ahead with full resolve to see them through to success; he would not allow anything or anybody to stand in his way. But for corporate culture, he decided not to follow through with strong direction on the "new day" he had introduced.

In addition to his introduction of the program to change the culture of the company, Drexel is remembered for a number of basic beliefs by which he evaluated his staff and set the pace for the organization:

- You are only as good as your last move. (This was Drexel's way of letting us know we could never rest on our laurels.)
- Growth covers up a multitude of sins. (He was referring to the large year-to-year growth in business BN had benefited from in the past several years.)
- If you make a mistake in the promotion of someone, don't live with the problem. Take care of it without delay.
- Our primary goal is to generate more cash by reducing capital expenditures and operating costs.
- We will not have one more person working for us than we need.
- The cradle-to-grave mentality I see in this company is at an end.
- We have some good people. What they need is better direction and leadership.
- Life does not go in a straight line.
- You don't have to like someone to be able to work with them.
- It's [railroading] a very simple business. You don't have to know too much about technology. The situations you run into require only simple solutions.

Drexel also is remembered for allegedly saying on one occasion, "This company is unmanageable." As one might expect, the response of some people was that for Walter, that might have been true. I cannot attest to whether or when he actually made that statement. However, I remember him reflecting quite often that the geographic spread of the operation, the fact that many employees (mainly train-service employees) worked for long hours without direct supervision, the legacy of outdated labor agreements, and the large amount of capital required every year to run the business, just to "stay even" on the condition of the track and equipment, were examples of conditions that made it more difficult to improve results on a railroad than in other kinds of business.

Drexel did see BN had some strong advantages; for example, we did not have to take the risk of huge investments in research and development to remain competitive. Also, our success or failure was not based on overcoming the big risks many industries have when introducing new products or services.

Drexel brought Thomas J. (Tom) Matthews, an executive with experience at Continental Airlines, to

BN to head up the Human Resources and Labor Relations departments. Matthews had worked under Frank Lorenzo, who had become famous for the bitter struggles Continental had with its employees. Needless to say, our union representatives and many employees became highly concerned over the prospect of having to deal with someone who'd had a major role in serious confrontations with labor. They had not yet recovered from the past three years of major downsizing of the workforce and the introduction of a much different style of leadership at the time of the Frisco merger. This concern turned to fear and animosity when senior management revealed the new agenda for revision of work rules, pay scale, and the ways in which future collective bargaining would be handled. The details of what ensued in this strategy are covered in chapter 25.

A number of other important initiatives were developed in the Drexel years, among them continued reduction in the size of the railroad's asset base, reducing capital expenditures, and making cash generation as our primary goal rather than improvement in the operating ratio, which historically was the major focus and basis for evaluation of the performance of a railroad company. Drexel, like Bressler, believed the railroad had evolved into a "harvest mode," which meant that investment should be minimized because the company had peaked and had limited potential for growth. By limiting capital expenditures and continuing to reduce the cost of operation, more cash would be generated, which in turn would be "dividended up" to the holding company for investment in other kinds of business that had higher returns and thought to have a better future. As a result the railroad company was to be viewed for its value as a cash cow.

Another highlight of "the Drexel era" was the relocation of the railroad company's headquarters from St. Paul to Fort Worth, and the move of its Operating Department to Overland Park, Kansas. Chapter 15 contains more comment on Drexel's decision to relocate upwards of six hundred employees and their families. Countless business reasons were advanced for making the expenditure for these moves. However, many people believed those reasons actually centered around the desire of newly hired executives to get relief from the high personal-income tax, cold weather, and left-wing populist politics of Minnesota.

After serving for two years as president and chief executive officer, Drexel was made vice chairman of the board. Darius Gaskins was then moved up from head of the Marketing Department to president of the railroad.

• D. W. GASKINS •

I would judge the reform of rail regulation over the last 30 years to be an enormous success. We are left with an untidy process but excellent economic results. . . . I am reminded of Winston Churchill's thought about democracy— that our regulation of freight railroads is the worst possible process except for all the other known alternatives.

...

My solution to falling rail rates was to begin to change the people responsible for setting rail rates. Specifically, we hired a group of savvy grain traders from our customers—international grain companies.

DARIUS W. GASKINS, JR., "REGULATION OF FREIGHT RAILROADS IN THE MODERN ERA: 1970–2010," *REVIEW OF NETWORK ECONOMICS*, DECEMBER 2008

HAVING BEEN ONE OF THE PRINCIPAL FOUNDERS and proponents of deregulation of the rail industry while serving at the ICC, Darius W. Gaskins was hired to head BN's Marketing and Sales Department in 1982. At that time, the rail industry had been operating in a deregulated environment for only about a year. Bringing

Gaskins in was a good move on the part of Bressler and Grayson since he understood the basis for rail economics and knew how best to manage under deregulation than perhaps anyone else in the country at that time. His background prepared him to lead a railroad company through the early stages of deregulation with success. Up to the time Gaskins came to BN, only Conrail seemed to understand what had to be done to take advantage of the opportunities ready to be seized by railroad companies. Others in the industry were struggling to figure out how to adapt to the changes they saw more as a threat or, at least, more of a problem than an opportunity to run their companies more as a business.

Gaskins served as the head of Marketing for two years before he moved up to replace Walter Drexel as president and CEO. Gaskins stayed with BN for seven years. There were some who noted he had rather limited executive experience when he came to BN and assumed responsibility for leading a large department, and very soon after that, to serve as CEO. However, he had gained management experience as senior vice president of Natomas North America, an oil-exploration company for about two years after leaving government service.

In becoming CEO of a large railroad company so soon, Gaskins had to hope BN's Operating Department had capabilities strong enough to "run the show" so he would be able to concentrate on building the strengths BN needed for success in the new deregulated environment. However, the changes in the structure and leadership Gaskins made in the Operating Department demonstrated that he understood very well where BN was falling short—it needed to be moving forward aggressively to improve service by applying and developing new technology and in understanding how to give better support to the new marketing initiatives he had begun to implement. Overall, Gaskins proved he probably was better prepared and more knowledgeable than any other leader in the rail industry on how to lead a railroad company through deregulation successfully.

In those years, BN led the industry in developing business-based programs with customers in all of the commodities it handled. Rapid progress was made in negotiating long-term contracts, setting service standards, and gaining commitments for the ownership and management of privately owned or leased freight-car

D. W. GASKINS WORK HISTORY

Bachelor of Science degree from the United States Military Academy

Ph.D. in Economics and Masters in Engineering from the University of Michigan

1963–67	Instructor (Captain, U.S. Air Force), Aerospace Research Pilots School
1973–75	U.S. Department of the Interior, various positions involving policy and resources
1970–73 and 1975–76	Assistant Professor, Department of Economics, University of California at Berkeley
1976–77	Director, Bureau of Economics, Federal Trade Commission
1977–78	Director, Office of Economic Analysis, Civil Aeronautics Board
1978–79	Deputy Assistant Secretary, Policy Analysis, Department of Energy
1980–81	Chairman, Interstate Commerce Commission
1981–82	Senior Vice President, Natomas North America
1982–85	Senior Vice President, Marketing and Sales, Burlington Northern Railroad
1985–89	President and CEO, Burlington Northern Railroad

SOURCE: www.railrunner.com/about/directors.php

fleets. For some time, BN was ahead of its competition in developing, presenting, and securing agreements for new and expanded services; in securing long-term commitments; and for its innovations in pricing. Gaskins's experience and education as an economist, together with his creativity in having a mind clear and not being bound up by the culture that railroads, regulators, and shippers had operated under for a long time, made it possible for BN to outpace its rail competitors in those early years of deregulation.

Gaskins's accomplishments are stated very well in a paper he wrote for the December 2008, issue of the *Review of Network Economics,* "Regulation of Freight Railroads in the Modern Era: 1970–2010." He refers to several initiatives that typified his approach to moving the company forward. One was to get new people in place who would know how to negotiate prices under deregulation on a basis other than to simply cut rates in order to hold the business. For the grain sector, people from the international grain trade were hired. Gaskins wrote, "These traders developed an auction system called COTS [certificates of transportation] which developed market information by selling 40 percent of BN's grain transportation in a forward market. The movement of the prices for these forward contracts informed our grain marketeers far better than a quiet chat in a golf cart." The certificates of transportation could be traded among the various grain shippers. The value of certificates traded moved in line with new developments in the grain markets.

Gaskins intensified the vital effort to get coal rates raised to the level where BN would get a reasonable return on the huge investment it had made upgrading its track and expanding its capacity to handle the coal. The effort to raise coal rates was started in the 1970s, before deregulation, but the freedom railroads gained under deregulation provided a much better opportunity for success. At the start of the first high-volume coal movements from the Powder River Basin, the rates had been set far too low, ascribed by Gaskins and others as "missionary rates." The electric-power companies were of course very difficult to deal with on this issue, since the cost of fuel and its transportation made up a very large part of their operating costs. On this issue, Gaskins wrote, "When we began to raise coal rates at the urging of our shareholders, we created a firestorm from our utility customers who had gotten very comfortable with BN's missionary rates. . . . BN lost several rate cases filed with the ICC during this era, but the incipient rise in coal rates was smashed be the competitive entry into the Powder River Basin by the Chicago and North Western Railway/Union Pacific Railroad [C&NW/UP] in 1984. We were able to demonstrate for the ensuing twenty-five years that two is a large number when considering rail competition."

In the years BN was attempting to get a resolution of the issue of long standing on the crew-consist issue, independent of national handling, Gaskins led an effort to use a BN subsidiary, the Winona Bridge Company, that would be allowed to operate on BN under trackage rights, but with its own crews. The wages paid the two-person crews handling trains of the Bridge Company would be low enough to make the service competitive with the costs of trucking companies. This was a very aggressive and innovative move, but in the court challenges that ensued, BN was unsuccessful in overcoming the very strong, "do or die" assault of the unions on this concept (also see chapter 18 for details on the decision to grant trackage rights to the Winona Bridge Company).

Another creative initiative developed under Gaskins's leadership was a program to sell or lease marginal light-density lines to investors who would establish new companies to operate and maintain them. With substantially lower costs, such operations would be able to handle business originating and terminating on those lines with at least a modest profit. All of the Class I railroads in North America picked up on this concept, once they learned how to move such proposals through the ICC for approval, now that they understood this was a way to avoid abandoning and losing the revenue generated on these marginal lines, and to avoid the lengthy legal proceedings required when abandonment was to be pursued. Overall, the program for line sales on BN and the entire railroad industry has been very successful. Gaskins deserves much of the credit for developing the concept and getting a large number of line sales and leases accomplished.

The biggest single sale and lease was that of 508 miles

of main line and several branch lines in the southern corridor of Montana (see chapter 8 for more detail on what was involved in the establishment of Montana Rail Link) in 1987. At the time BN decided to sell and lease this large amount of its railroad property, BN was being assaulted by Montana's political leaders, unions, the news media, and other parties for allegedly failing to live up to its commitments and for supposedly having a monopoly on the movement of products grown, mined, or otherwise produced in Montana. In his 2008 article, Gaskins related the reaction of Governor Ted Schwinden when he revealed BN's plans to sell this much of its railway: "When I told him that we were going to sell half of our Montana operation to Denny Washington, a prominent Montana businessman, the blood drained out of the Governor's face. It was no fun to beat up on Denny Washington." While the decision to sell this large piece of the southern corridor remains controversial to this day, it was an example of the new and very aggressive strategies Gaskins brought to BN in the years he headed the company.

Gaskins wrote very openly about the tension that existed in BN over investing in its railroad versus its holdings in energy, real estate, and natural resources: "A substantial portion of the railroad's cash flow was diverted during the 1980s to non-railroad activities. There was no corporate appetite for large, new investments in railroad operations. Essential rail investments were covered by taking on additional debt secured by railroad assets."

He expressed his dismay "that individual projects seemed to be justified on the basis of expected incremental returns, but the full cost of the whole BN network could not be recovered from projected revenues. Slowly, the picture improved as additional cost reductions kicked in. By the time I left the railroad in 1989, the outlook had improved enough to support a spin-off of the railroad with its debts into a separate, publicly traded company."

Gaskins's career with BN culminated in a showdown with senior officers of the holding company over the terms for spinning the railroad off from BNI's non-rail holdings. In the split, the railroad company was to take on all of BNI's debt. Gaskins was willing to accept that challenge, but he strongly (and successfully) resisted the attempt of BNI to take ownership of the land under the railroad from it and place it in BNI's real-estate company. This radical proposal for the transfer of ownership of the railroad's right-of-way was said to be necessary to get the value of the real-estate company up to a billion dollars to make it marketable in the spin-off of BN's non-rail companies. The land in question was where the track and facilities of the railroad were located. It was not to be limited to property owned by the railroad but no longer required for operating purposes.

It was completely unreasonable for the holding company to expect the railroad to give up ownership and control of the land on which its track and other components of its infrastructure were placed. It is unique and vital for a railroad to have control of its physical plant and the underlying land. Without that asset, it simply would lose control of its ability to control its destiny and maintain opportunity for future expansion or changes in the way its above-ground facilities are managed. Gaskins deserves a great deal of credit for having enough strength and courage to not back down from that challenge. If he had not succeeded, BN would have been left in a very weak position, and without the kind of control necessary to manage the foundation on which it was dependent for success and even its survival.

Another successful effort on Gaskins's part was his decision to clear out the few remaining senior-level managers who tried to manage the company in the intimidating and generally negative style that had been brought into the company in 1981. Gaskins practiced a style of leadership in which he wanted everyone in the company to have pride in their work, with incentives to follow and develop better methods in its operating and marketing functions, and in providing the kind of service that would attract more business. Vestiges of culture that ran counter to such values were eliminated.

Gaskins left BN in 1989. He was succeeded by Gerald Grinstein, a board member, who had served as vice chairman for three years. Grinstein had a degree in law and had served on the staff of U.S. senator Warren Magnusson of Washington. As CEO of Western Airlines, Grinstein had been given a great deal of credit for the successful merger of Delta and Western in 1987. He was given especially high marks by the unions representing Western's employees in negotiating the terms for combining their seniority with the employees of Delta, and in working through numerous other points of tension and concern that were part of that merger.

It was anticipated (and certainly hoped) by the people of BN that Grinstein would be able to take a more affirmative and less combative approach in such major issues as resolving the crew-consist issue and selling and leasing major parts of the core network. Other areas included efforts to subcontract or otherwise move work from BN employees to outside contractors and confrontational measures such as granting extensive trackage rights to a low cost operator. They believed Grinstein would appreciate the need for the company to provide a more supportive and encouraging style of leadership, and not continue the climate of confrontation and antagonism that had burdened the people of BN in a variety of ways since 1981.

• GERALD GRINSTEIN •

The standing joke was that they [Burlington Resources]
got the gold and we [the railroad] got the shaft.

...

A big mistake the BN made was not buying the MoP. It was a huge mistake.

...

I mean, people who define their lives in terms of the railroad.
That is an attribute that is not easy to come by.

GERALD GRINSTEIN, QUOTED IN
LAWRENCE H. KAUFMAN, *LEADERS COUNT*, 247, 295, AND 273

Gerald Grinstein became affiliated with BN as a board member in 1985. He was soon elected vice chairman and, in 1989, president and CEO. He held that position until 1995 when BN merged with Santa Fe. Among other professional pursuits, Grinstein served as president of Western Airlines from 1984 to 1987.

Grinstein had built a favorable reputation with labor unions from his success in protecting the interests of employees of Western Airlines when it merged with Delta Airlines. With that record of success, Grinstein was able to bring a spirit of optimism and hope to the people of BN who had worked under a culture of stress and transformation since 1980. Because of Grinstein's engaging personality, people at all levels of the company found him easy to talk with and receptive to ideas on changes that would benefit themselves and the organization.

Grinstein took over as head of the railroad company at the time of the spin-off of Burlington Resources in 1989, which left BNI with only its railroad, plus over $2 billion of debt that had been accumulated by the railroad and BNI's non-rail units. Grinstein and the entire team at the railroad faced an enormous challenge in working that debt down to a reasonable level (from a debt-equity ratio of about 80 down to 50 or less) to within a few years. To their credit, that goal was accomplished. However, it had to be done by deferring a substantial amount of capital expenditures needed in those years to improve the railroad's efficiency and enable it to build the additional capacity needed to move increasing tonnages of coal from the Powder River Basin.

By 1994 the debt had been reduced enough to allow acquisition of 350 new locomotive units equipped with AC traction motors, a very notable advance in technology. Also, the construction of additional second main track on parts of the coal corridors in Wyoming and Nebraska could finally be undertaken.

It was hoped that with Grinstein in charge, a breakthrough could soon be achieved in the long-standing dispute BN had with UTU on the crew-consist issue. An agreement was reached with employees working under the contracts with the former CB&Q, Frisco, C&S, and FW&D. However, even with the change in spirit and the general working environment under Grinstein, no progress was made toward finalizing an agreement with representatives of train-service employees working on the northern lines between the Twin Cities and the West Coast. Only with direct intervention by international officers of the UTU was the crew-consist issue finally settled.

Grinstein closed out his career with BN 1995 by successfully negotiating the terms for merger with Santa Fe. Overall, the merged company has done very well in accomplishing the goals of shippers, shareholders, employees, and the economic sectors it serves.

GERALD GRINSTEIN WORK HISTORY

1957	Graduated Harvard Law School Positions held on Capitol Hill: Administrative Assistant to U.S. senator Warren G. Magnuson Counsel to the Merchant Marine and Transportation Subcommittee
1978–1984	Law firm, Preston, Torgrison, Ellis and Hollman
1984–1988	President and COO, President and CEO, Chairman and CEO, Western Air Lines, Inc.
1987–1999	Non-Executive Chairman, Board of Directors, Delta Airlines
1987–1999	Vice Chairman, Burlington Northern, Inc.
1989–1995	President and CEO, Burlington Northern, Inc.
2004–2007	CEO, Delta Air Lines

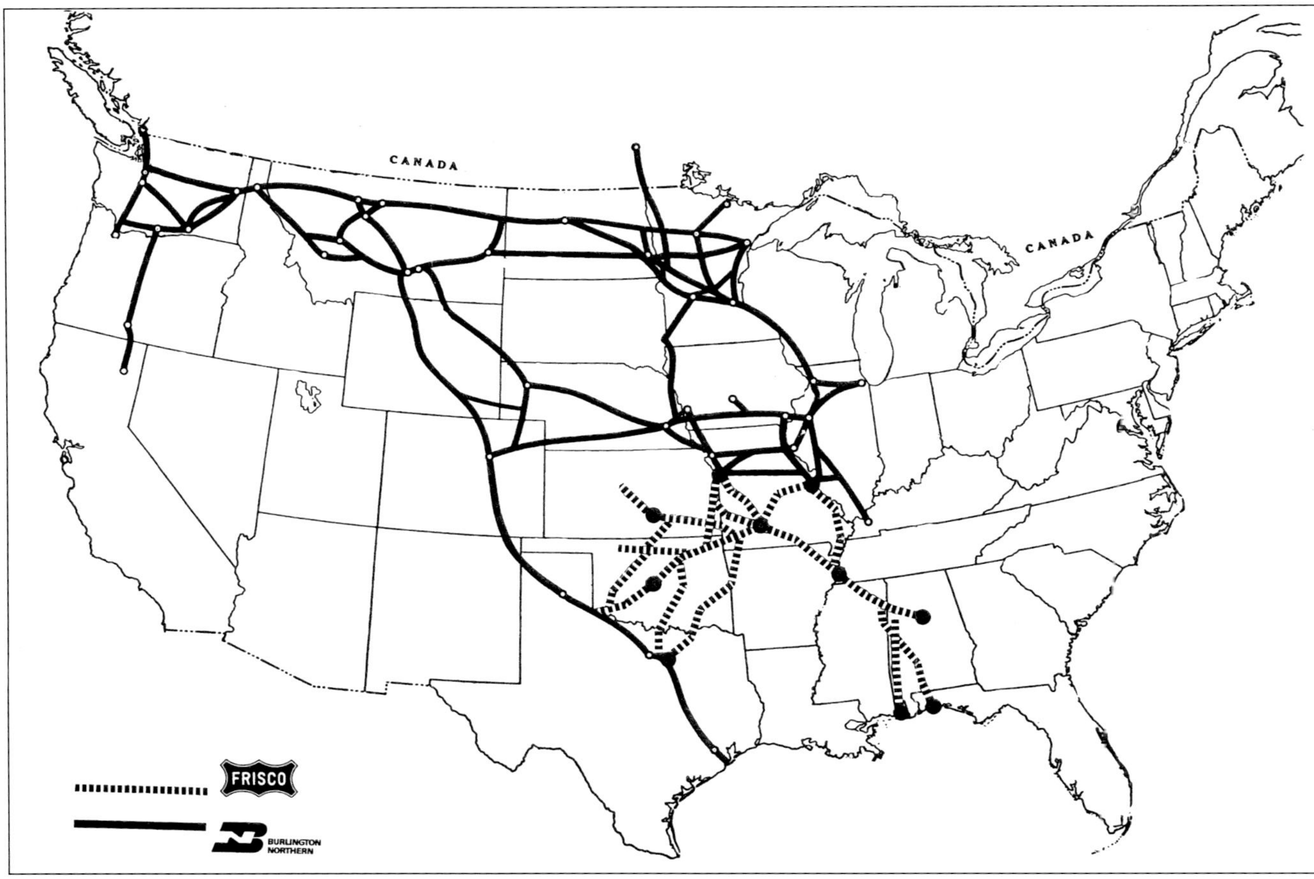

Figure 2.1. Map of Burlington Northern and Frisco routes.

CHAPTER 2

MERGER WITH THE FRISCO

• *expanding single-line service into the South* • *lessons applied in productivity, efficiency, and cost reduction* • *a new culture, controversial to this day* •

A FEW MONTHS AFTER L. W. MENK WAS elected president of the Burlington (CB&Q) Railroad, he made his first move toward merger with the Frisco (St. Louis–San Francisco) Railroad, his previous employer. Menk had the Burlington acquire 10 percent of Frisco stock during the time the GN, NP, and Burlington were pressing the ICC for a favorable decision on their application to merge. No formal application was prepared to include the Frisco in the merger at that time.

Early in 1967, the Burlington reported that these 220,000 shares were sold to Henry Crown, a Chicago industrialist who was reported to already be the Frisco's largest holder of outstanding voting stock. William J. Quinn, who succeeded Menk at the Burlington, advised a *Chicago Tribune* reporter, "someone might try to use the company's holdings in the Frisco to 'becloud the issues' in the pending Burlington–Great Northern–Northern Pacific merger case. Although we think the Commission (ICC) would not have been influenced by such efforts in its current reconsideration of our merger, we concluded that all doubt would be removed by acceptance of the Crown offer to acquire the stock." The writer observed that the purchasing price was not disclosed but was thought to be in the $11 to $12 million range. This purchase boosted Crown's holdings to about 16 percent, making him the largest holder of Frisco stock.[1]

Once that merger was consummated in 1970, we wondered how long it would be until Menk would again initiate action for BN to merge with the Frisco. Seven years later, in 1977, BN announced that it had undertaken a study with the Frisco to determine the benefits of merging, to develop the operating plan to be implemented upon consolidation, and then they would apply to the ICC for authority to merge.

SHOULD BN HAVE TRIED TO MERGE WITH THE MISSOURI PACIFIC?

Not long before the decision to pursue merger with the Frisco was announced, Robert W. (Bob) Downing, vice chairman and chief operating officer, and Norman Lorentzsen, then president and executive vice president, made an inspection trip over parts of the Missouri Pacific Railroad (MP). Downing Jenks, who had his roots on the former GN, headed the MP at that time. Downing and Lorentszen returned home with enthusiasm for the possibility of merging with the MP. When they approached Menk with this idea, though, he rejected it out of hand, saying that instead, BN would be making plans to merge with the Frisco.[2] Soon after, BN announced the plans. BN and the Frisco set up joint teams from all departments to develop plans and put together the data and other material that would be required in the ICC application.[3]

Following the announcement, the MP and UP began to explore the possibility of merging. With BN out of the

1 "Col. Crown Calls Frisco Good Investment," *Chicago Tribune,* February 19, 1967.

2 Refer to the Addendum for Lorentzsen's writings on this subject.

3 From writings that Norman Lorentzsen shared with the author and several conversations the author had with Mr. Lorentzsen on various subjects between 2012 and 2016.

picture as a potential merger partner, the MP needed to come up with plans to expand its system. The MP had a strong base of traffic originating on its lines. It was in an especially strong position along the Gulf Coast where it served many chemical plants that produced a large volume of high-revenue shipments—the chemical business was among the most lucrative traffic handled by any railroad company in North America. With its financial strength, the MP had been better able to exploit growth opportunities along the gulf than its major competitor, the Southern Pacific. The UP, of course, had prospered from the advantage of owning and operating a high-density main line between California and the Midwest. Once the BN decided to expand its territory, the UP knew it had to make its own move to expand its reach into the South.

R. C. GRAYSON TAKES THE REINS ON THE BN RAILROAD

Even before BN's Frisco merger was approved by the courts, Bressler hired Frisco's CEO, Richard Grayson, to head BN's Transportation Division. At the time the merger of BN and the Frisco was approved, the deregulation of pricing for the railroad industry had just occurred, Bressler had just been hired from Atlantic Richfield to head BN, Inc., which put him in charge of all units in BN's Transportation and Resource divisions. As a result, three major changes—two in leadership and one structural through deregulation—had hit BN in the same year. Thus began a total transformation of BN's policies, strategies, operations, and overall, its ways of doing business. It was the beginning of a string of upheavals in the company that would continue for the next fifteen years, well into the 1990s.

By the time of merger with the Frisco, late in 1980, the largest part of the programs for upgrading and expanding capacity to handle increased business had been completed. We were told that improvement in operating and financial performance was essential and could be accelerated greatly under direction from Grayson and the team of managers running the Frisco. This belief prevailed, even though BN had already produced much better results in 1979 and 1980 compared to previous years (note table on page 367 in *Burlington Northern: A Great Adventure*).

The level of improvement that started in 1979 was fully expected, not a surprise, since the heavy expenditures for roadway maintenance were to level off by that time. BN's leaders had been successful in securing the financing needed to move the vast tonnages of business out of the Powder River Basin. They had convinced the board and shareholders of the need to tolerate lower earnings per share for several years while a large amount of operating money was being put into upgrading the property. BN had successfully undertaken and managed a level of growth and property improvement that no other railroad had done since the time of construction of new lines to the West Coast in the 1880s and 1890s.

The Frisco was a mid-size railway of 4,658 route miles compared to the 24,618 miles BN owned, operated and maintained at the time. The Frisco had fairly light density even on its main lines, averaging less than 20 million gross tons per mile per year. About 30 percent of its business was overhead traffic (carloads bridged between railroads), a relatively high amount. Overhead business is always more vulnerable to diversion to competing railroads than business that originates or terminates on a railroad's line. The Frisco had done well in building up bridge traffic by providing good service between the UP over Kansas City and CSX and NS over Birmingham and Memphis. It also provided run-through service with the Santa Fe through Avard, Oklahoma. However, with more mergers and deregulation on the horizon by the late 1970s, the Frisco knew that it was likely that most of its overhead traffic would be lost. As a result, the Frisco needed to merge with another railroad or risk having to carve up its network by selling at least some of its lines to connecting railroads or to short-line operators. In any event, the Frisco stood to lose so much business that it could not survive as a strong mid-size railway company.

When Grayson was appointed president, the incumbent president of the Transportation Division, T. J. Lamphier, was made senior vice president–Transportation, Policy, and Analysis. In the original plan for organization, J. H. Hertog of BN was to retain his position as head of the Operating Department, and the Frisco's vice president–Operations, W. F. Thompson, was to work under Hertog as vice president–Region Operations. Just before the date of the merger, Hertog was made the senior vice president–Coal, and it was announced that

Thompson would head the Operating Department. That set the stage for radical change in priorities, methods, standards, organization, and leadership style. Together, these changes would bring about a difference in culture and a new approach to managing operations and maintenance activities.

Frisco officers were placed in the number two position in the maintenance-of-way section of the Engineering Department and in the car- and locomotive-maintenance functions of the Mechanical Department. Frisco managers were set up to lead change in other areas such as station services, operations analysis, and budgeting. In all sections of the Operating Department, officers of the former Frisco set the agenda, established the priorities, and "trained" managers at all levels on the new methods and standards that were to be introduced on the "old" BN property.

Officers who had worked for BN before the merger continued to head the five operating regions. A sixth region was established at Springfield, Missouri, at the time of merger, and was headed by a Frisco officer. Soon after the merger, when such vacancies occurred on any of the five regions on the "old" BN territory, Frisco people often were placed on them. At the same time, BN people were designated to fill vacancies as they occurred on the Springfield Region.

Integration was accomplished quite rapidly. Compared to most railroad mergers, the BN/Frisco merger was simple to consummate. There were only three common points—Kansas City, St. Louis, and Fort Worth—where operations had to be consolidated. The difficult part of this merger was imposing the culture and values of the former Frisco in former BN territory and in transforming the operating systems BN had developed in the ten years since it was formed.

THE CHANGE IN CULTURE BEGINS

The culture of the combined BN–Frisco was transformed by imposing a rough and tough style of management on the company. This way of managing was in sharp contrast to the values that were set up at BN at the time of the merger in 1970 and built upon in its first decade. An affirmative style of leadership had been practiced and maintained by all of BN's CEOs and department heads with consistency. BN had moved away from the mean-spirited, threatening, domineering, command-and-control style of leadership that had characterized some railroad companies and other old-line industries in the past. The new culture was imposed over the entire BN system within only a few months. For those who had been raised under an affirmative culture, adjustment to the new leadership style was difficult.

When the new organization for the merged company was formed, Ivan Ethington was set up as executive vice president, reporting to Grayson. Thompson and the two vice presidents in Marketing (one responsible for pricing and the other, for sales) reported to Ethington. Since Ethington had a strong, up-front personality and was a very capable officer, we believed he could hold his own and curb the excesses in the management style being invoked, and apply better judgment on decisions on personnel issues that were being made all too often in a "shoot from the hip" manner. Unfortunately, Ethington's health began to fail soon after his appointment, and in a few months, he retired. The position of executive vice president was not filled following his departure.

GRAYSON'S LEADERSHIP TRAITS

Grayson was an excellent railroad man, one of the most capable I have worked under. He was shrewd and highly knowledgeable and developed better systems for managing basic tasks in Operations and Maintenance than nearly anyone else I have either worked under or have learned about. For most people who worked for BN in those years, Grayson and Thompson are remembered mainly for the character of contempt created in the company and the bad treatment many people received. Consequently, not many BN people wish to recognize or give credit to them for the many improvements in methods and practices they established. Often when I have mentioned in conversation with former associates (including some who held senior positions in those years) that many good operating principles were brought to BN in those years, they will say, "name one."

The central theme during Grayson's time as CEO was clear and simple: "Be the low-cost carrier." He stated this objective over and over, in his communications within the company and with analysts and investors. It was a very effective message since every initiative undertaken by BN in those years could be tied to it. Everyone in the company came to understand what role their work was to have in meeting that objective. Grayson was not a charismatic or showy person who caught people's attention by tossing out catchphrases. But we soon learned that every word he spoke counted, and that it was wise to take it in and be sure you had your mind on his messages, because you would be accountable for putting what he said into action. This repetition in communicating basic messages and goals was very effective. Grayson added no embellishments or qualifiers that might distract one's attention on the heart of his messages.

The strong focus on reducing costs came about from Grayson's belief about what the rail industry would be hit with under deregulation. There would be strong and immediate pressure to reduce rates in establishing the long-term contracts to hold business. Our margins of profit would become even thinner unless we took action to reduce our cost base. BN caught onto this new dynamic faster than perhaps any other railroads. This is borne out by a look at the progress we made in lowering our operating ratio to the best in the industry by 1984 (see table 2.2).

Deregulation was the major force requiring large reductions in costs. In addition, there was a great deal of pressure from the investment community and BN's newly established holding company to improve the rate of return from the large investments that had been made in the past ten years to improve the infrastructure and expand its capacity. Also at this time, management throughout American industry was emboldened to take on the challenge of reducing labor costs following the Reagan administration's successful effort in confronting the air-traffic controllers when they went on strike in violation of federal law.

TO OVERCOME RESTRICTIONS ON REDUCING THE WORKFORCE AND NUMBER OF EXEMPT EMPLOYEES

The highest priority for the new management team was the reduction of the workforce, both scheduled and exempt. As mentioned earlier, employees on the payroll as of the date of merger in 1970 had lifetime job protection. Those hired after "M-Day" did not fall under that mandate. Whenever the new plans we developed for expense reduction ran up against the restriction of job protection, our policy was to find ways protected employees could be severed so we could proceed in making the reductions.

REDUCING THE HEAD COUNT

In offering severance of one year's wages or salary, it was believed there was "no better place to put your money." Severance payments on this basis produced a return on investment of 100 percent. The wage and benefit costs for employees designated as surplus were taken off the budget and expense statements of the Operating Department, and the responsibility for those costs was assigned to the Labor Relations Department. Labor Relations was then charged to sever those employees or reassign them to vacancies for jobs we expected to retain, within the limits of applicable labor agreements. Large numbers of surplus protected employees accepted offers of a year's pay as severance. Those who declined severance were assigned to "make work" jobs such as cutting up surplus freight cars. Others were placed in what became known as "rubber rooms" until they would decide to accept the offer of a severance payment or until a vacancy opened up for which they were either qualified or could be given some training to become qualified.

In the case of "older" exempt employees, once they could see the changes that were coming, most of them quickly signed up for the "early out" program. That basically amounted to a chance to retire at age 55 for employees with at least thirty years of service. Their earnings upon retirement would not be significantly different than if they continued to work. This gave exempt employees a way to end their careers with dignity and without having the fear of termination hanging over them. A great deal of institutional knowledge and experience was lost through the rapid exodus of so many experienced people in such a short time. On the other hand, it opened things up for the next generation of managers to advance sooner.

For those who remained on the payroll, it was interesting to observe how quickly they "united." Before the merger with the Frisco, some of BN's managers still had strong emotional ties and loyalty to the company they worked for before the 1970 merger that created BN. However, once they saw a new force coming in from the outside to govern BN, they became more united and loyal to BN. It was similar to how a family will rise up and unite against a common threat. But at the same time, those who were younger or chose not to retire had to overcome any feelings of resentment they had toward the new "system" and demonstrate they wanted to be on the new team. They had to become open to working with and for a group of people who had a very different background and under a very different style of leadership.

When the attitudes or job performance of those who did not "buy in" to the new ways of doing things were manifested, the new leadership dealt with them quickly and without patience. Often, they were given no second chance to show they had "come around" or "gotten the message." While often reprehensible, this approach did bring about the change needed to get new methods implemented quickly. But fear set in. When a new program for incentive compensation was set up, fear combined with greed to expedite change.

The new leadership put pressure on us to be sure all of our people were on "real jobs," to get rid of "the fat" and terminate anyone who was not performing well under the new standards. While unpleasant and stressful, this approach did clean house and flush out any marginal performers. It helped us put together teams of managers who had left the past behind and who were ready and glad for the opportunity to meet the new challenges and opportunities.

We made major reductions in the scheduled workforce, mainly in the ranks of non-operating employees. This was done through changes in methods: streamlining administrative procedures, investing in labor-saving equipment and technologies, and looking intensively at the amount of work produced by every position. On the Seattle Region, for example, we eliminated 50 percent of the authorized clerical and administrative positions. We mechanized and centralized a large amount of work at the regional level by investing in modern equipment. Authorizations for Expenditures (AFE) for acquisition of new equipment and making necessary track changes were approved without delay through the contingency fund set up for unbudgeted capital expenditures. If the savings we developed clearly were "hard dollar" savings and with a return on investment of 25 percent or more, these projects usually were approved the same day the AFE was received by the senior vice president–Operations. Approval was not held up for any undue or protracted analysis.

Next to the clerical force, the ranks of the Mechanical Department took the biggest hit. This came about primarily by an overhaul of methods and procedures used in car maintenance and inspection. Large cost savings resulted and "light" bad-order cars were repaired with less delay, and we were able to expedite intermediate inspections of cars in through freight trains. The most effective program was the mechanization of the car-repair forces that inspected inbound trains. With the equipment, tools, and supplies we provided, they could make minor repairs to cars while they still were in the train, rather than having to switch such cars out of the train and moving them to a fixed repair facility located somewhere in the terminal. With fewer cars having to go through a car-repair facility, the force was reduced. Service was improved by eliminating an average delay of two days to switch a car out, move it to the car shop, have it repaired, switch it into the classification yard, and finally, place it in an outbound train in the departure yard.

INCREASING PRODUCTIVITY OF LABOR, CARS, LOCOMOTIVES, AND MACHINERY

The size of the active locomotive fleet was reduced by improving the utilization of locomotives. The measure of the productivity of locomotives was based on the number of gross ton-miles per available horsepower on a system and region basis. Achieving target levels in this measure required short-term adjustments in the number of locomotive units we were allowed to have in active service. Management and responsibility for the low-horsepower fleet of locomotives used in local, yard, and helper service was moved from the system Transportation office to the regions. The size of a region's fleet of low-horsepower locomotives in active status was adjusted on a daily basis by local managers in line with short-term fluctuations in the volume of business being handled. The high-horsepower locomotive units continued to be managed by System Transportation personnel, who were held responsible for achievement of target levels of utilization, also based on the number of gross ton-miles per available horsepower. The result was a large decrease in the number of units in active service, which in turn reduced fuel consumption and the number of people needed for locomotive maintenance and servicing.

We achieved a quantum leap in labor productivity when we found we could close the locomotive maintenance shop at Auburn, Washington, where 150 units were assigned for maintenance. One of the commitments made for the 1970 merger was that the shop and yard at Auburn (former NP facilities) would continue in operation. However, a "forever" type of agreement needed to be broken in view of changing times, and with our need to make the cost reductions required for survival under deregulation. We simply told the employees and city fathers in Auburn that for twelve years we had maintained our commitment to keep those facilities open. But by 1982, we could no longer be stuck with the inefficiency those facilities represented. Richard Grayson told me to move ahead with closure and provided his personal support through all of the pressures and accusations of bad faith and that we were reneging on commitments BN had made long ago. Closing the shop and yard in Auburn was an emotional event in many respects, and without the changes in leadership in the Frisco merger, it is questionable if or when the facilities at Auburn would ever have been closed.

Next, we closed the locomotive maintenance at Hillyard (Spokane). Until 1982 Hillyard had been designated as system shop for heavy maintenance and overhauls. However, when System Mechanical came under pressure to reduce its costs, rather than simply closing the facility, they decided to turn the Hillyard shop over to the Seattle Region for management. We quickly determined it was not needed for running maintenance of the units under our responsibility and closed it. That decision enabled the reduction of about 250 people.

Making these reductions was painful, but they left us a lean, efficient, and more effective operation. Together, Dan Jaeb, the region director–Mechanical and the three division superintendents (Bob Seeley, Gary Widle, and Bob Howrey) on the Seattle Region were outstanding in their support of the agenda for reducing maintenance of equipment expenses. Together, they made consolidations in equipment maintenance facilities that could have been part of the operating plan for the 1970 merger, but were set aside at that time to help reduce opposition to the merger from labor unions and local communities. Similar stories of success in reducing costs could be cited for many other departments and locations.

IMPROVING PRODUCTIVITY IN ALL FUNCTIONS

From the outset of the Frisco merger, we were directed to improve the productivity of all mechanized tie gangs to the rate of installing four ties per man-hour. To reach this level required setting up each gang with a double set of equipment and increasing the gang from thirty-five men to forty-two employees. With an eight-hour day, 336 employee-hours were worked, which in turn required the gang put in no less than 1,344 ties. With gangs set up with thirty-five men and a single set of equipment under the old system, we had been used to getting between 700 and 800 ties placed.

Robert J. (Bob) Seeley, division superintendent, and Sam Melonas, assistant superintendent–Roadway Maintenance on the Portland Division, bought into the new concept and right from the start, their new 42-man gang exceeded the standard of four ties per man-hour. They even beat the productivity rate of the tie gang working on the territory of the old Frisco railroad at that time. The Pacific and Spokane divisions did not like watching the Portland Division outshine them, and quickly, Don Rogers, the region's engineer–Track, supported the effort by getting the machines and equipment maintainers in place, together with technical advice and support, and reorganized their gangs. With this much higher rate of productivity, the number of ties specified in the annual program could be increased within the budget limit. That alone was a strong incentive to produce at a higher and higher rate.

Prior to the Frisco merger, the policies of our Engineering Department did not allow us to "step down" curve-worn welded rail that had been replaced. Instead of using it to replace light-rail sections in sidings or yard tracks, we had to cut it up and load it out as scrap. Under the Frisco policy, any piece of welded rail, no matter how badly worn, was viewed as better than the old, jointed 65-, 75-, or 85-pound rail that was in those tracks. We were encouraged to use a locomotive or any other means to pull the recovered welded rail to a nearby location where is could be laid in secondary tracks with light-rail sections still in place.

Later, after new rail pick-up trains were acquired and put in service, we could move recovered welded rail to more distant locations, if needed. The word was put out by W. F. Thompson that henceforth, anyone who ever cut up recovered welded rail would be fired. We were allowed to lay the recovered welded rail in a new location without first having an AFE approved. All that was required was for us to make a list of the number of feet of rail and the location where we had laid the recovered, heavier rail and send the list to the accounting people, who would then correct the property records. In this way, none of us would get in trouble for doing work that had not been formally authorized. This was a good system for making use of an asset that still had plenty of life remaining, instead of cutting it up for scrap.

A new system that provided opportunities to do more "spot" maintenance on secondary tracks was the use of credits to operating expense for the value of scrap steel that we recovered from track removals. Grayson explained we would be allowed to credit the value of scrap we recovered in track removals or property cleanup against our operating expense. We could then apply the amount of such credits toward additional basic, non-programmed maintenance work that was needed. This system gave us a chance to catch up on small trackwork projects that had been set aside for many years in favor of large upgrading projects. It was of great benefit to have accounting systems set up that would encourage "the right things" to be done on a railroad, rather than restrict us. In addition to helping us to overcome deficiencies in maintenance, this new system provided an incentive to complete the removal of unneeded pieces of track in stations and yards, thereby cleaning up the property and turning unneeded assets (scrap steel) into cash.

ABILITY TO REDUCE THE SIZE OF THE ACTIVE FLEETS OF CARS AND LOCOMOTIVES

One of the major areas of success in the Transportation function was in management of the freight-car fleet. The processes we had been using were highly centralized and quite complex under the COMPASS system. Car management had become monolithic, lacking in flexibility and responsiveness to local needs or efforts to improve utilization and manage the size of the active car fleet. Instead of designing a new system for BN, it was decided that car management should be decentralized and accountability for its functions moved to the regions. The primary measure on which the regions were judged was the number of car-days per carload (a combination of carloads originated on-line and received in interchange) on each region. Any day that number moved in the wrong direction meant we had too many cars in active status on that region. To correct an unfavorable number required that more cars be put in storage and that more attention be given to moving more cars off the region with less delay.

As the size of the active fleet was reduced, there were fewer gross ton-miles to be moved, thereby requiring fewer locomotives and with fewer cars to be handled through yards. With fewer cars to be switched, fewer yard-switching assignments were needed. Yard congestion was reduced and in time, fewer trains had to be run to move cars. With fewer cars to be moved, there also were fewer cars to be inspected and found in need of repair; hence, an opportunity for the Mechanical Department to reduce its car-inspection and -repair force. The result was a more fluid, better functioning railroad. Such strong emphasis on the size of the active car fleet produced efficiencies throughout the Operating Department. The cascading effect was amazing.

The initiatives described may seem very elementary, easy to understand, and presumably, easy to implement. Individually, they are quite simple, but unless every one of them was targeted on consistently and supported at all levels of management, they would not get done at a high level of intensity. Further, it was not simple to manage or control the operation when dozens of new initiatives, standards, and best practices were all being implemented at the same time. If a narrow, single focus were applied to just one aspect of productivity at a time, it might have collide with other requirements, to their detriment. It is the job of operations supervisors to keep all of them going at the same time, and to make sure that progress on one initiative is not being made to the detriment of others.

SAFETY IN TIMES OF STRESS, UNCERTAINTY, AND DISTRACTIONS

During times of uncertainty and chaos in the early 1980s, there was the danger that safety would suffer. Despite all of the distractions, disruption of routines, changes in priorities, rumors of how much worse things may get, and inconsistencies in and resentment of many managerial directives, the numbers on safety performance show this did not happen during the time of upheaval that occurred with the BN–Frisco merger. Instead, safety showed considerable improvement for a few years. What brought about the improvement was the work done by all levels of field managers to communicate with employees about what was going on in the company and what else was likely to happen in the short term, involving the closing of facilities or initiating new methods and equipment that would result in additional layoffs or transfer of work. As soon as such information was passed on to supervisors, they were expected to communicate it. Even though much of that information was not good news for many people, at least they knew where things were headed. That removed some of the distraction that comes with uncertainty. Also, we emphasized the need to leave problems "at the gate" when coming to work, and maintaining focus on the work at hand.

Another factor with an effect on safety was the bind or closeness that developed between field managers and the rank-and-file employees. There was tension and concern among both the supervisors and the craft members over the way that both sides were being treated. Many employees heard, or observed firsthand, what their bosses were being subjected to, and the uncertain status of local supervisors who were still around. At the same time, employees feared for their jobs. Both groups had to endure a combination of tension, fear, resentment, and uncertainty of their status. This brought supervisors and employees closer together.

These factors caused both supervisors and employees to focus more intently on their work. They were less complacent or relaxed in performing their duties. Even though it was not a happy time, it caused people to concentrate on their work more intensely. While no one is likely to support or advocate having an adversarial environment as a means to improve safety, the fact that it raises concern over one's livelihood will cause many to push outside distractions and lower-priority matters aside. The numbers prove it is possible to manage (and improve) safety even in times of turmoil and low morale.

QUALITY OF PLANT AND EQUIPMENT NOT ALLOWED TO DETERIORATE

During the "Frisco years," the property was not run down either by making reductions in operating expenses for roadway maintenance or for capital expenditures for such vital work as tie and rail replacement, ballast renewal, or surface correction. Deliberate neglect of track quality had happened all too often over the years in the rail industry when new management teams were brought in. However, it cannot be said that Bressler, Grayson, or the priorities of the holding company required us to severely reduce the resources needed for keeping the track in satisfactory condition.

A look at table 2.1 clearly indicates that the quantities of material and the amount of capital authorized for roadway maintenance remained at about the same level from 1981 through 1983 as they had been from the mid- to late 1970s and into 1980. Beginning in 1984, the quantity of rail and ties installed increased considerably. No matter what else may be said about how the company was managed in those years, the new leadership cannot be rightfully accused of running down the property.

A MISTAKE?

Most of what is commonly remembered about the Frisco merger is the conduct of some of its people, going all the way to Gerald Grinstein's (CEO from 1988 through 1995) comment: "It [the merger with the Frisco] was a big mistake."[4] On the other side, some from the former BN still do not wish to acknowledge that some better operating and maintenance practices were installed on

---

4 Lawrence J. Kaufman, *Leaders Count,* 295.

BN in those years. A lesson learned in those times was the need for leaders at all levels to be looking outside of their organization for new and better practices. Some opportunities had been missed during the 1970s, when the entire BN was strongly focused internally on the upgrading and expansion projects that were vital to the company's future.

Table 2.1. RAIL AND TIE PROGRAMS, 1975–1985

Year	*New Rail (no. of miles)*	*Ties (in thousands)*
1975	255	2,420
1976	255	2,901
1977	388	2,881
1978	413	2,941
1979	586	3,039
1980	785	3,821
1981	688	2,750
1982	864	3,726
1983	660	4,655
1984	629	4,390
1985	668	3,699

Note: Starting in 1981, these quantities of material include what was placed on the lines of the former Frisco Railroad in addition to BN. At the time of its merger with BN, the Frisco consisted of 4,658 route miles, compared with to 31,420 miles on BN including its subsidiaries, the FW&D and C&S railways.

LESSONS LEARNED

An important lesson learned from the years following the Frisco merger was in the area of officer conduct. It is important for a CEO and others at the senior level to establish standards of conduct, "limits" in behavior, and examples of leadership style and practices that are forbidden and those to be emulated. People in such positions should be charged with setting an example for everyone to see as the kind of company we wish to be. Leaders should be expected to raise the level of skills and job performance of their people rather than simply looking for reasons to terminate or demote those who may not be fully proficient. "Anybody can fire"; developing people takes much more skill.

Whenever a new agenda is set in an organization, it is important for its people to learn what constitutes good performance. Those affected by change need to watch and learn from those who have mastered the new fundamentals and who are being recognized for their successes. It is important to learn to bury the past, regardless of its glories and what was accomplished. Take time to study, learn, and understand the "new system," how it works, and what will be expected of you. The sooner you understand, prepare, and buy into the new agenda, the better for you.

Table 2.2 OPERATING RATIOS, SELECTED RAILROADS, 1980–1986

Year	*BN*	*ATSF*	*UP*	*NS*
1980	91.5	89.7	86.5	80.1
1981	87.7	93.6	86.3	78.1
1982	88.4	96.1	89.9	82.9
1983	82.3	91.3	89.3	83.6
1984	78.7	90.4	89.9	79.6
1985	80.7	92.8	90.8	79.8
1986	87.8	90.8	81.9	80.1

Note BN's progress in reducing its operating ratio below 80 in 1984, which was the best performance of any U.S. railroad for that year. This was a reduction of just under 13 points in four years. BN's performance in the years following 1984 was affected by the UP's success in gaining a large part of the coal business originating in the Powder River Basin, and reflects aggressive price reductions applied to hold business following the deregulation of pricing. Finally, the driving force in the company became cash generation and payment of dividends to the holding company, rather than the operating ratio.

CHAPTER 3

DEREGULATION OF PRICING

The railroad's basic difficulty is legislative in origin; hence, only legislation can correct it.

J. M. BUDD, CHAIRMAN OF BURLINGTON NORTHERN, NO DATE, LOCATION, OR CONTEXT GIVEN

BRIAN SOLOMON, *INTERMODAL RAILROADING*

We've increased our economic performance tremendously since the late 1970s and raised our return on our assets from around two percent to more than 10 percent in 1984. And one of the major reasons is the new freedom to compete that the Staggers Act has given us. . . . I think the act has been an essential ingredient in the turnaround in the rail industry, and particularly in our company.

D. W. GASKINS INTERVIEW, *BN NEWS*, JANUARY/FEBRUARY 1986

DEREGULATION AS PROVIDED IN THE Staggers Rail Act was among the most powerful and effective initiatives that transformed the U.S. rail industry in the 1980s. Deregulation ranks at or above the positive impact of finally getting the size of train and yard-switching crews rationalized, getting governmental units to accept the social responsibility for passenger service, and learning how to make intermodal service profitable. It also led to taking advantage of the magnificent, unprecedented opportunity to move vast tonnages of new business from the Powder River Basin in Wyoming and Montana, and gaining the asset base and thereby the ability to restructure to enable the economies of scale inherent in the railroad business that would take hold.

The financial problems of much of the rail industry in the 1970s, namely, the bankruptcy of the Penn Central, Milwaukee and Rock Island railroads, made it clear to economists, regulators, and elected representatives at the national level that the era of the heavy-handed hold the government had held on the rail industry for so long was in danger of pushing even more of it into needing heavy government subsidies or even nationalization. It was finally recognized that railroads needed to be given the opportunity to compete with each other and against the other modes of freight transportation, which, in the case of trucking and inland waterway companies, had the advantage of operating on facilities or infrastructure built, maintained, and operated by the government. Under ICC regulation, railroads had great difficulty in responding to new business opportunities to compete with other modes, due to lack of flexibility and the timeliness needed to negotiate rates and other terms for their services. Instead of being able to compete in the marketplace, they had to work through the restricted and outdated practices of the rate bureaus and regulators.

Success in obtaining and holding on to business was based less on the creativity and negotiating skills of the railroad company's sales and marketing managers, and more on the level of personal relationships or friendships between them and their customers. Railroad sales personnel spent most of their time responding to complaints on equipment supply, delayed shipments, or requests for special handling of one kind or another involved in the movement of their customers' freight. They lacked the freedom needed to negotiate confidential rate contracts with their customers.

The first step toward deregulation came with the passage of the 4R (Railroad Revitalization and Regulatory Reform) Act of 1976. It allowed railroads a "zone of reasonableness" in setting rates with freedom—within specified limits—without having to first get ICC approval. It was a start toward moving the rail industry into the world of competition. Other provisions in the 4R Act removed some of the restrictions that impaired mergers, gave some relief in restrictions for approval of the abandonment of unprofitable branch lines, and prohibited states from taxing railroad property at rates higher than those applied on other commercial and industrial property. The relief granted in this legislation came during Gerald Ford's term as president.

The 4R Act also encouraged the ICC to move toward deregulation of rail intramodal service. Under its chairman, Dan O'Neal, regulators responded by offering partial deregulation of the traffic of fresh fruit and vegetables, as railroads had lost most of that business to trucks. In only three months, the volume of perishable business handled on the Southern Pacific and Santa Fe skyrocketed. Darius Gaskins replaced O'Neal shortly before the passage of the Staggers Act of 1980, which moved the rail industry much faster and further into the era of deregulation. Gaskins wasted no time in advancing the rule making for full deregulation of intermodal business that had been prepared shortly before his appointment. Gaskins and the ICC announced a favorable decision on this proposal in November 1980:

> The Congress expects us to undertake a careful examination of railroad regulation and eliminate or reduce restrictions on railroad price and service changes. In particular, the legislative history focuses on the need to pursue vigorously opportunities for exemptions. Congress has stated it is anxious for us to remove existing regulations barriers and reserve judgment on potential problems until after exemptions have been granted.[1]

The ICC's order covered both domestic and international intermodal business. From this point, the marketplace, and not the decisions of the historic rate bureaus and the ICC, would determine the railroads' success in obtaining and moving intermodal business.

ENTERING THE WORLD OF COMPETITION IN PRICING

Deregulation of the whole spectrum of freight soon followed. However, there was a lack of enthusiasm for the deregulation of pricing in some parts of the rail industry. Not all railroads were prepared for the cultural adjustment that would be required in moving from the relative comfort and predictability of working through the processes used in the past for review of proposed rates. Moving into a deregulated environment would require a new set of skills and would end the long era of managing under the bureaucratic, regimented principles they had worked under their entire careers. Instead, they would have to enter the world of competition, be able to negotiate contracts, and quickly make adjustments in rates in response to competition from other railroads and other modes of transportation. It was the need for making this kind of paradigm shift that caused Bressler and Grayson to hire Gaskins in 1982 to head BN's Marketing Department.

It was anticipated by those who advocated deregulation and pushed it through to signature by President Jimmy Carter that railroads would have the flexibility needed to raise their rates enough to improve their financial performance. However, with the trucking industry being deregulated at about the same time, and with the pressure on the railroads to lock up business with long-term contracts, they found themselves reducing rather than increasing their rates. Darius Gaskins wrote, "The shocking element of the story is the railroads' new freedom to adjust rates upward was overpowered by the new competitive reality. In the early years of the Staggers Act, railroad marketing departments had little expertise in rate making. . . . I discovered this world of falling rates in my new job at the Burlington Northern Railroad in 1982."[2]

---

1 David J. DeBoer, *Piggyback and Containers: A History of Rail Intermodal on America's Steel Highway*, 149.

2 "Regulation of Freight Railroads in the Modern Era: 1970–2010," *Review of Network Economics* (December 2008): 564.

Early in the game, Grayson saw perhaps better than anyone else in the industry what railroads would have to do as soon as the deregulation of pricing became effective. He told us that immediately, we had to undertake an all-out effort to reduce our costs. That gave rise to the theme, "Be the low-cost carrier," that we worked under in the early 1980s. That effort put BN ahead of its rail competitors. By 1984 our operating ratio was down to 78.7, the lowest of the large railroads operating at that time. Even with the downward pressure on rates in those years, we managed to reduce our costs at an even faster rate. And, we still were able to generate the cash we needed to sustain a large program for capital expenditures, without having to seek additional funding from outside sources.

Under the Staggers Act, the ICC could not direct a railroad company to reduce rates that were lower than 180 percent of variable costs as determined under the Uniform Rail Costing System. In establishing the 180 percent ceiling, Congress showed its understanding that the railroads had to be able to set some rates higher than their variable costs to earn enough to support reinvestment in their property and to earn a reasonable return on their invested capital. However, rates in excess of the 180 percent threshold level were subject to challenge to the ICC. Several electric-power companies and some grain shippers later used this provision against BN in an attempt to get the ICC to force the railroads to reduce their rates.

Under the leadership of Darius Gaskins, BN developed some unique and innovative programs that generated additional business and higher revenue. To accomplish that in the grain business, BN hired some experts from the international grain companies that were resisting our effort to apply new and better concepts for the pricing and movement of grain under deregulation. Among the concepts they introduced was an auction system for "selling" cars for grain transportation in a forward (futures) market. Forty percent of BN's grain-carrying capacity was put into a program called COTS (Certificates of Transportation). This type of program was new to the rail industry but had been a practice of long standing for barge and ocean shipping. Forward purchasing also was a common practice in the grain trade, in which grain might be sold several months before it is actually transferred from one party to another.

In BN's program, the COT certificates were offered in units of 54 cars, 26 cars, and single units on 14 major corridors used for grain movement. BN decided to offer the COT program as a substitute for transportation contracts after deregulation because the confidentiality provisions in contracts created problems in getting information about shipping prices to the grain markets. For grain shippers, the COT program established certainty that cars would be available for loading at a specific time. The certificates could be traded with other grain companies. As happened with ever-changing grain markets, the value of the certificates could move up or down. For BN, the program provided predictability for the movement of 40 percent of its large fleet of grain cars, as well as the opportunity to better schedule its operation. Car and locomotive utilization improved as a result. ICC commissioner Karen B. Phillips described the COTS program as "one of the few truly innovative carrier marketing programs arising out of the Staggers Act."[3]

ON TO A REAL SUCCESS STORY

The performance of the U.S. rail industry following the onset of deregulation in 1980 was impressive:

- Average rates per revenue ton-mile decreased 43 percent from 1981 to 1991, adjusted for inflation. Further reductions brought rates down to 60 percent of the 1981 level. Even with some increases in rates starting in 2005, average ton-mile revenue has remained 42 percent less than 1981.[4]
- The railroads' share of the intercity freight market (in ton-miles) increased from 35 percent in 1978 to 40 percent in recent years.
- Return on investment increased from an average of less than 2 percent in the 1970s to between 9 and 10 percent in 1996.
- The utilization rates for locomotives, cars, and track have doubled (based on mileage accumulated by equipment and on the gross ton-miles handled per mile of road).

---

3 David M. Cawthorne, "Burlington Northern Gets Final OK for Freight Car Futures Program" *Traffic World,* February 3, 1992.

4 AAR positions paper, "The Cost Effectiveness of America's Freight Railroads," May 2014.

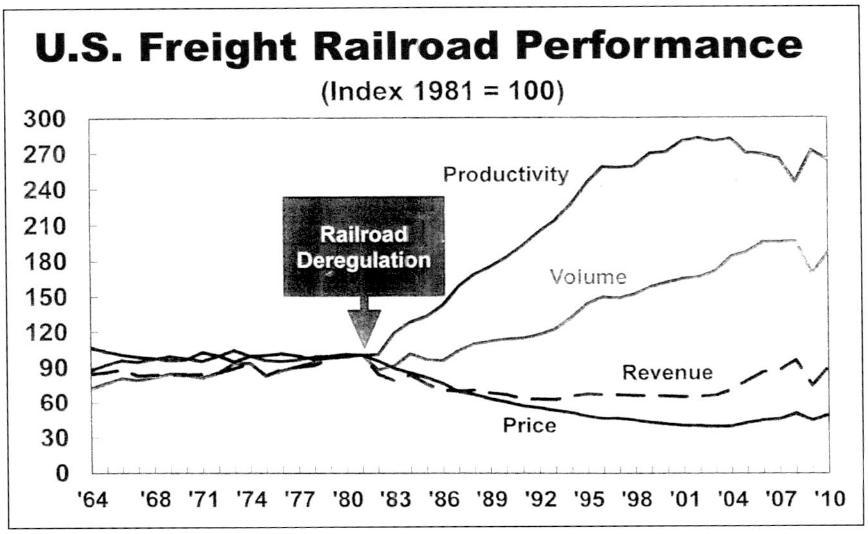

Figure 3.1. Association of American Railroads.

- Labor productivity has increased 400 percent (generally stated as the number of gross ton-miles per employee hour).
- Gains in productivity have been passed on to customers through lower rates.
- Average hourly wages and benefits for railroad employees have increased 116 percent, compared with a 103 percent increase in hourly wages for all U.S. workers.
- Railroad workers are in the top 2 percent of all American wage earners.
- In safety, employee injuries declined 84 percent from 1980 through 2013, and the train-accident rate fell 84 percent.

Those who have gained the most from the deregulation of pricing have been the users of rail transportation. The cost of freight service has been greatly reduced across the U.S. economy. Shippers have benefited from the ability to negotiate confidential, long term contracts for rates, and in many cases, for the standard of service to be provided. Once railroads were relieved of the restrictions they had in the old regulated environment, creative pricing and service packages could be provided that would generate more business for the railroad and enhance the capability of shippers to market their goods and to process the resource materials they must transport to run their business.

PART II

REVALUING RESOURCES

CHAPTER 4

ESTABLISHING A HOLDING-COMPANY STRUCTURE

You couldn't put such an array of assets together at any price.

RICHARD M. BRESSLER QUOTED IN "A RAILROAD FOR THE LONG HAUL," PAUL GIBSON, *FORBES*, APRIL 27, 1981

The second key objective is . . . to achieve a better balance between the transportation and resource business.

RICHARD M. BRESSLER, LETTER TO SHAREHOLDERS, BURLINGTON NORTHERN ANNUAL REPORT FOR 1982, PAGES 2 AND 3

SOON AFTER RICHARD BRESSLER MOVED IN as president and CEO of BNI, he made it known that both the Transportation and Resources divisions were underperforming units. He set two short-term objectives: the railroad would be made "one of the most efficient carriers in the industry," and "a better balance" between the transportation and resource businesses would be achieved. Resource activities would be expanded by new investments made in assets both on and off BNI–owned properties.[1] To these ends, a holding company was formed and the two major business units (Transportation and Resources) were restructured into eight independent operating companies.

Upon merging with the Frisco Railroad, several senior executives who had been with BN before the merger soon retired or left the company for various other reasons. For the Resources Division, Richard Bressler brought in a new slate of executives. Much of the senior management team that had been in charge of the oil and gas and the land and minerals units was soon replaced. This included Bob Binger, president of the Resources Division, and H. Leighton Steward, who had been hired to head the oil and gas unit only two years earlier.

Somer G. (Bud) Merryman, a vice president who had been with the forest-management unit even before the 1970 merger, was retained and named president of BNI Timberlands. Merryman held that position for two years. Fred Winegar continued to head Plum Creek, Inc., until 1982 when William Black, another executive with a long career at Plum Creek, replaced him. David Leland was hired from Southwest Forest Industries, Inc., to head Plum Creek in 1983. Other executives were soon recruited from outside BNI to head the newly formed companies established under the holding-company structure for oil and gas, land and minerals, and real estate unit.

Only a few months after joining BNI, Bressler began the process of reorganization into a holding-company structure. In his opinion, BNI lacked a clearly defined corporate structure for each unit of its business. Under the philosophy Bressler established for BNI's business

1 Letter from Richard M. Bressler to shareholders, BNI *Annual Report for 1981*, page 3.

units, each would have considerable autonomy. When a good return could be assured, support would be there from the holding company for making capital investments. Together with the CEO of each unit, the holding company would set targets for performance (mainly for the generation of cash flow), set incentives for management performance, and provide help in the preparation of a strategic plan. The management of each unit was expected to run it, assuming accountability for producing results at or above the target levels that had been set.

Bressler believed we would have greater success in attracting management talent for a specific type of business if BNI was organized into distinctly separate operating companies. With a holding-company structure, BNI would be in a stronger position to raise money in the financial markets when capital was needed to support a particular growth opportunity or increase productivity in one of the units. Under BNI's previous organization structure, the law allowed us to issue securities only for transportation purposes. When capital was to be applied to a non-rail activity, funds generated by the railroad would have to be diverted away from the railroad. Under a holding-company structure, funds needed by the non-rail businesses could be raised without dependence on the railroad and without having to draw money away from investments needed on the railroad.

Bressler was challenged as to how BNI would treat and manage its railroad company under the new structure. He asserted the railroad was the "crown jewel" among the companies that made up BNI, and for that reason, the financial strength and quality of the its property and equipment would be maintained.[2] As evidence that would be the case, Bressler pointed out that we spent 18 percent more on the track in 1981, his first full year as CEO of BNI, than in the previous year. Further, we planned to triple the amount spent for track-maintenance machinery in 1982. Overall, capital spending on the railroad would remain at a high level. Investments would be concentrated on projects that would improve productivity as well as maintain the quality of the roadway and equipment.

A lack of understanding—and a general lack of interest to listen and learn—caused some political leaders, union representatives, and the public in general to become fearful of adverse consequences for the railroad and its people. They felt certain that with a holding-company structure, money would be taken out of the railroad and applied in other lines of business. The result would be a general deterioration in the condition of the track, cars and locomotives. Service would deteriorate, customers would leave BN, and jobs would be lost. All in all, they feared a holding company would be the stage for ruination of the railroad. This kind of concern was so intense and long lasting in the northern states that in March 1982 Senator Max Baucus of Montana convened a hearing of the Senate Judiciary Committee where Bressler testified.

Having each line of business set up independently under the holding-company structure made it possible for them to focus on two primary goals: to increase operating income and cash generation, and to achieve particular goals unique to their business. In an interview Bressler gave *Forbes* magazine in 1981, he stated, "You couldn't put together such an array of assets together at any price."[3] What was needed in each company was the kind of leadership that would accept accountability for performance, and that had the resolve and ability to transform their company into a high-performance organization. Bressler emphasized repeatedly that the holding company would set targets of performance, establish incentives, and help the units deal with financing needs—the analysis and evaluation of proposed capital expenditures. Running the operation on a day-to-day basis and carrying out the plans for reaching the desired level of performance would be left to the management of the unit.

2 "Bressler: Railroad (is) 'Crown Jewel' of BNI," *Mgr,* a BNRR newsletter for managers and supervisory employees, April 1982.

3 Paul Gibson, "Burlington Northern: A Railroad for the Long Haul," *Forbes*, April 27, 1981, 120.

CHAPTER 5

AGGRESSIVE PLAN AND ACTIONS TO ENHANCE EARNINGS

LEADERSHIP PRACTICES UNDER BRESSLER

Executives who did not embrace or demonstrate the resolve needed to move their unit forward fell out of favor and were soon replaced. Not all of the executives Bressler recruited from the outside made the grade, either. Some of them left BNI within a short time. Bressler was tough, even with those who had appeared to be friends or close associates, when he concluded they were not able to operate to his standards. He appeared to play no favorites, and there was only one team in the company, his team.

From the outset of his tenure with BNI, Bressler focused on strategies that would unlock the value of the natural resources that the investment community saw as undeveloped or only marginally developed. He wanted to raise the combined level of revenue from those resources and other non-rail holdings to a level much closer to the amount of revenue and operating income produced by the railroad. At that time, the new management team felt the railroad had to prepare to take a long strike to break the unsustainable legacy of high labor costs and restrictive work practices that afflicted BN and the entire rail industry. To have the strength to take a strike of that duration would require a large "war chest" of funds generated by both the railroad and resource units. Bressler believed the management capability in those businesses had to be upgraded for BN to handle a challenge of that level. During this time, BN was building up the strength that might be needed to support the railroad, and the shareholders would be rewarded with higher returns as the resource units improved their performance.

CHALLENGE TO THE NON-RAIL UNITS

Bressler's comments on each of BNI's lines of business in the annual report for 1981 gave a general indication of the direction he would have each of them to take under his leadership. He also provided a somewhat "gentle" critique and hint of the agenda he had for each unit:

- FOREST MANAGEMENT In years past, as much as 33 percent of the contracts for timber cutting contained inadequate provision for cost escalation. In 1981 that amount was reduced to 13 percent. By 1983 no more timber would be cut under such provisions. Also, the ratio of timber cut to the harvest potential on land owned by BNI was among the lowest in the industry. BN planned to increase this ratio in future cuttings.
- FOREST PRODUCTS MANUFACTURING Plum Creek, Inc., was rated as one of the most efficient western producers, with high productivity from its workforce and facilities.
- OIL AND GAS The emphasis of Milestone Petroleum, Inc., was shifted to having exploration, development, and productivity done for the company's own account, both on and off land owned by BNI. Having a working interest was considered preferable

to simply collecting royalties and lease payments. The expenditures for exploration and development were doubled in 1981.

- COAL AND MINERALS The new management team increased exploration activity. Coal reserves were being consolidated into blocks of land large enough to support large-scale mining operations.[1]
- LAND AND REAL ESTATE A shift was made to retaining rather than selling land, as had been the norm in the past. With this change, a steady income stream could be built in joint venture agreements.

SHIFT FROM SUSTAINED YIELD TO AGGRESSIVE CUTTING

After Bob Binger left BN, Plum Creek took a much different direction in forest management. It made large clearcuts of as much as one square mile, which brought charges of wanton desecration of nature. Plum Creek claimed it practiced selective harvesting in 80 percent of its logging and that clearcutting was practiced in only 12 percent of its logging operations.

In 1990 Plum Creek's regional director, Bill Parson, was quoted on the issue of limiting timber cutting to a sustained yield basis: "We have never said we were on a sustained yield program, and we have never been on a sustained yield program. Let's get to the heart of it. Sure, it's extensively logged, but what is wrong with that?"[2] In the same article, Plum Creek established the annual rate of growth on its railroad land grant lands as between 210 and 300 million board feet per year.

Between 1984 and 1991, Plum Creek cut an average of 605 million board feet per year. Dave Leland, its CEO, stated, "Plum Creek had to accelerate its cut in 1982 and 1983 to even get up to a sustained yield cut [rate]." Plum Creek's expansion of clearcutting caused an uproar from environmentalists, the general citizenry, and some of the elected representatives, charging that it had over-logged its land. Congressman Rod Chandler (R–Washington) went so far as to call Plum Creek the "Darth Vader" of the state of Washington. Rick Holley, Plum Creek's vice president–Finance in the mid-1980s, recalled, "The parent company viewed Plum Creek as a liquidating entity. The idea was that once you cut the trees, that's it—you moved on. It was really an interesting time because we didn't know what was next for the company or where we were headed."[3] Holley was named president and CEO of Plum Creek early in 1984.

Under its new direction, Plum Creek cut timber far more aggressively than it had under the policies that Bob Binger had established during his tenure. BNI had minimized the controversial practice of clearcutting before the change in direction for the company. It changed from selective cutting to maximizing the return through "old-growth liquidation," away from the values many foresters have to nurture, protect, and sustain a company's timberlands. As happened throughout BNI's family of businesses in those years, the company replaced managers who had difficulty in making the adjustment to support a new agenda, and with it the need to change some of their beliefs, attitudes, or mindsets.

Professional foresters will argue both sides of the question as to whether clearcutting is a sound practice in forest management, if it is wanton or reckless, causing the destruction of a great natural resource. The comments made by Binger and the new management of Plum Creek reveal the vast differences in viewpoints at different stages in BN's history on how its forest resources should have been managed.

In the 1980s, Plum Creek was able to sell logs to countries in the Pacific Rim at high prices. It was exporting 60 percent of the timber it cut. Making those sales led to the clearcutting of the forests Plum Creek owned in Washington and Montana. To meet the demand, the harvest level was increased from 67 million board feet (mmbf) to 136 mmbf in 1963, and to 236 mmbf in 1986, the peak year.

1 Author's note: In an interview with *Forbes*, April 27, 1981, Bressler noted an agreement in which the buyer of coal mined on BN lands was paying only 16 cents per ton, per a contract negotiated twenty years before, compared to a royalty payment of $1 per ton or 12.5 percent of the selling price of the coal that would be expected in 1981.

2 Dennis Farney, "Unkindest Cut? Timber Firm Stirs Ire Felling Forests Faster Than They Regenerate," *Wall Street Journal*, June 18, 1990.

3 *Gratitude, Stewardship, Opportunity: 25 Years of Plum Creek*, a company publication.

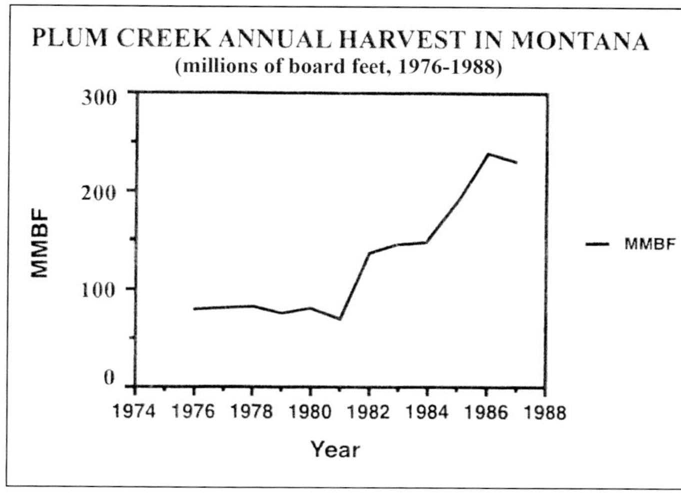

Figure 5.1. Note that the harvest ranged from 70 to 80 million board feet per year until 1982, when the cut was increased substantially and reached well over 200 million board feet from 1985 to 1988. In those years, Plum Creek resorted to clear-cutting to accelerate the earnings of its forest-management unit. TIMOTHY MATTHEW BECHTOLD, "NOW V. FOREVER: THE CONFLICT BETWEEN BUSINESS AND FORESTRY IN THE MANAGEMENT OF PLUM CREEK TIMBERLANDS IN MONTANA" (1992), THESES AND DISSERTATIONS, PROFESSIONAL PAPERS, PAPER 3108, UNIVERSITY OF MONTANA SCHOLAR WORKS.

Plum Creek was able to outbid smaller sawmills for the timber being sold off government-owned land, causing some of those mills to be shut down. In fact, Plum Creek closed the sawmills it owned as well. This led to a decline in employment and in the sales of finished lumber. The spotted-owl issue came later.

In 2016 Plum Creek merged with the Weyerhaeuser Corporation, another large producer of forest products and also a large holder of forested lands, making it the largest private land-owner in the United States.

STRENGTHENING THE OIL AND GAS UNIT

Early in 1981, John F. Greene was hired to head BN's oil and gas operation, which had recently been named Milestone Petroleum Company. At the end of 1984, the name of BNI's oil products company was changed from Milestone Petroleum to Meridian Oil Products, Inc. (MOPI). A new holding company, Meridian Petroleum Holding Company, was formed by combining the operations of MOPI and El Paso Exploration (owner of El Paso Natural Gas Company's non-cost-of-service properties and activities). Joseph Reid was hired to run the Meridian Holding Company in 1984.[4] Reid had served as CEO of Superior Oil Company a few years earlier. Reid stayed with the company until 1986, when he was replaced by Donald Clayton, also from Superior Oil. Thomas O'Leary, who had been president of the Missouri Pacific Corporation[5] before it merged with the Union Pacific, was hired as vice chairman of the board of BNI in 1982. He was charged by Bressler to build up the non-rail business in oil and gas and coal and mineral production, as well as real estate. O'Leary also managed the law and finance functions at the headquarters level. Travis Petty (also vice chairman) was responsible for natural-gas transmission, timber operations, and human resources. Richard Grayson, the third vice chairman, had responsibility for the transportation units (mainly the railroad company) and BN's international business.

ACQUISITION OF EL PASO GAS

The desired expansion of revenue was centered around exploration for oil and gas on land and mineral rights owned by BN and from companies to be acquired. The

4 *1984 Annual Report, Form 10-K, Burlington Northern, Inc.*, pages 7 and 15.

5 Note: At the time O'Leary was with the Missouri Pacific, Downing B. Jenks was chairman and CEO of the Missouri Pacific Corporation and John Lloyd was president of the Missouri Pacific Railroad Company. O'Leary headed the Missouri Pacific's holding company, Missouri Pacific Corporation. In addition to its railroad company, Missouri Pacific had interests in a pipeline for natural-gas transmission and a few companies in the Portland cement business.

first to be acquired was the El Paso Natural Gas Company, which owned a 22,000-mile pipeline for gas moving from fields in Texas and New Mexico to California. El Paso furnished about 50 percent of the natural gas consumed in California. It also was involved in exploration for gas, and owned reserves of gas in the Anadarko and San Juan fields in Oklahoma and New Mexico. BN acquired 48 percent of the common equity of El Paso for $621 million in a tender offer. The remaining 52 percent of El Paso stock was acquired later for an additional $681 million in cash and stock. The cash for this transaction was raised in part through the sale of BNAFI (Burlington Northern Air Freight, Inc.).

At the time BN made its move, El Paso it had been weakened by a write-off of $365 million due to a failed venture to move liquefied natural gas from Nigeria to the U.S. The volume of imported liquid natural gas declined severely after 1979, to the extent the four unloading terminals in the United States were shut down. Four tanker ships had to be put in storage and then scrapped between 1985 and 1987.

Although El Paso had a 25-year contract for the purchase of gas from Algeria, the energy minister demanded the price of gas be increased in line with the rapid increase in the price of oil. The minister demanded "thermal parity": that gas be priced at the BTU equivalent price of oil. He made the point that "a therm is a therm." Even with the intervention of the U.S. Government, no agreement on pricing could be reached that would keep the price of gas from Algeria on a "fair" basis with imports from other countries. Early in 1981, El Paso took a writeoff of $365 million, representing its uninsured value of the fleet of liquid natural gas tankers.[6]

In 1981 El Paso had sales of $4 billion and record earnings of $147 million. In 1982 the economic downturn resulted in an oversupply of natural gas, causing the price to drop. Net income that year dropped to $53 million. In 1984 federal legislation governing pipelines forced El Paso to shift from the role of a seller of gas to a distributor—it no longer owned the gas it transported. Instead, it served only as the transporter (a common carrier under open access) of gas, as a service to the owners or buyers of the gas. Prior to this change, El Paso had been set up to purchase gas from the producers, move the gas through its pipelines for a fee, and then sell it to distribution companies who served the consumers of the gas.

In 1988 El Paso Natural Gas made a charge of $230 million against pre-tax earnings when it faced a judgment of $602 million, resulting from disputes with gas producers over take-or-pay contracts that required payment for minimum quantities of gas to be shipped. From 1982 through 1985, El Paso had accumulated a liability (after settlements) of $110 million. The company faced additional exposure of about $500 million in 1986, plus another $430 million in 1987. Its cash flow could not possibly handle obligations of such magnitude. El Paso and other pipeline companies therefore had to seek regulatory relief through political action, in addition to restructuring its pricing and contract obligations and curtailing the acquisition of additional gas-producing areas. In 1987 the Federal Energy Regulatory Commission ruled that pipeline companies would have to assume full liability for 25 percent of their take or pay liabilities, put 25 percent into their commodity (variable) rates, and add 50 percent as a surcharge to their demand rate.

BN's reaction to this new basis for competition and the negative effect it had on the economies of scale inherent in the pipeline business was to separate the gas production part of El Paso's business from its pipeline system. The gas production properties were put into Meridian Oil, and the pipeline part of El Paso was spun-off.[7] Due to the problem of oversupply, El Paso had to allocate its purchases for several years. The affected suppliers brought suit. In a decision of the Supreme Court, the judgment against El Paso was reduced to $480 million.

BN's oil and gas operating income was $99 million in 1987. Due in part to a writedown of $605 million in 1986, oil and gas showed a loss of $586 million in 1986. Excluding the writedown, operating income in 1987 was $179 million. The pre-tax charge of $605 million was made to reflect the substantial decline in oil and gas prices.[8]

In spite of all of the challenges and undesired outcomes El Paso experienced from some of the decisions that it had made in the 1970s and 1980s, Bressler still

6 Richard H.K. Vietor, *Contrived Competition: Regulation and Deregulation in America.*

7 Vietor, *Contrived Competition,* 143, 157, 161, and 165.

8 *Information Statement Covering the Distribution of Approximately 87% of the Outstanding Shares of Burlington Resources, Inc.,* November 14, 1988.

maintained that El Paso would be a good investment for the long term. He was convinced that natural gas would be in great demand in the years ahead, and that with El Paso's low-cost operation, he would be able to generate a high return on its invested capital.

There were financial experts who questioned the wisdom of acquiring El Paso at that time. They viewed it as a weakened, troubled company with an uncertain future. In addition, El Paso's gas sales in California had declined, it had cut its dividend, and it carried $1.6 billion of debt. Still, Bressler determined El Paso would be a good fit for BN's agenda to expand its revenue from oil and gas. It would be another ten years before Bressler's decisions in the field of energy could be validated, at least from the perspective of a BN shareholder.

The takeover of El Paso Gas was termed "hostile." El Paso fought BN's initial offer and threatened to sell some of its assets to weaken BN's effort. In the end, peace was made. El Paso's CEO, Travis Petty, was made vice chairman of BN's board. Bressler had always spoken highly of Petty and his acumen for the oil and gas business.

Bressler's next move was to acquire Southland Royalty Company, another oil and gas company, for $695 million in cash in 1985. Again, there were experts who questioned this decision, since the price of oil had been declining since 1980, eventually getting down to $8 per barrel. In 1985 the federal agency charged with regulating pipelines would have to maintain the take-or-pay contract they had with gas producers. At the same time, customers of the pipeline company were not to be held to their purchase commitments. That part of the ruling allowed pipeline customers to take their business to pipelines offering lower prices at the time. These conditions caused BN to take a write-off of $605 million on the value of its holdings in oil and gas.

Following the acquisition of Southland, BN combined its Milestone Petroleum Company with Southland and El Paso's exploration and production unit to form a new company called Meridian Petroleum Holding Company, This combination made Meridian one of the nation's largest independent oil and gas operations. In this period of only about five years, BN had already succeeded in building the war chest it thought it would need to sustain the company through a lengthy strike on its railroad.

ADVANCES MADE IN PETROLEUM ENGINEERING

An indication of the capability and strength of BN's expanded and restructured oil and gas exploration unit was revealed in an interview of a petroleum engineer, Tom Dyk, who had worked for BR a few years earlier, in the 1980s. The interview was conducted by Gerard O'Brien, a writer for *The Montana Standard.* Dyk was asked, "What is your proudest moment in your career?" He answered:

> [While working for] Burlington Resources, a subsidiary of Burlington Northern Railroad[,] I was the General Manager of the Rocky Mountain Region. We developed the horizontal drilling technique. Because of that, we made one of the major oil finds in the region—in the Bakken region in northeast Montana, western North Dakota and a part of Saskatchewan. We drilled another section of that same formation in 1987 to 1992. That area has seen resurgence in the last five years.
>
> It was in the Red River formation in Bowman County, North Dakota, inside the Montana border near Baker. We tried horizontal drilling there in the main field, and recognized one of the horizons existed for miles as you headed east. It produced 10,000 to 15,000 barrels. You can access it for 5,000 feet. So we put acreage together and discovered a well in the Cedar Hills that could produce 800 million to one billion barrels. . . . We were able to hire the best and the brightest out of the schools at that time. Those people are now running their own major companies. Many came from [Montana] Tech or Texas schools or the School of Mines in Golden, Colorado. Businesswise, my proudest moment was when we discovered the largest oilfield in decades in the Rocky Mountains at the Cedar Hills field in 1992, over 800 million barrels of oil through the application of horizontal technology.[9]

Tom Dyk is now the CEO of the Axia Energy Company.

The oil industry credits Donald Clayton, who came to BN's Meridian Oil Company from Superior Oil as a senior vice president in 1985, for developing the horizontal-drilling technology that has made it economical to

---

9 Gerald O'Brien, "Tech a Family Tradition," *The Montana Standard,* quoted in mtech.edu/alumni/Profiles/dyk.php website for alumni of Montana Tech.

extract oil from the shale formations on land on which BN held mineral rights in North Dakota and eastern Montana.[10] The application of horizontal drilling by Meridian and the fracturing of oil shale has led to an economic boom in many areas and made the United States less dependent on foreign sources for oil. The vast additional quantities of oil being produced have made it far less expensive for industrial and household uses of energy. This new technique for drilling enabled Burlington Resources and Meridian to open major production in what had been somewhat marginal properties. Clayton was named president of Meridian in 1987 and remained with Burlington Resources until 1993. Gary Hovis, an analyst with Argus Research wrote, "He [Clayton] was a real builder in the true sense of the word. He brought them into the oil and gas business."[11] Clayton was also named to the Engineering Hall of Distinction at his alma mater, Louisiana State University for his leadership and contributions to the growth of the oil industry.

TAKEOVER OF TRACK-BALLAST PRODUCTION

Changes were made in other non-rail units as well. In the newly formed Meridian Land and Mineral Company, Bressler recruited a new CEO and other managers from the Anaconda Minerals Company. They soon got their eyes on the large quantities of ballast the railroad placed in its track every year as part of routine maintenance—mainly surface correction and undercutting programs—and for new trackage being built to expand our capacity. We needed access to good ballast sources at several locations throughout the system. Some were owned by the railroad and operated by contractors who crushed the granite or other type of hard rock to a standard size for use as track ballast. The contractors then stockpiled the ballast and loaded it into rail cars as needed by the railroad's track maintenance forces. The amount of ballast produced and loaded was large, amounting to several thousand carloads each year from the largest ballast sources. The Engineering Department negotiated purchase agreements with each of the contractors. Meridian Minerals soon advised it had plans to take over the production of ballast at our largest sources. The prices at each location were in excess of what we were paying the contractors we were using. We told the Meridian managers that if they wanted to make a bid for furnishing us ballast at one or more locations for the next maintenance season, we would consider their proposal along with those of other contractors.

The contingent from Meridian told us that we did not understand, that the decision had already been made that Meridian would be taking over the management of ballast supplies for us, and "here is the deal" under which we [Meridian] will operate. With their much higher prices, we would be able to put less ballast in the track than we needed, so why would we simply accept their proposal? Meridian told us they needed a large source of revenue in order to finance other ventures, among them providing rock for construction of buildings, roads, and other projects in metropolitan areas such as Dallas and the Twin Cities, where there were limited sources of aggregate. Of course, the projected tonnage for such markets would be small in comparison with the amount of ballast Meridian would produce for the railroad. Meridian needed the profit it would make from the sale of ballast to the railroad to finance the acquisition of new machinery for producing ballast, so it could increase its staff and build up the capability it needed to furnish aggregate to new customers. Finally, the production and loading of ballast would be more efficient when done by Meridian compared to the contractors we were using. We replied if that were the case, they should be offering us a lower price rather than the higher rate they had just announced.

The outcome was as we anticipated; that indeed the railroad would turn the ballast operation over to Meridian under its terms. That decision had already been made at the holding-company level. There would be no negotiation on the prices we would pay. In its startup, Meridian did a good job in furnishing ballast of the quality and on the schedule we needed it for our projects. However, this episode was an example of what the railroad

10 Louisiana State University College of Engineering, Hall of Distinction, Class of 1992–1993; "BR Shifting Its Focus," *Bloomberg Business News*, March 2, 1963.

11 "Burlington Resources Shifting Its Focus," *Bloomberg Business News*, March 2, 1993.

company was expected to do in support of new ventures of the non-rail business units. The cash we generated was "dividended up" to the holding company, which would then decide how much of it the railroad could use for its capital projects, and how much would be used for new ventures or acquisitions in oil and gas, forest management, land development, selling aggregate to builders or road contractors, or other ventures.

On the one hand, under the holding-company structure, each unit under BNI was expected to run its own show, and stand its own two feet. The railroad would no longer be able to rely on the earnings of the non-rail units to support its needs for capital, as it was alleged to have done in the past. However, under the new corporate structure, and with the railroad producing higher earnings, the table could be turned. Suddenly, the cash generated by the railroad might be applied to new non-rail ventures, and not for projects on the railroad.

Meridian Minerals revenue increased from $7 million in 1984 to $34.9 million in 1987. The sale of aggregates amounted to 75 percent of its revenue in 1987. Railroad ballast sales produced revenue of $18.4 million and "commercial sales" (aggregate sale to non-rail customers) amounted to $6.6 million. All but 3 percent of the Minerals Company's revenue came from the aggregates and royalties on the coal properties owned by BN and managed by Meridian. Without the opportunity to produce and sell ballast to the railroad, and collect royalties from the mining done by outside companies, Meridian Minerals would have generated very little income, as commercial sales of aggregates were only $6.6 million, or about one-fifth of its total revenue. Meridian Minerals should have been told to go out and make its own way, by developing new business opportunities and seeking a way to financing them, instead of "looking good" via income from the railroad company.

There was a bright spot in 1993, when Meridian Minerals announced the discovery of three million ounces of gold on land it managed near Salmon, Idaho. Three projects for mining gold in California under Meridian management were underway in 1988, at the time Burlington Resources was spun off.

In time, Meridian's ballast operation was turned back to other contractors. With strong contractors of long-standing back in the business of producing aggregate for the railroad, the ballast operation had made the full circle. The price for producing and loading ballast once again was negotiated between the railroad's Engineering Department and the contractor. In the case of the quarry just outside St. Cloud, Minnesota, one of the BNSF Railway's major sources for ballast, a contractor loads about six thousand carloads per year, more than a half million tons.

CHAPTER 6

PREPARATION FOR SPIN-OFF OF BURLINGTON RESOURCES AND PLUM CREEK

Greater percentage growth will come from our oil and gas business and our forest management operations during the next five years.

INTERVIEW WITH RICHARD M. BRESSLER,
BURLINGTON NORTHERN ANNUAL REPORT FOR 1980, PAGE 1

• *great success in new investments in oil and gas properties* • *culminated in a windfall for the shareholders* • *heavy debt burden placed on the railroad company, but gave the railroad freedom to be master of its destiny* • *preparing the railroad to go it alone* •

DURING THE 1980S, BN SPENT $1 BILLION to develop its resources. With cash flow from the railroad and by taking on substantial debt, BN invested $2 billion in El Paso Natural Gas and Southland Royalty. In 1988, when the non-rail holdings under BNI were spun-off, the debt was left with BNI (and, in turn, the BN Railroad, as BNI's only remaining subsidiary). This made BN Railroad the most heavily leveraged of any railroad company at that time. It was a big relief to the railroad when the resource-based companies were separated from BNI in the spin-off carried out in 1988. With each of the resource companies either sold or becoming independent, each was on its own in generating funds for capital expenditures, paying dividends, buying stock back, reducing debt, or any other use for the cash they were able to generate on their own.

It is interesting to note that Meridian Minerals was sold, rather than being retained under Burlington Resources, as was the case with the oil and gas unit. The oil and gas business was producing returns in the range of 40 to 50 percent, compared with about 10 to 15 percent in the case of Meridian Minerals and Plum Creek.

In 1988 a new corporate body named Burlington Resources (BR) was formed as a holding company for the non-rail companies. A publicly held company, 13 percent of its stock was sold through an initial public offering in July 1988. Only five months later, the remaining 87 percent of BR stock was distributed to BN shareholders. In 1989 Bressler turned his responsibilities over to O'Leary. The split of BR from BNI was set up to protect the investments made in valuable non-rail assets, in case of a nationwide rail strike that would prevent the railroad from operating.

PREPARING THE RAILROAD TO "GO IT ALONE"

As mentioned earlier, by 1987 BN had developed the financial strength it would need to get through a long strike by its rail workers, if that was what it would take to get relief from the high wage rates, stifling work rules, and excess manning required on its trains. The company was preparing to "go it alone" in the next round of labor negotiations scheduled for 1988. At that time, BN felt it could negotiate a better deal with its unions by withdrawing from national handling. For many years, all of the bigger railroads had given their proxy to a national committee that would conduct negotiations on their behalf. When major issues were involved, an impasse would usually be reached, as the carriers' committee and the unions worked through the course of procedures required in the Railway Labor Act. After following the series of prescribed steps and time intervals, the unions would become free to strike, and the railroad companies were empowered to implement the changes they had sought without success in the negotiations.

Toward the end of that long, drawn-out process, and with the threat of a strike looming, it was likely the president of the United States would convene a Presidential Emergency Board (PEB) as provided in the Railway Labor Act to study the dispute for thirty days and make recommendations for a settlement. The unions and the companies were then given time to consider the recommendations of the PEB and encouraged to negotiate further, in the hope of reaching a settlement. Most often, that would not happen. After a strike of two or three days, the Congress would intervene and pass legislation that imposed a settlement, generally following the recommendations of the PEB. With this kind of process for settling major differences and establishing the terms for a new contract, there was less incentive for serious collective bargaining with the sense of urgency felt in other industries. In other words, both parties knew the rail industry would not be allowed to take a strike.

The new leadership at BN, having no background in the rail industry, was prepared to "go to the mat" independently with the rail unions, to get a far more favorable settlement than they believed BN could possibly get through the long-established regimen of national handling. BN's dream for a breakthrough was shattered in 1987 when the U.S. Supreme Court ruled that secondary picketing was legal in the rail industry. Under that decision, the courts could not enjoin the unions from picketing and shutting down the operations of other railroads, even though they were not party to the strike against BN. That had happened in 1987, when the unions struck a small eastern railroad and placed pickets on the railroads with which that company interchanged traffic. By ruling that secondary picketing was legal, it would be impossible for one railroad to take a strike in hopes of reaching a settlement independently, without shutting down other railroads in the process. "The grand strategy of a natural resource war chest to withstand a show-down strike by the operating unions was thereby voided."[1]

It was important to protect the company's non-rail holdings from being drained or exhausted in the event of a strike; hence, the decision to move toward separating ownership of BN's railroad from its other companies. The result was the creation of Burlington Resources and the decision to spin it off from BNI.

GETTING RELIEF FROM RESTRICTIONS IN BONDS ISSUED BY THE NP IN 1896

To have the ability to transfer resources from the railroad company to the newly formed non-rail companies, BNI had to take on the historic challenge of getting relief from the restrictions in bonds issued by the NP in 1896. The restrictions required the NP and BN to certify to the bond trustee each year that an amount equal to or greater than earnings from the sale of resources or income generated by the resources had to be reinvested in the railroad. When that level was reached, the trustee could release the excess earnings to the company. Until this restriction could be removed, earnings from the resources could not be used for the benefit of the shareholders, but rather only for the maintenance of track and bridges. BNI first needed to be released from that general lien on 1.9 million acres of undeveloped property so it could be developed or sold.

A group of bondholders tried to stop BNI from getting relief from this restriction, which had its roots in J. P. Morgan's effort to raise funds for the NP as it came out

1 Donaldson, *Corporate Restructuring*, 113.

of bankruptcy. After protracted negotiations, both sides agreed in 1978 that BNI would pay the bondholders $35.5 million if they would agree to remove the historic restriction. For the issue of bonds due in 1997, that amounted to $14.75 per $100 face value. For the bonds with a maturity date of 2047, the payment amounted to $45.63 per $100. With this settlement, BNI gained the right it sought for the use of 2.4 million acres of land, plus surface and mineral rights to an additional 1.9 million acres.[2]

Burlington Resources (BR) merged with Louisiana Land and Exploration (LL&E) in 1997, giving it a large interest in the Gulf of Mexico, Louisiana, the Madden Field in Wyoming, Algeria, and the East Irish Sea. It was ironic that H. Leighton Steward was president and CEO of the LL&E when it merged with BR—Steward had left BN in 1981, not long after the restructuring began under Bressler. In the combined BR–LL&E, Steward was appointed vice chairman of the board.

With all of the success BR had in growing its business, Conoco Phillips decided to acquire it in 2006. The transaction was valued at $35.8 billion. All in all, the growth and success of BR and its predecessor units in the BN family was very impressive.[3]

BR sold assets it evaluated as unrelated to its core business of oil and gas. The Glacier Park Company, its real estate unit, sold the one million acres it held for $450 million. Plum Creek Timber Company formed a limited partnership and was spun off to prevent the possibility of a leveraged buyout. BR transferred $325 million of debt to Plum Creek. This was also done to take advantage of the law allowing publicly traded partnerships to be tax exempt, if at least 90 percent of their revenue came from natural resources. To gain that advantage, Plum Creek had to be split into two companies, one owning Plum Creek's manufacturing plants and the other, its timberlands. The manufacturing unit was required to take on the burden of $325 million of long-term debt the limited partners incurred in making the purchase of Plum Creek from BR, up from $2 million before the restructuring.[4] With the burden of interest payments on that amount of debt, the company would operate at a loss, and have no liability for taxes. Also, such a large amount of debt would likely keep the company from being bought out.

Plum Creek moved ahead to acquire additional timberlands in the Northwest, as well as in New England, Michigan, and the South. Together with the 1.4 million acres of timberland it acquired from Burlington Resources, Plum Creek became the largest private landowner in the United States, with about 6.8 million acres.

In 1999 Plum Creek converted from a publicly traded partnership (MLP) to a Real Estate Investment Trust (REIT). It then had all of its lands third-party certified in the Sustainable Forestry Initiative Program. Plum Creek was the first company to have this done with all of the land it owned. Plum Creek advised its unitholders that under an REIT, it could attract a broader base of investors, which should enhance investor value compared to continuing to run as a MLP. It would also reduce Plum Creek's cost of capital, thereby providing "a superior structure for growth."[5]

Plum Creek's policy on managing its timberlands is "harvesting trees at the best economically mature point in the life cycle of a tree. We manage our timberlands following sustainable forestry practices.... Plum Creek has committed more than 1.4 million acres to conservation partnerships. In addition, about 1.5 million acres are involved in Habitat Conservation Plans and agreements that provide for long-term management and protection of endangered wildlife across the country." Also, Plum Creek has certified all of its timberlands independently through the Sustainable Forest Initiatives, established to "insure sustainable forests far into the future." In reflecting on the policies BN had for forest management under Bob Binger in the 1970s, it would appear that in recent times, Plum Creek has taken several pages from the policies and values Bob Binger avowed and practiced.

Other non-core businesses sold by BR included 1.5 million acres of timberland, one million acres of real estate, 22,000 miles of gas pipelines, and some of its mining operations. Land and mineral rights in North Dakota and Montana with 20 billion tons of coal were sold to Great Northern Properties, a new privately owned

2 Rierman v. Burlington Northern, 118 F.R.D. 29, S.D.N.Y., 1987.

3 Conoco Phillips website.

4 "Now v. Forever: The Conflict Between Business and Forestry in the Management of Plum Creek Timberlands in Montana," Timothy Matthew Bechtold, thesis, University of Montana, 1992.

5 Letter to Plum Creek unit holders from Rick R. Holley, president and CEO, February 12, 1999.

company formed by the Corbin L. Robertson family and American Bailey Mining, Ltd., to acquire BN's coal-related assets. That acquisition made GNP the largest private owner of coal reserves in the U.S. GNP had no connection with either BN or its predecessor, the Great Northern Railway.

With the funds BR raised through the sale of these assets, it spent $399 million to acquire the producing properties of Unicon Producing Company. With its growth through acquisitions, BR ranked just behind six major oil companies. Although low prices for natural gas hurt BR, the acquisitions it made at low prices put it in a strong position by the time the prices for gas began to climb. BR was reported to be the low cost producer of natural gas. It was recognized for its utilization advance technology for horizontal drilling and advance reservoir simulation technology that gave it a cost advantage over its competitors. These new extraction methods also made it possible for BR to recover gas in areas that were thought to have been exhausted as far back as the 1950s and 1960s.

THE SPIN-OFF AND SEPARATION OF THE RAILROAD AND RESOURCES

The terms of the spin-off of BR from BNI provided that BNI (now made up entirely by the BN Railroad) would be saddled with debt of $722 billion, giving it a very high debt-to-equity ratio of 74 percent. A large part of that debt had been created to finance acquisitions of additional non-rail resources. Only 19 cents of that debt for each dollar of equity was assigned to BR. That put nearly all of the debt burden with BNI, whose sole remaining asset was the railroad company. Obviously, this gave the railroad a huge burden of debt to pay off. Such payments had to be given precedence over the railroad's needs for on-going capital investment to replace worn out or obsolete assets ranging from rail to locomotives to computers. BN became the most heavily leveraged railway in North America.[6]

The BN Railroad retired more than $500 million of the $723 million of debt it held in 1989 by using cash generated by operations, including the sale of receivables. The debt-equity ratio was reduced from 76 to 68 in just one year. A goal was set to achieve a ratio of 50 by 1994, which required that debt be reduced at an average rate of $200 million each year. This goal was accomplished in 1992, two years earlier than planned, when a ratio of 48 was reached.

In *Leaders Count,* Larry Kaufman provided a valuable and well-written account of action taken by Darius Gaskins (then president and CEO of Burlington Northern Railroad) when the terms for the separation of the railroad company from Burlington Resources were being finalized. Anyone who was associated with BN or with today's BNSF Railway owes a debt of gratitude to Gaskins for his success in protecting the railroad's interest. Without the courage, leadership skills, and sense of right and wrong that Gaskins displayed at that time, the railroad company probably would not be blessed with the strength, character, or stature it has today as a transportation company.

One of the terms for the breakup provided that the land "under the railroad" would be put under the ownership of a real estate company that would be separated from BNI. From the start of the negotiations, Gaskins explained that it had been agreed among the non-railroad people of BNI that the railroad would be turning property not needed for railroad operating purposes to BNI's real estate company for management and development. But when the value of that property fell short of the $1 billion the real estate company needed to operate on its own and set up an initial public offering, they then set their sights on taking ownership of railroad operating property as well. That would have included even the land under the railroad's track, maintenance shops, and support facilities. That kind of provision was of course totally unacceptable to the railroad.

After reviewing the issue with Bressler, Gaskins thought he had convinced him that the operating property would have to remain with the railroad. However, when the documents governing the breakup had supposedly been revised, and were now ready for signature, Gaskins found they still provided for transfer of enough railroad operating property to the real estate company so it would have the $1 billion of land it was after. Gaskins says he refused to sign the documents and vowed he would resign unless the operating property remained

6 Laura Sachar, "Rail Stripper," *Financial World,* January 10, 1989.

THE SPIN-OFF AND WHAT IT MEANT TO BN'S RAILROAD COMPANY

- Debt held by BN Railroad to increase from $1.3 billion at end of 1987 to between $2.5 and $2.9 billion.
- The new debt had been incurred by BNI's energy, mineral and real estate properties. Debt to be left with BNI, and not with the non-railroad properties to be spun-off.
- Burlington Resources (BNI's oil and gas subsidiary) wants to explore and buy reserves and must have a very clear balance sheet to be able to finance the transaction.
- BN Railroad will have to make estimated annual payments of $250 million to service the debt.
- The debt payment will still be lower than what the railroad used to turn over to the holding company each year, that usually ran at least $300 million and for one year approached $400 million.

Excerpts from David M. Cawthorne, "BN Rail to Have Far More Debt After Restructuring Finished," *Traffic World*, June 13, 1988, in which the writer quotes unnamed BN officers and Wall Street analysts.

under railroad ownership. Gaskins prevailed, saving the railroad from loss of ownership and control of its right-of-way and keeping it from having to pay rent to the real estate company for that land. That kind of payment might have reduced the railroad's net income significantly, and impaired it from making the kinds of investments needed for modernization, expanding capacity, and building its competitive capability to the level the company has been able to fund since it was formed in 1995.

Gaskins emphasized he was not against the plan for the breakup of BNI. In fact, he termed it as "a super plan" that he supported, adding, "It was the best thing that ever happened to the BN railroad when we got rid of the holding company. It was the best thing that happened to the real estate company and the other ones that couldn't make it, because the market proved they couldn't make it. They didn't go anywhere."[1]

Gaskins stayed on as president and CEO until the end of 1988. He was succeeded by Gerald Grinstein, who had served as vice chairman of the board of BNI since April 1987, and before then, as the head of Western Airlines. Grinstein had been given high praise for the relationships he developed with employees and in dealing with

1 Kaufman, *Leaders Count*, 245. The encounter described above occurred in late 1987. Gaskins is quoted directly by Kaufman at some length. The reader is referred to pages 244 through 247 in which Gaskins explains in detail how he handled the challenge of protecting the railroad's interest before signing the documents containing the conditions of the spin-off of BR.

Table 6.1. Success in Agenda to Reduce Debt, 1989–1994 (millions of dollars)

	1989	*1990*	*1991*	*1992*	*1993*	*1994*
Long-term debt	$2,233	$2,133	$1,982	$1,567	$1,737	$819
Equity 1,080	1,241	1,202	1,728	1,919	2,237	
Capital Expenditures	373	401	509	487	676	753
Debt to total Capitalization[1]	68	63	62	48	48	45
Operating ratio[2]	36	87	90	87	86	83

1 Expressed as ratio.
2 Ratio of operating expense to operating revenue.

Source: Burlington Northern, Inc., Annual Report to Shareholders, 1994

their concerns and needs in the preparation of plans for the merger of Western and Delta.

In the years following the spin-off of Burlington Resources, the railroad's capital expenditures had to be cut in order to help provide the funding necessary to reduce the huge amount of debt to a reasonable level in the next six years. Some of BN's senior officers recall how they had to hold back on the acquisition of new, more efficient locomotives and on projects needed to expand capacity on major coal routes in Wyoming and Nebraska that were badly needed to handle the ever-growing tonnages of coal. After about four years of success in meeting its goals for reducing debt, the railroad was able to increase its capital spending again. In January 1994 BN began taking delivery of the first of 350 high horsepower locomotive units equipped with AC traction motors in a four-year program costing $675 million. For details on the characteristics of these locomotives, refer to chapter 19. Also, a program was started to build second-main-track mileage on lines in need of additional capacity.

At the time of the restructuring, Gerald Grinstein's evaluation of the "deal" the railroad got from it was widely quoted: "They got the gold and we got the shaft." In those dark days, and with the uncertainty in the company's history, it did not hurt to put a little humor into the situation. Also, it showed that the boss understood and agreed with the people of the railroad that they had been handed a burden and a great challenge in the restructuring. Grinstein recognized they had worked under difficult—at times unreasonable—conditions, ever since the reorganization and change in management that started in 1981. Having to cut capital spending to work off the debt was no laughing matter. But at least, managers and employees could see some hope on the horizon, now that there would no longer be any "infant industries" or new members of the corporate family who would be put in line to receive the cash generated by the successful efforts of the railroad and its people.

CHAPTER 7

EVALUATION OF RESULTS

Isabel H. Benham, a noted rail financial analyst, challenged Bressler as to the effect the decision to load up all the debt on the railway would have on the railroad company's bondholders. Bressler replied, in part,

> to your other point about the leverage at the railroad, I agree that it is too high and it was not planned that way. Because the railroad had thrown off excess cash in recent years, the restructuring was designed to essentially take two years' excess cash flow in advance and give it to Resources. That amount of additional debt we were comfortable with in any viable scenario; however, the amount of the ETSI[2] settlement took us by surprise. As you know that $175 million settlement occurred at the end of 1988 and by that time there was already a minority interest in Resources which effectively shut the door on any reshuffling of the debt load. Reduction of debt is now the number one priority at BNI and I am confident it will be accomplished.
>
> To your final thought as to whether or not there will be sufficient capital available to meet the future requirements of the industry, I was surprised that you did not mention the problem of sub-par profitability of the industry. If the BN or any other railroad can achieve the profitability it should have, I have no fears about obtaining the required capital.[3]

A writer for *Financial World* magazine viewed the issue of debt load much differently: "these days there are no J. P. Morgans around to look after their (bondholders) interests—only managers with juicy stock options and apparently no concerns about leaving a business that's encumbered with debt."[4]

Gordon Donaldson, an author and a Harvard Business School, 1955–93, professor, made a very revealing comparison of BN's financial performance compared to that of the entire rail industry and of Union Pacific, specifically. Donaldson noted that total equity returns (combination of capital gains and dividends paid), "(for BN) virtually doubled from 10.60 percent to 20.74 percent" from Bressler's arrival in June 1980 to the split of Burlington Resources from BN made in May 1988. By December 1990 the return on equity increased to 29.59 percent. With these results, BN outperformed both the total of the rail industry and that of Union Pacific, its chief rail competitor and a company that also held large non-rail assets during those years. Donaldson concluded, "the benefits from the spin-off of resources are quite clear. The evidence of shareholder benefit speaks for itself."

To its credit, the railroad company worked the debt off, bringing its debt-to-equity ratio down from 74 percent in 1988 to 45 percent in 1994. In so doing, some large, high-priority capital expenditures had to be set aside or delayed in those years. Among those projects were the

---

2 ETSI refers to Energy Transportation Systems Inc., a consortium organized to build a coal-slurry pipeline from the Powder River Basin to electric-power plants in the Midwest strongly contested by the rail industry.

3 The report was entitled, "The Forgotten Bondholder and the Impact on Rail Capital Programs," issued by Kane Research, Inc., May 11, 1989. Donaldson, *Corporate Restructuring*, 129.

4 Laura Sachar, "Rail Stripper," *Financial World*, January 10, 1989.

Table 7.1. TOTAL EQUITY RETURN (AVERAGE ANNUAL RETURN)

Interval	BN	*Rail Industry*	UP
1971–May 1980	10.63%	13.29%	18.45%
June 1980–May 1988	20.74	12.21	8.83
June 1988–December 1990	29.69	11.36	7.98

SOURCE: Donaldson, *Corporate Restructuring*, 134.

replacement of locomotives that were being kept in service beyond their economic lives, capital expenditures needed to expand capacity to handle the ever-increasing tonnages of coal originating in the Powder River Basin, and applying new technology in track maintenance on parts of what had become the world's heaviest-tonnage lines. Having to defer these and other important projects set BN back on its agenda to improve service and increase productivity at a faster rate through investment in new technology. After the debt was reduced to a much lower level, it took BN several years to catch up on the deferrals it had been forced to make because of the heavy debt load it was left with when Burlington Resources was spun off.

In the long run, the railroad company, its people, and its customers all benefited from finally becoming free of the internal financial gymnastics that went on in the company as funds were transferred or reallocated among the vastly different companies within BNI. Once the breakup occurred and the railroad worked off the debt burden—and merged with the Santa Fe—it flourished. It was back to the stage it had set by 1980 to produce high returns on the capital it had invested since 1970.

The ten years of disruption from restructuring and serving as a cash cow for other lines of business under the BN banner had finally passed. Even though it took five years for the railroad to unload the burden of debt, at least it was closer to once again becoming the master of its destiny. Likewise, the non-rail companies that had been formed or acquired and nurtured by BN could now go out on their own and have the freedom to make their mark in the marketplace, without being held back to "share their wealth" or possibly be restructured in some way to serve the needs of other companies in the "family."

In evaluating the Bressler years, one must focus primarily on the amount of gain that was realized by the shareholders. Certainly, pain was endured by many constituencies in the process, including many of the people of the companies BN owned, restructured, or sold. Bressler walked into BN at just the right time to reap the benefit of the huge investment BN had made to enable it to take advantage of the opportunity for growth that was (and perhaps always will be) unique in the North American rail industry. Also, Bressler benefited from the opportunity he seized to move "wealth" from one unit of the company to others, which amounted to one company having to sacrifice what it had produced in order for the new or acquired companies to get established and, hopefully, grow and prosper.

Gordon Donaldson summed up the overall benefits of the restructuring led by Bressler very well: "There is . . . no denying the improvement brought by the restructuring process of the 1980s, slow and painful as it was. As of April 30, 1993, the market value of the four publicly held companies aggregated $13.3 billion. The market value of Burlington Northern during 1980 was less than $1 billion."[5] Bressler stated often that an organization's first priority was to increase shareholder value. Clearly, the shareholders benefited greatly from the initiatives undertaken under Bressler's direction in the thirteen tumultuous, unsettling years in which he headed BNI (refer to table 7.2 for details on value of common and preferred stock).

Getting the resources unit separated from the railroad was a blessing for all concerned: from employees and executives to shareholders, the entire investment community, and anyone else who had concerns over the performance of the company and how it should be managed. Having ownership of the vast array of non-rail assets had been a matter of contention for the entire history of BN and for the former NP in the years leading up to the eventual merger with the GN and Burlington. It might have been best for all concerned if the NP's non-rail assets

5 Donaldson, *Corporate Restructuring*, 132.

Table 7.2. History of BN Common and Preferred Stock

Date	Event
March 2, 1970	BN formed by merger of CB&Q Railroad Company, Great Northern Company, and Northern Pacific Railway Company Terms of exchange of stock: CB&Q 3.25 shares of BN for one share of CB&Q GN one share of BN for each share of GN plus one-half share of BN preferred for one share of GN common NP One share of BN for one share of NP
May 27, 1980	Two-for-one stock split
November 21, 1980	BN merger with SLSF (Frisco) Railway Company 1.9 shares of BN for one share of SLSF and one-half share of BN 2.125 preferred for one share of SLSF
December 13, 1983	BN merger with El Paso Company El Paso: one-fourth share of BN Adjustable Rate Preferred Stock at a stated value of $48 per full share plus $12 (without interest) for one share of El Paso Adjustable Rate Preferred was redeemed December 1, 1986, at $48 plus accumulated dividends of $14.83 per share for December, 1983, through December, 1986, for previously unexchanged El Paso shares
February 3, 1984	Two-for-one stock split
December 1985	BN merger with Southland Royalty Company An all cash transaction @ $17 per share
June 1, 1986	Redemption of preferred stock BN 2⅛% (call price of $26.40) BN $9 (call price of $102)
December 1, 1986	Redemption of BN Adjustable Rate Preferred (cash price of $48)
July 7, 1988	Initial Public Offering of BN Resources (wholly owned subsidiary of BN) at $25.50
December 31, 1988	Spin-off of Burlington Resources. BN shareholders received 1.7431 Shares of Burlington Resources, Inc., for each share of BN. Spin-off shares (BR) were issued at $32.695 per share.
June 30, 1992	Burlington Resources spun-off El Paso @ .23939 shares of El Paso per share
July 15, 1993	Redemption of BN 5½% preferred stock at $10.00 per share plus a accrued dividends of $0.067222 per share
September 22, 1995	Merger of BN and Santa Fe Pacific Corporation to form Burlington Northern Santa Fe Corporation BN shares exchanged one-for-one. Santa Fe Pacific shares Exchanged .41149345 BNSF for each share of Santa Fe Pacific.
November 10, 1995	Redemption of 6¼% cumulative convertible preferred shares at $52.1875 plus $0.7465 accrued unpaid dividends
September 1, 1998	Three-for-one split of BNSF stock
March 31, 2006	Burlington Resources acquired by Conoco Phillips. Each share of BR common stock was converted into the right to receive $46.50 in cash and 0.7214 shares of Conoco Phillips common stock.

had been spun off to NP shareholders in some way before the effort to merge the four railroads was undertaken. Very likely, that would have been difficult—if not impossible—to accomplish at that time because of the terms of the NP bond issue of the 1890s. Also, without the earnings and value of the resource holdings, it might have been far more difficult for BN to raise the large amount of money needed to upgrade and expand the capacity of the railroad in the 1970s.

BN's franchise or business base proved to be very valuable and solid. Its railroad network and capability to deliver freight fit in well with the economic base it serves. Also to be included in the value of BN's franchise are the skills and work ethic of the thousands of its people who are very dedicated to railroading as a profession and a way of life. Having relief from the mandate to funnel the railroad's earnings to "sister" companies, or for the railroad to become dependent on the earnings of those companies at some time has added greatly to the company's capability to finance improvement and expansion projects that improve its operating performance and its ability to compete more effectively. The proof of the value of the franchise and the ability of the railroad to make it on its own is evident from the success of today's BNSF Railway. For many years, our predecessors argued that with relief from excessive government regulation, from the losses incurred in the passenger business, and with work rules rationalized, the rail industry would be a strong and viable part of the American economy. That has happened. All we needed was the chance to be freed from those types of restrictions, so we could operate like other kinds of business.

PART III

REDUCING THE ASSET BASE

CHAPTER 8

SEVERING A VITAL CORRIDOR

CREATION OF MONTANA RAIL LINK

Our whole railroad is for sale. If someone offers a decent price, all or part of it is for sale.

HOWARD KALLIO, BN CORPORATE RELATIONS STAFF MEMBER,
QUOTED IN "BN'S MISSOULA LINE IS ON THE BLOCK,"
MISSOULIAN, NOVEMBER 25, 1986

• *we will not have two main lines between any two junctions, terminals, or common points* • *decision to sell a vital link in a major corridor* •

TO HELP REDUCE THE ASSET BASE, THEREBY improving the rate of return on assets, BN's Operating Department was directed in the early 1980s to examine locations where there were parallel or duplicate routes between terminals or junctions. Also at that time, a system-wide study of alternate routes was underway. Wherever we were maintaining alternate routes between nodes or terminals, we were to determine which route should be retained as part of BN's core system. "Through" traffic would be taken off the other route, which would then be relegated to local service only. Without the through traffic, the maintenance standard could be lowered. If there was not enough local business to operate the line profitably, it would be abandoned or sold to a short-line operator.

COMPARISON OF ROUTES

The corridor between Laurel and Sandpoint was by far the biggest of the corridors to be studied, by any measure. It presented the greatest opportunity for consolidation of traffic between two junctions or common points. The most direct of the two routes was the former NP's line of 561 miles via Helena and Missoula. The alternate route, 101 miles longer, was the GN route via Great Falls, Shelby, and Whitefish. In the 1970 merger plan, the NP line was designated the segment to be used as the preferred route for traffic moving between the Pacific Northwest and Kansas City.

We had to determine whether it would be best to make the improvements on the secondary main line between Laurel and Shelby to handle the through traffic that would be diverted, or if it should be downgraded to the status of a branch or feeder line that would handle only the locally originated grain business. The NP route had been selected in the operating plan for the merged company because of the advantage it had in distance and in having centralized traffic control (CTC) in service on all but the ninety-two miles between De Smet and Paradise. BN maintained the entire line to a high standard after the 1970 merger. Freight trains were authorized to operate at 60 miles per hour except for a few locations with heavy curvature, primarily on the mountain passes just west of Livingston and Helena.

Over the entire distance of the GN line between Laurel and Shelby (321 miles), there was no signal system in service. Most of the sidings for meeting trains were too short and spaced too far apart to accommodate the much longer and increased number of trains we would have to run on that line. These characteristics greatly reduced the capacity of the line. In contrast, the NP line was laid with heavy rail of main-line standard. There still was a considerable amount of 90-pound rail on the GN line at that time that would soon have to be relaid with heavy continuous welded rail, if all of the through trains were to be diverted from the line via Missoula.

A major advantage for the GN line via Great Falls was its much more favorable grades, a maximum of one percent. On the NP line, there were heavy grades where the line crossed Bozeman Pass west of Livingston and over the Continental Divide on Mullan Pass west of Helena. However, the former NP line via Missoula had been designated the preferred route between the Pacific Northwest, Kansas City, Texas, and Denver due to its shorter mileage, and because it had been upgraded and maintained to a very high standard (see table 8.1 for a comparison of the two lines). It also had sufficient capacity to handle the anticipated growth in international business, whereas the GN line via Great Falls would have required heavy expenditures for upgrading the track, and in time, to expand its capacity with CTC and additional and longer sidings.

The NP line had a strong base of local business, with several large lumber and paper mills. The line via Great Falls served several grain elevators, also an excellent source of revenue, as well as two sawmills and a wallboard plant. An exhaustive study was made to determine what amount of capital investment would have to be made on the Great Falls line if it were to handle the "through" trains being operated via Missoula. That would include several siding extensions between Laurel and Shelby, relaying much of the line with heavier rail, and some heavy maintenance work needed on five tunnels between Mossmain (between Laurel and Billings) and Great Falls. Because there were clearance restrictions on running excess-dimension ("high-wide") loads through these tunnels, the tunnel floor needed to be lowered by undercutting. Also, one tunnel (known as the Rimrock Tunnel) of 2,517 feet twelve miles west of Mossmain had a wood lining and was recommended for "daylighting," a major project. A few miles west of Great Falls, the track through an area known as the "Manchester flats" on a high, unstable fill had required frequent surfacing for many years. To handle a steady flow of much heavier tonnage would have required further engineering inquiry and likely a line change or other major capital expenditure to correct the problem.

These are examples of conditions that would have to be dealt with before the Great Falls line could be designated the better of the two lines for the long term. Having lower grades alone was not enough to overcome these disadvantages. On the line via Missoula, CTC would be taken out of service, some sidings removed, and track maintenance greatly reduced. With the number of trains being operated on the northern corridor between Shelby and Sandpoint at that time, no problems in capacity were anticipated with the addition of the four to six daily trains to be diverted.

DECISION TO SELL ONE ROUTE

The outcome of the study favored retention of the Missoula line as the preferred route. While this was not the result desired by those leading the effort to reduce the asset base, it was accepted. A new approach was then taken, that of attempting to sell the former NP line to a local investor. Gene Thayer, who was prominent in Montana politics and the founder and president of Montana Merchandising, Inc., a grain-trading and -shipping company with facilities at several locations in the grain-producing areas of the state, was the first party approached. When Thayer declined the opportunity, contact was initiated with Dennis Washington, a resident of Missoula and the owner of a successful construction company. A few years earlier, Washington had acquired a large copper mining operation near Butte from the Atlantic Richfield Company (ARCO). The mine, smelter, concentrator, and refinery had been developed and operated by the Anaconda Company for many years before ARCO assumed ownership in 1977.

Anaconda had been seriously weakened in 1971 when its operations in Chile were nationalized. Also at that time, copper prices plunged on the world markets. Prices stayed low after ARCO took over, and it soon shut down

Table 8.1. COMPARISON OF GRADES AND MILEAGE BETWEEN LAUREL AND SANDPOINT

Via Great Falls (former GN line)

Line Segment	(PERCENT GRADE) WB	EB
Laurel–Great Falls	0.6	1.0
Great Falls–Shelby	0.6	0.6
Shelby–Summit[1]	1.1	
Whitefish–Sandpoint[2]	1.0	1.0

1 Approaching Summit, there is now a grade of 1.1% for 3.5 miles as a result of a line change made in the late 1960s to reduce curvature. Previously, the grade was 1.0%.

2 These are the grades on the new line built to accommodate construction of the Libby Dam, completed in 1970. Previously, the maximum ascending grade was 0.25% westbound and 0.7 % eastbound.

Via Missoula (former NP line)

Line Segment	(PERCENT GRADE) WB	EB
Bozeman Pass	1.9	1.8
Winston Hill	1.0	1.0
Mullan Pass	2.2	1.4

Comparison of mileage:

Via Great Falls	669
Via Missoula	573
Difference of 86 miles	
Bozeman Pass	1.9

all of the mines and smelting and refinery operations it had just acquired. ARCO had to contend with labor strife, declining copper prices, and onerous environmental issues were on the horizon. In 1983 ARCO closed the famous Berkeley pit and Continental mine at Butte, the concentrator and smelter at Anaconda, and the copper refinery at Great Falls. ARCO is reported to have sold its mining properties to Washington for $18 million. Washington also had to invest $8 million to cover the cost of reopening the mine.

Washington's fortune was good in that copper prices rebounded strongly shortly after his purchase. The basis for his decision to purchase the property was the value of the mining equipment, which he thought could be sold for use elsewhere, but when the price of copper revived, Washington determined the mine could be operated profitably. He then put the resources in place to reopen the Continental pit on a limited basis. Washington became a folk hero in Montana for what he had accomplished.

> "Always bring in the best experts around to run businesses you don't understand. I never hire someone to run a business unless he's smarter than I am."[1]

> "Every person will get a break at some time in their life, but not everyone will recognize it or have the ability to use it. The best you can do is be prepared."[2]

Washington resumed mining operations under a new company, Montana Resources, Inc. Soon, three hundred people were employed, producing 50,000 tons of copper-molybdenum ore per day. The ore is run through the concentrator, and the copper concentrates are then shipped to China for refining. Three million employee hours were worked without a lost-time injury after Washington's takeover. His workforce in the mining operation he re-started was non-union, a point that raised a red flag with the BN workers when they learned that Washington would be the owner of the lines to be acquired by and operated as Montana Rail Link (MRL). However, MRL negotiated contracts with two railroad unions to represent its employees soon after start-up.

Darius Gaskins wrote, "I remember a meeting with the Governor of Montana in 1988 [Ted Schwinden]. who was very annoyed with our rail operations in his state. When I told him that we were going to sell almost half of our Montana operation to Denny Washington, a prominent Montana businessman, the blood drained out of

1 Richard L. Stern, "Denny's Always the Low-cost Producer," *Forbes*, May 15, 1989.

2 Dennis R. Washington, 2007 Inductee into American Mining Hall of Fame, quote in "Mining Foundation of the Southwest."

the Governor's face. It was no fun to beat up on Denny Washington."[3]

It did not take too long for political leaders, shippers and the general citizenry to accept and become generally satisfied with the start-up of MRL under Washington's ownership. BN leased the main line for sixty years and sold the branch lines to Washington for MRL. He also acquired 100 cars and 62 road and yard locomotive units, and assumed the leases for 700 cars needed to handle the volume of locally originated and terminated business it expected to handle at startup.[4]

BN gave MRL trackage rights on the sixty-two miles of its main line between Spokane and Sandpoint. Until 1992 BN retained ownership of the 52-mile segment of main line between Helena and Garrison. In that way, BN retained the control it needed for access to a phosphate mine near Garrison and to connect with the Montana Western Railroad's line between Garrison, Silver Bow, and Butte for interchange with the UP. At that time BN was bridging a fairly heavy volume of business between the UP at Silver Bow and the Canadian Pacific at Sweetgrass, consisting mainly of diatomaceous earth used in oil drilling, potash, and chemicals. When BNSF gained operating rights on the UP into Stockton, California, under the terms of the UP–SP merger, BNSF was able to move business it had been interchanging with UP at Silver Bow on a single line haul to and from California. That loss of business through Silver Bow put the Montana Western (MW) into financial difficulty. BN reacquired the Garrison–Butte line, thereby regaining access to Butte and a connection with the UP at Silver Bow. BN then leased the Helena–Garrison segment to MRL.

EVALUATION OF RESULTS

BN agreed to use MRL to bridge a minimum of 115,000 cars per year between Laurel and Sandpoint.[5] This business remains in the BN account while it is being hauled over MRL. BN has retained its role as the rate-making carrier. BN furnishes enough motive power to MRL to move its business, and MRL manages the operation and maintain the roadway. Bridging traffic for BN amounts to about two-thirds of MRL's total volume. Having a base of business that large eliminates much of the downside risk for MRL. For BN, having a strong, low-cost, reliable operator in place to handle a large amount of its long-haul business has proved to be a satisfactory arrangement.

MRL's customers have rated its service quite high, and its safety record has generally been good. I made a hi-rail trip over MRL from Missoula to Billings in 2008 and was glad to see the property had been well maintained. In the sale and lease agreement, MRL is required to maintain the track to BN standards and allow BN to inspect the railroad to determine if those standards are being met. Also, a number of large capital improvement projects had been completed, including additional CTC, siding extensions, rail relays, and headquarters buildings for roadway-maintenance crews. It was encouraging to learn that MRL had the resources to undertake an $18 million project to improve the track, clearances, drainage, and stability in the 3,896-foot-long tunnel at the summit of Mullan Pass. To prevent overheating of locomotives, the horizontal clearance was increased three feet and the vertical clearance, five feet. The tunnel was shortened by 400 feet, and the roof was strengthened by placing steel arch supports at two-foot intervals. While the improvement project was underway, part of the tunnel roof collapsed, blocking the line for more than a month. To be able to undertake and complete a single project of that magnitude without outside assistance is certain indication of the financial strength of a railroad the size of MRL.

3 Darius W. Gaskins, Jr., "Regulation of Freight Railroads in the Modern Era: 1970–1010," *Review of Network Economics*, December 2008.

4 "Rail Link Reveals Data on BN Deal," *Journal of Commerce*, November 17, 1987; Kyle Brehm, "The MRL Story," *Trains*, April 1990; Kathleen R. Keeney, "Senators Seek Investigation of BN Line Sale in Montana," *Traffic World*, October 26, 1987. The main line was leased rather than sold due to provisions in bonds issued by the Northern Pacific in the 1880s that would not be redeemed until 2047. At that time MRL would be given the option to purchase the main line. The purchase price of $160 million was said to include the value of the 60-year lease payments, and $27 million for the value of the branch lines, equipment and facilities acquired.

5 R. W. Downing, retired vice chairman and chief operating officer, BN, in letter to the author, July 5, 2009.

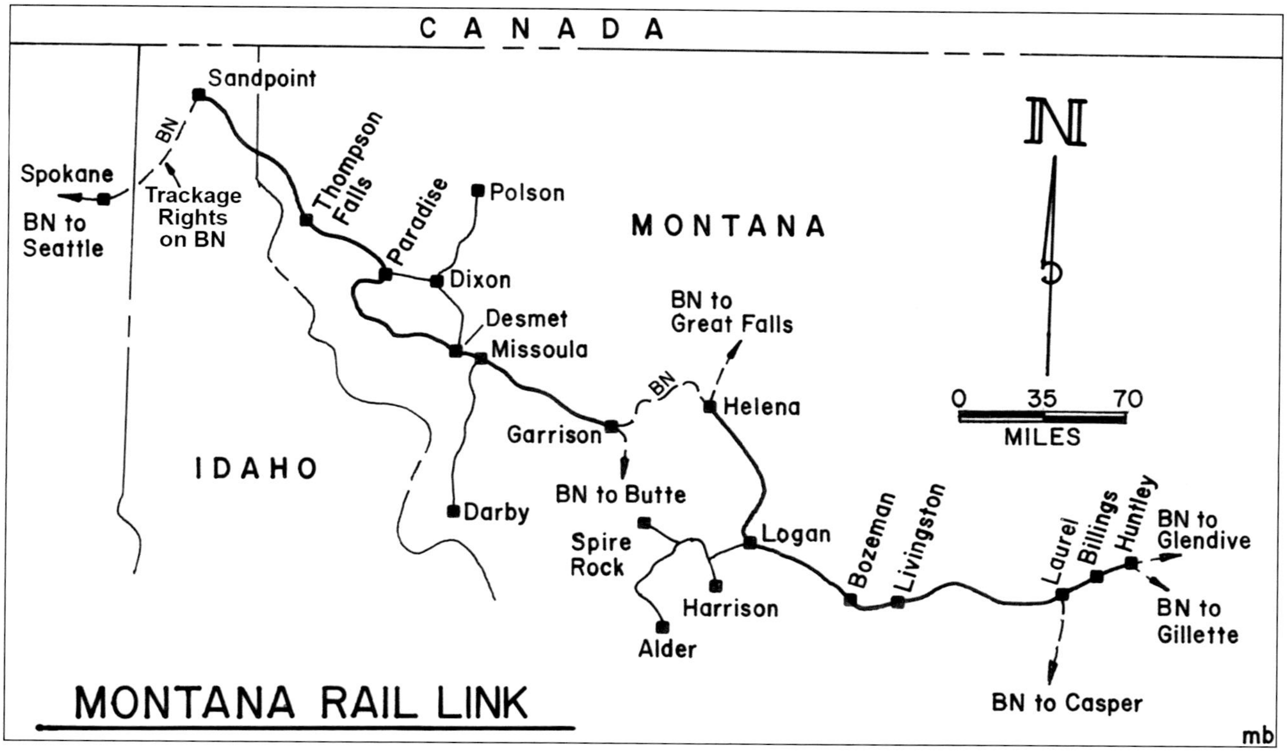

Figure 8.1.

Using 1988 (the first full year of operation for MRL) as the base, the number of employee hours worked was 29 percent higher ten years later. Using train miles as a second measure, business increased by 17 percent in the first 10 years. It must be recognized that the increase in these numbers very likely was tempered to some extent by the operation of more heavy-tonnage unit trains bridged for BN and perhaps by running less local train service, which is labor intensive and involves running light tonnage trains. Also, it is likely that employee hours were reduced in those years by increased mechanization of maintenance work and automation of information handling tasks. Overall, though, it appears there was a steady growth in business in MRL's first decade. At the time of this writing, about twenty-seven years after MRL's startup, the amount of business had increased substantially, to the point where additional investment may be needed in the infrastructure to increase line capacity.

IMPACT ON EMPLOYEES

For many BN employees, the sale to MRL was difficult and caused a great deal of resentment against BN. Some train-service employees chose to exercise their seniority at Havre or Whitefish rather than relinquish the seniority, job protection, and wage guarantees they held on BN and go to work for MRL. When they exercised their seniority on jobs on the "northern tier" (BN's preferred route, the former GN line), they displaced some junior employees who were holding regular positions. Some cases of vandalism, harassment, and unpleasant behavior occurred between the employees of the two groups as they adjusted to working with each other, similar to what had happened at Spokane and a few other locations at the time of the merger in 1970.

Having to move their families or commute a distance of over one hundred miles to and from Whitefish or Havre was a hardship for employees who had never expected to be forced either to move and follow their work, or to remain at their home terminal, give up their seniority and merger protection, and face uncertainties in taking a job with a new company. Most of BN's non-operating employees stayed and went to work for MRL. BN paid $25,000 to any employee who would hire out with MRL.

The choices made by many BN employees to not go to work for MRL forced it to recruit and train a large number of people in time for the start-up of operations. Experienced railroaders were hired from many different locations throughout the country, including many who had lost their jobs when the Milwaukee shut down its West Coast extension in 1980. MRL entered into agreements with the Brotherhood of Locomotive Engineers (BLE) to represent operating employees, and the Brotherhood of Maintenance of Way Employees (BMWE) to cover employees in other crafts.

The agreement MRL made with the BLE provided for a two-person crew on through freight trains, consisting of an engineer and an assistant engineer. Up to then, BN had been unsuccessful in getting an agreement with the UTU to reduce its train crews from four to two employees on the lines of the former GN and NP. On yard-switching crews and some local trains, MRL assigns "utility employees" to work on the ground. Instead of battling the UTU on the crew-consist issue, MRL came to terms with the BLE on the number of employees to be used on trains and on yard-crew assignments. The UTU was left out of the picture.

Upon completion of the agreement between MRL and the BLE, a joint statement was issued by Bill Brodsky, president of MRL, and R. E. Dean, vice president of BLE: "The agreement reached today is based on a cooperative, profit-sharing approach to labor-management relations. . . . The agreement will permit MRL to compete effectively and will permit employees represented by BLE to share in MRL's success." However, Ron Dean made it clear at the same time that the BLE continued to oppose the transfer of BN's line to MRL ownership.[6]

A few hours after MRL took over the ownership and operation from BN on October 31, 1987, a person yet unknown managed to engage three coupled locomotive units into action at Livingston, causing them to run unmanned and out of control up the grade to Bozeman Pass. On a curve on the downward slope, the three locomotives derailed and turned over on a curve at a speed estimated at 80 miles per hour. The result was damage of $3 million. A person termed a "vagrant" was found injured in one of the locomotive units. It was determined that he lacked the technical expertise one would need to get the locomotives moving.[7] The FBI launched an investigation.

Within a few days of start-up, things settled down and the transition was made from BN to MRL, even with challenges still going on in the courts, and not withstanding tremendous opposition and political pressure in many forms from elected representatives at all levels of state, local and federal government. To head up MRL, Washington hired William H. (Bill) Brodsky, who had started his career in the Engineering Department of the Milwaukee Road in Montana. Before coming to MRL, Brodsky held a senior position in the Operating Department of the Santa Fe. He recruited a management staff of experienced railroad people from the Milwaukee, BN, and several other railroad companies. According to an article in the same issue of *Forbes*, MRL made a profit of $33 million on revenue of $120 million in its first year of operation. A report in *Trains* magazine stated that MRL was able to pay off its debt in only four years.[8]

MRL was fortunate that of its property was created out of BN's Rocky Mountain Division, which had won the award for being the best in safety in many years. Only the yard at Laurel and the twenty-five miles of road between Laurel and Huntley had not been under that division. With that strong tradition a strong safety culture had been built over the years, going back into the 1950s, under the NP. However, with many BN operating employees opting not to go to work for MRL, a high percentage of the workforce had to be brought in from the outside. This provided a real challenge for MRL's managers and employees, to orient the workforce in the use of safe work practices and to instill safety as its first priority. In its early years MRL's employees had a frequency ratio in excess of 10. Over the next several years, the ratio was bought down to a much lower level, to a very commendable record of 1.2 in 1998. That performance brought MRL up to the standard of the prior Rocky Mountain Division, earning it a gold medal from the Harriman Institute for Safety for the best

6 "Union Opposes Rail Sale Despite Signing Contract," *Livingston (Mont.) Enterprise*, September 15, 1987.

7 "Vandalism Mars Takeover of Lines in Two States by Montana Rail Link, Inc.," *Traffic World*, November 9, 1987.

8 Steve Glischinski, "Main Street of Big Sky Country," *Trains*, April 1993.

performance among the Group B–size railroads. Over the same period, the ratio of train accidents per million train miles was reduced by about two-thirds.

ATTEMPT BY BNSF TO BUY IT BACK

Rob Krebs, the first CEO of BNSF, attempted to persuade Washington to sell his railroad back to BN, but had no success.[9] With the success Washington has had in his investment in MRL, it seems likely he would expect to have the opportunity presented to him to acquire more lines rather than to give up his ownership of MRL. Washington is well past age 70, and it will be interesting to watch how he sets up his investments for the long term. Obviously, BNSF will want MRL to stay in good hands for movement of its overhead business. Washington has two sons who are in charge of the Washington Group's marine operations and the short-line railroad it acquired in British Columbia a few years ago. They hold seats on Washington's board, and it appears they are being trained and positioned to manage the company's holdings when the time comes.

With the closing of most of the lumber and paper-manufacturing plants located on MRL, it would be interesting to compare its current value with the value it had when it was created over twenty-five years ago. In January 2010, MRL advised that its on-line originating business had fallen so much that it was reducing its freight-car fleet from 2,200 cars to 600 cars.[10] Without BNSF's overhead business, it is likely there would no longer be enough local business to support an asset base as large as MRL has in its roadway and support facilities. MRL would have to reorganize and scale back to the kind of operation that is typical of most short line railroads. However, in view of the projections for increases in the amount of coal, grain, and oil moving west for export, that is not likely to ever happen. It is more likely that MRL will need to expand its capacity to move unit trains over the mountain passes. If it is not practical to build more capacity over Mullan Pass, MRL may even have to look at putting its line over Homestake Pass (via Butte) back in service. It might also become necessary for BNSF to expand the capacity of its line between Laurel and Shelby with CTC and additional sidings.

To many people, the wisdom of the decision BN made selling this important part of its preferred route between the Pacific Northwest and Kansas City to a third party remains questionable. Turning ownership of that line over to an outside party was an important part of the goal BNI had at that time to reduce its asset base. It also eliminated the need to allocate the capital annually for rail, tie, and ballast renewal, to own and maintain a fleet of cars for online loading, and the general enhancements needed every year on a railroad to maintain service and the quality of the operation. Leasing the line served to spite the Montana politicians, news media, and pressure groups that had targeted BN and other large corporations for many years as the root cause of the lack of economic growth in Montana, which they alleged made it difficult for its farmers, ranchers, and much of its general workforce to be able to earn enough to live and work at the standard they desired.

From the operating and service standpoint, it appears MRL is a well-run railroad. It performs highly in moving BN's carload and unit-train business within an elapsed time that is satisfactory. MRL has a good reputation for service with the industries located on its line. It is generally credited with running an operation that is safe and has also developed a reputation as "a good place to work." Being able to finance a major purchase such as the sixteen new SD70AC locomotives, and to invest $18 million to overcome the historic problems in the Mullan tunnel clearly indicates the company has financial strength. There may not be any other regional-size railroad company that could finance such projects and acquisitions without some amount of outside assistance.

Considering that MRL has to bear the cost of operations and maintenance over two mountain passes, along with several tunnels and large bridges, in tough winter conditions, it performs well. BN is fortunate the risk it took in selling and leasing over 900 miles of its railroad has not turned out to be the severe detriment to its operation that some thought it might be at the outset. This is a credit to Bill Brodsky's success in recruiting and developing a competent, professional force of railroad managers and employees.

9 Don L. Hofsommer, "An Interview with Robert D. Krebs," June 7, 2008, at Lake Forest, Illinois, for the Railroad Executive Oral History Program.

10 "Montana Rail Link Cuts 46 Jobs; Cites Closed Mills," *Billings Gazette*, January 13, 2010.

CHAPTER 9

LINE SALES TO START-UP ENTREPRENEURS

In examining the impetus behind the recent deregulatory efforts in the railroad industry, Congress has sought to free the union-management relationship from time-consuming, "process oriented" bureaucracy imposed by various regulatory statutes and allow the sagacious, invisible hand of the free market economy to reorder rapidly that industry's economic difficulty.

RULING WRITTEN BY JUDGE GERALD W. HEANCY, 8TH U.S. CIRCUIT COURT OF APPEALS, QUOTED IN DAVID M. CAWTHORNE, "U.S. SUPREME COURT LIKELY TO REVIEW RAIL LINE SALES," *TRAFFIC WORLD*, JUNE 6, 1988

THE STAGGERS ACT OF 1980 PROVIDED A means for large railroad companies to sell or lease marginal, low-density lines to start-up entrepreneurs or businesses outside the rail industry. BN moved aggressively to take advantage of this new provision that made it possible to carry out such sales quickly and with a minimum of bureaucratic and administrative processes for both the railroad and potential buyers to deal with. The line-sales program enabled BN to remove unproductive, low return assets from its books. For some lines, it eliminated the need to invest just enough capital in the roadway and equipment from year to year to keep such lines in operation until they would become candidates for abandonment.

The new owners and operators of these lines were able to set wages lower than what BN had to pay its unionized workforce. They could perform track and equipment maintenance with either low-cost contractors or employees who could work across the historic craft lines of train crews and maintenance personnel. As a result, a short line could operate these low-density lines profitably.

BN sold or leased these low-volume, low-density lines at a low price that made financing reasonable for prospective buyers. The new railroads were not required to report their financial results to the ICC, as had been required of all railroads, including short lines, before the Staggers Act became effective. The new short lines and BN entered into contracts that required the short line's business to be handled as part of the BN network for a specified payment.

Line-sale programs have worked well over the entire rail industry. About 25 percent of all carload shipments are originated or terminated on short lines. These new railroads have had a good record of success in building up their on-line business by giving close attention to details in service performance and in managing their costs. They have developed good relationships with their customers and work cooperatively with BN's market managers and local operating supervisors where their lines connect with BN's network.

The BN line-sales program made it possible to continue rail service on hundreds of miles of marginal lines that would have become candidates for abandonment. Railroad jobs have been saved and customers continue to have the alternative of rail service. By keeping trucks off rural highways, less money has to be appropriated by states and counties for maintaining and upgrading their roads. As small companies, the short lines sometimes find it difficult to finance major maintenance involving bridges, large programs to replace rail and ties, and other types of work that go beyond small, routine "spot" maintenance work. In such cases, short lines may look to the FRA, state-sponsored programs, or shippers associations for financial assistance.

The Staggers Act gave the ICC the authority to assure prospective owners of the new short lines they would be exempt from labor protection and would not have to assume existing labor agreements between the selling road and the unions. Also, the short line was not required to give priority in hiring to employees of the Class I railroad who would be displaced by the sale.

BN employees who were adversely affected in short-line sales were allowed job protection under the New York Dock Conditions, which apply in mergers and acquisitions. Under these provisions, the wage and benefit levels of employees who were adversely affected by the sale must be maintained for six years. In most cases, however, they were able to exercise their seniority to other positions at nearby locations. It is unfortunate that the labor unions did not attempt to make agreements with BN for lower rates of pay for employees working on lines that are marginal and may become candidates for sale or abandonment. If wage costs could have been reduced enough to make these lines even modestly profitable, BN might have been able to retain ownership of them. However, since rail unions generally are not prone to give up anything they have gained in the past, even to save jobs, the prospect of setting up such a low-cost operation within a large railroad has always been unrealistic. One major exception occurred on the Milwaukee Road in 1978, when the UTU agreed to reduce the number of brakemen on a group of trains being set up to handle new intermodal service between Chicago and St. Paul. It was only because the Milwaukee was in desperate financial condition at that time that it was able to gain a concession of that magnitude.

BN reacquired the Washington Central, the short line operating the former NP line east of the Cascades, when it decided to reopen the line over Stampede Pass. It also reacquired the 80-mile line between Glendive and Snowden, Montana, that connected the transcontinental lines of the former NP and GN. Apparently, the importance of having this line available as a detour route in case of an interruption to service was realized when the line was no longer available due to the condition of its track or another factor limiting or preventing its use. Late in 2012, BNSF also reacquired the 126-mile line between Ferry and O'Neill in northeastern Nebraska. A new ethanol plant and a high-capacity, rapid grain-loading facility coming into service on the line raised BNSF's interest in repurchasing the line. In the years ahead, it will be interesting to see if BNSF will initiate another effort to regain control and ownership of the 560 miles of main track that were leased to Montana Rail Link in 1987.

In southeastern North Dakota, the decision to sell the former GN line that runs diagonally between Wahpeton Junction and Casselton (via Kindred) remains questionable. Having that line available for connection with the former GN line between Breckenridge and Minneapolis would provide a good alternate route to the preferred route through Dilworth. With the large number of oil and coal trains now moving via Dilworth, trains often have to be held back while preceding trains are stopped in Dilworth for a crew change or having to go into the yard to set out or pick up cars. Use of this line would be preferable to the north-south line between Moorhead Junction and Breckenridge, which is the long way around the "triangle," nine miles longer, that must now be used. When the line via Kindred was removed from the BN network, flexibility and line capacity were lost. With a volume of about sixty trains per day now being run through Casselton, the time may have come when the alternate route via Kindred should be reacquired by BNSF and maintained for 40 miles per hour.

CHAPTER 10

POPULISM IN MONTANA

Throughout its history, Montana's culture of populism caused the election of many politicians who blamed the railroads, mining companies, and forest-products-manufacturing companies for whatever ills they thought befell the state, its farmers, ranchers, and workers. Together with the news media, the politicians have used heavy rhetoric against business in general, thereby giving Montana a reputation for being anti-business. Pat Keim, formerly division superintendent at Havre and later BN's legislative representative in Montana, offers this perspective: "Montana's population is rooted in agrarian populism of the early 1900s and the reaction to what many perceived as the overarching reach of the Butte-based Anaconda Copper Mining Company operations into the economic and political affairs of the state. These two forces coalesced into a strong and continuing opposition to large businesses and out of state-based corporations in particular."[1]

The flames of resentment against BN for allegedly being a monopoly, reducing employment, and not retaining large work centers in Montana were fanned when BN was successful in challenging Montana's 14 percent property tax in 1984. BN argued in court that under the Railroad Revitalization and Reform Act of 1976, railroads could not be taxed at a higher rate than other businesses. BN won the case. The state legislature soon passed a bill to restore the higher tax rate, with language the legislature thought would protect the increase, if or when it was challenged through the courts again. BN's property taxes in Montana doubled to $17.5 million per year. Montana's director of Revenue, Jon La Faver, acknowledged that the increase made Montana the second-highest among all states in property-tax burden, as a percent of operating revenue.[2]

In an interview in the *Billings Gazette,* Wayne Hatton, vice president–general manager of BN's Billings Region, stated objectively and forcefully that such political decisions and other actions taken in recent times the McCarty Farms lawsuit[3] could affect BN's decision on maintaining work centers or making new investments in Montana:

> Taxes, regulations and an uncooperative state of government make Montana a tough neighborhood for the Burlington Northern Railroad. Montana's unfavorable business climate could force the company to place discretionary building projects—and other jobs—in other states. If you live in a neighborhood where someone takes a shot at your every six months, what would you do? . . . If you [had] less cost and less trauma in any other state, what would you do? . . . We're getting the word that we're not welcome here.[4]

Hatton added that a new law increasing property taxes was sending a signal to other kinds of businesses as well that they are not welcome in Montana. Further, the state had a law requiring cabooses on freight trains. Another one required that railroads maintain a station agent in all county seats and in all communities with a population over 1,000, unnecessarily costing BN $2.4 million per year. La Faver responded that the legislature would

1 Pat Keim to the author, conversations and emails.

2 Robert Ekey and Paul J. Holley, "State Off Track, BN Says," *Billings Gazette,* October 17, 1985.

3 Refers to a lawsuit filed jointly by Mc Carty Farms and the Montana Department of Commerce, challenging that BN's rates for transporting wheat and barley were unreasonable.

4 Ekey and Holley, "State Off Track, BN Says," *Billings Gazette,* October 17, 1985.

be reluctant to grant relief to BN on such issues "until the railroad listens to their concerns about grain rates."

It was interesting to note that some communities in Montana filed suit against the State Revenue Department, challenging the increased amount of property taxes BN would have to pay. Pat Keim recalls, "These suits resulted when BN's legal challenges to the property tax increases caused the courts to hold the disputed amount in escrow pending the outcome of the case rather than allowing the Department of Revenue to collect and distribute the money to the local and county taxing entities. The local entities therefore could not set their budgets and their recourse was to file suit." Also, BN reported that a delegation from North Dakota visited its regional office in Billings to encourage the company to move its operations to their state. In the same interview, Hatton stated that "any decisions made by BN would not be in form of retaliation for past practices, but business decisions."[5]

In any event, BN would continue to run trains, maintain its track, and provide service to its customers in Montana. "Jobs may suffer [but] we're going to be here," Wayne Hatton told the writer for the *Billings Gazette* in 1985. The decisions BN made on the future of facilities and routes it had in Montana in the next two to three years indeed would have to be judged as business-based, and not as retaliation or for political reasons. These decisions included:

- the sale and lease of 940 miles of railroad to Montana Rail Link in 1987,
- closing and sale of the heavy maintenance and running maintenance facilities in Livingston in 1986,
- closing of its locomotive maintenance facility in Havre in 1991,
- closing of the regional office in Billings in 1986.

BN continued to operate its locomotive-maintenance facility at Glendive and its rail-welding plant at Laurel. The shop at Glendive was upgraded to handle the increased number of locomotive units being put in service for the coal corridor running between the Powder River Basin and power plants in Minnesota and Wisconsin. BN retained ownership and management of its "high line" through northern Montana, its secondary main line between Laurel and Shelby, and several branch lines. In looking back at the decisions BN made in those times, they were unpopular and evaluated by many as those of a greedy, mean-spirited company. However, an objective evaluation shows that they were strategic and business-based. They were sound decisions as shown by the test of time, except possibly for the sale and lease of lines from which MRL was created. It could be argued that the decision to turn the main line between Laurel and Sandpoint over to a new operator never served a real business purpose for BN. Perhaps the best basis for this contention is the effort Rob Krebs made soon after the BN–Santa Fe merger to acquire that property from the Washington Group and put it back under BN management.

Since the years of turmoil and confrontation in which BN made the decisions to close some of its work centers, BN and BNSF have continued both to maintain the infrastructure to a very high standard for the overhead business they move across Montana, and to handle the large tonnages of grain and forest products they originate. Both companies have worked cooperatively with the agri-business interests in Montana to develop a series of modern grain-loading facilities and transportation services that has opened new overseas markets for grain produced in Montana. Lower rates that reflect the economies of scale from running heavy-tonnage trains on a disciplined basis have been established. Thousands of new, higher-capacity grain cars have been acquired. Employees are provided with the safest and most modern, productive equipment and tools available for maintenance of track, bridges, signals, and rolling stock. The hundreds of people BN and BNSF have employed in Montana are among the best-paid industrial workers in Montana or anywhere else in North America. By any standard, the operation in Montana is safe and efficient, one in which its citizens and their elected representatives in government can take great pride.

Shortly after the BN–Santa Fe merger, the locomotive-maintenance shop in Havre was reopened, staffed, and equipped to maintain a hundred locomotive units it had just acquired. Also, a headquarters office for BNSF's Montana Division was established in Billings.

5 Robert Ekey, "BN Ponders Its Future in Livingston," *Billings Gazrtte,* October 27, 1986.

CHAPTER 11

CONTENTION OVER SHOPS AND FACILITIES IN MONTANA

Yesterday's managers can't promise what tomorrow's managers will do.
WARREN MCGEE, RETIRED CONDUCTOR, IN
JOHN HAINES, "BN CLOSURE NO SHOCK TO MAN WHO FOUGHT RAILROAD MERGER,"
BOZEMAN DAILY CHRONICLE, NOVEMBER 7, 1985

• issue of locomotive shops in Livingston, Havre, and Glendive • dispatching center moved to Seattle • region office in Billings closed • new rail-welding plant and car-repair shop built in Laurel •

IN THE YEARS WHEN THE PROPOSED NORTHern-lines merger was being reviewed by the ICC, there were loud protests over concern that the large locomotive maintenance and repair facilities in Livingston would be closed. The railroad companies agreed to keep the Livingston shops open for at least ten years. After the merger, employment in those shops actually increased from 670 to 935. Community leaders were so amazed and elated at these results that they put on a recognition dinner and a full weekend program of celebration in 1975. They expressed pleasure and appreciation for the success of the merger they had fought, and which instead had benefited Livingston, the employees of the former NP, and the many people BN had hired and trained for work in Livingston since 1970.

L. W. Menk attended the dinner and spoke favorably about the future of railroading in Montana. Even Warren McGee, who had been the head of the Livingston Anti-Merger Committee that had told the ICC the terrible things that would happen if the merger was approved, spoke highly to Norman Lorentzsen of BN's living up to and exceeding its commitment. At that time, McGee was still working as a conductor for BN. When Lorentzsen questioned about the complete flip-flop in his attitude, McGee simply said something to the effect of "Just keep proving me wrong."[1]

CLOSURE OF THE LIVINGSTON SHOP

This turned out to be a high point in relations between BN and the political and opinion leaders in Montana, as it was not long before the state raised property taxes on BN and a new slate of executives took charge. They put the new "be the low-cost carrier" theme fully in place, requiring an examination of all work centers, with an eye to closing as many as possible. The Livingston shops

1 Conversation with Norman Lorentzsen, July 2012.

soon became a target. Those facilities might have been closed soon after the 1970 merger, had it not been for the concerns expressed by the ICC regarding the demands of the combined group of citizens, rail workers, political leaders, and the news media that the Livingston shops would be closed.

There was some pressure from within BN that the capacity of the Livingston heavy-repair section of the shops had to be retained for the long term because of the large increase in coal business. However, since there still was unused capacity for heavy repairs at the shops in West Burlington, that argument alone did not prevail. Also, new shops with capability for performing heavy repairs had been put in service at Northtown and Alliance. Improvements in the design and performance of newer locomotives also resulted in a longer time between failures and made it possible to extend the interval between periodic overhauls.

In 1985 BN announced plans to close the back shop at Livingston where the heavy-maintenance work was done. The portion of the shop used for running maintenance—servicing and routine maintenance on locomotives between trips—would be retained, but the major part of the employment was in the back shop. Employees who were to be cut off at Livingston were entitled to exercise their seniority to West Burlington or other major mechanical facilities such as those in Alliance, Lincoln, or Northtown. BN contributed $1 million to a charitable trust the City of Livingston would administer for the general social and economic well being of the community.

The entire shop complex was sold to Dennis Washington in 1987, in addition to the roadway and equipment he was to acquire to form MRL. Under Washington, the back shop was re-opened, and the running maintenance facility was kept in operation. The back shop was set up as a business unit called the Livingston Rebuild Center (LRC). BN and a number of other railroads and locomotive leasing companies had heavy-maintenance, overhaul, and rebuild work done at the LRC's facility.

Once BN announced its decision to lease the mail line between Sandpoint and Huntley and sell several branch lines to a third party, the State of Montana really turned on BN. Closing the shop at Livingston added greatly to the widespread belief that BN made those decisions to get even with the state's elected leaders and the general anti-business mentality prevalent in Montana.

CLOSURE OF THE LOCOMOTIVE-MAINTENANCE SHOP IN HAVRE

In 1992 BN announced the closing of its locomotive maintenance facility at Havre, located on its preferred route between Chicago and the Pacific Northwest. At that time, over two hundred people were employed in that facility. The shop at Havre was built in the 1940s during the years of conversion from steam to diesel-electric motive power. Havre was selected at that time because it was at about the mid-point of the GN's main line between the Twin Cities and Seattle. It was assumed that locomotives on through trains would have to be limited to a run of about a thousand miles and then swapped out of through freight and passenger trains for servicing and maintenance. With the newer, improved locomotives put in service in later years, it became apparent that this limitation was unnecessary. Further, changing locomotives at an intermediate point adversely affected utilization. It was far more efficient to perform routine maintenance at the end points. Therefore, closure of the shop in Havre was felt to be in order at the time.

After these closures, the only large BN–owned maintenance facilities remaining in Montana were the locomotive shop in Glendive and the rail-welding plant at Laurel. The medium-sized yard and car-repair facilities at Laurel and Missoula had been turned over to MRL. There was some pressure with BN to close the shop at Glendive as well, but for a host of good reasons, the decision was made to keep it in operation. A shop was needed at some point between the mines in the northern part of the Powder River Basin and Superior, Wisconsin, for maintaining the locomotives handling the large number of coal trains for Cohasset, Superior, and Becker, Minnesota, that were running on the former NP main line.

Once it was decided to delay, or perhaps never open, the new locomotive-maintenance shop planned for Mandan, there was no reasonable alternative to keeping the old shop at Glendive open. Closing the shop at Glendive and having to run those locomotives out of route into Alliance or Northtown for maintenance would have had an adverse effect on utilization and required BN to put more units in that service. Hence, it was concluded finally that the shop in Glendive should be retained and upgraded.

The office for the Billings Region, headed by a vice president–general manager and a large staff of mid-level managers, was closed in 1986. The centralized dispatching office that had been set up in Billings in 1985 was closed and moved to Seattle. Ten years later, the dispatchers who had relocated to Seattle had to move again, along with all of the other regional dispatching centers on BN, to the new network control center set up in Fort Worth.

Shortly after the merger with the Santa Fe, 154 new locomotive units were acquired. Since they were to be primarily used in grain, intermodal, and merchandise service on the northern corridor, it was decided that the shop in Havre should be reopened to handle maintenance of these new units. Also, a new headquarters office for the general manager of the Montana Division was set up in Billings.

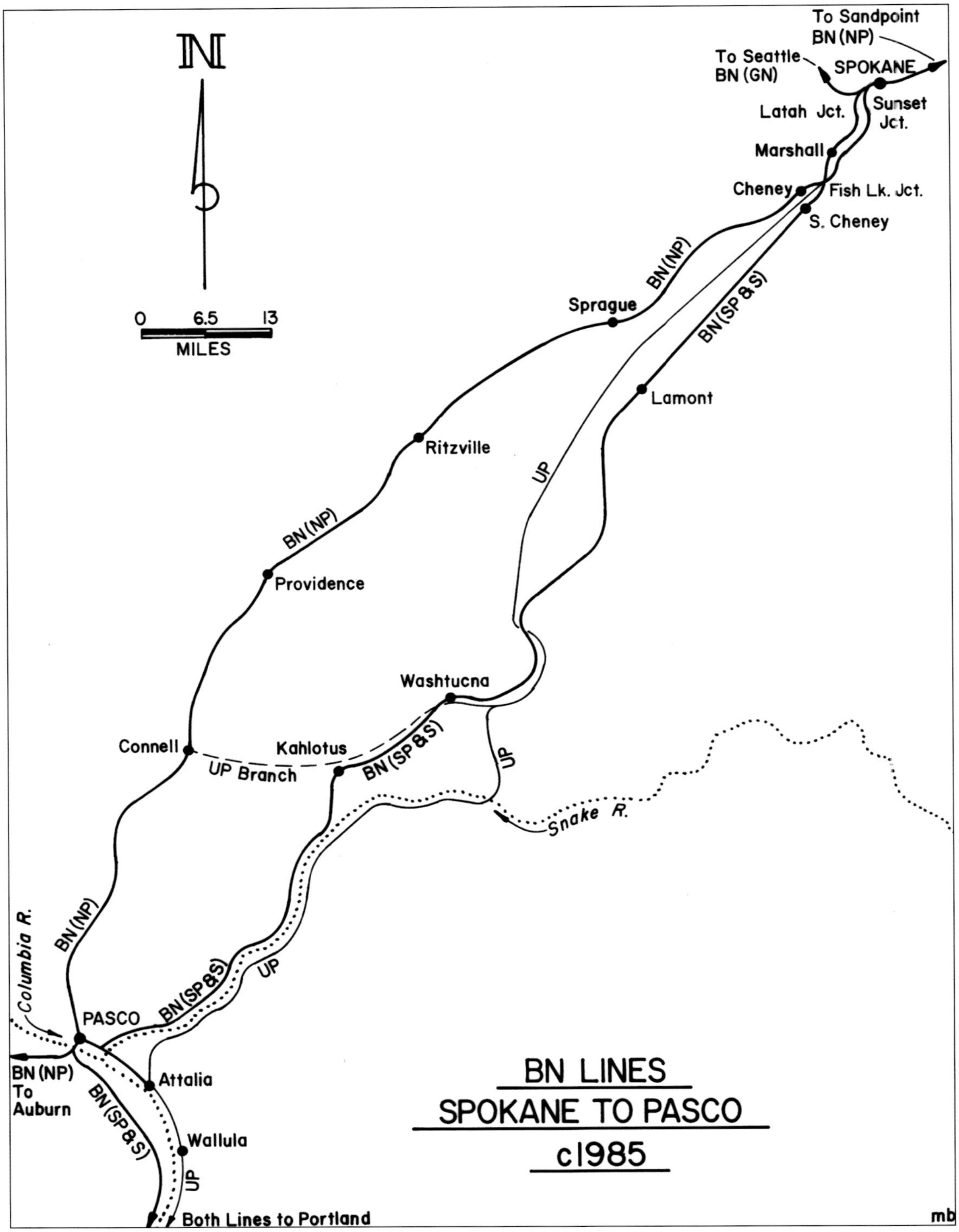
N
0 6.5 13
MILES
To Sandpoint
BN (NP)
To Seattle
BN (GN)
SPOKANE
Latah Jct.
Sunset Jct.
Marshall
Cheney
Fish Lk. Jct.
S. Cheney
BN (NP)
Sprague
BN (SP&S)
Lamont
Ritzville
UP
BN (NP)
Providence
Washtucna
Connell
Kahlotus
UP Branch
BN (SP&S)
UP
Snake R.
Columbia R.
BN (NP)
PASCO
BN (SP&S)
UP
BN (NP)
To
Auburn
Attalia
BN (SP&S)
Wallula
UP
Both Lines to Portland
BN LINES
SPOKANE TO PASCO
c1985
mb

Figure 12.1.

CHAPTER 12

DECISION TO ABANDON A "CROWN JEWEL"

SPOKANE–PASCO

We will not have more than one route between two terminals or junction points.

• decision to end the use of the lowest-grade route to the Pacific • abandoning one of the network's "crown jewels" •

IN ANNOUNCING THE PLANS OF THE GN AND NP to build a new line on the north bank of the Columbia River, James J. Hill stated, "We will build a road of such character of construction as has not before been built west of the Rocky Mountains, of low gradients and slight curvature.... It is finishing the work we started out to do and we must carry to completion."[1]

The Spokane, Portland and Seattle Railway (SP&S) was the last link in the transcontinental system that Hill planned and built to standards that would allow it to surpass its competition. With the advantages the SP&S had through its ability to operate with a low ratio of locomotive tractive effort or horsepower-to-train weight, and having maximum curvature of only 3 degrees and minimum grades, it was a dream for operating and maintenance people.

Only twenty years before Hill announced these plans, the NP had completed construction of its main line between Pasco and Spokane. Hill was challenged on the need for the SP&S to build a line parallel to the NP for those 145 miles. Because the NP's line had grades of 1.0 percent eastward and 1.15 percent westward, and considerable curvature, Hill was determined to build a line that was better engineered. The new line built for the SP&S had a grade of only 0.4 percent ascending eastbound and maximum curvature of only 3 degrees. Westbound, the only ascending grade was 0.8 percent for three miles west from Fort Wright, at the east end of SP&S ownership, followed by 13.5 miles on an ascending grade of 0.4 percent to Marshall.

To meet Hill's mandate to keep the grades and curvature to a minimum, the SP&S built on an alignment that required construction of five large steel-trestle bridges over streams and coulees between Spokane and Pasco. Heavy grading was encountered in getting the line built through several rock formations. The result was a well-engineered line that allowed a low-cost operation in operating heavy-tonnage trains in either direction.

To take full advantage of the favorable characteristics of the SP&S line, BN ran its heavy-tonnage westbound unit grain trains on it between Spokane and Pasco.

1 James J. Hill addressing a gathering of business leaders at the 1905 Lewis and Clark Centennial Exposition at Portland on his plan to complete construction of a new line with low grades on the north bank of the Columbia River.

Having the capability for directional running between Spokane and Pasco provided BN with plenty of capacity and eliminated the delays for meeting trains that are inherent on a single-track railroad. Both the SP&S and NP lines were operated under timetable and train-order authority, with an automatic block-signal system.

The nearly continuous, gradual descent made by heavy westbound unit grain trains for about 370 miles on the SP&S line between Spokane and Vancouver kept fuel and locomotive costs to a minimum. In 1980 the daily volume of freight trains ranged between twelve and sixteen, evenly split between the two lines. The density of traffic was not great enough to justify what was in effect a double-track railroad. However, since the two main tracks were already in place, it made sense for BN to use both lines. To convert one of the lines to a single-track operation would have required a large capital investment to build longer and more evenly spaced sidings and install CTC on either line. There were about 131 miles of 112- and 115-pound conventional bolted rail on the SP&S line that would have to be replaced sooner if all of the tonnage were to be run on that line.

While virtually all of the SP&S line between Vancouver and Pasco had been relaid with continuous welded rail (CWR), the old conventional bolted rail east of Pasco had not yet been replaced with CWR, since it carried lighter tonnage than the line west of Pasco. Most of the business interchanged between the NP and SP&S was routed through Pasco, which meant that nearly all the tonnage the SP&S moved on its line east of Pasco was business interchanged with the GN at Hillyard (Spokane). Since it was expected that international business would increase in the years ahead, it was felt that existing capacity of the "double-track" railroad should be retained. BN believed it would be best not to convert one line or the other to a bi-directional, single-track railroad and then to abandon all or part of the other line.

Beginning in 1980, the direction of the company changed dramatically, with new management coming in at the senior level. Operating strategies and policies were being transformed as we adjusted to the new deregulated environment we were moving into, and the long-term effect it would have on the amount and types of business we would be handling in the future. Operating methods were being overhauled as well following merger with the Frisco Railroad. On top of all that change, the economy fell into a deep recession in 1981. Among the many initiatives BN undertook at that time was a drive to improve the return on invested capital. That was to be accomplished mainly by reducing capital expenditures and the size and value of the asset base. A major part of that effort was the identification of duplicate or alternate routes that could be scrapped or sold. Among the alternate routes studied were those between Laurel, Montana, and Sandpoint, Idaho; Seattle and Spokane; and Pasco and Spokane.

Since the lines of the former NP and SP&S closely paralleled each other, that corridor became a prime target for line rationalization. A detailed study was undertaken to determine which line should be retained and upgraded enough to handle all of the business. In those years it was feared and assumed by several members of senior management that the volume of business handled by railroads was not likely to increase in the years ahead. Among the many factors considered in our study of the two lines were the following:

1. Operating costs, primarily the amount of fuel consumed and train-crew wages.
2. The amount of motive power required in view of the significant difference in grades. With the very low grades on the SP&S line, heavier trains could be run, and with less motive power than was required on the parallel NP line. Less fuel was burned and trains could be operated with a lower horsepower-per-ton ratio, i.e., fewer locomotive units were required.
3. Investment required in rail, ties, ballast, and drainage to bring the track up to the standard required to handle the additional tonnage if we were to establish a single-track operation.
4. How much of either line could be abandoned.
5. Comparison of the cost required to build enough capacity with longer sidings, additional sidings, CTC, and some segments of second main track.
6. Running times for various classes of freight trains—grain, coal, intermodal, and general freight.
7. Cost of maintaining rockslide-detector fences and removing fallen rock between Pasco and Washtucna on the SP&S line.

8 Cost of bridge maintenance.
9 The amount of locally originated and terminated business on each line.

Much of the 130 miles of conventional bolted rail on the SP&S line would soon have to be relaid. A relay of that magnitude would be expensive, and as is the case with any rail relay, it would have a low return on the invested capital. The main arguments for retaining the SP&S line were because it had much more favorable grades and curvature, so that the rate of fuel consumption would be lower, less motive power would be required, and the running times for all classes of trains would be lower. However, those advantages were not enough to offset the cost of relaying nearly 130 miles of rail and maintaining the line as a second main track. There was considerable local business on the NP line, so most of that line would have to be retained even if the SP&S line was designated the preferred line for through trains. There was virtually no local business at any station on the SP&S line.

Some BN managers cited the exposure the SP&S line had to rock slides in a few locations between Pasco and Washtucna, in support of their recommendation to install detector fences and provide enough money each year for a preventative program for scaling rock, which could come loose and fall or roll down to the slide fence. The engineering and maintenance people of the SP&S looked upon the matter of rockslides as just one more item of roadway maintenance they were required to deal with, and not as a serious safety or costly maintenance problem.

The result was a decision to discontinue use of the SP&S line, remove the rail, and turn it over to a state authority for use as a biking and hiking trail. However, BN reserved the right to put the line back in service if deemed necessary in future years.

Table 12.1. Comparison of Routes of NP and SP&S between Pasco and Spokane

	NP	SP&S
Length (mi.)	145.4	146.4
Maximum grades		
westbound:	1.2% (5.3 mi.)	0.8%* (5.2 mi.)
eastbound:	1.2% (2.9 mi.)	0.4% (36.5 mi.)
Curvature (no. of curves)		
1 degree	56	63
2 degrees	64	28
3 degrees	32	21
4 degrees	33	
5 degrees	2	
6 degrees	18	
TOTAL	215	112
Total delta (degrees)	5231	3172
Gross tons per mile per year (1980):	20.1 M	11.8 M

* Westbound, the entire line was on a descending grade except for 3.3 miles of ascending grade of 0.8% and 14.1 miles of 0.4% grade in the first 17 miles west of Spokane, after passing Latah Junction.

During the study, BN evaluated the possibility of acquiring the right-of-way of the branch line the UP had recently abandoned between Connell, where it crossed the NP line, and Washtucna, on the SP&S line. By that time, the UP had removed its track, but the UP advised it would be willing to sell the land to us. This alternative would have required construction of twenty-nine miles of track, but would have allowed abandonment of the fifty-nine miles of the SP&S line between Pasco and Washtucna. This included the area where slide fences were maintained to detect rockslides. Having a line on the old UP grade would also have provided a faster, more direct route for trains using the SP&S line to enter or depart from the hump yard at Pasco. However, when it was decided that the NP line alone would be sufficient to handle all of the business projected between Spokane and Pasco, any further consideration of acquiring the UP right-of-way was dismissed. Also, building twenty-nine miles of new track would have been costly, and not in keeping with the mandate to avoid making large, new investments in the railroad, except those with a high rate of return, based on "hard dollar savings."

In the end, the only significant disadvantages of the SP&S line were the small amount of locally originated and terminated business it had in comparison with the NP's line, plus the cost of replacing the conventional bolted rail. We made a thorough analysis of all the factors involved, but all of the "eyes" that were focused on the issue had to conclude that the only option we had was to retain the former NP line and abandon the SP&S line. We had to come to this conclusion because of the mandate we had to abandon one line or the other. The only argument we had for retaining both lines was to preserve the capacity of the "double-track" railroad for long-term growth, assuming of course, that one had some faith that business would recover when the recession ended and that international trade would expand in the years ahead.

With the buildup in business that began in the late 1980s, many BN people regretted the decision to shut down and abandon the SP&S line. It became clear that both lines should have been retained. Fortunately, BN had the resources to finance major capital expenditures to increase the capacity of the NP line and otherwise improve it enough to offset some of the disadvantages of having only a single-track railroad located on fairly heavy grades. CTC was installed over the entire subdivision, 14.5 miles of second main track were built on the grades of one percent in both directions from Providence, double track was extended four miles east of Pasco, and nine sidings were extended.

In 2014 BNSF announced plans to add more miles of second main track and extend a number of sidings on its single-line route between Spokane and Pasco. Apparently, even the high density of traffic moving on that corridor in these times is not enough to tip the scale in favor of restoring the SP&S line to service. Even with those improvements, the NP line still will remain a far less efficient line than the one built by the SP&S. The right-of-way of the SP&S line was placed in a "bank."

Bob Downing was a mild-mannered, intelligent and knowledgeable person who always expressed his views on railroading in a calm, reasoned manner. However, the decision to discontinue the use of the SP&S line in favor of the NP line was one that upset Bob. Each time I visited him, he expressed his dismay that the leaders of BN in the mid-1980s had so little understanding or respect for the fundamentals of railroad engineering and operations that they would force their people to dismantle a line of railroad with such favorable characteristics. There were a number of other decisions made in those years that Bob found in violation of the norms, values, and principles that he and other leaders had established on BN in its early years, but the decision to discontinue use of the SP&S line disturbed him the most. Time has proved Bob's assessment to be valid. Unfortunately, errors in judgment of this nature are exceedingly expensive to correct. Once made, they usually are forever.

CHAPTER 13

RATIONALIZING YARD AND TERMINAL FACILITIES

• GAVIN YARD (MINOT, NORTH DAKOTA) •

• closure of a showplace facility, the pride of the Great Northern Railway •

IN 1956 THE GN OPENED A NEW HUMP CLASSIFICATION yard five miles east of Minot, North Dakota. It was named in honor of Frank J. Gavin, who served as president and chairman of the GN from 1939 through 1951. Gavin Yard was built at the junction of the GN's main line to Minneapolis and the line to the head of the lakes at Duluth–Superior. It was used primarily to block cars in eastbound trains for delivery to the connecting lines at Minneapolis, and cars for the principal destinations of traffic headed west—to the SP&S at Spokane, and to Seattle, the Everett–Bellingham area, Great Falls, Whitefish, and Havre. A large part of the classification yard was designed to handle grain that originated in western North Dakota and eastern Montana and was brought into the yard at Minot for grading and then held for orders following sale. The greatest benefit of the yard was in giving relief to the series of GN's yards in the Twin Cities that were not designed to efficiently handle the switching of large volumes of cars coming from the West, and not able to do the extent of blocking needed for westbound traffic moving beyond Minot.

No matter where a railroad decides to build a new yard, there always is room for debate on whether the location turned out to be the best. It was argued by some that the yard should have been built much closer to Minneapolis, in or near Willmar, or right in Minneapolis. Any of these locations would have enabled the GN to also block eastbound traffic originating east of Minot or on the Sioux City line, for connections at Minneapolis. Unfortunately, the GN did not own enough property anywhere in Minneapolis or St. Paul that was flat or large enough for a hump yard. A yard in Willmar would not have been in the location needed to handle the business moving on either the St. Cloud line or the line between the Twin Cities and Duluth/Superior. By the early 1960s, it was decided in the consolidated operating plan that a large new hump yard would be built on NP property at Northtown on the north side of Minneapolis.

The operating plan specified that Gavin Yard would continue to play a major role in handling business on the preferred route, even after the new hump yard would be put in service at Northtown. However, not long after the new yard at Northtown was opened, it became apparent that Gavin Yard was no longer needed for classification of traffic moving on the northern corridor. Northtown was much better located to handle such work and had sufficient capacity. That made it unnecessary to retain Gavin Yard as a major hump classification yard, in the supporting role it was supposed to have in the merged company.

Since there was a great deal of pride in the design and operation of a yard as new as Gavin, the possibility of closing it as a major hump yard and changing its role to local service only about sixteen years after it opened was not well received by many BN people. Over the years, large yards become "institutions" in the culture of many railroads. Many of its officers consider it a badge of honor to have worked in a large yard that, at least by reputation, is a tough, challenging place to manage. In the case of Gavin Yard, it was well designed and had been maintained as a real showplace. Unlike many railroad yards, the atmosphere at Gavin Yard had always been orderly and businesslike, and not in a constant state of frenzy or chaos, which was the impression one would have in observing some other large yards in that era.

In addition to Northtown being able to handle more volume and make more blocks of cars than envisioned in the merger plan, other factors were in play by the early 1980s that led to realization that Gavin Yard could be closed as a major hump yard. One was the shift of merchandise business to intermodal equipment. Trains made up of intermodal shipments originating at end points on the system did not require classification by humping at an intermediate yard. New commercial practices in the marketing and sale of grain led to the use of unit trains, thereby eliminating such costly practices as having to hold carloads of grain at yards for inspection and sale for two days or more before the railroad could finally release and line them for movement to destination. That change took a large amount of switching out of Gavin Yard and freed up several tracks in its classification yard.

The result was much less need for Gavin Yard as an intermediate facility for classifying large volumes of cars in either direction. The hump was shut down and the yard was reconfigured into a flat switching yard large enough to handle local needs only. Gavin Yard served the GN and BN as a major hump yard very well for twenty-six years (1956 to 1982), but the time had come to rationalize it down to the level of capability that BN needed to maintain at Minot for local business. For many people with a GN heritage, shutting down the hump and removing several miles of track was an emotional event: the end of an era.

· HAUSER, IDAHO ·

· decision not to build a large, new hump classification yard ·

THE CONSOLIDATED OPERATING PLAN FOR THE 1970 merger called for construction of a new terminal complex on property acquired shortly before the merger at Hauser, Idaho, twenty-four miles east of Spokane. Because Spokane was at the hub of five main-line subdivisions, it was thought to be the preferred location for a large classification yard in the western part of the system. It would have a role as critical to the flow of traffic as the new yard to be built in Minneapolis. While the NP had built a modern hump yard at Pasco, only 125 miles west of Spokane, having such capability located at Spokane would be far more beneficial in the consolidated operation.

From the time of the merger in 1970 to 1982, only nine tracks were built on the property at Hauser. Construction of the new yard was delayed in order to finish building the yard in Minneapolis. Also, by the mid-1970s, BN had to use all the capital it could raise for the major expansion and upgrading projects required to handle the projected tonnages of coal to be moved out of the Powder River Basin.

By 1982 those large projects were completed, and the railroad company's earnings had improved enough to allow the opportunity to undertake construction of the full-scale project at Hauser. Serious consideration was given to building the new yard even in the face of pressure on the Operating Department to reduce the asset base. A yard of the size projected would have cost at least $50 million.

In the analysis we made of the current and anticipated flow of carload business in the Pacific Northwest, we found it had decreased considerably from the 1960s, when the consolidated operating plan was prepared. More and more bulk traffic such as grain was moving in unit trains, and a large amount of merchandise traffic had been shifted to intermodal equipment. Productivity

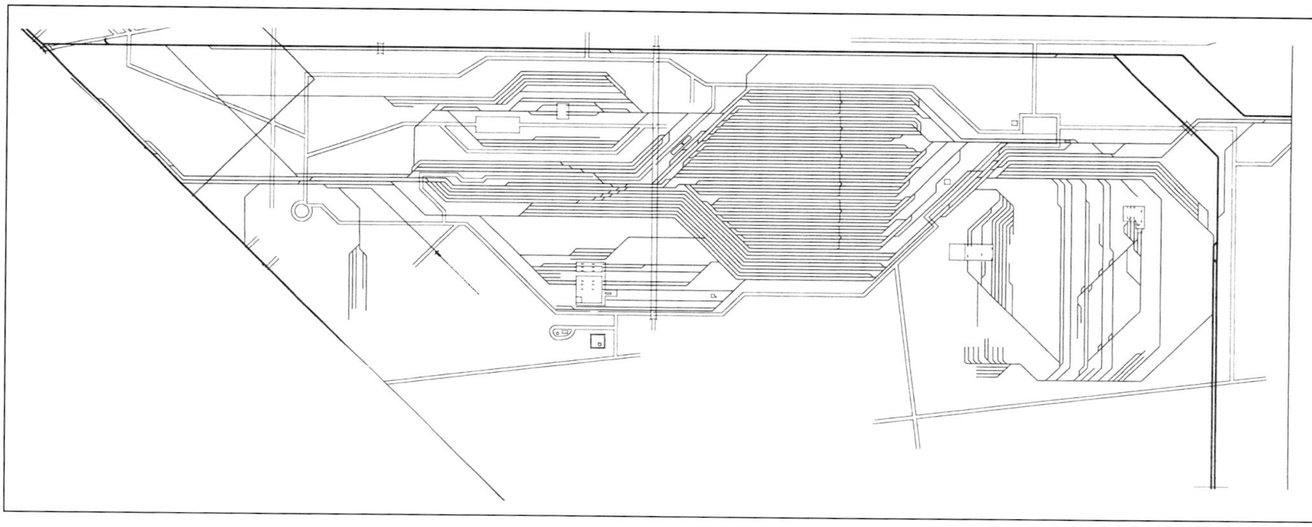

Figure 13.1. BNSF schematic (dated 2005) for the new yard BN opened at Galesburg in the early 1980s. Very large savings were made in maintenance costs in several ways: the application of new technology to the switching and routing of cars; processing information needed to insure connections; and car-movement schedules were made from an inbound train to the designated outbound train for each car handled through the yard. The new yard opened with thirty-two tracks in the classification yard (the herringbone series of tracks below the hump.) After merger with the Santa Fe, capacity has been added in a series of projects over several years, increasing the classification yard to sixty-three tracks, along with the addition of four tracks in the receiving/departure yard. A new locomotive-maintenance shop was built to offset closure of the shop in Cicero to make room for expanding the intermodal facility. BNSF RAILWAY COMPANY.

had been improved enough at existing yards for us to conclude that we could avoid making the investment for the full capability originally intended for Hauser.

In 2004 BNSF completed a technologically advanced locomotive-fueling facility for "through" trains at Hauser. It consists of three signaled main tracks and the capability to fuel trains moving in either direction. A motive power consist of four locomotive units can be refueled in forty-five minutes. Hauser has also been established as the crew-change point for trains operating on any of the four subdivisions that reach Spokane. The yard is also equipped with twelve tracks used for yarding trains terminating or to be held and for general switching. It serves as an "overflow" yard for the main switching yard (Yardley) in Spokane.

· GALESBURG, ILLINOIS ·

· rebuilding of an obsolete two hump classification yard ·

IT WAS EASY TO DETERMINE THAT A BETTER USE of capital at that time was to modernize the large yard at Galesburg, which was labor intensive, in a generally rundown condition, and being operated with technology from the 1930s and '40s. Because the return on investment was highly favorable, capital was committed to completely rebuild the yard at Galesburg. It turned out to be a good decision, with the improvement in service and reduced costs that were realized. In the past thirty-five years since the new yard was completed, it has been expanded several times, and it serves a vital role in the network of today's BNSF Railway.

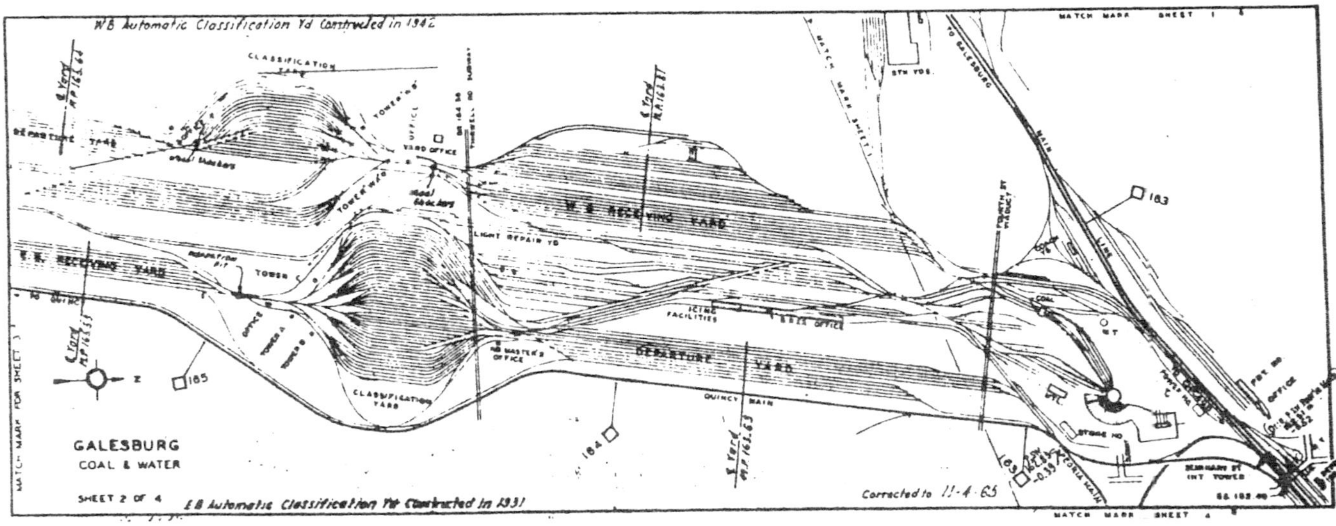

Figure 13.2. A schematic of the old two-hump classification yard at Galesburg, which was dismantled and replaced by a new single hump in the early 1980s. CB&Q RAILROAD COMPANY.

· OTHER TERMINALS ·

Closings and consolidations of yards at other locations contributed to the goal of reducing the asset base. In the Twin Cities, construction of a large, modern hump yard at Northtown made it possible to close eleven yards. When large yards were closed in Denver and Spokane, property was freed up for commercial development or various kinds of public projects. The sale of land and the removal of large quantities of track material and large support buildings contributed toward reduction of the asset base. At the same time, this consolidation of operations into fewer yards made operations more efficient.

PART IV

INNOVATION AND NEW DIRECTIONS

CHAPTER 14

"CHANGE YOUR DEPARTMENT"

Early in 1981, department heads were given a mandate to "change your department." Soon afterward, they were evaluated as to their ability and willingness to undertake the kind of transformation that would reduce costs, improve the effectiveness of their department, and bring the attitude and commitment of its staff members in line with what it would take to meet the new goals, standards, and accountability expected for the performance of their unit. This included acceptance of the concept of incentive-based compensation, rather than an attitude of entitlement and complacency, in which they would believe life in the company would continue to run in a straight line, and that fundamental changes were not needed.

To change a department could mean relocating its headquarters to another city, decentralizing some of its responsibility out to the regions, changing out some key management personnel, redefining its mission, or changing the department's goals and priorities to better support BNI's new agenda. Whatever needed to be done to apply the mission, strategy, and new approach to managing the railroad was required in all of its departments and functions. When it was determined the current leadership of a department was not up to working in the new culture, junior executives were promoted or experienced executives were brought in from outside the company to initiate rapid change.

Every department was expected to reduce the size of its staff and the layers of management in place to run it. Some of the smaller, less-vital staff support departments reduced their head count by as much as 50 percent. In so doing, department heads had to examine all of the activities and processes going on in their departments that had been built up over the years. They had to determine if responsibility for any of those functions should be decentralized to the regions, or if they should simply be dropped if maintaining them would contribute little or no value to the new objectives their departments were expected to meet. Making such transformations was difficult for some managers who had a long-term association with BN and a predecessor company in a particular function or activity. Many senior and mid-level managers who were above age 55 chose the "early out" program and retired. Since this program allowed them to decide whether to accept that offer, those who accepted it were able to leave with dignity, and not be seen by others as having been forced to leave.

That opened opportunities for promotion to younger people who had no strong allegiance, sense of ownership, or empathy with past practices. As with the executives brought in from the outside, they were able to move right in, reduce the staff, and establish quickly which functions were vital and which had to be dropped. They also made the moves necessary to eliminate costly, cumbersome bureaucratic practices that had been built up over the years, slowed decision-making, and often restricted the "doers" in the organization from being as effective as they could be.

Many examples of how transformation was carried out in the departments could be cited. Among them was the transfer of responsibility to the regions for the fleet of low-horsepower locomotive units that were required for local service, yard switching operations, and the secondary trains operated within a region. Responsibility for utilization of the freight-car fleet also was decentralized. The result was a profound improvement in utilization that made it possible to reduce the number of low-horsepower locomotives and cars that needed to be owned and maintained.

In the Mechanical Department, changes in inspection and repair procedures reduced the number of cars awaiting repair, and the time required to make repairs. Changes in the assignment of machinery and work methods used on large track-maintenance gangs resulted in vastly improved productivity.

The system signal shop was closed and its functions were sent out to the regions. The primary accountability for managing costs—in line with the new goals and standards set for improving productivity in all operations and maintenance functions—was established as the responsibility of the regions. Some departments, among them Labor Relations, Information Systems and Human Resources, assigned and relocated a key staff member to work under each region. By working directly with the region staffs, less time was required for decision-making, and the need to raise questions and requests for approval or assistance to the headquarters level was greatly reduced.

To speed up the process for the approval and funding of new operating and maintenance projects that had a quick payback period, a contingency fund was set up. This made it possible to avoid the delays for approval that would occur if these projects had to be placed in line with the normal capital-budgeting cycle that might not start until several months later. Being able to get a large number of projects with a high rate of return and "hard dollar" savings approved and completed quickly was a big factor in reducing the operating ratio. It required a fundamental change in the working relationship between the Operating and Finance departments.

TRANSFORMATION OF THE INFORMATION SERVICES UNIT

Another noteworthy example of how a department was changed was evident in the transformation of the Information System Services Department (ISS, also known as the Management Information Services Department in earlier years). With the demands from user departments for more analytical tools and detailed reporting, ISS had come under increasing criticism, to the point of being viewed by many as ineffective in its ability to respond to important needs. To deal with the many challenges and problems, Eli Wackstein was brought in from El Paso Gas to head the department. In an interview reported in *BN News,* Eli stated, "I had to overcome the department's reputation of not being effective. . . . We've had to earn confidence and change attitudes by implementing a successful new organization. There is improved credibility among employees who are in contact with the ISS Department. There is much excitement and enthusiasm because they can request new projects and get results."[1] Some of the improvement in the perceived effectiveness of the department resulted from its decision to place a few staff members in the user departments and the operating regions.

There were cases in which the head of a department was retained, but with one or two "change agents" added to his staff. They were to be given a free hand in implementing new methods that would quickly reduce costs and improve productivity. In applying this approach to initiating change, the department head had to become amenable to giving a wide latitude of responsibility and authority to individuals designated for such a role.

A number of promising younger managers were lined up with mentors who would help train them on the new agenda being established in a particular department or functional area. Some of them were also provided the opportunity for cross-functional training, in order to help broaden their knowledge of the new business practices being introduced, and to prepare them as candidates for promotion. It was interesting to observe how well many managers who were transferred out of the headquarters environment and out to the field adapted to their new role. They became effective contributors by having to work closely with line managers to improve performance of the unit. This kind of role was far better for them and the company than when they held an administrative or analytical position at headquarters, charged with enforcing regimented procedures that often were slow, cumbersome (causing "paralysis by analysis"), and counter-productive to the introduction of new methods or technology that was badly needed in meeting new objectives.

1 "An Interview with Eli Wackenstein," *BN News* (August–September 1985): 17.

OPPORTUNITY FOR RAPID ADVANCEMENT

During the process of transforming the departments, a great deal of the expertise of experienced executives was lost, mainly through retirement. Some who left the company were well liked, having built a big following within the company, and were considered effective leaders and managers. The other side of the coin was that younger people of promise could advance much more rapidly than they would have under the pace of management succession that existed before the early-out program. Many of the executive positions that were vacated did not have to be filled.

If nothing else, these times of rapid and fundamental change got everyone's attention. Managers at all levels examined themselves as to the level of competency they had developed, whether they were performing well enough to be evaluated as promotable, and to be sure their job performance would clearly show they were"on the team" and "hitched to the plow." Everyone knew there was no room or refuge for those who were "on the fence," or who thought, "this, too, shall pass."

Overall, the methods employed to restructure the company and its departments in ways that would enable it to achieve its new objectives and business practices were effective. Some mistakes were made, and "overkill" or injustices occurred. There were a few cases in which a second effort toward transformation had to be undertaken when it was found necessary to replace executives who had been brought in only a few months before. The tough decisions on personnel matters were made quickly. The results from these changes in leadership style and culture and the general mandate to "change your department" are borne out in the much lower operating ratio and the overall improvement in financial results BN achieved within two years after the transformation was started.

CHAPTER 15

RELOCATING HEADQUARTERS OFFICES

No, We're Not Moving

HEADLINE IN THE APRIL 1982 ISSUE OF *MGR.*, A NEWSLETTER ISSUED PERIODICALLY IN THE EARLY 1980S

BN's Operations Department Has Moved South

BN NEWS, JULY 1983

BN Considers Move of Some St. Paul Staff

MGR., DECEMBER 14, 1983

Fort Worth Move Completed

BN NEWS, OCTOBER, 1984

He [Bressler] encouraged geographic dispersion of headquarters. "You pick good people and get out of their way. If you are physically separated you don't get on each other's nerves from constant contact."

GORDON DONALDSON, *CORPORATE RESTRUCTURING*

Having to make a change in one's job location and residence is a way of life that railroad operating managers readily understand and accept. It is part of the process of "going through the chairs" in advancement—in becoming familiar with the operating characteristics and requirements of the prominent parts of the railroad's network. However, any possibility for the relocation of any headquarters department will raise emotions, anxiety, and resistance of those who work at the "home office" and who have never had to experience or even think about a transient nature in their jobs.

For the 1970 merger, there was no question the headquarters of the new company would be in St. Paul. GN and NP occupied a large, recently modernized building in downtown St. Paul, built under James J. Hill's direction, so where else could headquarters possibly be? It was natural and fully expected that the headquarters staff of the Burlington (CB&Q) would be relocated from Chicago to St. Paul. There was some grumbling from people who had their roots in the Chicago area about the high income tax and colder weather in Minnesota, as well as having to live in a somewhat less "exciting" city than Chicago. However, most of the Burlington people adjusted quickly to the change.

Such was not the case starting in the early 1980s, when Bressler decided to set up a holding-company structure and move about a hundred people to Seattle. Many of those involved in this change had never been required to relocate in the past when promoted or to broaden their experience. Even the escape from Minnesota income tax to a state with no income tax, and the prospect of living in one of the world's most scenic locations, with boundless opportunities for outdoor recreation, was not enough to quell the concern of some over relocation. No one had ever dreamed that headquarters—or even a part of it—could possibly be moved out of St. Paul.

OPERATING DEPARTMENT "SPLITS" TO OVERLAND PARK

Imagine what the initial reaction was when the word got out that some or all of the force in the railroad company's General Office might also have to relocate. Quickly, this possibility moved past the rumor stage when Bressler declared that the large departments of the railroad should decide where their headquarters office should be located. It didn't take long for the Operating Department, then headed by W. F. Thompson, to decide it should move south, at least in the direction of "back home" for the people of the former Frisco. Kansas City was soon determined as the best place for the Operating Department to be located. It was close to the mid-point of the system, at the crossroads of several major corridors of the BN network.

Bressler was in full support of the Operating Department going off on its own, to move away from the interference and hammering he had seen it take from other departments to advance their agendas, often of limited value. The Operating Department needed to be kept free to work on reducing its costs and improving bottom-line returns. The new problems of living in or near Kansas City—high humidity, the tornado season, frequent electrical storms, and the loss of easy access to Minnesota's ten thousand lakes—were said to pale when compared to getting away from the burdens of the high state income tax, cold weather, and the policies of the left-wing Democratic-Farmer-Labor Party that some saw as putting expanded governmental control over their lives. Reflecting on this controversial matter, Bob Garland recalled, "except for the personal savings in state income taxes, I know of no unbiased evidence that shows the claimed benefits of such a move could not have been achieved without it."[1]

The decision to move about two hundred people of the headquarters office of the Operating Department to Overland Park, Kansas (a suburb of Kansas City), was announced late in 1982. The move into leased space in a new office building was completed in June 1983.

The headline, "No, We're Not Moving" appeared in an article written for the April 1982 issue of *Mgr.*, a newsletter sent to exempt (management) employees. The article covered by that headline read as follows: "Contrary to rumors circulating throughout the company, BN has not sold its St. Paul offices, nor does it have plans at this time to move its headquarters to Kansas City or any other U.S. city." The article continued with a quote from Chairman Richard Grayson: "That's not to say we haven't considered the idea, and we continue to review our situation. It's news to no one that Minnesota's business climate is not the best in the U.S. Its corporate and personal income taxes are among the highest in the nation. . . . We'd be negligent if we didn't continue to evaluate this climate and its effects on our business."

THE REST OF THE RAILROAD—TO FORT WORTH

By November 1982 (seven months later), that position had changed. BN advised a study was underway on a possible move of some headquarters employees out of St. Paul. Among the locations being considered for the new headquarters of the railroad company were Chicago, Denver, Fort Worth, and Lincoln. It was no surprise when the announcement was made early in 1984 that the headquarters offices of the Executive, Sales and Marketing, Law, Personnel, and Labor Relations would be moved to Fort Worth.

Everything about Fort Worth contained the attributes for a business location that appealed to the new management team's preferences: no state income tax, a pro-business political and social climate, no cold weather, and the chance for BN to be identified with the host of progressive large companies that had moved out of the congested, high-cost, high-tax, and generally stifling

1 E-mail messages, Robert Garland to author, November 2015.

environments of large cities in the eastern and midwestern sections of the country. Also, it was felt by some that BN would be in better position to attract new management talent in a more spirited and dynamic area than could be found anywhere in the Twin Cities or the Upper Midwest, for that matter.

Relocating four hundred families to Fort Worth was expensive, and for many of them, who were not accustomed to or ever expecting to have to move, disruptive to their lives. The company had invested a large amount to modernize the General Office building in St. Paul in recent years, including installing air conditioning, replacing the windows, and modernizing some floors (including the executive level). Since BN owned the building, there were no lease or rental payments to make. However, it still was an old building and felt by some to be too much of a vestige of the past. The environment of the building James J. Hill had constructed sixty-five years before to house both the GN and NP headquarters offices was believed to stifle opportunities to make the changes needed in BN's culture and in the ways employees approached their jobs.

A large number of ties and many miles of new rail could have been purchased and put into the track for what was paid to acquire equipment and furnishings for a new office, make lease payments, and move the families and household goods of employees. We had been telling the people of the railroad for the past four years that we had to get our costs down, spend less on capital projects, and that wages, salaries and benefits had to be cut for the company to survive and prosper in its new deregulated environment. To many people, spending millions to relocate to lavish new headquarters at Overland Park and Fort Worth was inconsistent with such statements.

Most BN people soon put such concerns aside and got on with the new program. What was important was to learn how you and your job fit in with the new ways of doing business, i.e., how to work in what had become a competitive, market-driven environment, and away from the historic bureaucratic, regulated, and burdensome practices of the past. Getting out from under the burden of the high state income tax was a relief to many, as was having a chance to thrive and develop in the exhilarating environment of the great and proud state of Texas. Most BN people quickly adapted to the new environment. Many have continued to live in the Fort Worth area after retiring.

OPERATING DEPARTMENT "REJOINS" THE COMPANY

It wasn't long until the decision was made to move the headquarters staff of the Operating Department from its new headquarters in Overland Park to Fort Worth, to get them back with the rest of the company. Having a large department with responsibility for a very large budget and the work of thousands of employees separated from the rest of the organization had proved to be counterproductive to establishing teamwork as an important value for the company and its people. The use of the telephone, e-mail, and video conferencing was not enough to overcome the disadvantages of separation. The time and expense for travel between Overland Park and Fort Worth were high. It made no sense to allow department heads to locate their offices according to personal preference, or what they thought was a better location than where the CEO and the heads of other departments were located.

Soon the spacious offices in Overland Park were vacated, and the operating team was relocated again. By the time of that move, plans were being made to centralize all of the dispatching, station, and yard office functions and customer-service staffs and create a new operations control center, making it necessary to have far more space than was available or suitable in downtown Fort Worth for the kind of equipment and work layout that would be needed. Moving the headquarters staff of all departments to a new campus environment in a suburban area near Fort Worth would make it expedient to get all of the railroad company's departments and functions in a single location.

The old General Office building in St. Paul was sold at the end of 1984. BN retained space for the functions it had decided not to relocate (Accounting, Information Services, and the Purchasing and Material staffs) due to the high cost of moving the equipment and the large clerical staffs involved. At the time, BN employed 1,550 people in the functions that remained in St. Paul. After merging with Santa Fe in 1995, the functions of those departments would be moved to other locations on the new BNSF system.

The office for the Billings Region, headed by a vice president–general manager and a staff of mid-level managers, was closed in 1986. The centralized dispatching office that had been set up in Billings in 1985 was closed and moved to Seattle. Dispatchers from the division headquarters offices in Havre, Missoula, and Glendive had been moved into Billings in order to reduce the size of the dispatching force and the amount of supervision it required. Ten years later, the dispatchers who had been relocated first to Billings, and then to Seattle, had to move again, along with all of the other regional dispatching centers on BN to the new network control center being set up in Fort Worth.

CHAPTER 16

GIVING UP SENIORITY

• we want our officers to be totally committed and not have their seniority to fall back on •

IN THE RAIL INDUSTRY, THERE WAS A LONG-standing practice of allowing employees to retain their seniority after promotion to an "exempt," i.e., a managerial or technical position. Employees promoted out of the ranks would retain their position on the seniority roster of whatever craft and location they were working in at the time they were promoted. It was viewed as an incentive to get employees to seek and accept opportunities for promotion. By being able to retain their seniority, promoted employees would always have "something to fall back on" in case the promotion they accepted did not work out well, either for them or the company.

There were many senior executives at BN and other railroads who had gotten their start in a job in which there was union representation. They took great pride in having started "at the bottom" in a craft position and then advancing in the hierarchy of management. For many of them, it was a badge of honor. Most of them were college graduates.

Management personnel who had been hired directly after completing their college education or recruited from another company or organization never worked in a position in which they would establish seniority. However, there were some railroad companies that encouraged the college graduates they hired to take a union-represented job for a short time to "get a [seniority] date" established before they officially began their management training program. The GN was among the companies that maintained this practice.

There were hundreds of first-line supervisors and middle-management-level personnel who had retained their seniority rights as permitted and encouraged under this policy. It was an accepted practice that caused no apparent problems in loyalty or devotion to the principles or work practices espoused by management. Each year there would be a small number of managers who would choose to resign from their exempt position and exercise their seniority. Usually, that was done for personal reasons—having family members who could not cope with a requested or required transfer, or if the management position to which they had been promoted turned out to be a mistake for either or both the company and the employee. Again, such cases were relatively infrequent.

NOTHING TO FALL BACK ON

With this tradition in place from the establishment of railroading as a big business in North America, it was a surprise and a shock throughout BN when some members of the new team of senior executives who came in the early 1980s strongly advocated that all managers who had seniority would have to decide "which side of the fence" they chose to be on. If they wanted to retain their exempt or managerial position, they would have to give up their seniority.

It was felt that if they continued to hold seniority after promotion, they might become disloyal or otherwise to be unable or unwilling to stand up for management in times of confrontation with the labor unions, or whenever they would have to deal with poor job performance or cut the jobs of individuals in groups they had worked with before they were promoted. It was expected that these managers probably did not really have their hearts in their jobs, knowing they had their seniority to fall back on when the going got tough, as was expected when BN would implement its plans to take on the unions to get substantial changes in work rules and reduce the compensation of railroad employees to a "market level." The new management wanted to be sure that all of its exempt employees would be fully on board and not lose heart and walk away in the event of a long-term strike over the changes BN needed in work rules and on the manning of train and yard switching crews.

In these years the management organization already had been terrorized at all levels through the transition to a leadership style of fear and intimidation. Along with that new way of doing things came ridicule from a set of new executives over what they saw as the "cradle to grave" culture that railroad people expected as a condition of employment. They thought railroad managers were grossly overpaid, that we had an entitlement mentality due to having a pension plan and health insurance coverage that was much too generous, and on top of that, because many managers had retained their seniority. As a result of being so well taken care of, they said we had a culture in which "nobody ever leaves." What was needed, in their opinion, was to put more of everyone's compensation and job security at risk—to have it based on individual job performance combined with how well the company did in meeting its goals. There would no longer be any "sure things" in terms of compensation and benefits.

With all of that uncertainty building up, it was alarming to many of BN's managers that they might also have to give up their seniority if they were to retain their management position. With continued reductions in the number of management positions in BN, together with new standards for evaluating job performance, it was becoming hard to know how long one might be able to hang on. If they would no longer be able to return to the ranks in case they were dismissed from their exempt position, there would be nothing left for them at BN. This was especially alarming to those who did not have a college degree or specific training or qualification for work outside of railroading. Those who had started their careers in train service (i.e., conductors, brakemen, engineers, or yardmasters) were especially vulnerable if they lost their job in management and also had to relinquish their seniority.

All of this turmoil, with its threatening atmosphere and uncertainty, caused people throughout the company to lose faith and trust in its new leadership. For many, it no longer was a good place to work. These conditions were major distractions, and for those who held safety-sensitive jobs, a matter of increasing concern. Fortunately, when yet another change was made at the top level of management in 1988, this controversial matter was allowed to dissipate. For the company, this was fortunate, since a large number of first-line supervisors in particular might have decided to play it safe by giving up their exempt positions and going "back to the tools," keeping their seniority.

Through all of the restructuring of policies and culture in the North American rail industry, no other large railroad company has fostered or implemented a policy requiring its managers to give up their seniority. The perception of some in senior management that retaining it was a problem was unique to the management BN had in place in the mid-1980s.

In recalling the turmoil the new management caused on this issue, it was both amusing and gratifying to find a quote of chairman and CEO Lou Menk in the "Merger Special" edition put out by *BN News* at the outset of BN's merger with the Frisco Railroad: "I still hold my Frisco seniority as a train dispatcher and a telegrapher. I'm number one on both lists, the unions gave me a special dispensation." It is clear that Menk still valued his seniority, even after reaching the level of CEO and long after he had left the Frisco to head the Burlington.[1]

JOB RANKING TO COUNTER GRADE CREEP

Another initiative that caused angst among many exempt employees was the new policy for evaluation or "ranking" of their job performance. We were to assume that in any of our departments or work units that about 10 percent were performing at a low or marginal level. About 10 percent deserved a ranking of superior or outstanding, and the balance (about 80 percent) would be ranked as competent. It was believed this forced ranking was appropriate in every work unit and that there

1 "BN, Frisco Join Forces," *BN News*, special edition (January 1981): 7.

were managers who should be evaluated as marginal or lower. They would then be put on a development plan to improve their performance. If an employee with such evaluation failed to progress to a level considered satisfactory or competent within a specified period (generally, three or four months), he or she would be terminated.

Over the years, "grade creep" had occurred, causing far too many exempt employees to be evaluated as 4 or 5 (superior or outstanding). Being graded a 3 (competent) was being given only to those considered borderline or approaching termination. Obviously, being graded as competent should have been thought of as good, but with so few being ranked at that level, it was not. It was almost unheard of for anyone to be graded marginal or unsatisfactory.

In the process of regrading, a large number of managers fell from a 4 ranking to a 3. Most of them took this as a real slap and resented the fact that they would likely receive much lower annual merit increases in salary as a result. On top of that, they had to expect they would no longer have their seniority to fall back on in case they were given a grade of a 1 or 2 in the forced redistribution of grades.

What this amounted to was applying the old-fashioned bell-curve concept used by many teachers at the junior-high-school level. It assumed that management had for certain made mistakes in selecting people from the ranks for promotion or in hiring from the outside. Certainly, that had happened on occasion, but to insist that 10 percent of those holding exempt positions were unsatisfactory performers was grossly in error.

However, as much as we disliked the forced distribution concept, we had to recognize that grade creep had occurred over a period of time. There was a tendency on the part of too many managers to rate many of their people as superior or outstanding rather than competent. Holding appraisal sessions with one's direct reports often is stressful and certainly not easy if their performance is not good. Without training on how to conduct an appraisal, there will be a tendency to avoid unpleasantness and the possibility of confrontation simply by grading too high. Only those who would be evaluated as promotable to a higher level because of their definable, superior job performance should have been rated 4's or 5's. There probably is no organization in which more than half of its exempt force should be rated in the two top categories of superior or outstanding. Finally, we needed to get across to exempt employees that a rating of competent is very satisfactory, and they should not take that rating to mean they were thought of as mediocre or that they were in danger of being demoted or terminated.

CHAPTER 17

INNOVATIVE INTERMODAL SERVICE

Innovative Intermodal Service

A LOGO USED ON TRAILERS ACQUIRED IN THE MID-1980S

• *growth through innovation; making it pay* •

EACH OF THE ROADS THAT MADE UP BN experienced rapid growth in intermodal service in the 1960s. Converting their service from boxcars to truck trailers for manufactured products was necessary in order to retain business that more and more shippers were ready to transfer to truck service. Large intermodal terminals were built and expanded more than once in large cities, including Chicago, Seattle, the Twin Cities, Kansas City, and Denver.

Also in those years, more and more imported consumer goods were being moved in the new containerized service offered by ocean shipping companies, who then started to use rail intermodal service to move their containers to inland points. For example, several Japanese steamship companies began to move containerized shipments of consumer goods into Chicago for distribution to stores and warehouses. The Matson Steamship Company acquired a large number of 24-foot containers to ship canned pineapple from Hawaii to the mainland, with consumer goods as a backhaul.

The freight forwarders that operated in large freight houses leased from the Burlington in Chicago converted rapidly from loading westbound freight in boxcars and refrigerator cars to trailers. The historic use of rail cars had greatly reduced the empty mileage for cars being returned west for lumber and fresh fruit and vegetable loading. Once the forwarders shifted to trailers, it became easy for them to shift their business away from the Burlington to other western railroads, if they became the least bit dissatisfied with the Burlington's service on a single day. Even though the profit margins were thought to be lower when freight moved in trailers, the railroad companies could see there would be no turning back from the transition away from rail cars.

At first, trailers were simply added to the general merchandise trains. In the early 1970s, special intermodal trains were set up on the corridors where a heavy volume of intermodal equipment was moving. On BN, Nos. 1 and 2 (the "Overland Mail") were set up to handle California business, and No. 3 (the "Pacific Zip"), for business moving to the Pacific Northwest. Eastbound, No. 4 operated from Seattle with containerized shipments and imported automobiles. Because the business moving in intermodal service was highly competitive, and the intermodal terminals still contained only a few short tracks on which cars could be loaded and on which trains were made up, the early intermodal trains were quite short, generally not more than thirty or forty cars. Also, it was thought that intermodal trains had to be kept short to help insure they would operate on schedule.

These trains were overpowered, usually with three or four of the new 3,000-horsepower locomotive units and with only about 2,000 gross tons. Very often this was more power than was used on general freight trains of 6,000 tons or more. The horsepower per ton of train weight on the intermodal trains would be in the range of three or four to one, compared to only about one to one on a conventional freight train. All of the expense for this additional motive power cut into the already low margins for intermodal business. This caused considerable internal debate as to whether we should stay in the intermodal business at all or, at least, not put such high priority into moving it. However, since its growth was seen as a bright spot in the traffic picture for railroads, senior management decided not to exit the intermodal segment of business or change the priority we were giving it.

THE NEED TO RE-INVENT INTERMODAL SERVICE

Although intermodal business was growing, the sales force was reporting difficulty in getting shippers who were using trucks for some or perhaps all of their business to shift much of it to rail intermodal service. To begin to really grow this kind of business, we learned we would have to commit the resources needed to improve service reliability, especially within terminals; reduce damage to freight caused by "the railroad environment," i.e., slack action; simplify the historic system for setting rates; and generally reduce the bureaucracy that shippers said they encountered when trying to use rail intermodal service. And, to improve profitability enough to produce a more satisfactory return on the capital employed in intermodal service, BN would be required to reduce the size of its on-board train crews. Those employees were being paid far more than over-the-road truck drivers.

To move the company forward on those and other issues of major importance to the future of intermodal service on BN, its intermodal marketing group was restructured in the early 1980s. A new team of managers with a blend of backgrounds in sales, operations, and finance was bought in. It was headed by William E. (Bill) Greenwood, whose most recent assignment was superintendent of the Alliance Division. Bill also had held a position in the Corporate Planning Department. Bill recruited a team of managers who would be challenged to learn and develop the quality of service that BN would need to move its intermodal service up to the level of performance needed to become competitive with the trucking industry.

For a host of reasons, that was to be a very difficult assignment. It was a time in BN history in which some senior managers had little confidence in any agenda intended to grow rail business. These were the years in which BN was fighting hard to get the rates on coal raised enough to get a satisfactory return on the huge capital investment made in the preceding ten years in order to be able to handle the increase in coal tonnage. The idea of investing more money to finance growth in another line of business would not be well received. Deregulation had just hit the rail industry, driving rates down in the new competitive environment. Because the intermodal business already was marginal at best, there was a lack of enthusiasm for new initiatives that would have to be undertaken and supported by other departments, particularly finance and operations. Even within the Marketing Department to which the intermodal unit reported, there were managers who did not have much enthusiasm for intermodal service as the wave of the future—and they were reluctant to get behind efforts to better meet the needs of our shippers and other shippers who were not using rail service of any kind.

Having a number of senior officers from the former Frisco Railroad setting the agenda for BN at that time was yet another hindrance, since the Frisco had not been a pacesetter in the rail industry in managing intermodal operations or growing that line of business. All of these factions would have to be won over by the new team of intermodal managers if much progress was to be made in the next few years.

The ways in which Bill Greenwood established and provided leadership for the team that transformed BN's approach to intermodal business was covered very thoroughly in *The Wisdom of Teams*.[1] An entire chapter is devoted to the workings of the intermodal team, which achieved high levels of performance in a short time. To be given such recognition is an indication of the magnitude

1 Jon R. Katzenbach and Douglas K. Smith, *The Wisdom of Teams* (Harvard Business School Press, 1993).

of challenges the team faced, and the success achieved through strategies they developed and put into action.

> This situation [BN's allegedly having the poorest intermodal service, equipment, and ramp facilities of any railroad at that time, and its general pessimism for intermodal business] represented a performance challenge, to say the least.... By the end of the 1980s, the intermodal team ... moved the company from last to first in intermodal business in the industry and had created a billion dollar business.[2]

In accepting the challenge to improve BN's performance in the intermodal field, Greenwood put together a team of similar "believers" to make it happen. David H. (Dave) Burns, one of the seven principals who formed this team, believed the writers of the book had

> failed to do justice to the few farsighted BN leaders who were instrumental in providing startup funding, and then greater funding as the concept began proving itself. ... While the intermodal startup capital costs were small compared to the enormous costs to gear up for coal, they were not insignificant for a railroad just finishing up an unparalleled remake of its operating plan.[3]

CONSTRUCTION OF INTERMODAL HUB CENTER TERMINALS

Intermodal strategy and service were revamped starting in 1982, in BN's decision to aggressively reshape its operation and create more opportunities to grow that line of business. An important part of the strategy for growth was to build intermodal terminal facilities with the types of equipment and the kind of track layout needed to increase capacity, flexibility, and reliability of performance. In establishing these terminals as "hub centers," 126 small outlying "circus ramps" were consolidated into 22 hub centers to increase the volume needed to replace the old ramps with new lift equipment and enable more dedicated intermodal trains to be run. That in turn would help speed up the movement and reliability of intermodal shipments.

Following a presentation to senior management on the new program, authority was given to set up two hub centers, at Portland and the Twin Cities. At the outset, there was considerable skepticism in the company on whether there was any merit to the hub concept; hence, only those two projects were approved as demonstration projects. Portland and the Twin Cities were evaluated as the most challenging locations, and perhaps, the most likely to fail. However, the hub-center concept proved so successful in those cities that within a short time, they were established at twenty more locations, giving BN a system-wide network of terminals equipped with good information technology and handling capability for containers and trailers that customers found they could rely on.

Dave Burns, the general manager of intermodal terminals at the time, recalls that all hub centers envisioned in the expansion program were established within eight years, by 1990. The rate of year-to-year growth in intermodal business was impressive. In the case of the Twin Cities hub, business increased 42 percent in just the first year after it was opened. Over the entire system, the volume grew by 25 percent just from 1984 to 1985, which caused BN to recognize the early success of the program and authorize rapid expansion to the full hub center program.

"For the small intermodal team" Dave wrote,

> it meant learning and honing entirely new skill sets, late nights and much discussion. Santa Fe and Conrail were helpful in configuring track layouts, trailer and container staging areas, and traffic and gate flow patterns, often within limited space of availability. Paving had to be sufficient to support mobile lift equipment carrying loaded units approaching the standards required for airport runways. But just as it had during the coal explosion, BN Engineering got on board quickly with enthusiastic talent and creativity. All of this contributed to the initial hub construction being completed within eight years. And most are still in operation after 30 years of heavy use.[4]

Dave also pointed out that in those years, a number of satellite hubs were established "where we would track trailers from, say, BN's Birmingham to Atlanta [150 miles off the BN rail network] where customers would pick up

2 *The Wisdom of Teams.*

3 David H. Burns, "Deregulation and the Rise of Intermodalism," October 2012.

4 Letter, D. H. Burns to the author, May 7, 2014.

Julian Woolford was appointed Terminal Manager for the new intermodal hub center in Portland when it was constructed and opened in 1982. In presenting the hub center concept to senior executives, the newly formed intermodal operating and marketing unit requested authority to open 22 hub centers throughout the BN system. Only two locations, Portland and the Twin Cities, were approved at that time. Portland was designated only because it was thought to have the lowest potential for growth and overall success. It would therefore be the best test for the concept. To the credit of Julian Woolford, his staff, and the system intermodal team,* both hub centers were soon judged as very successful, exceeding all targets set. Authority was then granted to establish the other 20 hub centers designated in the plan for expedited and greatly improved intermodal service.

* The team consisted of Bill Greenwood, Ken Hoepner, Mark Cane, Dave Burns, Emmett Brady, and Bill Berry.
Source: Jon R. Katzenbach and Douglas K. Smith, *The Wisdom of Teams*, 27–49.

and deliver them at a facility we rented space in. This was an attempt to extend BN's reach beyond the physical end points. Some of these worked out but others became too costly to make a profit. But it was a good illustration of intermodal's bias for action—try something! If it doesn't work out, stop."[5] Overall, the new group of intermodal managers had great success in innovation that brought increasing attention to BN's desire and ability to provide non-traditional service and pricing to the marketplace.

Of all the projects and initiatives the intermodal group took on in the early to mid-1980s, the one that became the most visible, complex, contentious, and required the highest level of commitment across all departmental lines was the new "Expediter" service. It was a test of wills across the company and of the unions that represented the Conductors, Locomotive Engineers, and Brakemen across the BN system. The Expediters were to be short, experimental trains that would provide service competitive with the non-regulated trucking industry between a series of key markets. These trains would operate with two-person crews and no cabooses. The new service would be operated to achieve 100 percent consistency in meeting service standards from the cutoff at origin to the availability of trailers at destination. The intent was to give shippers more affordable and dependable service in short-haul corridors.

The network of designated corridors for the Expediters would provide service that was fully competitive with trucks in price and reliability. The trains would operate on each day they were scheduled without fail, even if the volume of business happened to be very low on a given day. An all-out effort was started by the intermodal group, together with the Labor Relations and Operating departments, to educate employees and their union representatives on the economics of existing railroad service that would have to be overcome to make the new Expediter service cost competitive and profitable. This was certain to be a tough sell, even though the plan for two-person crews was to be applied only on trains that would be handling the new intermodal business.

5 Letter, D. H. Burns to the author, February 25, 2014.

At the outset, the unions and employees feared the company would soon put existing business of all types on the Expediter trains and then be able to eliminate the conventional-type trains that handled the company's regular business—from that, many jobs in train service. Operating such short, low-tonnage trains ran into the face of the best historic operating standards that were set up to run heavy trains with the lowest ratio of locomotive horsepower per trailing ton needed to get a train over the road on schedule.

The most significant and challenging break from traditional railroad practice was the need to operate the Expediter trains with a two-person crew. With the standard crew of four or five employees, railroad intermodal service was not cost competitive on hauls of less than six hundred miles. Getting the unions representing the operating employees to understand, trust, and accept that as reality was the biggest challenge in setting up the new operation. A great deal was at stake in the ensuing negotiations for an agreement on crew size that would make it possible for BN to get back business that had been lost to low-wage, non-union, deregulated trucking companies. For the start-up of Expediter service, all runs were to range from 300 miles to 750 miles on the territory of the former Frisco Railroad.

After enduring the cultural changes, aggressive cost cutting, and new leadership style that came into BN in the early 1980s, it was difficult to convince operating employees to work cooperatively with management on a new program that would require them to give up the manning level and other job conditions they felt they had "earned" over the years. A high level of trust and confidence in the motives of management had to be restored before any amount of progress could be made on such an agenda. To help build a partnership, BN intermodal personnel brought operating employees with them to meetings with potential customers for the new service, so they could hear first-hand what level of rates and service performance would be needed to convince those shippers to at least try using the new service.

THE INTRODUCTION OF EXPEDITER SERVICE

These and other challenges were overcome to the extent needed to allow some experimental Expediter trains to be operated with two-person crews. The ultimate test of whether management would stand by its commitment would come on the days when there would be only two or three trailers to be moved. On one occasion, the crew assigned to an Expediter schedule operated with only a locomotive unit, and no cars. The point to be made was that the Expediter trains would be operated every day they were scheduled and not be annulled or consolidated with another train to be run sometime later in the day, if too few trailers were tendered for movement.

Not long after the general chairmen of the former Frisco territory agreed to the use of two-person crews, the general chairmen for the former CB&Q territory saw the benefits of that agreement and agreed to the same conditions. In the summer of 1985, additional Expediter trains were initiated between Chicago and Memphis. In September 1986 Expediter service was established between Chicago and the Twin Cities. This corridor quickly became the most successful. At the outset, only 10 or 15 trailers were carried each week, but by the end of the year, BN's Expediter trains on that corridor were carrying up to 1,200 trailers per week. As much as 70 percent of this volume came from trailers diverted from over-the-road trucking service.[6]

On the northern tier of the BN system, between the Twin Cities and the Pacific Northwest, efforts to make a similar agreement for reduced size crews were unsuccessful. The general chairmen who represented Conductors and Brakemen working on the lines of the former GN, NP, and SP&S were unwilling to agree to having two-person crews even on trains that would handle new business exclusively. As a result, no Expediter service was established on those parts of BN. Additional strategies undertaken by BN in an effort to reduce wage costs and develop new business on the northern tier are covered in Part V herein.

The Expediter concept proved so successful that more corridors were added to the network in 1987 on lines of

6 John F. Strauss, Jr., *The Burlington Northern: An Operational Chronology, 1970–1995*, 51.

the former Frisco and the CB&Q where two-person crews could be used. With this large growth in volume, the trains were getting longer. It was then agreed that Expediter trains operated with a two-person crew would be limited to forty cars. The on-time performance of the new Expediter trains and the availability of shipments for pickup at destination was outstanding, at 95 percent. Another strong indicator of success was that 99 percent of the shipments moved in Expediter service arrived damage-free. Prior to the Expediter concept for service, a major complaint about intermodal service was the amount of blocking and bracing that had to be used by shippers to help prevent damage from slack action and rough handling in long trains.

From 1982 through 1986, BN's total intermodal business increased two and a half times, from 200,000 to 500,000. Within the areas of BN where Expediter service was introduced, the number of intermodal shipments increased from 5,000 to 50,000 in just one year.[7] On top of that, BN advertised that the prices for its Expediter service were as much as 50 percent lower than what trucking companies were charging. To help insure that the features of trucking service that were so dear to customers would be baked into its new Expediter service, BN hired a number of trucking managers to run its intermodal terminals.

This success of the Expediter service was a real shot in the arm to BN personnel as they watched its rapid growth. It ran contrary to the general mood that had prevailed in BN for the past few years: that there were no growth opportunities for rail service. Hence, BN people had concluded there was little point in trying to innovate or seek new business from markets that had either dropped rail service or perhaps had never used it. Even the huge increase in coal being moved in unit train service was looked down upon by some officers, due to the rates being set too low on several movements, and because the return on the capital we had invested still was too low. Even though much of the intermodal business produced a low margin of profit and still was a small percentage of BN's total revenue, most BN people found it refreshing to see such impressive growth happening within a very short time. It definitely helped promote a "can do" type of attitude among many whose spirits had been dampened in the many years of cost-cutting and reduction in the infrastructure that had been the company's main agenda since mid-1980.

The general chairmen of the UTU and BLE who represented employees on the territory of the former Frisco and CB&Q deserve a great deal of credit for the leadership they showed in convincing employees of the importance of supporting this new market initiative. They put their jobs as elected representatives on the line when they asked employees to trust management that reducing the size of train crews was necessary and important to the future of the company.

While the Expediter program was successful in growing the intermodal business, it still was far from enough to bring intermodal business up to the level of growth and profitability needed to justify further investment in equipment, terminals, and the kind of information systems that would be necessary, even in the short term. With strong competition from deregulated truckers, there was little opportunity to raise prices. Part of the solution would have to come through the development of equipment that would be far more efficient than truck trailers for domestic shipments.

THE INTRODUCTION OF DOUBLE-STACK EQUIPMENT

Containers owned by ocean shipping companies had been in use for international shipments since the early to mid-1960s. Railroad companies had invested in large gantry cranes in their intermodal terminals to handle containers, which had the advantage of a much lower tare weight than trailers, since the "wheels" for over-the-road movement of containers could be left behind when they were loaded on a rail car or a ship. Containers had less aerodynamic drag, less weight, and could be moved with less fuel consumption.

Small groups of design experts from the car-building industry, together with some imaginative people from the rail and ocean shipping industries began to work on conceptual designs for cars that would handle containers

7 "BN Runs New Expediter in Chicago–Minnesota Lane," *Traffic World*, October 13, 1986; "Innovative Intermodal Service, a Matter of Attitude," *Progressive Railroading*, November 1986.

stacked two high. Accomplishing that would meet the need for getting more revenue freight into less linear footage on a train, and much more concentrated use of each piece of rail equipment. The cars for this service would be articulated—permanently coupled in groups of five, with each of the three intermediate cars "sharing" the truck of its adjacent car or "platform."

In this concept, less tare weight would be required, since there would be fewer end platforms, draft gears, couplers, and trucks in each set of five platforms. Capacity was freed up for additional revenue-producing tonnage, and more train length was available to move more revenue units. By requiring fewer sets of couplers and draft gears in the five-unit "car," there would be much less slack action, which answered the crying need for intermodal equipment that would reduce the amount of damage to freight, and require less dunnage for freight susceptible to damage from shifting or excessive impacts. There was no need to install end-of-car cushioning devices, which further reduced the tare weight of the new double-stack equipment. Trucks with a capacity of 125 tons were used on the intermediate sections.

Most importantly, a train of double-stack cars had twice the carrying capacity of a train with only single-deck cars. The movement of containers in international service was soon converted mainly to double stack equipment. The economies in this kind of service gave railroad companies a significant cost advantage over truckers. Further, these economies provided a strong opportunity for conversion of domestic intermodal service from trailers to double-stack containers. With trailers, domestic intermodal service had not been cost competitive on hauls of less than about six hundred miles. Double-stack service shortened the break-even point to the range of about five hundred miles for most commodities. With each train of double stacks handling at least twice as many intermodal units, fewer trains were required, thereby increasing line capacity. In some specific locations, moving containers stacked two high may have reduced the pressure to lengthen sidings to handle the increasingly longer trains that would have been required with single-level cars.

Most double stack container trains loaded at Seattle or Tacoma carry about 7,000 gross tons and 280 containers, for a length of about 8,000 feet. This type of train is a far cry from the typical intermodal train of the 1970s that carried only 30 to 40 cars, each with two trailers, for between 2,000 and 3,000 tons and powered by three or four high-horsepower locomotive units.

BN made an aggressive move into domestic containerization in the late 1980s by setting up a new organization called "BN America." The new service used only a lightweight container designed and owned by BN. Other types of containers with a heavier empty weight and owned by others would not be accepted and moved in the BN America program. Changes in "standard" railroad intermodal procedures were made to improve quality in drayage service, billing, and dispatching, as well as in terminal operations. Those improvements helped BN's domestic container service to grow rapidly and accelerated the transition from trailers to containers throughout the rail industry.

CHAPTER 18

THE WINONA BRIDGE COMPANY

TO BECOME A LOW-COST OFFSHOOT

It's just as phony a setup as the Montana Rail Link setup.
They both hinge on BN's cash, with their ultimate purpose of side-stepping labor contracts.

GARY BLAKELY, A BN EMPLOYEE AND MEMBER
OF THE UNITED TRANSPORTATION UNION, QUOTED IN
"BN OFFSHOOT TO RUN HI-LINE," *BILLINGS GAZETTE*, NOVEMBER 28, 1987

• *a new low-cost operator to function as "a railroad within a railroad"* •

OF ALL THE INITIATIVES UNDERTAKEN BY BN in its effort to restructure the cost base of the railroad, the proposal to grant trackage rights to a low-cost operator on the entire length of the northern corridor raised the highest level of employee resentment, distrust, hostility, and contempt for the company. The proposal centered on the use of an obscure subsidiary called the Winona Bridge Company, that had owned and operated a drawbridge and 1.07 miles of track between East Winona, Wisconsin, and Winona, Minnesota.

The bridge had been owned jointly by the Burlington Railroad and the Green Bay and Western (GB&W) Railroad. BN held two-thirds of the capital stock and the GB&W, one-third. The bridge was built for access to industries on the Minnesota side of the Mississippi River, of which Bay State Milling Co. was the major customer. The bridge was closed in 1985 due to the need for heavy repairs on the trestle approach to the drawspan. Also, it was not designed to handle 100-ton cars. In 1987 BN bought the GB&W's share of Winona Bridge.

A STRATEGY TO DRASTICALLY REDUCE LABOR COSTS ON THE NORTHERN CORRIDOR

In 1987, when BN proposed to grant trackage rights to Winona Bridge to operate intermodal trains to and from Seattle, the bridge company had five employees. None of them were qualified to operate a train. Operating employees would have to be hired or transferred from BN to run the new operator's trains. The purpose of BN's proposal to have a new, low-cost operator on its northern corridor was to be able to attract what BN termed "new business" using intermodal equipment. The plan was for Winona Bridge to have lower labor costs than what BN had in its contracts with the UTU and BLE, making it possible to generate business BN could not price competitively due to its higher labor costs.

Starting in 1980, BN had been trying to convince its employees and their representatives of the need to lower its costs by reducing the size of train crews from four employees to only two. After a protracted effort, BN was successful in making agreements for reduced crews for its "Expediter" service on two-thirds of its system. However, on the northern corridor, BN had no success in making an agreement for similar service with reduced crews. About 88 percent of the portion of the northern corridor between St. Paul and Seattle consisted of lines of the former GN, and 12 percent of the NP. The 101 miles between Winona Junction, Wisconsin, and St. Paul had been owned by the former Burlington. Operating employees were still working under the contracts with the former owners of these line segments, since there had been no success in negotiating a common schedule of agreements for BN.

Having had no success in negotiating an agreement for reduced crews on the northern corridor, BN requested authority from the ICC to grant trackage rights to its wholly owned subsidiary, the Winona Bridge Co. Under this agreement, Winona Bridge would have the right to pickup and setout intermodal shipments only at St. Paul, Spokane, and Seattle, at least at the outset of its operations. In time, BN advised it might extend such authority to other intermediate stations. Since Winona Bridge had no contract with either the UTU or BLE, its employees would be either new hires or employees who would agree to transfer from BN and work under the pay scale and other provisions established by Winona Bridge.

The concept advanced by BN was similar to the "airline within an airline" structure that many large airline companies set up in the 1980s, mainly for service to small market areas. A major difference between the rail and airline application was the nature of the infrastructure and technology used by each industry. The only infrastructure needed by an airline is that of terminal facilities and a traffic-control system owned and operated by a government agency. On a railroad, the infrastructure to be used by a new operator would have to be private property—the track, bridges, and signal system owned by the established railroad company—and on which the scope rules from a closed shop agreement in which only employees who are governed by the contract negotiated between their employer and the union that represents them may handle the company's business.

When trackage rights were granted to Winona Bridge, the unions first petitioned the ICC for reconsideration, but without success. The UTU then appealed to the Eighth Circuit Court of Appeals. The UTU and BLE also served notice on BN through Section 6 of the Railway Labor Act on the basis that the agreement granting trackage rights to Winona Bridge constituted a unilateral change in the collective bargaining agreement with BN. In March 1988 BN sought injunctive relief against a threatened strike. The unions argued that the labor agreements in effect with BN should extend to Winona Bridge as well, which of course would preclude Winona Bridge from negotiating any kind of new agreements with BN with lower wages, a reduced crew consist, reduced benefits, and changes in working conditions.

Most of all, the unions feared BN would divert its "regular" business, i.e., business not limited to new intermodal shipments, to Winona Bridge. They saw that as an even greater threat that would come six years later, once the labor protective conditions under the trackage rights agreement would terminate. Mel Winter, general chairman who represented the Conductors and Brakemen working under the GN and SP&S schedule of agreements, took a very strong position against the establishment of operating rights to Winona Bridge.

COURT RULING: WINONA BRIDGE CO. IS NOT A NEW ENTRANT

In 1988 the case moved to the Seventh Circuit Court of Appeals which ruled that the trackage-rights agreement could be consummated but that employees were entitled to protection from the unilateral change in the collective bargaining agreement BN was attempting to make. The court asserted BN was showing "anti-union animus." Further, in contrast to the cases in which airlines were setting up non-union subsidiaries, BN was attempting to shift business to a non-independent carrier that was in reality an extension of BN. In reality, Winona Bridge was not a new entrant in the area of service and competition.

In its ruling, the court was persuaded by the union's fear that

> the extreme result being an eventual wholesale shift of business to Winona Bridge, while the cumulative amount of business of Burlington and Winona Bridge remains constant. Burlington's argument would apparently consider as new business every customer who calls hereafter for service on this Northern Line. . . . To hold otherwise [to not stop the operation BN contemplated for Winona Bridge] would undermine the Railway Labor Act. A carrier would be free to evade virtually every collective

> bargaining agreement on the flimsy assertion that the "new" business is business that the carrier could not have obtained while operating under the collective bargaining agreement.[1]

Thus ended the creative attempt to set up a low-cost operation to handle the additional intermodal business BN believed it could attract with lower rates than it could offer under its current cost base. That left BN in the position of having to try once again to persuade employees and the unions to agree to reduce the size of its train crews. After several years of protracted confrontation, international officers of the UTU were brought into the negotiations. Finally, five years later, in 1993 agreement was reached that would give BN the ability to reduce the size of its train crews, and gain a cost base closer to that of rail competitors that had signed crew consists agreements a few years before, and that had put them in a more competitive position with the trucking industry.

At one point during the dispute, the management of Winona Bridge invited the UTU and BLE to negotiate on a contract that would apply only to the employees it would hire. The unions declined that invitation. If BN thought that setting up Winona Bridge as an operating company would drive its employees and the unions representing them to negotiate a new crew consist agreement and to reduce their pay and benefits, they were disappointed. Instead, it caused the unions to dig in even deeper to protect and keep what they had gained in contract negotiations over a long period of time. As mentioned earlier, it would be another five years before BN obtained the agreement to reduce the size of train crews that it had sought for so long.

---

1 862 F.2d 1266, Burlington Northern Railroad Company, v. United Transportation Union, Brotherhood of Locomotive Engineers v. Winona Bridge Railway Company, United States Court of Appeals, Seventh Circuit, Decided Nov. 18, 1988, and 851 F.2d 1056, M. M. Winter, Petitioner, v. Interstate Commerce Commission and United States of America, Respondents.

CHAPTER 19

INDUSTRY-LEADING ADVANCES IN MECHANICAL

Completion of the types of projects discussed in this chapter made BN a leader in programs and innovation in the maintenance of equipment function. Considerable attention and recognition was given to BN's Mechanical Department in rail-industry trade journals and in the proceedings of professional engineering associations. Through all of the changes and improvements BN made in its equipment and mechanical facilities in those years, the emphasis on safety made BN a safer place to work, and provided a strong foundation for improving service and the return on invested capital.

USE OF FUEL TENDERS IN LOCOMOTIVE CONSISTS AS AUXILIARY FUEL TANKS

The addition of fuel tenders enabled the purchase of large quantities of diesel fuel at the least-expensive locations on the system, extending the interval between the time a locomotive was placed in helper service and when it would have to be taken out of helper service and moved to a servicing location for refueling. Generally, locomotives equipped with a fuel tender could stay out in helper service for about thirty days, compared to only about a week when used without a fuel tender. The tank cars converted for service as fuel tenders were equipped with the power cables and air pipes needed for multiple-unit operation, so they could be placed anywhere in a locomotive consist. On intermodal trains operating between Chicago and Seattle, five stops en route for refueling were eliminated, reducing the elapsed time. A total of seventy-eight tank cars were assigned to service as fuel tenders. Modifications were made on four hundred road locomotive units to draw fuel from the tank cars in that service. Five-hundred-gallon auxiliary lube-oil tanks also were added on the SD40-2 units, since lube-oil consumption would increase in line with the increased amount of fuel being burned by locomotives in a consist equipped with a fuel tender.

In a few years, the extent of the fuel-tender program was reduced due to the heavy stress the tank-car structure was subjected to when it was in a locomotive consist, and because of concern of the coal-marketing experts that the weight of the tender and the fuel it carried were displacing revenue coal tonnage that would otherwise be hauled in the train. Moreover, the tender added to the length of the train. In a few years, the price of diesel fuel dropped dramatically from where it had been in 1981 when the concept of the fuel tender was introduced. The fuel-tank capacity on new locomotives was expanded to 5,000 gallons, which further reduced the advantages of having fuel tenders included in the locomotive consist. It was not long until the use of fuel tenders was limited to helper locomotive consists based at remote locations such as Crawford Hill on the Alliance Division.

CLOSURE OF SMALLER LOCOMOTIVE RUNNING MAINTENANCE FACILITIES

The maintenance facilities at Cicero, Superior, Tulsa, Birmingham, Memphis, Spokane, Vancouver, Washington, North Kansas City, Minneapolis Junction, and Havre were closed. Running maintenance was consolidated into the larger, more-efficient shops at Alliance, Lincoln, Northtown, Springfield, and Seattle.

CONSTRUCTION OF A NEW LOCOMOTIVE-MAINTENANCE AND -SERVICING FACILITY AT GALESBURG

A new shop was included in the rebuilding and modernization of the hump yard that was completed in 1984. When plans were made to convert the hump yard at Cicero to an intermodal terminal, BN decided it would be best to replace the capability of the locomotive-maintenance shop at Cicero with a new facility at Galesburg, since nearly all non-unit trains enroute to Chicago and connecting lines to the east would be run through the yard at Galesburg for classification. The new shop was designed to handle the maintenance of 250 units.

Not long after the shop was opened, it was set up to handle locomotive truck repair, more so than running maintenance. This was done to support the West Burlington shop, which was not equipped with a drop table for handling trucks. It turned out that the capacity of the new shop at Galesburg was not needed for locomotive maintenance, its intended use, until the late 1990s when BN increased the size of its locomotive fleet and required more capacity for maintenance. At that time the Galesburg shop was set up for running maintenance to be done under contract with General Electric.

IMPROVED PERFORMANCE OF THE LOCOMOTIVE FLEET

Gross ton-miles per locomotive horsepower increased from 42,000 in 1982 to 66,000 in 1989. Mean time between failures (average for all types of failures) for high horsepower locomotives increased from 27 days in 1985 to 73 days in 1989. This was the pay-off from technical training, the use of quality practices and input from employees.[1]

AC (ALTERNATING CURRENT) TRACTION MOTOR–EQUIPPED LOCOMOTIVES

For many years, experts in motive-power technology did not think AC traction motors would be suitable for installation on locomotives used in heavy-duty freight service on North American railroads. Starting in the early 1980s, BN challenged both locomotive manufacturers to develop AC motors for use on its locomotives in heavy-tonnage service. In 1991 the Electro-Motive Division of General Motors (EMD) entered into a partnership agreement with Siemens AG of Germany to begin such development. Siemens had designed and built electric propulsion systems for railroad locomotives used widely in other countries, and was evaluated by EMD and BN as well suited to develop AC motors for the freight locomotive market in North America.

Getting two prototype SD60MAC units in service in 1991 and two more in 1992 for testing has been evaluated by many experts as the most innovative advancement in locomotive technology since the FT-type units designed for road freight service were offered for purchase shortly before World War II. Based on its favorable evaluation of the performance of the prototype units, BN placed an order with EMD for 350 SD70MAC units valued at $675 million. A commitment of this magnitude was needed by EMD and Siemens to insure a return on the large amount of capital they had invested in developing the prototype models, as well as to perfect the technology they employed and to get set up for production. The large and impressive commitment BN made to this new locomotive model was unprecedented in the rail industry. Paul Schneider, an author of books on the design and technical performance of locomotives, wrote, "[In the past] the attitude of most U.S. railroads has been, 'Let someone else work out the bugs [in a new model], then we'll look at it.' "[2]

In 1993 the four prototype SD60MAC units were delivered to several other railroads for testing. Those units remained under lease to BN until 1998, when they were returned to EMD in exchange for two SD70MAC units and electronic upgrades on four other units.

It should be noted that BN made this large financial commitment not long after the restructuring in 1988 in which the railroad company was saddled with $2.3 billion of debt that had been accumulated by both the Transportation and Resources divisions. With the unfavorable debt-equity ratio that resulted, the railroad had to work this debt load down to a sustainable level within a few years. To make that possible, capital expenditures

1 Gus Welty, "'Preventive' Payoff is Big," *Railway Age*, June 1990.

2 Paul D. Schneider, *Burlington Northern Diesel Locomotives: Three Decades of* BN *Power*, 74.

had to be limited quite severely. Clearly, BN's executives and board members recognized the great advantage to be gained by applying the AC technology through their decision to increase capital spending and authorize the large purchase of AC units, even with the heavy load of debt BN faced at that time.

The higher tractive effort produced by the AC units made it possible for BN to use only three locomotive units on coal trains that had required five DC units to move over Crawford Hill, as well as on the new line between Donkey Creek and Orin Junction and on the route used by trains destined to power plants in Colorado and Texas. On the flatlands east of Alliance and on the Nebraska Division and the coal routes on the Chicago Region, two AC units could replace three SD40-2 or similar types of units equipped with DC motors. In the years when only the DC technology was available, the C&NW and UP combination had a cost advantage over BN due to their lower grades, requiring only three units rather than five on its route leading out of the Powder River Basin. Once the new AC units were in service on BN, it gained an immediate competitive advantage over the UP, by needing fewer units in coal service and being able to substantially reduce its costs for fuel and locomotive maintenance.

For some time, GE showed no interest in developing AC technology for its traction motors, but once BN placed its large order with EMD, GE changed its thinking and soon developed locomotives that were competitive with EMD's SD70MAC. By the late 1990s, over 3,000 AC-equipped locomotives had been manufactured by EMD and GE for the railroads of North America. The work done by BN to advance AC technology paved the way for the Union Pacific, Canadian Pacific, CSX, and later other railroads to adopt it to their great advantage.

Following is a summary of the technical and operating advantages of AC traction compared to DC:

- Having a higher rate of adhesion, from 33 to 38 percent for AC units compared to 21 percent for SD40-2 units equipped with DC traction motors.[3] Together with HTCR[4] radial trucks, and anti-wheel slip systems, which allows a proportionate increase in the tonnage rating for the locomotive. Starting adhesion may be as high as 45 percent, which in turn makes starting tractive effort much higher.
- Locomotives equipped with AC traction motors are not limited by the short time ratings (maximum amperage) of DC motors, due to the difference in the speed-torque characteristics inherent in AC motors. This difference makes a higher tonnage rating possible at low speeds without risk of damage to the traction motors from overheating.
- Having no brushes and commutators makes AC motors less costly to maintain and gives them a longer life.
- AC traction motors are not susceptible to the problem where ground relay action caused by blowing snow getting in the traction motors, which occurs with DC motors in winter conditions.

EXPANSION OF LOCOMOTIVE REBUILD WORK AT CONTRACT SHOPS

A program to upgrade older locomotive units was started at the West Burlington shop in 1974. The company had determined it could no longer justify the purchase of new low- and medium-horsepower units to replace the old F-type units and the GP7, GP9, SD7 and SD9 units acquired in the 1950s. The rebuilding and upgrading of older types of units was expected to extend their service life by fifteen years. By the end of 1976, fifty-nineunits were upgraded. To take advantage of the lower costs of outside contract shops, the rebuilding of three hundred smaller, low horsepower GP30, 35, and 40 units was contracted out in 1987. The contract shops provided a four-year new-locomotive warranty for these units. They were rebuilt at 65 percent of the cost of a new locomotive with similar characteristics.

3 The rate of adhesion varies somewhat according to operating conditions (e.g., whether the top of the rail is wet or covered with oil) at the time.

4 HT stands for "high tractive;" "C" is the mechanical designation for a three-axle, three-motor truck, and "R" stands for "radial." The HTCR radial truck design allows for "self-steering" capability that provides greater adhesion in traversing curves and lower wheel and rail wear, and requires less maintenance. The locomotive trucks are able to "turn" as they round curves, which reduces the amount of resistance between the rail and wheels.

Table 19.1. Comparison of Characteristics SD70MAC and SD40-2 Locomotives

	SD70MAC	SD40-2*
Horsepower	4000	3000
Weight (fully fueled)	415,000 pounds	415,000 pounds
Type of traction motors	3-phase AC	D77/78 DC
Adhesion rate—starting	45%	25%
Adhesion rate—continuous	35%	21%
Starting tractive effort	175,000 pounds	87,155 pounds
Continuous tractive effort	137,000 pounds	82,100 pounds
Diesel engine	16 cyl. 710G3B	16 cyl. 645E3
Fuel injection system	electronic	mechanical
Air brake system	Knorr electronic	26RL

* For SD40-2 units purchased for unit train service

INNOVATION IN LOCOMOTIVE OWNERSHIP AND MAINTENANCE

In partnership with the Finance, Planning, and Transportation departments, BN's Mechanical Department developed a highly innovative partnership with both locomotive manufacturers for the ownership and maintenance of new locomotives. Under this program, EMD and GE were required to assume responsibility for the maintenance of their own products. With the targets set for locomotive performance and availability in the contract, it was expected the manufacturers would have a strong incentive to improve the quality of the locomotives they built. By having a third-party arrangement for ownership, BN did not have to include the value of the locomotives in this program on its balance sheet, a big step toward reducing BN's asset base and its goal for a higher rate of return on invested capital (refer to chapter 20, "Power by the Hour," for additional details on this program).

SHOP-BETTERMENT COMMITTEES

To encourage worker participation in improving work processes and addressing productivity issues, BN set up a series of joint labor-management committees in its system shops in the early 1980s. At the Havelock and St. Cloud shops, the committees made a strong case that heavy repairs to damaged privately owned coal cars should be made "in house" instead of at outside contract shops owned by third parties. Due to the contract shops having lower labor costs, car owners designated them for such work, rather than allowing BN to repair the cars in its shops. Under the rules covering the repair of damage to privately owned cars, the car owners were compensated by the railroad company for the cost of repairs under the rates established by the Association of American Railroads (AAR) for labor and material. The car owners could pocket the difference between the higher costs they were reimbursed under the AAR rates, and the lower price they would have to pay for repairs done at the contract shops.

Even with the disadvantage of BN's shops had with higher labor costs than the generally non-union contract shops, the employee committees figured out a large number of changes in work methods and developed some innovations in shop machinery that would reduce BN's costs below the AAR rates it was paying to the car owners. The margin between BN's costs and the AAR rates was wide enough to convince BN management to agree to have the repair work done "inside." Inspectors sent to our shops by car owners found the work done in BN shops was of excellent quality, and they accepted our decision to have the repair of damaged cars done at BN's shops.

We had our numbers audited by BN's experts in costing

and car repair to ensure there would be no reason to challenge or question the numbers that showed our people could do the work at a lower cost. BN employees took great pride in being able to find ways to beat competitors who employed lower-cost labor. It was a classic case of a change in "corporate culture" in action, in a meaningful way that benefited both employees and the company.

In addition to the repair of damage to cars owned by outside parties, the committees reviewed BN's proposals to contract out other types of repairs, as well as the bids BN received from contract shops for such work. Generally, it was found that BN's shops could perform heavy work such as complete locomotive overhauls at a lower expense. However, for repair of components, the contract shops usually came in with lower costs. A big disadvantage to BN employees was the small number of components involved in these projects and, thereby, not having the economies of scale needed to spread high fixed costs and higher labor costs over a large number of components. Because BN's shops were efficient in overhauling locomotives, the company was able to make offers that were competitive with contract shops in overhauling locomotives owned by other parties. It wasn't long before about 15 percent of the work being done on the outside was brought back to BN shops—a success that provided additional BN jobs.

RAPID-RESPONSE CREWS

Two-person crews consisting of an electrician and a machinist were first set up at Alliance to respond to calls for on-line equipment failures on trains and other mechanical matters that were delaying and disrupting the operation of trains. The new concept worked so well that it was soon expanded to road territory out on the entire division. These crews were on duty on a 24/7 basis to respond to calls for assistance from conductors, engineers, and dispatchers. A rather strict qualification process had to be used to insure that employees working on this kind of assignment were experienced and knowledgeable and could work without a great deal of direction. Once they were out on the territory, far away from a shop, they were on their own in facing an unpredictable variety of challenges.

This kind of capability for rapid response was vital in a territory with a high density of traffic, helping to insure there were no failures to have empty trains in position to load at the time scheduled at the mines. If a BN train could not make it to a mine as scheduled, there was the danger that a UP train in the area might be diverted to load at that mine, with BN losing the revenue. If that happened, it might be several hours before a new slot would become available for loading the BN train that was delayed.

In 2010, when BNSF entered into an agreement with the shopcraft unions for the Rapid Responder positions, there were fifty-six positions at ten locations in Nebraska, Wyoming, Colorado, and Kansas. The agreement provided that "A Rapid Responder will be required to perform all troubleshooting and repairs to expedite train movement, which they have the qualifications and equipment to perform, regardless of craft affiliation." The company has the right of selection for each position, regardless of seniority and craft affiliation. All in all, the agreement represents the very positive attitude the company, its employees and the unions took toward meeting the need to have experienced and highly capable people available to assist train crews when the operation on high density lines is interrupted due to a mechanical failure or a warning given by a detection device.[1]

An article in the 2011 *Reflections* newsletter for the Powder River Division contained several statements from members of responder crews that reveal what made this program so successful:[2]

Larry Reinhart commented, "We relieve a lot of pressure for everybody. It is a lot of fun and more of a challenge than routine maintenance in the shop or on the road truck."

Gary Galey noted, "We are here to expedite movement from the rear to the front [of a train]. What takes someone else hours takes us 15 minutes. It is a win-win situation."

Jeff Synak stated, "While we are challenged to learn other crafts, we also lean on each other quite a bit to get knowledge we don't possess individually."

1 Memorandum of Agreement Between BNSF Railway and the three shopcraft unions effective October 12, 2010. This item was located through an internet search.

2 "Responders Make Rapid Impact," *Powder River Reflections* newsletter, 5th ed., 2011.

Mark Craney, a trainmaster with road territory, added: "They have had a positive impact on velocity. . . . By being on the scene, these employees can potentially prevent a locomotive unit from being set out, which positively impacts velocity. . . . They are huge time savers and their actions reduce risk for other employees."

When necessary to get technical advice, the responders may call on such expert sources that are available on a 24/7 basis as the mechanical office at the Alliance shop, the airbrake section at the Lincoln shop, or GE's technical center.

In a high-density operation, it is vital to avoid any and all delay to trains running between terminals. A delay to one train will soon cause other trains to have to stop and be pushed back until the disabled train can start moving again, or if that is not possible, moved with assistance from another train to a location where it can be moved off the main track. The chain reaction that follows will throw empty trains off their schedule for loading, disrupt the plan for calling crews on duty, and possibly cause some crews to be relieved due to reaching their limit for time on duty. Because those costs are enormous with even one occurrence, it is mandatory that preventive "zero defect" work be carried out to head off in-service failures of equipment, signals, and track. Given that there still will be some failures despite best efforts to prevent them, it has been found to be well worth the expense of the responder crews available to help minimize delays and their cascading effect on the operation.

CHAPTER 20

POWER BY THE HOUR

. . . the railroad doesn't buy the locomotives; instead, it buys the electric power generated by diesel-electric locomotives on a megawatt-hour basis.

. . .

The locomotives have been spending far less time in the repair shops and more time hauling revenue freight.

BOB WIEDRICH, "POWER-BY-THE-HOUR: A RAIL SUCCESS STORY," *CHICAGO TRIBUNE*, APRIL 16, 1989

TO HELP REDUCE ITS ASSET BASE, BN sought new concepts that would reduce its ownership of locomotives and the need to own and operate facilities for locomotive maintenance. Another objective was to get the locomotive manufacturers to take more responsibility for the performance, i.e., reliability and availability of their locomotives. In 1986 BN and EMD created a totally new concept to meet BN's needs and interests.

The agreement provided for purchase by BN of the output of electric power generated by one hundred SD60-type locomotives to be leased by Oakway, Inc., a subsidiary of Connell Finance Co. BN would make payment for the use of these locomotives on a "power by the hour" basis, specifically, the number of megawatt hours it used from the output of the locomotives' generators. This meant that BN would bear the expense of those locomotives only when they were actually in service and "pulling freight." The time they were out of service for maintenance or due to in-service failures would be borne by the manufacturer. Obviously, EMD had a strong incentive under this program to maximize availability and reliability. Once EMD assumed such responsibility for the performance of its product, it would have the incentive to come up with design modifications and improved maintenance practices that would reduce its costs and enable it to receive more income from BN. A minimum quantity of 240,000 megawatt hours in a six-month period was set, on a "take or pay" basis. Oakway would perform maintenance on the hundred new units, using its own shop and employees, including supervision.

It was no surprise that BN's employees challenged the loss of work they thought they were entitled to under the "scope" rule that was imbedded in all historic labor-management agreements in the rail industry. Getting this concept for locomotive ownership and maintenance responsibility in place did not come easily. The unions representing BN shopcraft employees (primarily machinists, electricians, boilermakers, and sheet-metal workers) called it "a management ploy to skirt union contracts." BN's senior vice president for Labor Relations, James B. Dagnon, stated, "There was a great deal of acrimony between us and labor for about a year before we could make a deal. A lot of people said our philosophy was to bust the union."[1]

A nationwide strike was threatened, but the courts ruled this was a "minor dispute," as defined under the

1 Ira Rosenfeld, "Locomotive 'Power-By-The-Hour' Largely Stalled at the Station," *Traffic World*, July 22, 1991, page 30.

Railway Labor Act; hence, one that should be settled by arbitration. A strike was averted, and in October 1987 BN agreed that work on the Oakway units would be performed by its shopcraft employees.[2] BN agreed to hire thirteen former BN employees and thirteen former EMD employees. They would work under supervisors employed by Oakway. Also, routine and scheduled running maintenance work on the hundred units would be performed at a shop owned and operated by Oakway.

Initially, the Oakway units were maintained at a shop in Weston, Colorado, leased from the Colorado & Wyoming Railroad. Later, EMD invested $5.4 million in a shop formerly owned by BN in North Kansas City, a location much more centrally located. Major repair work (overhauls) would be carried out at BN's system locomotive shop in West Burlington, Iowa. A similar agreement was made with GE for maintenance of a group of one hundred new B32-8–type units in a specified area inside BN's locomotive shop in Lincoln, Nebraska. LMX Corporation (Locomotive Management System, a subsidiary of General Electric set up for leasing locomotives) was set up by Oakway to manage this operation for GE. The agreement with Oakway was for fifteen years for the SD60 units built by EMD, and for LMX, ten years. The EMD units BN used under this concept were assigned mainly to unit coal trains. The four-axle B32-8 units built by GE were used in general freight service. In case of failure to achieve the agreed upon level of performance, EMD and GE were required to furnish replacement locomotives from a reserve pool they owned and maintained

The intent of these agreements was to put pressure on each manufacturer to design, build, and maintain locomotives to a higher level of performance. By having direct responsibility and the rewards and penalties for the performance of their products, it was expected the locomotive builders would be able to learn more about the problems and deficiencies of their product, and would also have a strong incentive to develop fixes to overcome them. And, as mentioned earlier, by not having to own or lease these locomotives, BN would not have to include them in its asset base. This strategy to reduce locomotive ownership was an important part of BN's drive to increase its return on invested capital.

In April 1989, two years into the "Power by the Hour" concept, Edward J. Bauer, BN's vice president–Mechanical, provided his evaluation:

> Time will tell, but right now, the program is a rousing success. I think that the rest of the industry will demand that builders become more closely involved in responsibility for maintenance of the locomotives they produce. We've been struggling with the builders for years to get more reliable locomotives that would give us 92-day maintenance intervals. . . . In 1985, we started our own program internally to improve the quality [of reliability]. But we also felt there was a real lack in the design and quality of new locomotives. And, the cost of new locomotives was accelerating at a rapid pace without a commensurate increase in quality. The locomotives are doing better than expected, with failures occurring on an average of 75 to 85 days. And that provides us with a real competitive advantage.

At that time, for locomotives owned by BN, the average number of days between failures was in the range of only twenty-five to thirty-five days.[3]

In 1989 BN acquired one hundred additional SD60 units and assigned them for maintenance at its shop in Glendive, Montana. EMD supervised the work of the BN employees under a "shared facility" concept. Although the Oakway SD60 and B32-8 units built in the mid-1980s are no longer in service on BN, the power-by-the-hour concept has been extended to some of the newer models BNSF has put in service. Evidence of the success of this program to shift responsibility for locomotive availability and maintenance has been the extension of the prescribed maintenance interval from thirty days to ninety-two. This change was agreed to by the FRA in 1980.

With improved availability resulting from less out-of-service time for maintenance and fewer on-line failures, locomotive utilization has improved significantly. The corresponding result is that fewer locomotives are needed in BNSF's active fleet, and the return on the investment made for motive power has improved. Some

2 Ira Rosenfeld, "Locomotive 'Power-By-The-Hour' Largely Stalled at the Station," *Traffic World,* July 22, 1991, page 30, and BN *News Update,* October 1987.

3 Bob Wiedrich, "Power-by-the-Hour: A Rail Success Story," *Chicago Tribune,* April 16, 1989.

of the capital once needed for locomotive replacement and overhaul was either freed up for other investment purposes or to reduce the size of the budget for capital expenditures.

Soon after BN developed the program, the UP and Santa Fe entered into similar arrangements in which EMD and GE managed the work of their employees. However, the acquisition of locomotives under the power-by-the-hour was not embraced by other railroads. The manufacturers agreed to it on BN in years in which they were receiving only a few orders for new locomotives. That made them amenable to such a radically different concept, in order to get more units into production. Once the demand for new locomotives picked up again, and with the vast improvement in the performance of newer models, the desire of both the locomotive builders and the railroad companies to expand on or extend the original agreements began to fade.

CHAPTER 21

RESEARCH AND DEVELOPMENT FOR THE FUTURE

I don't want our suppliers determining what new technologies we adopt and the rate we adopt them.

...

In the petroleum industry ... we know we are not being aggressive enough if we are not hitting dry holes. I want you to hit some dry holes.

S. R. DITMEYER'S RECOLLECTION OF STATEMENTS OF R. M. BRESSLER IN A DISCUSSION ON THE APPROACH TO BE TAKEN ON R&D ON BN.
KAUFMAN, *LEADERS COUNT*, PAGE 226

RICHARD BRESSLER DIRECTED THE SENIOR management of the railroad company to set up a Research and Development (R&D) Department. Steven R. (Steve) Ditmeyer was hired from the Federal Railroad Administration (FRA) to organize and manage a small group of technical experts to develop opportunities to employ technology that may have been overlooked by the rail industry, or perhaps, not sought after. Ditmeyer had a strong technical background, with a degree in Industrial Management from Massachusetts Institute of Technology and having served as associate administrator for R&D activities at the FRA.

Bressler felt that a strong R&D effort could help breathe new life into an industry that appeared to him to be operating with outdated technology that was holding it back. Bressler's strong interest in it was seen by many BN people as inconsistent and in contradiction with the pessimistic views that he was reported to have expressed on the rail industry's future. However, Bressler also had stated his belief that the railroad was the "crown jewel" of BN, and he wanted it to be seen as the best performing railroad in the United States, equipped with good tools and equipment.

Bressler and Burlington Northern Railroad president Walter Drexel admonished that any innovations in technology or operating methods BN developed that would give BN a competitive advantage would not be shared with the rest of the rail industry. This mandate ran in opposition to the ways in which companies in the rail industry had worked together over their history, by being willing to share plans and information on developments they had made. Leaders in the rail industry believed that in an industry as interlocked as the railroads were, their overall performance would improve if better methods and technology were shared and put in place across the industry.

In addition, much of the industry's R&D was carried out by the Association of American Railroads (AAR), which made the results of its research available to all of its members. Bressler did not evaluate the AAR's contribution in R&D very highly. He felt the amount of R&D the AAR undertook was insufficient—some of its projects were incremental, limited in scope, and would not develop the kind of technology the industry needed to modernize, economize, become more competitive, and increase its return on investment. Bressler felt the railroad supply industry should be carrying out much more R&D. However, he recognized that many of the suppliers in the rail industry were small and rather weak, making it difficult for them to undertake the level of R&D that was needed. Also, most of the suppliers operated in a reactive mode rather than one of pushing the rail industry forward by developing better tools and systems to meet its challenges.

TO APPLY AVIONICS TO A RAILROAD OPERATION

Perhaps the best example of Bressler's commitment to moving BN ahead in the use of technology was his belief that the technology used in avionics might have application in the rail industry. Bressler was well acquainted with senior executives of Rockwell International, a leader in avionics, through his membership on Rockwell's board. Bressler directed Ditmeyer and me to take a small number of our signal (train control) experts to a meeting with the Collins Air Transport Division of Rockwell at its headquarters in Cedar Rapids, Iowa. A partnership was soon developed with Rockwell, and within about two years, Rockwell and BN developed a fully operational system for "train control." It was called the Advanced Railroad Electronic System (ARES, called "air-eez" for short). The new system provided capabilities and improvements in safety and the train-control function:

- ARES employed technology that would intervene automatically to prevent collisions, stopping a train if the engineer failed to comply with signal indications, exceeded the authorized speed, or failed to stop the train before going beyond the limits (location) to which it had been authorized to operate.
- Improved protection for workers conducting on-track maintenance or inspection.
- In addition to features that could enhance safety, ARES had the potential for integration into the operating systems for managing the utilization of cars and locomotives, to increase the capacity of a line segment, monitor the "health" of a locomotive while in service on a train, and to evaluate the performance of the train's locomotive engineer.
- With on-board display of signal aspects, the need for maintaining wayside signals would be eliminated.

Clearly, the systems build into ARES could prevent some accidents and disruptions to operations by overcoming the danger of human error and employee negligence. It also held the potential for re-engineering and overhaul of the systems and methods used to manage line of road operations and service delivery. By 1987 ARES was set up as a 250-mile "closed loop" operation on the lines serving the Mesabi Iron Range in northeastern Minnesota. The new technology worked well, right from the start. It met all expectations for safety and reliability. ARES was well accepted by the train operating employees, dispatchers, and the track-and-signal-maintenance personnel involved in the demonstration project.

Frank Christopherson was working as a locomotive engineer on the Iron Range during the time ARES was tested in the field. In the oral history Frank provided on his fifty-three years of railroad service, he described the kinds of tests made and how the ARES system functioned: "I did not find any deficiency in the system as many times I tried to confuse the system or override it and was unable to do so."[1]

Frank described a test in which he was directed to attempt to run his train beyond the location to which it was authorized to operate:

> A situation was created where we had a track warrant to milepost 15.9. We were directed to overlook the warrant and proceed past this point. Two miles before MP 15.9 we received a reminder on the TSI screen of the end of track warrant authority. We continued on and about ½ mile further a yellow-printed warranting appeared on the TSI screen. As we continued the yellow became red and a buzzer sounded. When no action was taken to reduce the speed of the train, the air started to set and controls became inoperative. We came to a stop very nicely, short of the fouling point of the track warrant. We tried this

1 *Frank Christopherson: Locomotive Engineer, Leader and Volunteer*, an oral history conducted by Tom Gannon and Tim Schandel, compiled by Earl J. Currie into an essay for the Lake Superior Railroad Museu, December 2011, page 62.

> test a number of times and it worked every time. We also tried to start the train again without a new track warrant to proceed and again, we were stopped before passing the fouling point. In another test we tried going over the speed limit in a slow order area and again, we received a warning on the TSI screen, followed by the warning light and buzzer. When no action was taken to slow down, again, the ARES on-board intervention system stopped us short of the slow order.

At the outset of the field testing of ARES, Frank recalled the first time he was directed to attempt to pass a red "stop" signal without stopping, and then, obtaining authority from the dispatcher to pass it at restricted speed as required by the operating rules. To not stop before passing a signal in stop position has always been a "cardinal sin" that would result in dismissal. Frank was not about to get trapped by such a directive in case the ARES technology did not cause the train to stop before passing the red signal. When a railroader's job is on the line, he or she will refuse to comply with a directive in violation of the rules. Frank therefore insisted on having a train order in his hand authorizing him to pass that particular signal when displaying a stop indication for the purpose of that test.[2]

The tests made on the Iron Range over the next five years validated ARES as a functional and reliable system that met the standards of performance BN had set as it was developed. BN thoroughly evaluated ARES and the benefits it could produce in safety and improved productivity. However, the expense of $350 million for implementation on the entire BN system at that time was formidable.[3] There were many less-costly high-priority projects with high "hard dollar" rates of return on investment that had to be undertaken in preference, in addition to the large amount of capital needed every year on a railroad to keep its track, bridges, cars and locomotives at the standard required for safety and efficiency. After the railroad company and BN's resource-based units were spun off in the restructuring of 1988, the railroad was saddled with a heavy debt load. Capital expenditures had to be reduced for several years to enable the company to work its debt down to a more reasonable level. Because of the very high cost of installing ARES and the relatively low return anticipated, ARES had to be shelved.

During the time ARES was under development, a coalition of other large railroad companies, the AAR, some railroad signal-equipment companies, and consultants began to develop a new system to be called the Automatic Train Control System (ATCS), intended to develop capabilities similar to what we were doing with ARES. The ATCS group put pressure on BN to disband its work on ARES and agree to join them in support of developing ATCS. When they were unable to convince us to drop ARES, they asked us to share with them the technology we had developed with Rockwell, so they could evaluate it as the standard for the rail industry. The ATCS team and some of the senior operating officers of other railroad companies resented and complained about our position that we would not give away or share proprietary technical data or design information about our methods and procedures that we thought would give us a competitive advantage. Bressler believed that position was part of the shift the rail industry was undergoing, from being heavily regulated to operating in deregulated, market-based, competitive environment.

The capabilities of the kind of Positive Trail Control (PTC) system that had to be installed by 2015 were developed by BN for its ARES program twenty-five years earlier. Today's PTC started with the vision and direction Bressler had for the application of technology developed for other industries, together with the expertise BN had in signal, engineering, and mechanical functions.

USE OF ALTERNATIVE FUELS

Exploring opportunities for using alternative fuels for locomotives was the second major project for BN's R&D group. Bressler was convinced that the railroad should be preparing to switch to natural gas, since it was available in large quantities and at 70 percent of the cost of diesel fuel per unit of energy. Further, the enormous holdings of gas and oil reserves on land owned by BNI's energy companies could make inexpensive natural gas readily available.

2 Oral history taken by the staff of the Lake Superior Railroad Museum.

3 "What Price Railroad Safety?" *Baseline,* www.baselinemag.com/c/a/Projects-Management/What-Price-Railroad-Safety

Early in 1986, a successful test run was made with a GP9-type locomotive fueled by natural gas, on a train operated from Minneapolis to Superior. This unit was equipped to burn either natural gas or diesel fuel. For operation below throttle notch five, it used diesel fuel. Natural gas was found to be the most efficient fuel when the unit was operated at notches five through eight. The switch from one fuel to the other could be made with a single control. In 1991 two SD40-2 units were converted to gas.

It was more efficient to handle natural gas in a liquefied form rather than as compressed gas. Tender cars with a capacity of 25,000 gallons of refrigerated liquid methane, a highly purified version of natural gas, were used on trains operated with the two SD40-2 unites. The testing was done on coal trains loaded at mines in Montana and destined to an electric power plant at Becker, Minnesota, a round trip of 1,700 miles. Overall, the testing program went well. Energy Conversion, the company that developed the modifications needed for the prime mover to burn methane, advised the engine could be run two to three times longer between lubrications and oil and filter changes. Further, the engine life cycle could be extended by as much at 40 percent.[4]

Over-the-road testing with the two SD40-2 units continued until 1995. On a technical basis, converting to methane for fueling high-horsepower locomotives in service on a high-tonnage railroad was feasible. At the time of this writing, conversion to natural gas for fueling locomotives has not been undertaken by any North American railroad except on a test basis. Construction of a system of new fueling facilities would be expensive, in addition to the substantial cost of converting a large fleet of locomotives to burn methane. Having to build fuel tenders also would be costly, and placing them in trains would add to the gross weight of the train, making it necessary to reduce the tonnage of revenue freight that could be handled. Electro-Motive, the manufacturer of railroad locomotives, advised BN that its 16-710 diesel engine—rated at 3,800 horsepower on diesel fuel—would be able to produce only 3,000 horsepower with methane, a significant difference that would have to be endured until EMD could overcome it with a design change in the prime mover it was producing the time the tests were underway. When the price of natural gas skyrocketed in the late 1980s, BN shelved any plans it may have had for equipping more locomotives to burn gas.

Testing of natural gas–fired locomotives thus ended in 1995. In 2011, when the availability of natural gas expanded so rapidly, several railroads renewed their interest in reducing their dependence on diesel fuel. Canadian National has retrofitted two locomotives to run on fuel with a mixture of 90 percent liquid natural gas (LNG) and 10 percent fuel. BNSF is working with General Electric and Caterpillar's locomotive manufacturing unit to develop test locomotives that will use LNG.

The economics in favor of LNG have widened greatly in recent years. Diesel fuel cost an average of $3.97 per gallon in 2012, compared to 48 cents for the equivalent amount of energy in LNG. However, the cost of retrofitting a diesel locomotive to burn LNG and acquiring the tanker unit to carry the gas is said to add 50 percent to the cost of a locomotive unit. Today's BNSF is in a much stronger financial position to undertake a large capital program such as a changeover to LNG than BN was in the late 1980s. Whether today's economics will be favorable enough to drive railroads to convert to natural gas has yet to be determined.

BN began to pursue a number of other interesting R&D projects in the mid-1980s that held the potential to improve its operations and maintenance functions. Among the most challenging and highest potential projects were the following:

- Acoustic bearing detectors, for pre-failure detection of defective wheel and axle bearings before overheating and failure occur.
- Communications network control, to provide overviews of individual communications sub-systems, to assist in problem resolution.
- A partnership to identify the technology needed for a new type of locomotive that would use micronized coal or a coal gasifier.
- Develop a train energy-management system to validate fuel consumption for various types of trains and equipment in service on main routes.

4 Presentation by Jared Loidolt, Transportation and Logistics student at the University of Wisconsin–Superior, April 2012.

- Wheel-stress measurement to validate the requirement to remove discolored wheels thought to contain internal stresses.
- Tests of radial trucks designed to reduce truck hunting, fuel consumption, and wheel wear.
- Use of lightweight materials such as aluminum and reinforced plastic on freight cars.
- Test of new types of intermodal cars to reduce fuel consumption and to increase stability, braking capability, and forces imparted to the track structure.
- Developing alternatives for disposal of defective ties removed from the track.

R&D programs were developed in partnership with suppliers and the test center operated by the AAR. Success in these and other R&D projects helped move BN into position as an industry leader in innovation, safety in train operations, and operating performance.

Tension arose from time to time in the process of budgeting for R&D projects. With the pressure underway to reduce capital expenditures and to maximize earnings in the short run, R&D programs were seen by some senior executives (including some who had come to BN from outside the rail industry) as an easy mark to hit in process of reducing the capital budget. Since they viewed the railroad as a cash cow, without much of a long-term future, why would we want to invest in R&D–type projects that might take a long time to develop, and with a questionable return on the capital that would have to be invested?

WE MAY HIT SOME "DRY HOLES"

In budget sessions in which Bressler participated, that position ran head-on with the views he had on the value and necessity of having substantial programs for R&D. Bressler went so far as to say that he fully expected we would hit some "dry holes" as we progressed such projects, drawing from his experience in the oil industry. There were times when Bressler was critical of those who made presentations for budgets for the Operating Department for not being aggressive enough in seeking more major, ambitious projects. At the same time, all of us were mindful of his mandate to find ways to reduce capital spending for the "basics" we needed every year to maintain the roadway and equipment to an adequate standard. At times it was difficult to know where to draw the line. Whatever budget amount was finally arrived at for R&D would not be set until Bressler considered all of the arguments and provided direction as to how much we should spend for R&D projects.

CHAPTER 22

SOURCING BY PURCHASING AND MATERIAL DEPARTMENT

Doerr acknowledges that many Roadmasters were skeptical of the program at first. "There was a trend at BN to hold onto materials and save them for a rainy day. And many didn't believe that we could deliver the materials as quickly as we promised them."

BN NEWS, MAY–JUNE 1983

MOST RAILROAD HISTORIANS FOCUS ON the work done by the persons who hold senior executives and on operations, the acquisition of cars and locomotives, and major engineering projects. There are few who delve into the activities and accomplishments on such support departments as Accounting or the Purchasing and Material function. In writing this history of BN, I was fortunate that one of the senior leaders of each of these departments was willing to take time to download recollections of his departments' role in shaping BN in its early years. The writings of Bob Garland and Norman M. (Norm) Doerr provide an understanding of the business processes they were in charge of, the challenges they had to deal with, and innovations they put in place to better support important elements of the company's work.

Soon after the merger, fifty store locations were set up to serve large and small equipment-maintenance facilities and the track, bridge, and signal-maintenance forces. The prospect of applying the capability of computers was intended to simplify the complex, cumbersome systems established over the years to protect railroad companies from theft, over-ordering, or general abuse of company property. Senior executives and managers at all levels were being challenged to move faster into the modern age of material management by learning how inventory levels could be reduced and how the procurement processes could be improved.

Norm Doerr, who moved up to become vice president of the Purchasing and Material Department, recalled a field trip when George Arneson, a roadmaster in Spokane, showed him a track bolt, asking, "Do you know it takes seven pieces of paper to get this from the Material Department?" Over the next few years, the processes for ordering, delivering, and accounting for material were greatly improved. George Arneson's daughter, Georgene, was among the younger managers who developed new systems and advanced to positions of responsibility in the Material Department.

Computer technology and capability were advancing rapidly, and BN soon acquired new IBM mainframe computer capability to replace both the Univac I, acquired by GN in 1957 to handle payroll accounting and to support inventory management, and a Univac III computer that had been acquired in 1963. Norm recalls his attempt to sell the old Univac computers to business and governmental organizations throughout the United States and Europe was unsuccessful. Knowing the Univac computers had to be moved out to free up space for new computers needed to meet the demand for new applications, Norm finally contracted with a local scrap dealer in St. Paul to lower them from a window on the fifth floor of the General Office building with a large truck crane parked on the street below for the value of the scrap metal they contained. Norm wrote, "It cost us far more in lost man hours as just about everyone in the building was hanging out the windows or was down on the street watching them lower the units to a truck bed."

An interesting "social" episode involving the merger of the material management function occurred when eight managers in the Twin Cities terminal requested a meeting with Norm to disclose the accumulation of informal unauthorized transactions that had been made before the date of the merger. He recalls,

> Dan Mullner spoke up first and said they had borrowed various material from each other for many years and was wondering if they had to pay each other back now that we were merged. I could see them all cringe when Dan finished speaking and were waiting for the "shoe to drop." I remember thinking how I had worried about getting all these guys to pull together and here they were, on a first-name basis. The fellow at Daytons Bluff had borrowed 20 car sets of lubricator pads from the fellow at Northtown. Someone was short of car oil used to lubricate the journals of freight cars and had borrowed 880 gallons, yet another owed someone six locomotive traction motors. I started to laugh and soon they were all laughing but none had the slightest idea why. I told them to charge materials to the account that had benefited and go about their business. You never saw a happier bunch in your life.[1]

It was a good example of how railroaders of all specialties cooperated and supported each other to help make things work when any of their associates needed help, and even if he or she was working for a competitor.

Norm made an aggressive push to handle all purchase orders on EDI (Electronic Data Interchange, as applied ot the exchange of data between a supplier and a user) and soon had 86 percent of the orders transmitted electronically. Engineering drawings were scanned and stored electronically, which greatly simplified the ordering of track, bridge, and signal material. At the same time, invoices from suppliers were handled via EDI. That next step made it possible for suppliers to draw down from a separate BN account instead of submitting invoices on paper and waiting for payment. Each roadway or signal supervisor was provided a bar-coded catalogue listing only the items in place on the track or in the signal equipment in service on his or her territory. Their orders for material would be transmitted to their assigned store in a few minutes instead of the weeks or months it often took under the old system.

TO TRANSFORM P&M TO A SERVICE ORGANIZATION

It was important to establish trust and credibility in the new system—that the material requested would actually be delivered. Norm Doerr and his staff prepared truck routes and delivery schedules that would provide delivery at least once each month. The trucks picked up scrap material to take back on each trip. The delivery trucks were semi-trailers equipped with a boom to facilitate loading and unloading of all types and sizes of material. RESBU—the responsibility budgeting system, a process of expense control, put in place in all departments those years—was a deterrent to over-ordering. The new system was soon seen as an improvement over the old practice of loading material for several delivery points in one box car. "Company material" shipments often were given low priority in movement and there were all-too-frequent cases of material being appropriated before it reached its intended delivery point.

One of the most significant achievements in the revamping of the Material Department was the reduction in the number of locomotives that had to be kept out of service each day "awaiting material." It had become common to find from twenty-five to thirty locomotives in that status at a time of rapid traffic growth when every locomotive owned by BN should have been out pulling freight. With an improved delivery system, the number of units held for material was reduced to one quarter percent of the fleet, or no more than five or six units. At the same time, the inventory of locomotive parts was reduced by 60 percent. Norm reported, "Our inventory of parts and supplies in the early 1990s was only half of the inventory we had on hand in 1980, while our turnover ratio was improved to well over two times per month for most classes of material. The total number of stores

1 Conversations and e-mail messages, Norman Doerr to author.

was reduced from fifty to twenty-one. These accomplishments were made by dedicated employees using every form of technology available."[2]

TO PUT THE FORMER FRISCO IN SHAPE

Norm has written an interesting commentary about his department's findings on the property of the former Frisco in the early days of its merger with BN. In the inventory of unapplied material in the storehouses and in the field taken upon merger, Norm found the amount of material charged out was far in excess of reasonable needs, based on the standards used on BN. Norm described the task of moving the excess charged-out material back to the stores as "gargantuan." He wrote, "This resulted in huge credits to operating expenses. One of our accounting managers told me that the value of the charged-out materials was equal to what we paid for the SLSF!" This resulted in huge credits to operating expenses. During those years, the company's operating ratio was reduced from the high 90s to the low 80s.

Norm recalls,

> This meant we had to find some way to make improvements without spending capital dollars. It was well known that the merchandise from derailments was often sold for pennies on the dollar, so we contacted our Freight Claims Department. Bill Marshall and Joe Wheeler in that department were very helpful and turned over those items to us that we could use. We of course gave them credit and used the items to upgrade our facilities. As an example, a box car loaded with office furniture was involved in a derailment. The furniture sustained very little damage but the customer refused the entire load, thinking that they could settle with the railroad and then buy the furniture back for very little. That backfired as we took the entire load and used it to upgrade the office furniture in a number of our stores. Morale improved immediately.[3]

On the former Frisco, most of the operating and mechanical buildings and facilities were modern and well maintained. However, the facilities used by the Material Department on that railroad that did not measure up to the standard of "a super railroad," a term that was ascribed to the Frisco property by a number of BN officers who were involved in preparing the plans for the BN–Frisco merger. Norm found it necessary to obtain authority to build a new storehouse and office building at Springfield through the formal capital budgeting process. He wrote,

> After a year of meetings and sometimes heated arguments, we finally secured funds . . . to build a new store with modern storage racks and equipment. . . . The old office was deplorable and beyond rehabilitation. . . . The concrete floor in the storehouse building was cracked and very uneven, creating all kinds of walking and tripping hazards. How anyone would allow such conditions to exist and expect people to work safely is unbelievable. This project was too big to be handled informally through resourcefulness, by self-help, a "boot straps" approach.
>
> The response of employees working on the former Frisco property was outstanding. They worked hard at learning the new inventory control system and computer systems, while the safety record improved by leaps and bounds. They appeared to want to be the best at everything we did in the department. As an example, Gary Morris, one of the truck drivers, asked to use one of our tractor-trailer units to enter a safe driver contest held by the State of Missouri. He won first place. Another Springfield store employee, Larry Edwards, was instrumental in helping make a fork lift truck safety video that was used to train new fork lift operators throughout the entire railroad.

The action taken to remedy these poor working conditions confirmed the old adage that if you give people good tools and a decent place to work, they will respond very positively in their attitudes, and their quality of work and productivity will improve dramatically.

2 Norman Doerr, conversations and e-mail messages, to author.

3 Doerr, conversations and e-mail messages, to author.

CHAPTER 23

INNOVATIONS IN MAINTAINING A HIGH-TONNAGE RAILROAD

• reaching 400 million gross tons per year, the highest tonnage anywhere in the world • adapting and developing the new technology needed to extend the service life of rail, switch components, and ties • improving the methods used for track inspection, maintenance planning, and response to defects that could disrupt the heavy flow of trains •

BY 1979, THE INVESTMENT WAS PAYING OFF

By far the heaviest part of the programs for track upgrading and the expansion of capacity were completed by 1980 on the Denver and Chicago regions, as well as on the C&S and FW&D. While some very necessary and important work was still in progress, there was a general satisfaction throughout the company with the amount of work that had been done, the quality of the work, and the fact that coal trains were running at or at least much closer to the planned cycle time. With less money being spent for basic maintenance work, there was some improvement in the operating ratio in 1979, and BN's net income finally began to increase. The financial projections for 1980 and beyond looked favorable.

Major capital projects such as the new Donkey Creek–Orin line, the mechanical facilities at Alliance, the new bridge at Rulo, and the addition of many miles of second main track and CTC also had been completed. Most of the track on the major coal corridors had been upgraded to the strength needed to handle heavy tonnages of coal. Through it all, many operating and maintenance managers, from first-line supervisors, up through the region vice presidents and department heads, had developed into strong, effective managers. They were qualified to lead a company that had been transformed in the past five years.

By the end of 1979, there was good reason to celebrate—or at least to pause briefly with satisfaction—on what had been accomplished, but only for a moment, because already the gross tons per mile we were accumulating were much higher than experienced anywhere else on BN, or in North America, for that matter. It soon became clear that the established standards and the approach to track maintenance and inspection that had been adequate in the past would have to be revamped for the lines on which we were moving tonnage at those unprecedented levels.

DONKEY CREEK–ORIN LINE

In August 1984 C&NW acquired 50 percent ownership in ninety-one miles of the new line between Shawnee Junction and Coal Creek for $76 million in 1986. Joint ownership with C&NW was extended an additional eleven miles to the north, to East Caballo Junction, for $27 million to enable it to serve four more mines. Under the agreement with C&NW for the costs of maintenance and operation, BN continued to dispatch and maintain the line. C&NW furnished the crews and motive power for its trains. Future capital expenditures were to be split 50/50, and the cost of maintenance was shared on a gross-tonnage basis.[1]

The entire new line of 113 miles was completed in November 1979. It became the world's heaviest-tonnage line, handling 400 million tons of coal (combined total for BN and C&NW/UP by 2008). It was opened as a single-track railroad, but as business grew, segments of second main track were added from year to year. By early 1982, 23.6 miles (19 percent of the line) of second main track were in service. That was expanded to 50.5 miles by October 1988 (40 percent). The entire line was under a two-main-track operation in 1997. As business continued to grow, more line capacity was needed. A third main track was completed on the entire joint-line mileage in 2007, and a fourth main track of twenty-onemiles was opened for service over Logan Hill in 2008. The additional capacity was needed to move the high volume of trains efficiently and in order to meet service requirements. Having such a large number of heavy-tonnage, slow-moving trains with a low power-to-weight ratio moving over many miles of one percent grades required much more capacity than if they had been running on a territory with much lighter grades.

In addition, it was necessary to have enough capacity to allow some segments of track to be taken out of service on a daily basis for track inspection and to conduct various levels of track maintenance. To facilitate maintenance, the new main tracks were built on track centers of 25 feet, much wider than the old standard of 14 feet used by BN. This change made it safe and practical for track maintenance in inspection work to continue while trains were passing on the adjacent main track.

1 See chapter 30 in *Burlington Northern: A Great Adventure* for a discussion of what led to C&NW, and later, UP, acquiring part ownership of the line and gaining access to the mines.

INDICATION OF UNEXPECTED HEAVY WEAR ON NEW RAIL

One of the first indications was a report Donald R. (Don) Rogers made in 1981 of heavy wear on the rail on curves on the Donkey Creek–Orin line in Wyoming. This new 127-mile line had been built in stages from 1975 through 1979. The maximum curvature was only 3 degrees. The rail was laid new and had been in service for less than three years by that time. The wear was not the result of a deficiency in maintenance or quality of the rail. It was a surprise to everyone. Our maintenance experts had not anticipated that rail laid so recently would already be in need of grinding to re-profile the rail and thereby head off corrugation, as well as to prevent rail defects from developing and to extend the life of the rail.

On the fifteen miles of the "new line" between Donkey Creek and the junction to the Belle Ayr line, it still was a challenge to maintain surface and line due to difficulty in keeping the embankment stabilized. Piling had to be driven on both sides of the track on fills. A large, 72-inch culvert on a 15-foot fill had to be replaced. A 24-hour track patrol was set up to run ahead of trains, together with a speed restriction of 10 miles per hour on about half of the line. Past efforts to deal with the problem of having bentonite clay in the subgrade would continue to haunt large parts of the railroad west of Edgemont as well, for years to come. These conditions required a heavy, ongoing maintenance program.

The installation of continuous welded rail to replace the jointed 39-foot rail obviously eliminated the need to maintain thousands of joints. However, even the few remaining joints between the quarter-mile long sections of rail soon became a maintenance problem, with the accelerated tie wear and mud pumping up through the ballast that occurred as the rail flexed under passing trains. The solution was to weld those joints in the field with a process called thermite welding. However, due to problems in making quality thermite welds, that practice had been forbidden by BN until the Frisco merger in 1981. With a heavy concentration of training for members of a gang dedicated to thermite welding, the Frisco had found that good-quality field welds could be made. Field welding was then approved for the combined BN–Frisco system.

In 1984, soon after Roy Buchanen became the vice president–general manager of the Denver Region, he stormed into the headquarters office of the Operating Department in Overland Park with a long list of deficiencies he had observed in the quality of work performed on the coal routes over the previous ten years. Getting authority for a major program to make field welds was his highest priority. Having money authorized to deal with the mud already coming up at "weak" points such as at switches, bridge ends, and road crossings, and at the transition between cuts and fills was next on the list. The message was that poor-quality work had been done up to his arrival on the scene and that millions of additional dollars would have to be spent to overcome the deficiencies of the past.

Of course, such tirades and accusations are of the "blame it on [George] Bush" nature, and the continuing rivalry between some BN and former Frisco people, but most of it was the result of the increasingly heavy tonnage being run over the line on the previous ten years. The approach taken earlier was not to try to put the blame on maintenance officers at any level, but instead to recognize that a new approach to maintenance had to be developed to detect, correct, and prevent problems from developing to the point where speed restrictions had to be imposed and before general frustration would set in throughout the company.

HEAVY, ONGOING MAINTENANCE WORK WOULD BE REQUIRED

We immediately contracted for a large program of undercutting and shoulder ballast cleaning, and surfacing, plus the field welding of joints. To this day, large programs of undercutting and shoulder cleaning are carried out on hundreds of miles every year on the major coal corridors. Expenditures for ballast remediation were found to be far more economical and longer-lasting than having out-of-face surfacing done on an annual or even biannual basis.

TO EXTEND RAIL LIFE BY GRINDING

In the early to mid-1980s, a learning curve led to the development of new methods to extend the life of rail. Changes in "rail management" were developed in those years by the new heads of the Engineering Department—W. A. Thompson,[2] Bill Glavin, Jerry Masters, and Mike Armstrong—greatly reduced the amount of capital needed each year for rail replacement. Re-profiling of rail by grinding and using new, improved methods for lubrication of rail on curves made it possible to extend rail life far beyond historic levels. Also, by not having to take track out of service as frequently to replace rail, there was less interruption to the cycles of unit train equipment. This led to a reduction in penalty payments that had to be made to train crews for delays on the road, for excess time held at their away from home terminals, or having to be relieved on the road under the twelve-hour law.

Profile grinding is necessary to keep the point of contact between wheels and rail in the center of the rail head, so the stress in the rail will be carried down the path designed into the track structure. Through a program of profile grinding, surface defects on rail can be eliminated, thereby reducing the stress and the generation of defects that will require rail to be changed out. As a result, rail life can be determined by the amount of wear on the head of the rail instead of the rate of defects occurring. BN increased its rail-grinding pass miles from about 2,000 miles in 1981 to 16,000 in 1986. Bill Glavin determined that by spending $13 million for rail grinding in 1988, BN saved $35 million in the purchase and laying of replacement rail.[3]

In a presentation to the American Railway Engineering Association (AREA) in 1989, Glavin summarized the success BN had in extending rail life through its enhanced program of rail grinding:

Without a program to greatly extend rail life, curves as light as 2 and 3 degrees would have to be relaid every

---

2 Author's note: Refers to W. A. Thompson, vice president, Engineering effective in 1985, and not W. F. Thompson, executive vice president–Operations on BN from 1980 through 1983, and before then, vice president of Operations of the Frisco Railroad.

3 "Meeting the Maintenance of Way Challenge," *Railway Age,* June 1991.

Table 23.1. TRAFFIC DENSITY, MAJOR COAL CORRIDORS
(millions of gross tons per mile)
(includes coal and all other commodities)

Corridors	*1955*[1]	*1975*	*1982*	*1989*	*2009*
TO KANSAS CITY					
Gillette–Alliance	5	29	86	117	185
Gillette–Orin[2]	–	40	65	92	402
Alliance–Ravenna	8	27	92	114	226
Ravenna–Lincoln	9	31	91	111	226
Lincoln–Napier	8	10	50	64	137
Napier–Kansas City	14	17	59	70	152
TO MINNESOTA AND WISCONSIN					
Gillette–Sheridan	5	21	21	48	50
Sheridan–Huntley	5	11	23	49	71
Huntley–Mandan[3]	14	29	43	48	74
Mandan–Casselton	17	31	45	50	63
Casselton–Fargo	15	29	59	95	123
Fargo–Staples	16	36	56	65	102
Staples–Minneapolis	16	35	48	50	77
Staples–Superior	9	6	14	18	26
TO COLORADO, OKLAHOMA, AND TEXAS					
Orin–Northport	5	5	65	64	100
Alliance–Northport	5	5	46	59	?
Northport–Brush	2	6	47	52	61
Brush–Denver	12	15	54	56	79
Denver–Pueblo[4]	–	–	57	44	79
Pueblo–Texline	–	–	42	63	86
Texline–Fort Worth[5]	–	–	41	40	78

Corridors	*1955*[1]	*1975*	*1982*	*1989*	*2009*
To Illinois					
Lincoln–Pacific Junction	18	44	52	97	142
Pacific Junction–Galesburg	12	36	35	34	115
Galesburg–Aurora	27	28	26	34	66
Aurora–Chicago	31	45	52	62	98
To Minnesota and Wisconsin					
Via Sioux City					
Ashland–Sioux City	6	6	10	17	27
Sioux City–Willmar	4	6	12	21	24
Willmar–Minneapolis	18	23	11	17	40
Minneapolis–Superior	3	7	9	15	21
Casselton–Willmar[6]	13	15	16	–	–

1 Efforts to locate a density chart for BN for any of its early years, from 1970 through 1974, were unsuccessful. It became necessary to use instead the 1955 data prepared for the merger application. It should be noted that in the period from 1955 to 1970, the only significant changes in tonnage on the lines of the component roads involved mainly the decline in coal moving out of southern Illinois, a large decrease in the movement of "natural" iron ore from the Mesabi Range in Minnesota, and fewer single-car shipments of general merchandise to and from small stations. Business on some lines in the Pacific Northwest increased in those years due to general economic expansion.

2 Line opened for service in 1978 for the entire distance between Gillette and Orin. Includes tonnage moved in trains operated by the C&NW and Union Pacific starting in 1984.

3 Tonnage shown is east Glendive, the area of heaviest tonnage.

4 Tonnage is not shown prior to 1982, before the C&S and FW&D were merged into BN.

5 Tonnage includes both the former FW&D line between Texline and Amarillo and the former Santa Fe line via La Junta, which have been operated on a directional running basis since the BN–Santa Fe merger of 1995.

6 Upon sale of the portion of the line between Casselton and Wahpeton Junction to a short line in 1987, through tonnage was diverted to the line via Fargo and Staples and the line between Moorhead and Wahpeton Junction (via Comstock).

Table 23.2. AVERAGE EXPECTATIONS FOR RAIL LIFE (MGT)

	1981	*1989*	*Type of Rail*
On tangent track	650–750	800–1400	standard carbon
Curves 1 degree and less	300–350	800–1100	standard carbon
Curves 2 degrees and less	175–200	500–700	*
Curves 3 degrees and less	125–150	300–500	*

*In 1981, Curvemaster/Japanese head hardened rail; in 1989, head hardened/fully heat-treated rail.
SOURCE: W. E. Glavin, "Rail Grinding: The BN Experience," AREA Proceedings, 1989.

year, as gross ton miles (GTM) grew to 150 and beyond in a year's time.[4] It is interesting to note that in 2013, considerable rail on tangent track with nearly two billion accumulated gross tons was still in service. Neither the defect rate nor the amount of head wear had reached the threshold level for replacement of that rail. Having maintained a consistent program of grinding is credited for the ability to keep rail in service for such a much longer life.

In 1990 the standard for new rail was changed from 132-pound rail to 136-pound, to gain three-sixteenths inch of steel and thereby allow more grinding passes and thereby extend the life of the rail. In more recent years, the 141-pound section has been adopted as the new standard for heavy tonnage lines.

INSTALLATION OF CONCRETE TIES

Also in the mid- to late 1980s, BN began to place concrete ties on its heaviest-tonnage lines with 50 million or more gross tons, and on curves of 2 degrees and more. Concrete ties were expected to have a life of fiftyyears, compared to about twenty-five to thirty years for wood ties on tangent track in areas of moderate rainfall and humidity. On high-degree curves in heavy tonnage territory, wood ties were lasting only five to six years. Concrete ties were expected to last twenty years on the same curves.[5]

With concrete ties, the interval between cycles for surface correction on high-tonnage lines would be extended from every other year to every third year. The track structure would be stronger, which would help maintain gauge and alignment in curves. Altogether, these benefits would reduce the amount of time the train operation would have to be interrupted, which had been for several days each year, for some type of maintenance work or replacement of track components. Since curfews for trackwork have a major effect on coal-train cycle times, any maintenance practices that would reduce the need for curfews would be of great benefit. In 1988 BN reported plans to install 3.5 million concrete ties through 1992 on 1,300 track miles. Also, the program included placement of concrete ties in turnouts at selected locations on lines of 50 million gross tons per mile per year.

MAINTAINING QUALITY IN THE BALLAST SECTION

Productivity in tamping (correction of track line and surface irregularities) was vastly improved with the introduction of new technology. Continuous-action tampers

4 "Meeting the M/W Challenge," *Railway Age*, June 1991.

5 "BN Increases Safety and Reduces Costs: A Concrete Example," BN *Technical Bulletin*, July 1988, and M. N. Armstrong, "Concrete Tie Experience on BN," *Bulletin 716*, American Railway Engineering Association, 1988.

were acquired that could operate in continuous motion by being able to tamp two ties at a time. This capability made it possible to extend the distances tamped per day, thereby completing the job faster and reducing the time of interruption to train service. The use of the new dynamic track stabilizer made it possible to restore stability of the track much sooner following tamping, thereby reducing the duration of speed restrictions.

As mentioned earlier, the quality of ballast proved to be an ongoing and increasing challenge as tonnage grew. Increased track time and money for spot surfacing became necessary to deal with the increasing number of trouble spots. If fouled ballast is allowed to remain in place, track quality will deteriorate and lead to speed restrictions and danger of derailments due to deviations in cross level, alignment, and the degradation of ties and fastenings. It was soon determined that undercutting to about eight inches and shoulder ballast cleaning would be more effective and reduce the amount of time that track would have to be taken out of service for maintenance over a period of three to five years. Generally, about 60 percent of the ballast is recovered in the process of shoulder cleaning.

BN improved the quality of the ballast used on its heaviest-tonnage lines in Wyoming and Nebraska by using granite ballast produced at its quarry at Ryder, Oklahoma, and at a source on the UP at Sherman Hill in Wyoming. The granite ballast was harder and therefore found superior to the Guernsey ballast that had been used on these lines when they were upgraded in the 1970s and early 1980s.

BN increased its program for undercutting and shoulder cleaning on its lines in Nebraska, Wyoming and Colorado from about 500 miles in 1984 (its first heavy year for ballast remediation) to nearly 800 miles in 1988. It has been necessary to increase those programs even beyond that level in subsequent years on BNSF's heavy tonnage routes. In 2011, for example, BNSF programmed 4,850 miles of shoulder cleaning and 700 miles of undercutting across its system.

NEW DESIGNS FOR TURNOUTS

Turnouts (switches) in main tracks are a high-maintenance component in the track structure but vital—they allow trains to cross over from one main track to another, to go on a diverging route at a junction, or to move on and off sidings to meet or pass other trains. In the mid-1980s, BN estimated that turnouts took 40 percent of its total budget for track maintenance. The short, abrupt angles in turnouts require trains to reduce speed, thereby reducing line capacity, causing delay to trains, and increasing fuel consumption. To reduce that cost and the amount of time track had to be taken out of service for turnout maintenance, BN developed new designs to reduce the high forces generated in turnouts by passing trains, and to allow trains to move on diverging routes or in and out of sidings at higher speeds. Bill Glavin, BN's system chief engineer at the time, stated, "These turnouts are another example of BN differentiating itself from the rest of the industry."[6] Using tangential geometry to reduce the entry angle, trains going through the turnout side could maintain a speed of 50 miles per hour instead of having to reduce to 35, as required with the design of turnouts previously installed. The most favorable applications for the new turnouts were on crossover switches and at the ends of double track.

Another innovation in turnout design developed by BN in those years was the swing-nose (movable point) frog. It was designed to eliminate the gap that exists in a conventional frog where the two rails intersect. Due to this lack of continuous contact with the rail, wheels passing over the transitional gap create very high force levels on both tracks and the equipment passing through the frog in a turnout. On BN's high tonnage lines with over 50 million gross tons per year, conventional railbound frogs had a service life of only twelve to eighteen months. During that time, the frogs had to be weld-repaired at least three times. The track had to be taken out of service for up to six hours each time, which adversely affected the cycle time of trains. The expense for welding and for such frequent replacement of an expensive track component was increasing rapidly.

---

6 "High Speed Turnouts," *Technical Bulletin,* a publication of BN's Engineering Department, September 1990.

The new design for frogs was used on lines handling over 100 million gross tons per year, with an anticipated lifespan of five to seven years.[7] W. A. Thompson is credited with identifying and promoting the use of swing-nose frogs and other innovations in turnout design, following his study of those applications on railroad lines in Australia, United Kingdom, and France.

Don Dill, roadmaster on the Alliance–Ravenna line, found that the specially designed swing-nose frog required no welding and only a light amount of grinding even after 70 MGT had passed over it. In that territory of nearly 150 MGT per year, a standard rail-bound Manganese frog had a life of less than a year.[8] Improving metallurgy and welding and grinding practices also helped extend the lives of turnout components, such as switch points and frogs.

These are examples of innovations and changes in track-maintenance practices that were found necessary as the tonnage built up to unprecedented levels. To handle the tonnages that increased to a level far above projections made in 1980, more and more additional miles of main track were built on all subdivisions on the Alliance Division and on the Nebraska Division's line between Ravenna, Lincoln, and Pacific Junction. A third main track was built on the entire BN–UP joint line, plus fifteen miles of fourth main track. By 1994 the capacity of the joint line was increased to 185 MGT and to 400 MGT in 2007. On one segment of the joint line, 445 MGT were handled in 2008. As the number of miles of main track in service was expanded, it became necessary to allocate more funds for maintenance, inspection, and replacement of the various components of the track structure as they wear out.

ENHANCED INSPECTION AND RESPONSE SYSTEM

Among other new and additional maintenance and inspection practices established for safety and to reduce the number and duration of interruptions to the train operation were the following:

- Inspecting track on a seven-day basis
- Operating the track-geometry car six times per year instead of the "standard" of twice yearly on main lines
- Assigning a rail-testing vehicle exclusively to the 127-mile joint line
- Walking inspections of areas requiring heavy or frequent maintenance due to unstable soil conditions
- Having night-response crews during the winter months, including a night roadmaster, due to the high frequency of broken rails
- Setting up a "maintenance blitz" to reduce the duration of time required for seasonal maintenance work; in a typical three-day blitz, the same work could take over a month if it was managed instead as individual projects
- Use of ground penetrating radar to test the density of ballast 16 inches deep, to identify the locations of fouled ballast
- "Quick response" equipment for small tie-replacement programs makes it possible to get machinery clear of the track within thirty minutes, far less time than required to move conventional machines in the clear on a support track so trains can get through the work area.

It is important to recognize that capital expenditures for the many large expansion projects and heavy annual-maintenance expense were financed in the face of an overall reduction of 35 percent in coal rates from 1985 to 2004.[9] Accomplishing this is a real credit to those who were able to drive down the operating and maintenance costs by improving both labor productivity and the return from investments BN had made in its roadway and equipment.

SEVERE DETERIORATION OF TRACK DUE TO COAL DUST

In May 2005 BNSF and UP suddenly found a totally unanticipated problem with the track on the new line they jointly owned between Shawnee Junction and East Caballo Junction. Two derailments involving fourteen and twenty-nine loaded cars derailed and blocked all three

7 "Swing Nose Frogs," *Technical Bulletin*, October 1988.

8 "BN 'SWATS' Track Maintenance Chores," *Railway Track and Structures*, October 1987.

9 Report of U.S. General Accounting Office (GAO), 2005.

main tracks. There had been an unusual amount of rain and snow that spring, and it was found that on about half of the 295 track miles of the line, the ballast had become severely fouled by coal dust. The accumulation of coal dust prevented rainwater from draining from the ballast.

With such heavy rainfall in the normally arid climate, the ballast had turned into gumbo—"coal dust goop," as some termed it. This new type of mud formed from the coal dust that had built up in the ballast in the twenty-five years the line had been open. When the wet coal dust dried, the badly fouled ballast hardened into a consistency not unlike cement and eroded the concrete ties. Without proper drainage, the track structure became weakened to the extent that it began to go out of alignment, and its surface became so irregular that the rails spread apart. Damage also resulted to concrete ties, switches, and the track on bridges.

Under the maintenance agreement between BNSF and UP, BNSF was responsible for maintaining the line. During the time required to clear the derailed cars and put the damaged track back in service, and during the several months of heavy track rehabilitation to restore the ballast condition, the UP was hampered even more than BNSF since its trains had to traverse all of the affected area. BNSF could get some relief from the congestion that developed from having so much track out of service by routing some of its trains for Texas and Oklahoma out the north end of the line at Donkey Creek, and then on the circuitous route through Alliance that BN had used before the Orin line was completed all the way to Bridger Junction. Both railroads took a heavy hit on their revenue for several months while extensive track rehabilitation was underway. Deliveries to customers were impaired, leading to severe criticism of both railroads. Government regulators and political leaders undertook investigations to bring out to the public where the fault lay.

It should be noted that the buildup of coal dust was not a complete surprise. BNSF had had a large program of three hundred track miles for ballast cleaning and undercutting on its coal lines in Wyoming and Nebraska in the previous maintenance season. Even so, its maintenance officers did not anticipate that coal dust could develop into such a major problem in so short a time, or that when it was mixed with rain and snow, the ballast section would be so severely weakened. In the previous fall, senior engineering officers from both companies had made a joint inspection of the line, and apparently the UP officers did not find reason to take exception to BNSF's maintenance practices. With the UP's long history of maintaining track at a standard of excellence, they surely would have raised a "red flag" and put a lot of pressure on BNSF to correct any current or potential problems they observed at that time.

The immediate fallout from having to take track out of service for heavy, emergency work was severe. Fewer trains could be run, and some of the power companies had to begin importing coal bought on the spot market from foreign sources, or at least, had to eat into their stockpiles or purchase electricity from other power companies to keep up with their demand. UP issued advice of a force majeure condition to its customers through an embargo that remained in effect until March 2007. Under the embargo, the UP would not deliver coal to any new customers in order to give it a better chance to protect service to its existing customers. UP claimed it lost $30 million of revenue per month while the embargo was in effect.[10] In total, rail delivery of coal in 2005 was 20 million tons below the level BNSF and UP had committed to move to their customers. This shortfall in deliveries continued into 2006.

To reduce the amount of coal dust blowing from each train, the railroads and the mines determined a change to lower the "profile" to which coal was loaded above the cars' side sills and topped off that would be effective. Together with a "topper agent" (chemical to make dust stick to chunks of coal) or a "surfactant," these practices would reduce fugitive dust by 85 percent. BNSF mandated this be done at shippers' expense and installed monitors along the track to verify that the amount of coal dust was being reduced. The shippers protested to the Surface Transportation Board (STB), a new federal agency established after the ICC was abolished to handle some, but not all, functions previously held by the ICC, that this burden of expense should fall to the railroads, but in December 2013 the STB ruled in the railroad's favor.[11]

10 Fred W. Frailey, "Powder River 'Blowout' Sends BNSF, UP Reeling," *Trains,* September 2005.

11 Douglas John Brown, "STB Backs BNSF on Coal Dust Issue," *Railway Age,* December 17, 2013.

Fortunately the amount of coal-dust emissions decreased as coal trains move away from the loading points. BNSF immediately adjusted its plan for track maintenance to make enough machinery, labor, and track material available for an all-out assault on the problem. Fouled ballast was removed on more than half of the line by undercutting. Turnouts were rehabilitated, defective concrete ties were replaced, and the ballast section on deck bridges was renewed. Track gangs worked on a seven-day basis, including nights. It took all of the 2005 maintenance season and part of 2006 to make enough progress in removing temporary speed restrictions and to free up enough miles of main track to be able to make up the shortfall in the amount of tonnage delivered.

Since that time, ambitious undercutting and shoulder-cleaning programs have been carried out every year to keep ballast from becoming so fouled from coal dust and mud pumping up through the subgrade that speed restrictions are required. Such programs and other initiatives in track maintenance are required to help insure that loading schedules can be met and that unit train cycle times will be maintained.

PART V

LABOR: IN TRANSITION TO A LOW-COST OPERATION

CHAPTER 24

UPHEAVAL IN THE 1980S

This is the last industry to eliminate its archaic labor practices.

. . .

Railroad labor is basically overpaid and underworked.

. . .

We're using the efficiency of capital to overcome the inefficiencies of labor.

RICHARD M. BRESSLER, QUOTED IN JAMES COOK,
"ALL ALONE BY THE TELEPHONE," *FORBES*, NOVEMBER 16, 1987

• *to achieve fundamental change in the wage structure of union-represented employees* • *full assault on the crew-consist issue* • *revolutionary recommendations from Presidential Emergency Board (PEB) 219* • *reflections on labor strategies employed* •

UPHEAVAL IN THE 1980S

Overall, we had been developing healthy relationships with employees and their representatives. The operation was improving, thanks to better training, and good tools and equipment. It also helped that employees had the opportunity and desire to apply their talents, knowledge, and experience to move the company forward. There were some struggles, setbacks, and disagreements along the way, but overall, BN was becoming an even better place to work. This affirmative work environment seemed to be coming to an abrupt halt early in 1981, when a number of seemingly cataclysmic events took place within just a few months:

- The first was the coming of Richard Bressler to replace Norman Lorentzsen as president and CEO of BN, Inc.
- Next was the appointment of Richard Grayson to head the railroad company and BN's other transportation units.
- Merger with the Frisco Railroad and several Frisco executives moving into high-level positions in the railroad's Operating Department.
- Deregulation of railroad pricing that would require a major effort to reduce costs enough to offset the anticipated reduction in rates necessary to retain and develop business in the new competitive environment.
- These factors combined to launch an all-out assault on BN's high labor costs, to increase earnings and increase the return on the heavy capital investments made since the 1970 merger.

The new management team focused immediately on the need to reduce the cost of the lifetime job protection to which BN was obligated under the terms of the agreements made in the late 1960s. Large numbers of jobs in the non-operating crafts were reduced. Strategies were developed for achieving fundamental changes in the railroad's cost structure, by reducing the size of crews on trains and yard switching assignments, and to reduce overall wage expense to a level where BN would

A CONFRONTATIONAL MANAGEMENT APPROACH TO LABOR ISSUES

STATEMENTS MADE BY RICHARD BRESSLER IN AN INTERVIEW WITH FORBES MAGAZINE REVEAL THE driving forces behind BN's strategy toward historic labor-management agreements and rates of pay that had been built up for decades in the rail industry. Following are some of the highlights from that interview:

- "This is the last industry to eliminate its archaic labor practices."
- "We're using the efficiency of capital to overcome the inefficiency of labor."
- ". . . even with 20,000 people gone, the dollar cost of our wages is about equal to what is was four or five years ago."
- ". . . independent truckers have undercut the Teamster-imposed wage scales that used to dominate the trucking industry's cost structure."
- ". . . a trucker puts a box [shipping container] on his truck and drives on through with his wife or a helper, whereas we change crews ten times a wage rate that's two and three times as high."

SOURCE: James Cook, "All alone by the telephone," *Forbes*, November 16, 1987, page 83.

be able to price competitively with the over-the-road trucking companies.

BNI and its railroad concluded that to accomplish change of this magnitude might require the company to withdraw from the historic, industry-wide practice of national bargaining on wages, benefits and work rules. Instead, BN would negotiate directly with the unions representing its employees. Right from the start, it was recognized that BN might have to take a strike. By first building up the revenue BNI was receiving from its non-rail activities, it was expected the company would be able to tough it out long enough to obtain the level of wage and work-rule concessions needed to improve its return on invested capital and to reduce its costs enough to insure long-term survival in the new deregulated environment.

Employees and union leaders were given this message over and over. Needless to say, they were not about to give up any work rules or provisions for arbitrary payments they felt they had "earned" over their history, whether they were obtained through contract negotiations, past practice, or built up over the years from favorable arbitration awards. Being pressured by a new group of executives—brought in from outside the rail industry and from the former Frisco Railroad for a consensus to make revisions to costly work practices or excessive manning of trains—did not convince employees and union leaders to even consider agreeing to make such fundamental changes.

During this time, a concerted effort was made to educate employees on the realities of railroad economics.

Discussions held during those sessions revealed that many employees had a real interest and a good understanding of the subject. Generally, the union officers participated well in the dialogue, but in the end, they viewed the facts and realities as problems for management to cope with, rather than trying to load them onto the backs of employees. The unions expressed little or no willingness to move toward making changes in the historic, uneconomic, outdated, counterproductive work practices that we said were holding us back from growing our business, keeping BNI from making a satisfactory return on its investment in the railroad, or that prevented us from being able to lower our rates to a level competitive with the trucking industry.

AN ASSAULT ON SURPLUS POSITIONS

As soon as Richard Grayson took over as president and CEO, BN went into an aggressive, all-out program to reduce costs in every activity and every department. To reduce the ratio of wages and benefits to revenue to a respectable level, the headcount had to be reduced dramatically. The initial focus was mainly on the size of the clerical force, and the number of car and locomotive-maintenance facilities, and the number of employees in the maintenance of equipment function. The clerical force had become bloated because of the complexities of the COMPASS system and the cumbersome administrative load resulting from the general bureaucracy that had built up since the 1970 merger.

In the case of the mechanical forces, there still were a number of shops at common points that had not yet been closed and would not be needed if better work methods and productivity standards were put in place. Also, a number of those shops were managed by the mechanical staffs on the regions and, as such, were not the direct responsibility of the headquarters Mechanical Department. Too often, the regions had generally been reluctant to close any mechanical facilities they controlled.

In addition, there was no policy in place for dealing with employees who would become surplus if shops were closed or if clerical forces had been reduced. To get a program for reduction of forces underway, Grayson told line management that they should no longer hold back on eliminating jobs even if employees protected under the 1970 merger agreement would then become surplus. Those employees were to be turned over to the Labor Relations Department to be severed at some level of buy-out or transfered to other kinds of work to other locations. If they would not accept a severance payment, they might be ordered to report every day to a designated area for employees who had no work. At some locations, surplus clerical employees were put together as a crew to dismantle and cut up retired or damaged freight cars for scrap that we did not plan to repair. This practice caused quite a stir among the employees, unions, and the news media. It was thought to be a demeaning, disrespectful method of handling employees who had no job, through no fault of their own, even though they may have declined opportunities to be transferred or become qualified for other kinds of work.

Those who criticized this practice failed to acknowledge that those employees were still being paid, since they were entitled to lifetime job protection under the merger agreement. If they had lost their jobs in virtually any other business or organization, they would likely have been out on the street with no income until they were able to get hired elsewhere. Also, the employees we had in surplus status were allowed and encouraged to take time away from their designated reporting area to look for work, or to use a telephone at their reporting location to seek other opportunities. Nevertheless, it was a difficult period in BN history, as we tried to deal with the problem of people whose jobs were declared surplus.

As we scaled back on the number of work centers, a number of exempt (salaried, non-union) personnel also found themselves in a surplus category until they could be placed or transferred to other positions. The entire situation showed that even a benefit as generous as lifetime job protection had its downside. Instead of having to endure the indignity of being a surplus employee in order to continue collecting the compensation surplus that employees were entitled to receive as protected employees, they might have been better off if they had been given some amount of severance pay, cut their ties with the company, and begin to seek other employment.

At the same time that we were aggressively eliminating jobs in each and every activity, department or work center, work was underway on a strategy for confronting the need to reduce the number of employees we were required to work on trains and yard switching crews, and to bring our wage expense for operating employees down to a level that would enable us to set lower, more competitive rates.

A HEAVY HITTER TO APPLY NEW STRATEGY ON LABOR ISSUES

In 1983 Walter Drexel brought Thomas J. (Tom) Matthews, an executive who had managed labor matters at Continental Airlines, to BN to head the Human Resources and Labor Relations departments. Matthews had worked under Frank Lorenzo, who was famous for the bitter struggles Continental had with its employees and managers. Our union representatives and many employees became highly concerned over the prospect of having to deal with an executive who'd had a major role in such serious confrontations with labor. The people of BN had not yet recovered from the previous three years of major downsizing of the workforce and the introduction of a much different style of leadership after the Frisco merger. This concern turned to fear and animosity when senior management revealed its new agenda for revising work rules, changing the basis of pay, and the ways in which the company planned to conduct collective bargaining in the future.

Matthews was brought in to lead the charge on the restructuring of relationships with labor and to draw up a strategy for obtaining revisions to the work rules and practices that were limiting our ability to price competitively. To put both managers and employees on notice as to our needs and that we were committed to moving ahead to achieve our objectives, Matthews began a system-wide campaign of education and communication. What he developed and presented was an aggressive statement about the kind of corporate culture we were moving into, and how important it was for every person employed by BN to "get on the team." Of course, it would take much more than a PowerPoint multimedia slideshow to change a company's culture. Instead, the leaders in the organization needed to begin conducting themselves in accordance with the new set of values and leadership practices they espoused. Leaders who did not "fit" would either have to change their ways or be replaced.

Many sessions were conducted with employees to explain what had to be done to make BN more competitive in a deregulated environment. We were going to have to reduce our costs for wages and benefits from their current level. Employees became aware that we were training and qualifying more operating officers for service as locomotive engineers in the event of a strike. They were being trained on a training simulator at the Illinois Institute of Technology (IIT), a new tool at that time, and by learning how to run trains on a 99-mile section of the secondary main line between Brookfield and St. Joseph, Missouri, that had been taken out of service pending abandonment. This kind of initiative and numerous statements made by management clearly let employees know we were serious about making changes in the historic labor agreements and in the way business was conducted between labor and management on BN. The company was getting in position to take a strike if necessary in order to get the unions to agree to substantial changes in work rules in all crafts, in manning requirements, and in the basis of compensation. It was to be an extension and acceleration of the tumultuous times we had endured since 1980.

CHAPTER 25

OVERHAUL NEEDED IN WORK RULES AND THE BASIS OF PAY

• to be able to apply technology and improved work practices •

PLAN TO NO LONGER BARGAIN NATIONALLY

In June 1987 BN announced a series of proposed changes in the work rules and pay practices that it had been discussing with employee groups and their elected representatives for the past four years. BN had gone all out in preparing its people for the strategy it felt was needed to overcome its bloated wage costs and work practices that prevented its employees from working as efficiently and productively as it thought most employees would want. Part of BN's strategy was to not give its proxy to the National Carriers Conference Committee for national negotiations to be started in 1988. Instead, BN would negotiate separately with its unions, expecting to get a better settlement on issues and opportunities that were thought to be unique to BN, at least more so than on the other large railroads.

There were no indications on the part of the unions to want to negotiate any major structural changes in the system of mileage-basis for compensation of train crews, together with the layer upon layer complexity of agreements for arbitrary payments, or the issue of crew consist (the number of employees used on crews in road and yard service). The general chairmen were determined to hold on to what they had "earned" over the years, beginning mainly in the years of government control during World War I, followed by a long series of additional provisions established in awards (decisions) made by Public Law Boards, precedents made in settling disputes over time claims, in the interpretation of existing agreements, negotiations on "local" issues and a host of "vest pocket" agreements made over the years. All of this had built up a complex, inefficient, costly web of work practices and rules for compensation for operating employees that BN felt had to be changed.

In the long history of the rail industry issues on compensation and work rules, most of the changes that had been made to improve productivity and reduce manning costs had come through mandates in congressional legislation that was based on the recommendations of Presidential Emergency Boards, which were appointed as a last resort when negotiations reached an impasse and a strike was either threatened or carried out. As a result, the leaders of railroad unions and, to some extent, the staffs of labor relations and the National Carriers Conference Committee were not "deal makers." In having Congress in effect settle disputes, the unions could not be blamed by employees for changes in work rules that resulted in the reduction of employment or changes in work practices with which they had been comfortable for a long time, however inefficient and outdated they may have become. At the same time, railroad executives and their Labor Relations officers knew they would not be allowed to take a strike to try to force the unions to yield on work rules, manning, or the historic basis for compensation of train and yard crews.

Starting in the early 1960s, some progress had been made in modernizing the basics under which operating crews worked. These changes came about largely through intervention by Presidential Emergency Boards and other governmental units. Following are principal changes made in work rules from the early 1970s to 1987:

- A move toward elimination of firemen on nearly all assignments in freight service
- Establishment of a new program for training of Locomotive Engineers
- Elimination of full crew laws that required more than two brakemen on a crew in some states
- Ability to establish longer (interdivisional) runs in through freight service by combining adjacent crew districts of nominally one hundred miles or by extending runs beyond their historic end points
- Allowing road crews to deliver inbound trains to interchange points or to the yards of connecting lines rather than being limited to terminating their runs at the historically designated terminal of their run
- Elimination of cabooses starting in the early 1980s
- In crew consist agreements made in the early 1980s, the ability to reduce crew size by one brakeman on trains of less than seventy-one cars and on some yard crew assignments.

These changes were important but still far from the extent of revision needed to get the level of productivity and flexibility BN needed to be more cost competitive and to improve its rate of return on invested capital.

In the early years of the BN merger, an effort was made to put together a single, consolidated set of agreements governing the work of road crews. The same set of rules would apply on the lines of any of the former roads. This was accomplished for the non-operating employee groups, but any such change was resisted by the unions representing road train employees. As a result, even after the merger, operating crews were still working under the same schedule of agreements they had at the railroad they worked for before the merger took place. Even the employees hired after the merger worked under the agreements of the former roads. The general chairmen representing employees working in the territories of each former road were encouraged to come up with a consolidated schedule. In doing so, they often picked the most costly and most restrictive provisions from each schedule. Assembling those parts into a new consolidated schedule of agreements would have given BN even higher wage costs (estimated at 40 percent greater) and more restrictions on operations than we already had. Hence, this initiative had to be dropped. It would have been desirable if this process had been conducted jointly between the general chairmen and Labor Relations experts before the merger. However, it might have become so contentious and complex that is would have stood in the way of getting union approval for agreements on job protection, wage guarantees, and the implementing needed to put the merger into effect. Today, 43 years after BN was formed, operating employees still work under the old schedules established well before the 1970 merger for each of the roads that make up today's BNSF.

TOWARD NEW, REVOLUTIONARY CONTRACTS

For negotiation of new contracts in 1988, BN proposed to break through this legacy of intransigence and arrive at a completely new set of agreements that would overcome the cost disadvantages it had in trying to gain business lost to trucks over the years. Success in this undertaking also would give BN the flexibility it needed to make its service less restrictive and more appealing to potential customers. With the new set of realities we faced under deregulation, BN challenged the new leadership team it had put in place to figure out a way to make a great leap forward and overcome historic restrictions and the failure of past efforts to modernize operating methods and eliminating wasteful work practices.

With this background to work from, BN proposed a number of changes in work rules and pay practices.

For the operating crafts:

- Two-person crews for all new business and Expediter-type trains (the newly established intermodal trains)
- Three-person crews on all other types of trains

- Employees to be paid on an hourly basis rather than on the historic mileage basis
- Elimination of the host of arbitrary payments, special allowances, and penalty payments that had built up over the years

For the non-operating crafts (maintenance of way, clerks, dispatchers, signal and communications, patrolmen, and yardmasters):

- Rates of pay for new hires to be competitive with outside industry wages, to be subject to a five-year progression
- A given craft would no longer have exclusive right to specific tasks or categories of work
- Management would have flexibility in assigning and changing headquarters and territories, starting times, rest days and meal periods
- A $30 per diem payment for a worker required to be away from headquarters overnight
- The right to furlough employees for up to five days per month at 60 percent of the basic rate
- The right to hire temporary employees on an as-needed basis
- All shop craft employees to work as composite mechanics

For both operating and non-operating employees:

- A flat flexible time bank for vacation, holidays, sick leave, and bereavement leave
- Claims and grievances to be resolved in six months or less through expedited appeal and arbitration procedures.[1]

---

1 David M. Cawthorne, "BN Proposes Major Overhaul in Work Rules, Pay Practices" *Traffic World*, June 22, 1987; *Summary of Proposed Labor Agreements,* Burlington Northern Railroad, June 1987, a pamphlet issued to employees and union representatives.

CHAPTER 26

CHANGE IN DIRECTION ON THE CREW CONSIST ISSUE

• to put BN on equal footing with its rail competitors •

BN'S AGGRESSIVE AND UNPRECEDENTED plan to challenge the unions to revise work rules and manning and work practices took a real blow when the courts approved the use of secondary picketing. If employees had gone on strike against BN in protest of such changes, they also had the right to picket the facilities of other railroads. That would soon have brought most, if not all, railroad service in the country to a halt. At that point, the courts and Congress would have issued orders and/or passed legislation requiring employees to return to work, and probably would also have handed down the terms of settlement for the dispute between BN and its unions.

The likelihood of such action became apparent to officers at BNI and the railroad company who had hoped the strategy they planned to invoke would cause only BN to be struck. The earnings from BN's non-rail holdings would enable the company to take a long strike if necessary to achieve the fundamental changes they were looking for. Once it became apparent that instead, secondary picketing would occur, BN lost interest in attempting to overhaul its labor contracts and for that matter, in maintaining ownership of its railroad company. It then moved ahead with the split of its rail and non-rail based businesses.

By that time, Gerald Grinstein was on board as vice chairman of BNI. Since the strategy of confrontation had not produced the results BN had planned and hoped for, it was thought by many observers that perhaps the conciliatory, collegial spirit Grinstein had applied so successfully when he negotiated with employees at Western Airlines might be more effective in obtaining the desired changes that BN's approach had failed to produce. Thus, BN was cast out from the leadership of officers whose confrontational approach to labor had produced little if anything toward a positive outcome.

BN did not serve Section 6 notices under the Railway Labor Act, which would start the process for negotiating the changes it proposed in June 1987. Instead of giving its proxy to the Carriers Conference Committee to negotiate on its behalf, BN began holding a series of problem-solving sessions to work through issues with the heads of the unions. The outcome of the work of Presidential Emergency Board (PEB) 219 on the crew consist issue and other proposals was far more favorable for the rail industry than was anticipated by BN management. Upon learning of the board's recommendations, BN knew it would be far better to go into national handling through the Carriers Conference Committee than to continue to try to go it alone. Of course, this reversal back to national handling could apply only to matters involving the UTU groups that had filed Section 6 notices, i.e., those representing employees on the territory of the former CB&Q and Frisco railroads. Since the general chairmen representing the GN, NP, and SP&S had not filed Section 6 notices, BN could not employ national handling to deal with them on the crew consist matter or on any other issues.

For a time BN thought that withdrawal from national handling as part of the National Carriers Conference Committee would enable BN to negotiate contracts that would better meet its needs. This possibility was first considered in 1984, just before national negotiations were slated to open for a new contract. In December 1989 BN announced it would be in national handling only for health and welfare issues. At that time BN stated it did not plan to enter national negotiations for any other issues.

BREAKTHROUGH ON MILWAUKEE ROAD

The issue holding the greatest potential for reducing the head count and wage expense was over the size of crews on trains and yard switching assignments. Going back to 1963, the recommendations of a Presidential Emergency Board, and congressional action to implement them, provided railroads the means to eliminate firemen from diesel locomotives. Also in that settlement, a few brakemen's positions on designated runs could be eliminated, although most of those positions were restored in negotiations a few years later. Nothing further was accomplished in reducing train-crew personnel on any railroad until 1978, when the Milwaukee Road, by then in bankruptcy, negotiated an agreement with the UTU to reduce the crews on certain designated intermodal trains to a cConductor and engineer only, and to having only one brakeman on most of its other freight trains.

In consideration of its financial condition, the Milwaukee was able to negotiate a crew consist agreement well in advance of other roads. In its negotiations, the Milwaukee offered the incentive of operating three new intermodal trains each day and in both directions between Chicago and the Twin Cities with reduced crews. Without a reduction in crew size, the company argued these short trains would not be even modestly profitable. To get the additional jobs, the UTU agreed to allow the use of reduced crews. Operation of this new service also was part of a demonstration project sponsored by the FRA. The agreement provided for the elimination of one brakeman position on the new intermodal trains and on certain designated freight trains. Employees who worked trains with a reduced crew were entitled to payments from a productivity fund. In 1982 the Milwaukee was able to extend the agreement to cover all train and yard switching assignments.

The Milwaukee's success in getting the crew consist agreements described above caused other companies in the rail industry to begin an all-out effort (and in the face of the moratorium) to confront the UTU with demands to eliminate both brakemen on all through freight trains and to reduce to one brakeman on runs in which some amount of intermediate switching work was planned. The railroads were unsuccessful in that effort, and no progress was made under mediation on that important issue. The threat of a strike loomed again. The UTU—which was to be hit harder than any other union by the ambitious plans to reduce labor costs that BN and the other large railroads were advancing—stood to lose a large part of its membership and was determined to stand its ground on the crew consist issue.

THE REVOLUTIONARY RECOMMENDATIONS OF PEB 219

A Presidential Emergency Board (PEB) was appointed by President George H. W. Bush in 1990. The board recommended the crew consist issue be handled locally rather than having the board make a recommendation that would have to be applied on the same terms on every railroad. However, the board recommendations provided for binding arbitration in case such local negotiations reached an impasse.

Article 23 of the 1984 national agreement with the UTU contained a moratorium that forbade both management and the unions from progressing any proposal to change the portion of the agreement pertaining to car limits, train lengths, and special allowance payments, prior to the attrition of all protected employees, which would be the year 2024. The moratorium could be waived only by mutual agreement. This provision made it unlikely that any relaxation in the crew consist agreement signed in 1984 would ever come about. However, when the crew consist issue came before PEB 219 in 1990, Chairman Robert Harris had to come up with a line of reasoning to work around this restriction. He did so on the basis that since he was charged with working through issues of compensation, the PEB was within its rights to develop and issue recommendations that would supersede even the limitations in the moratorium.

Mr. Harris had served on the National Mediation Board and on the National Labor Relations Board, as staff director on a U.S. Senate committee and as an arbitrator and mediator on numerous cases in the airline and railroad industries. He had been appointed to serve on Presidential Emergency Boards by every president since Ronald Reagan. Harris was known by many as "a man of immense courage and integrity." Wendell Bell, assistant vice president in Labor Relations, at one time served with Mr. Harris on a public law board and recalled, "He [Harris] knew what changes were needed, what had been put off for decades, and was determined to get the industry there, but without savaging the employees in the process. And, astonishingly, he did it, in one fell swoop."[1]

The unions were greatly upset with the Board's recommendations on a wide range of issues and went on strike on April 17, 1991, the date the Board's recommendations were to become effective. Within 24 hours Congress took action to end the strike. It was not long before the Presidents of three unions, the UTU, the Brotherhood of Locomotive Engineers and the Transportation Communications Union (representing the Clerks) were voted out of office.

UTU members who worked on BN's "southern tier," the lines of the former CB&Q Railroad, ratified a crew consist agreement on October 28, 1991. This vote was especially important for BN since a law passed by Congress following a pro-longed dispute allowed the C&NW to eliminate one Brakeman position on its crews effective May 22, 1989. In December, 1991, about two and a half years later, the C&NW and the UTU agreed to terms for elimination of the second Brakeman position, which reduced its crews to a Conductor and Engineer only.[2] Having that agreement in place gave the C&NW a real competitive advantage in negotiating rates for moving coal. A crew consist agreement governing the C&S and FW&D railways had been ratified seven years before, in 1984.

1 Wendell A. Bell, retired Labor Relations attorney, BN and BNSF, conversations and e-mails with author.

2 H. Roger Grant, *The NorthWestern: A History of the Chicago and North Western Railway System,* 241.

INTRANSIGENCE ON NORTHERN TIER OF BN'S NETWORK

On the "northern tier," the lines of the former GN, NP, and SP&S, it took five years, from 1988 to 1993 for BN to finally gain the benefit of an agreement allowing it to reduce the size of its train and yard crews. Once it would have an agreement covering the northern tier, BN projected it would achieve savings of about $100 million per year, enough to reduce its operating ratio by two points. Getting an agreement in place became a top priority matter for BN. Its progress was watched closely by the investment community and by customers and competitors. The number of employees to be reduced in train and yard service would be in the range of 1,100 to 1,500 of the approximately 3,500 UTU-represented employees working on its northern tier. The process of obtaining an agreement with UTU officers representing those employees proved to be a lengthy, frustrating, and divisive issue between management and a group of employees who were a primary and very important link in BN's system for service delivery.

Employees in each of the three former roads that made up the northern tier were represented by a general chairman. However, Mel Winter, who represented those working on the former GN territory, clearly stood out as the spokesman and leader of the group of three general chairman. Winter showed no inclination to negotiate an agreement and appeared to have no concern for BN's need to be cost competitive with the other railroads that already had crew consist agreements in place, including its major competitors, the C&NW, and Union Pacific.

Winter hired out as a Brakeman on the GN at Willmar, Minnesota, and soon became active in union matters. He advanced quickly to the position of general chairman for the road crews on the entire GN system. He grew up in St. Cloud and had wanted to start his railroad career there, but when he learned the GN was not hiring there, he was able to get hired at Willmar. Winter was instrumental in developing the implementing agreements needed to put the plan for train operations into effect on the consolidated railroad. Most of BN's "preferred route" for trains running between Minneapolis and Seattle was to be on lines built by the former GN.

One of the two exceptions in which the NP's main line was designated as part of the preferred route was the segment between Minneapolis and Casselton, North Dakota, a connection between the NP and GN lines about twenty-five miles west of Fargo. To enable the former GN employees based at Willmar and St. Cloud to follow their work to the NP line, Willmar crews were given seven allocations, and two allocations went to St. Cloud crews in the NP's chain-gang pool, which consisted of twenty-two crews at the time. GN employees who were forced to take these allocations had to relocate to Minneapolis. As would be expected, there was some friction between those with a GN pedigree and the NP employees who found they had to share what had been exclusively their work with a new element of people who had been their rivals for nearly a hundred years.

Mel Winter was the representative for the GN road crews who lost their positions in the chain-gang pools at Willmar and St. Cloud when nearly all of their trains were shifted to the former NP route. Together with the abandonment of several branch and secondary lines in central Minnesota, there was very little work left for crews based at St. Cloud. Those crews and several other from Willmar were forced to take the allocations in the chain gang based at Northtown. This was a tough blow for the St. Cloud and Willmar employees, and it struck right in the territory where Winter began his career and still held seniority.

In handling the crew consist issue of the late 1980s, Winter decided in 1988 not to file the standard Section 6 notice to the company as required under the Railway Labor Act, to indicate desire to amend provisions in the existing contract between the UTU (i.e., in Winter's "territory") and the company that would expire in 1988. Nor did BN serve a Section 6 notice on the UTU for employees working under the GN contract. In writing for *Traffic World*, Ira Rosenfeld described how the Section 6 notice fit into the negotiating process and why it was not used by either party in this case:

> The Section 6 notice is the first step in the lengthy negotiation process spelled out in the Railway Labor Act. Issuance of a notice . . . advises the other side of the desire, within 30 days, to change the existing labor agreement . . . If no agreement is reached, either party may request mediation by the National Mediation Board . . . There is no requirement to accept a settlement. Local union members say their reasons for not filing Section 6 notices are rooted in mistrust of both their employer and the UTU's national leadership. Burlington Northern officials publically say they waited for the union to make the first move. Privately, they say it is not in their interest to file the notices, "not because we will eventually get a cheaper deal, but because we will get one better suited for BN."[3]

When the company notified Winter that it wished to begin local negotiations on a new crew consist agreement, as required in the PEB's report, Winter announced that because he had never served a Section 6 notice on the company, he was not governed by the PEB's report. When challenged to explain why he had failed to issue a Section 6 notice, Winter replied, "The BN is not serious in reaching a settlement. They want to break the union. We haven't talked to them at all. We just don't trust them."[4] In another interview, he stated, "The carrier likes to say that they have changed and relations have improved with the workers, but it is all just lip service."[5]

International officers of the UTU said that because the outcome in the PEB's report was so unfavorable, it turned out that Winter made the right decision by not entering into national handling and risking real damage from the outcome. In defense of BN's decision not to have filed a Section 6 notice, James Dagnon, senior vice president–Labor Relations, was quoted as saying, "Today's railroads are more diverse than just western and eastern, rich and poor. It is harder to get a [national] consensus on what fits than it is working alone."[6]

Also at that time, Dagnon reported that BN and the unions were participating in joint problem-solving talks. He said that progress was slow because "We are not used to the local level and we have to learn that we can trust each other." Dagnon added there had been no meaningful progress in the negotiations, which by that time had dragged on for fifteen months.[7]

3 Ira Rosenfeld, "3,500 Burlington Northern Workers Boycott National Rail Labor Talks," *Traffic World*, April 15, 1991.

4 Ira Rosenfeld, "Burlington Northern and Unions Dance, but It's Not Clear Which Is Leading," *Traffic World*, December 11, 1989.

5 Rosenfeld, "3,500 Burlington Northern Workers Boycott National Rail Labor Talks."

6 Rosenfeld, "Burlington Northern and Unions Dance, but It's Not Clear Which Is Leading."

7 Rosenfeld, "Burlington Northern and Unions Dance, but It's Not Clear Which Is Leading."

To add to the complexity of handling these negotiations locally, Gerald Grinstein, vice chairman of BNI at that time, sent a letter over his signature to employees, advising that BN intended to negotiate locally instead of nationally. Grinstein sent this letter while Darius Gaskins still was president and CEO of BN's railroad company. Grinstein succeeded Gaskins later, in 1988. With the success Grinstein had had several years earlier in negotiating with unions on the terms for the merger of Western Airlines with Delta (Grinstein was president and CEO of Western at that time), it appears he felt he could also be successful in settling issues between BN and its unions. The task turned out to be more challenging and complex than perhaps Grinstein or anyone else could have anticipated. It may be that so much distrust and resentment had built up through the 1980s, from all of the highly controversial issues created in those years, that it proved to be impossible to make meaningful progress even on an issue as important and complex as getting this new agreement had become.

As would be expected, personalities came into play as well. Even Grinstein's record of success in working with labor, his leadership skills, and other favorable attributes alone were not enough to move BN toward settlement of the crew consist issue. Part of the process BN used to force the UTU to get serious about the need for a crew consist agreement for its northern tier was to get a ruling from the National Mediation Board (NMB) that BN was not required to deal with all the individual general chairman representing each of the former roads that made up BN. With a favorable ruling, the UTU would have to designate a single representative to negotiate with BN. Individual general chairmen such as Mel Winter would no longer hold the power to negotiate for the group of employees they had been elected to represent. The NMB ruled in BN's favor, that since BN was "one company," each union should designate a single representative.

BN then advised the international offices of the union that it would no longer deal with all of the individual local officers, and that they should designate a single representative as their negotiator. The UTU did not respond. Late in 1991, BN sought arbitration on the issue of getting a crew consist agreement in place to cover its northern tier. BN made this request after a federal court ruled against the union's suit that was intended to block BN from implementing the PEB ruling. The court ruled that BN and the UTU should take their case back to the NMB. However, the arbitration panel ruled it did not have jurisdiction to settle the dispute, since neither BN nor the UTU had filed Section 6 notices. As a result, the arbitration panel ruled that BN and the UTU were exempt from the terms the PEB put forth for other railroad companies that had remained in national handling. BN appealed to a federal court to overturn the arbitration panel's ruling, arguing that its decision could place BN at a competitive disadvantage. As would be expected, Winter stated, "The panel did a terrific job."[8]

THE UTU "INTERNATIONAL" MOVES IN

The crew consist issue was finally resolved when officers of the UTU International decided to intervene. Although the International had held to a position of "hands off" and allowed the UTU locals on the GN, NP, and SP&S to handle the matter per past practice, it apparently found it untenable to have crew consist agreements in place on all other railroads, and on every other part of BN except on the northern tier. An agreement covering UTU–represented employees on the northern tier was reached in March 1993. It provided for severance payments up to $80,000 per employee. Employees who became surplus could choose not to accept the voluntary separation payment and instead be paid $60,000 over a period of eighteen to forty-eight months, as designated by the employee. If not recalled to active service by the end of that period, those employees could remain in volunteer surplus status, but without compensation, until recalled. If an employee declined either or both of those options, he or she would be placed on reserve status and be paid at 75 percent of their previous twelve months' earnings, or at 75 percent of the basic five-day yard-helper rate, whichever amount was greater. Employees in reserve status were required to return to active status within fifteen days of being recalled. Also, they would be called back to work ahead of employees who had elected to take the $60,000 payment and be placed on volunteer surplus

8 "BN Asks Court to Order Mediation in Labor Dispute," *Traffic World*, January 27, 1992.

status. In addition, all employees on the northern tier received a signing bonus of $5,000.[9]

Certain terms in the agreement governing the northern tier were "sweeter" than those provided in the agreement covering the southern tier that was made a few years earlier. BN agreed to extend all of the terms that were more favorable in the agreement just made for the northern tier to employees on its southern tier.

The failure of BN management to be able to negotiate a crew consist agreement with UTU officers representing employees on the northern corridor may have been the result of a buildup of animosity over unprecedented initiatives such as the strategy that led to the creation of Montana Rail Link, the pain endured by many people following the Frisco merger, and the demeaning attitude of some senior executives toward the railroad as a business, the work performed by its employees, and their level of compensation. No other North American railroad company had set up confrontations of these types in attempting to reach an agreement on the crew consist issue. It is fair to say that BN gained little or nothing from the strategies it employed to try to force the union representing operating employees on the northern tier to back down.

However, this long story about the confrontation BN had over the crew consist issue on the northern tier was not the result of an attitude of vengeance or misguided reasoning, although it might have been part of the problem. According to many employees, Winter simply did not believe that freight trains should be run with a two-person crew and no caboose. He chose to protect the old style of operation with every weapon he had. He set out to do everything possible to stop, or at least to delay, the reduction of employment that would result from a crew consist agreement. He was not on the side of the employees who wanted him to sign an agreement that would provide them the severance payment of as much as $80,000 so they could afford to leave BN and pursue other employment opportunities. Instead, Winter was adamant that the number of jobs in train service that the company was required to fill under existing agreements would not be compromised to any extent.

Through all of this confrontation with BN management, Mel Winter, as the general chairman of the UTU representing Conductors and Brakemen operating under the contract with the former GN, became a folk hero to many employees. It was reported that Mel received standing ovations at meetings he held with employees during and following the time of confrontation with BN management on the Winona Bridge issue. Employees believed Mel's "one-man stand" on that issue kept BN from imposing either a system of reduced compensation, or one that would shift some or all of its business to the new low cost carrier. The old adage, "People will behave according to the way they've been treated," may apply here as well. Thus ended the long, stressful ordeal BN had been under to obtain a crew consist agreement that would place it on a competitive footing across its system. It had been a long struggle, and much work lay ahead of BN management at all levels to rebuild morale and get employees to focus on matters that would improve safety, service and general operating proficiency. As chairman of the General Chairman's Association (consisting of all of the general chairmen of the unions representing both operating and non-operating crafts on BN), Winter's strategy and attitude appeared to have had considerable influence on employees and union leaders throughout the company.

It is important to note that of all the crafts within the railroad's workforce, the conductors, brakemen and firemen (the firemen also were represented by a UTU predecessor) took the biggest hit in the railroads' efforts over the past fifty years to reduce employment and wage expense. This started with the elimination of Firemen, followed by the loss of jobs at the end of passenger service, the reduction of local and branch-line service, increasing train length, operating fewer work trains to unload track material, and the elimination of cabooses and full-crew laws still in effect in several states. With a crew consist agreement in place, the conductor was the sole remaining UTU–represented employee on a crew. He or she would now have to ride the locomotive instead of the caboose and do the head brakeman's work as well as the conductor's, a major shift in the culture and work environment of a train crew.

9 Burlington Northern Railroad Annual Report for 1994.

CHAPTER 27

INTRODUCTION OF REGIONAL GANGS

• to achieve stability and improved productivity •

ANOTHER OUTCOME FROM THE WORK OF PEB 219 was the provision for allowing large track gangs to work beyond the limits of the historic and small seniority districts. It was highly inefficient for railroads to have to disband such gangs when they had completed their work in one district and the company was ready to move the gang's track machinery and gang supervisors to a project within another seniority district. Having to abolish all of the jobs and leave the workers behind who had been working on the gang and then bring on an entirely new set of workers was a disruptive, very costly, inefficient, and slow process.

Often, time was required to qualify a new set of machine operators. Under the labor agreement, they had to be allowed thirty days to satisfy the management that they had become qualified to operate the particular machine they bid on. If they were disqualified or if they decided they did not want to operate that machine, the employee next in line had to be afforded the same opportunity. While this was going on, there was no qualified operator available to run the machine. If too few employees bid on positions in the gang, the company would have to hire new employees and train them. The employees who were on the gang while it was working in the previous district had to exercise seniority on whatever positions they could hold. Often, there were not enough vacancies available for all displaced employees, and some would have to be furloughed.

One of the rulings of the PEB made it permissible to establish large production gangs on a system or regional basis. This allowed the gang members to cross seniority lines and stay with the gang for the duration of its programmed work. It gave them a good change to be employed on the gang for its entire work season. Those employees were provided lodging, an allowance for meals, and reimbursement of expenses to return home on their scheduled days off. Very importantly, the rate of pay for employees working on the regional gangs was about 30 percent higher than on comparable positions that did not involve extensive work away from home.

As a result, the skill level of employees and the productivity of the gangs increased. These jobs became very popular with maintenance-of-way employees. We usually received many more bids than we had positions on the gang. With a turnover rate that was much lower, employees were able to get used to working with each other, and a solid, competent team of workers evolved early in the maintenance season. When the gang was disbanded at the end of the work season, employees could exercise their seniority on local section gangs or track-inspector positions. Employees who did not wish to be away from home for up to two weeks or so at a time on a regional or system gang could continue to work on jobs in a local area instead. No one could be forced to take a job on one of the large regional or system gangs.

The recommendations developed by the members of PEB 219 gave railroad companies what they needed to revise work rules and manning practices that had restricted them from the flexibility they needed to improve their service, to become more cost competitive with other modes of transportation, and to improve the efficiency and quality of work performed by large track maintenance crews. The changes in labor matters that quickly evolved from the PEB recommendations were as important to railroads as the freedom in pricing they gained under deregulation and in adopting new technology. The PEB board members demonstrated remarkable insight, understanding, and appreciation of what the railroads needed to break out of the bonds of old labor practices that were holding them back and, in the long run, depriving railroad employees from the chance to have a career in an industry that would have a good future.

Chairman Robert Harris deserves a great deal of credit for the leadership he applied in preparing recommendations that led to such substantive results. On the day that two other carrier representatives and I gave a presentation before the board on the need for updating the work rules governing large track-maintenance gangs, we could sense from the questions asked by Harris and his fellow board members that they were seeking the kind of background information and arguments they would need to support the changes we advocated. During the hearings, Harris was very firm in dealing with attempts to distract the board from the points we made as a team. He became very impatient when bluster and frivolous challenges were made by the opposition. Harris even took time to compliment us during a break following our testimony. Needless to say, we were well pleased when we saw that our recommendations for changes were largely adopted by the board in its report. Harris deserves a great deal of credit for his part in overhauling many outmoded aspects of railroad labor practices.

CHAPTER 28

REFLECTIONS ON STRATEGIES EMPLOYED IN THE 1980S

how best to achieve fundamental change

IT IS INTERESTING TO REFLECT ON THE approach BN took regarding labor strategy beginning in the early 1980s and up to 1988 when the resource-based units of BN were separated. What came out of all the turmoil, tension, and anxiety that was created in those years? Did BN accomplish any more from the approach it took with labor compared to the measured and much more "standard" approach the other large, successful railroads maintained in those years? How much opportunity to enlist support from employees on issues of mutual concern to the industry and its employees was lost? What was gained from the public pronouncements of some senior officers that expressed contempt and ridicule of the work performed by railroad employees, and the record of success they and the company had built in its early years? In retrospect, it appears things could have been done better, under a more affirmative approach to labor strategy. It seems likely that better results could have been obtained in a shorter period of time, and a lot of grief could have been avoided for both rail workers and management.

From 1981 to 1990, BN reduced employment 40 percent, from 55,347 to 32,905. This reduction was made by applying new technology, implementing the best practices for managing maintenance and operating costs, and selling marginal branch lines. The amount of business handled by its employees grew nearly fourfold, from 60.9 billion revenue ton-miles to 234.3 billion. Employee productivity increased from 1.278 million revenue ton-miles per employee to 7.120 million. With the overall reduction of about 50 percent in rates that had to be made to retain business in the years after deregulation, BN and other railroads were forced to aggressively reduce their operating costs. With the entry of the C&NW into the Powder River Basin in 1984, BN had to reduce its rates enough to retain as much business as possible. Together with the tonnage the C&NW was able to capture, BN suffered a decline of $578 million in coal revenue. Richard Bressler expressed to a writer for *Forbes* magazine, "The sad part of it is, even with 20,000 people gone, the dollar cost of our wages is about equal to what it was four or five years ago. If we hadn't done it, the railroad would be bankrupt by now."[1]

Even with the large reduction in employment, BN's labor costs still were too high to enable it to price competitively with non-union truckload carriers. Bressler added that the efficiency of capital had to be employed to overcome the inefficiency of labor, but even that, together with the large reduction in the workforce, was not enough. It was unlikely that an agreement could be made in the foreseeable future with the unions to reduce basic wage rates, unlike what the workers in the auto industry and some other manufacturing sectors had agreed to concessions when pressed by the leaders of struggling industries.

In the rail industry, being able to continue paying high wages over several decades has required management to make large and on-going reductions in the number of people on the payroll. Large, fundamental changes in

1 James Cook, "All Alone by the Telephone," *Forbes*, November 16, 1987.

costly work rules and manning requirements have been possible only through outside intervention, through Presidential Emergency Boards congressional legislation, or the rulings of arbitrators. As a result, rail workers continue to be among the highest paid of any group of industrial workers in North America.

During the times of confrontation with organized labor on wage rates, manning, and other work rules, the basic truths, values, and character traits that are vital to building and maintaining constructive relationships became self-evident. Clearly, efforts to manage by the use of fear and intimidation were counterproductive to the need for both parties to define areas of common interest and concern that they should focus on. They needed to find ways that would help them understand each other's needs, and then negotiate agreements that would move the company and its people forward.

A mean-spirited, demeaning style of leadership should not be tolerated at any level of management in dealing with employees, or by managers in dealing with each other at any level of the organization. Likewise, crude, vulgar, threatening, and vindictive language must not be used when issuing directives, criticisms, or orders for corrective action. Generally, the ways in which people behave and respond will reflect the way in which they have been treated. BN lost a lot of ground in the 1980s by the attitudes and unduly aggressive approach to employees and unions used by some of its officers, as well as the kinds of strategies they tried to employ to bring about change.

The problem was not in having a historic "command and control," militaristic culture in place—railroad people recognize and accept the need for structure, order, and consistency in conducting operations and maintenance activities. Rather, it was the use of threats and the demeaning behavior of many managers of that time. Important decisions affecting the employees' future and that of the railroad itself were being formulated and carried out by a few leaders who showed little respect for them, either individually or as a group, or even for the company those managers were working for.

The years of turmoil on BN manifested how vital it is to have leaders in place who have the trust and respect needed to make progress on matters of safety and other matters of high priority. Having such capability is vital in the unforgiving environment of rail operations. To get employees on board with a program for continuous improvement in safety and service performance, and to gain their support for introducing new technology and updated work practices, a spirit of trust and confidence must be established. That spirit must be nourished by having managers at all levels of management who demonstrate they know the business of railroading, who want to run "a good railroad." They must show that they believe in the business of railroading, that it has a good future if it is run right. Company officers must be able to demonstrate they have the ability and the resolve to fix problem situations, have the influence needed to correct legitimate problems, and know how to recognize and take advantage of new opportunities that will make an operation run better.

They must be seen as fair and approachable, and be known and trusted to follow through on their commitments. Employees must be treated like professionals by managers at all levels showing respect for what they do, day in and day out, to make the railroad run well. Managers must be willing to listen to input from the people who are doing the work of the railroad for their ideas on how things could and should be improved, and for early warnings on problems that need to be dealt with and not allowed to fester and become big issues.

With relationships and a culture of this kind, employees, union representatives, and managers can become united behind efforts that will help grow the business, make progress in meeting the company's standards for service and financial performance, meet the challenge the company will face during downturns in business, or in dealing with afflictions from external causes. Railroading is a tough, unforgiving business, but employees do not expect sympathy or have to be coaxed along. Instead, they expect to be treated fairly and have a management in place that is known to be good at the business of railroading. There must be a strong corps of leaders who can be counted on to make decisions that are smart and sound for the benefit of everyone concerned. Employees will then have respect their company as a good place to work, in which the rewards and job satisfaction are more than simply getting a paycheck. With good morale, and the spirits of confidence and trust imbedded in that culture, employees will apply their skills and talents in support of sound efforts to make the operation safer, more orderly, and better disciplined.

PART VI

SAFETY: REBUILDING THE FOUNDATION

CHAPTER 29

SAFETY IN TIMES OF TURMOIL AND RAPID CHANGE

• heading off the distractions to keep focused on the work • maintaining safety as the first priority for everyone at all times and on every task • keeping your eye "on the ball" •

THE EARLY 1980S WERE A TIME OF TURMOIL and tension on BN. This was brought on by the new culture imposed by the senior leaders who moved in with the Frisco merger, as well as with the massive reductions in personnel being made across the board. A large number of the company officers who had at least thirty years of service, making them qualified for retirement, left within a few months. A great deal of managerial strength, knowledge, and expertise was lost within a few months. While that opened up many opportunities for younger operating and maintenance officers to advance, not all of them were ready to effectively handle the responsibilities of a higher-level job, and some needed time to grow into their new assignments.

Despite those disruptions and the amount of distraction caused by the chaos and tension that ensued, safety did not deteriorate in those years, as one might have expected. From the vantage I had as a region vice president–General Manager in those years, I attribute that to the resolve of region and division officers not to let that happen. Good progress in improving safety had been made on BN, and the leaders in field operations and maintenance simply would not allow it to be taken away from them and the people they supervised.

Also, when times get tough, such as when layoffs occur, and the priorities and operating practices are changing, people will pay closer attention to their work. With the tension and uncertainties they face, they are not complacent, and they do not take safety for granted out on the job. Together, these "new negatives" cause them to pay more attention to what they are doing, making them less prone to becoming victims of complacency or inattention. In any event, the employees and their managers worked well together in those times to keep safety from deteriorating. They accomplished this by their own volition. For the most part, safety was given no particular attention, nor was much concern for safety expressed on a day-to-day basis by most senior-level officers in those years. This is not to say they did not care about safety, but only that a concern for safety was not openly manifested in their leadership style or their set of values. BN people—who had grown and developed under the style of leadership we had before these changes in management came about—noted that less top-down emphasis was being given to safety. It was up to managers and employees at the division and shop levels to continue to manage and direct safety, as they had been taught.

A SERIOUS SETBACK IN SAFETY

Starting in 1985, safety took a reversal on BN. In the next six years, it became steadily worse. In this book I am not speculating or stating my opinion on what was behind that unfavorable trend. I will leave that to others who were there, working for the company at that time. By 1991 the frequency ratio had deteriorated to 13, which made BN by far the poorest performer in safety of any of the large railroad systems. In 1993 John Chain was put in charge of safety. General Chain had been hired in 1991 to head the Operating Department as executive vice president, after retiring from the U.S. Air Force, where he headed the Strategic Air Command. Only two years later, he was reassigned and directed to put all of his efforts into overcoming BN's dismal record on safety. In his new role, Chain retained the title of executive vice president.

With the strength of Chain's leadership qualities and the resources and authority he had command of, BN's performance in safety was turned around very quickly and impressively. He led the BN team very well in making the railroad a much safer place to work. By 1994 the frequency ratio was reduced to 3.9, down to about where it had been ten years before. In BN's annual report for 1994, Chain was given a very high, well-deserved tribute for the success of his efforts: "Jack Chain . . . took on the challenge of making BN injury-free in 1992. The record to date and the high expectations for the future are to a very large measure the result of his tireless work." Of course, credit for this kind of success does not rest solely with Chain. It took the commitment and strong desire of people across all of BN, in all specialties, and at all levels to resolve to work once again at the standard and level of professional capability needed to run a safe railroad.

Chain established himself as a real champion of safety. He went out into the field to listen to employees, and then responded aggressively and quickly to deal with complaints about conditions affecting safety and morale. Employees saw that he had the authority to make decisions to correct conditions, adopt improved work practices, and acquire better tools and equipment. Chain used that authority effectively, which helped win the hearts and minds of the employees. Chain related especially well to the train crews, whom he likened to the flight crews, who were considered the real core of the Air Force. He was able to inspire employees to work at their best, with pride and knowledge that there were high level people in the company who respected them and the work they did on the railroad.

For a host of reasons and anecdotes that could be cited, Chain had not been a good fit as the head of the Operating Department. Some of the problems in morale he encountered in leading safety might have been, at least in part, the result of the hyper-critical, negative ways in which it is said he sometimes treated the junior-level officers who were doing their best in working through the tough day-to-day problems that arise in running a railroad. However, serving as the head of safety was a perfect fit for Chain at that time in BN's history. The record speaks for itself.

Too often in the past, people assigned to lead the Safety Department of a railway company were capable, respected operating and maintenance officers whose careers had peaked. However, they were not always the best suited for the responsibilities of a chief safety officer. While the basic accountability for safety rests with the line operating and maintenance officers, it still takes a good Safety Department at the headquarters level to develop new programs and methods to meet current and new challenges, and to help keep the awareness for safety at a high level in the organization. With the leadership skills Chain had mastered in his military career, he clearly had those capabilities and much more. BN was fortunate he did not leave the company when he was replaced as the head of operations. In the years since BNSF was formed in 1995 safety has continued to improve. The frequency ratio was soon reduced to less than 2.0, which put BNSF close to the level of the best performers in the rail industry.

CHAPTER 30

MAKING THE OPERATION SAFER

• three serious accidents in 1984 • the urgency to recover, restore, and rebuild safety • understanding and overcoming the root causes of accidents and injuries •

A COLLISION AT WIGGINS, COLORADO

Although the overall trend in the frequency ratio for employee injuries had become more favorable by the mid-1980s, that record was clouded by three serious train accidents in 1984. The first accident occurred at Wiggins, Colorado, between two opposing trains in CTC territory. Five crew members were killed and two were injured. The National Transportation Safety Board (NTSB) determined the cause to be failure of the crew of one train "to comply with restrictive signal aspects.[1] . . . Contributing to the failure of the Engineer and Fireman was their consumption of alcohol and fatigue resulting from their voluntary lack of sleep during their off-duty time, aggravated by irregular work/rest cycles."[2]

COLLISION AT NEWCASTLE, WYOMING

The second accident occurred at Pedro, Wyoming, a siding near Newcastle, nine days later. In its report, the NTSB stated, "the probable cause of the Newcastle accident was the failure of the Engineer and Head Brakeman of Extra 7843 East to operate their train in compliance with restrictive signal aspects because they were asleep or, in the case of the Engineer, otherwise impaired. Contributing to their failure was the use of marijuana by the Engineer, as well as the fatigue of the Engineer and Head Brakeman due to their voluntary lack of sleep and unpredictable working hours."[3]

---

1 The NTSB's use of the term "aspects" instead of "indication" is in error. A signal "aspect" is what a crew member sees, i.e., the color of one or more signal lights. A signal "indication" is the definition or statement of what a crew is supposed to do upon observing a given aspect. That may be to stop the train or reduce its speed to a maximum number of miles per hour. If a signal aspect is green, the indication is "clear" and the crew may then operate the train at the speed authorized at that location. If it is red, the train must be stopped before any part of it passes that signal.

2 NTSB Report No. NTSB/RAR-85/04, "Railroad Accident Report, Head-on Collision of Burlington Northern Railroad Freight Trains Extra 6714 West and Extra 7820 East, Wiggins, Colorado, April 13, 1984 and Rear-end Collision of Burlington Northern Railroad Freight Trains Extra 7843 East and Extra ATSF 8112 East Near Newcastle, Wyoming, April 22, 1984." Note this was a "combined" report, covering both accidents.

3 NTSB Report No. NTSB/RAR-85/04, "Railroad Accident Report."

To this day, it is distressing and unnerving to recall the circumstances surrounding these accidents. The loss of life and the factors contributing to these accidents were alarming, to say the least. Further, it was disturbing to read the NTSB's criticisms of BN's supervision of train operations on the Alliance Division where these accidents occurred. Following are highlights from that part of the NTSB's report:

1 Concerning the accident at Wiggins:
   - First line supervisors (trainmasters and road foremen of engines) were not getting out on their territory at night, nor were they riding trains as often as they should.
   - There was a lack of resolve on the part of local supervisors to support the effort of the owner of the lodging facility at Akron (the away-from-home terminal of crews) to forbid "alcoholic beverages and illegal drugs" from the premises.
   - The NTSB surmised that the efficiency tests (on-the-job "surprise" tests made of crews to assess compliance and proficiency on the operating rules) were not of the quality sufficient to be effective.

2 Concerning the accident near Newcastle:
   - The NTSB surmised that operating supervisors did not work at night and that there was little contact between the crews, working between Edgemont and Gillette, and their supervisors, who were alleged to be overloaded with administrative functions that confined them to their offices.
   - Operating officers were found to be young and inexperienced, as were the crews they supervised. The NTSB alleged that the supervisors of that territory had been given insufficient training on the operating rules, limiting their effectiveness in their role, not only as "enforcers," but also as "teachers" who were able to interpret and communicate on the application of rules with the employees they supervised.
   - The NTSB believed that because traffic in the territory had at least doubled in the five years preceding the accident (actually, traffic had increased by ten-fold over the ten years preceding the accident), the number of supervisory positions, specifically at Edgemont, was inadequate. In fact, two such positions had been abolished not long before this accident.[4]
   - The NTSB went on to accuse BN of a general failure to "keep supervisory levels apace of traffic appear to be a direct result of BN management policy. The senior vice president of regional operations said he believed BN ought to rely more heavily on Conductors and Engineers for the management of its train operations and, thus, avoid over-managing the employees. . . . The Safety Board believes that it is absurd for BN management to charge its supervisors with the responsibility for training and testing the employees to gain their increased compliance with its rules, and then justify reducing the supervisory force on the premise that the employees ought to be able to supervise themselves."

A QUESTION OF PROFICIENCY OF FIELD SUPERVISORY OFFICERS

Clearly, the NTSB's report contained strong statements about the quality of the supervisors it interviewed or otherwise learned about in the course of its investigation. At the time of the accident near Newcastle, BN had some excellent, seasoned officers in place—assistant superintendents, trainmasters, and road foremen of engines—who were experts in the operating rules and procedures, as well as the labor agreements and the standards of service at which the operation was to be run. Certainly not all supervisors were lacking in experience and general competency. There were some officers in place on the division who understood the priorities of their jobs.

Among those priorities was to know the competency of the operating crews working in their territory, to make quality efficiency tests according to the company's standards, to require compliance with operating rules and safe work practices, and to be out on the railroad with their people close to 100 percent of the time and not

4 See page 168 for details on staffing levels on the Alliance Division during the years of rapid growth in the number of employees working in train operations.

confined to their offices. Those officers had the confidence and experience needed to coach and train employees, especially those who were newly hired as brakemen and those recently promoted to conductor or engineer. Before they were assigned to what had become the most challenging division to manage, they had established a record of success in their careers. Any of them would have come through with high ratings had they been interviewed and evaluated by the NTSB. To what extent, if any, those experienced officers were interviewed was not covered in the NTSB's report.

At that time, there also were some young, largely untested, inexperienced officers assigned to this heavy territory. The NTSB's statement on the level of experience and overall capability of those officers is based on the facts and information from those interviewed. For some of them, it was like they had been "thrown to the wolves." Instead of being given their first assignment on the toughest division on BN, they should first have been assigned to light-density territories or terminals where the pace was slower and they could be closely supervised and mentored by their bosses and other more experienced officers. Putting younger officers out on the most demanding territories on the railroad, where there were unprecedented challenges, was not fair to them, their bosses, the workers they supervised, or the company. The Alliance Division was no place for amateurs. As mentioned earlier, many of the officers on that division were more experienced, technically competent, capable, and had been selected for positions on the Alliance Division from a list of those who were promotable, young enough to have a lot of energy, and eager to "show their stuff" in the "big leagues" of railroading.

It should be noted that the Alliance Division was not the only place of great challenge in those years. The Nebraska Division (named the Lincoln Division until 1976) and much of the Chicago Region also had hired large numbers of new people. The managers on those territories also had the everyday challenge of getting large numbers of trains over the road safely and on schedule in the face of the massive track upgrading projects underway. Among the locations of great challenge on the Chicago Region were Galesburg, Aurora, Beardstown, and Centralia, Illinois; and Ottumwa and Creston in Iowa. Many of the officers who held these very demanding supervisory positions in those years on the Alliance Division and the other territories just mentioned advanced to much higher levels in the Operating Department in the next several years. To be clear: contrary to how the NTSB characterized the level of competency of our supervisors, we did not have an "amateur hour" with no competent people out there running the show at all places and at all times.

COLLISION AT MOTLEY, MINNESOTA

The third major human-caused accident in 1982 occurred near Motley, Minnesota, on June 14. Two opposing trains collided head-on on a single-track line operated under timetable and train order authority. There was no signal system (ABS or CTC) in service on this subdivision. The dispatcher cleared a coal train to operate eastbound from Staples, but overlooked a westbound empty coal train, thereby setting up the conflict in granting authority for the eastbound train for movement on the main track. Three employees were killed and four were injured, one seriously. The cost of damage to cars and locomotives was $3.9 million.

The dispatcher had been qualified for service only a short time before the accident occurred. In the NTSB's report (Report No. NTSB/RAR-85/06) of the accident, the NTSB noted the dispatcher was working his second tour of duty since being qualified for that position. Further, he had no experience in railroad operations before he was admitted to the course for training new dispatchers. In a recent consolidation of division dispatching offices, some experienced dispatchers had elected not to follow their work, which created the need to train new dispatchers. The NTSB was critical of the process BN used in selecting and training candidates for dispatching positions, and also of the lack of oversight on the part of the chief dispatcher on duty at the time of the accident.

Post-toxological testing of the blood of two of the crew members who were killed in the accident revealed blood-alcohol concentrations of 0.13 percent and 0.138 percent. When the FRA announced that finding, the engineer's family and many of his co-workers expressed indignation toward the FRA. Throughout his career, the engineer had been known to be a teetotaler. To have him charged with the consumption of alcohol, and with that some culpability to the cause of the accident, was completely wrong, based on their knowledge and observation of his conduct in his long career. Because of this reaction of indignation, the FRA decided to have tests conducted at two other laboratories. In the evaluation of the two new tests, toxicologists concluded the presence of alcohol was due to fermentation that occurred in the span of several hours from the time of the accident to the time the engineer's body was recovered in the wreckage.

The NTSB stated, "expert toxological opinion indicated that all of the alcohol could have been accounted for by postmortem decomposition was the source of the detected alcohol levels." Following its analysis of the specimens, the toxocogist of the Minnesota Bureau of Criminal Apprehension advised the NTSB, "my opinion, that the majority, if not all of the alcohol that was found in the blood, is from bacterial decomposition." The NTSB added, "There is a lack of clinical data regarding postmortem alcohol generation." A separate test conducted by the Armed Forces Institute of Pathology confirmed the conclusion of the Minnesota state agency.

To his credit, the FRA administrator, John Riley, traveled to Superior and met with the families of the employees and apologized for the statement that the engineer had alcohol in his system at the time of the accident. It goes without saying that those days were a time of extreme stress and difficulty for the engineer's family, his co-workers, and the entire family of BN people. For the three surviving crew members, urinalysis testing for alcohol and drugs were negative. Neither blood nor tissue samples could be obtained for one of the engineers due to the extreme severity of the fire and injuries that destroyed most of the tissue.

In its statement of the cause of the accident, the NTSB was critical of BN's methods of selecting, training and supervision of dispatchers: "The National Transportation Safety Board determines that the probable cause of this accident was the Burlington Northern Railroad's inadequate selection criteria which resulted in the placement of an individual without sufficient training and supervision into the safety critical position of train dispatcher."

INITIATIVES TAKEN TO MAKE THE OPERATION SAFER

Each of the three serious accidents in 1984 occurred in a different type of operation and in three different areas of the railroad. The collision at Wiggins was on the main line between Chicago and Denver. Wiggins is twenty-four miles west of Brush, the junction of that main line and the Brush–Northport–Alliance line. Heavy tonnages of coal were moving on the Brush–Denver segment, although the trains involved in the collision at Wiggins were handling general merchandise of "mixed" commodity, single-car shipments. Before the "coal boom," this line was operated mainly for West Coast merchandise and passenger trains moving between Chicago and Denver.

Newcastle was in the heart of the coal territory, on the main corridor between Edgemont and Gillette, where the number of trains per day had increased from generally four to six per day to thirty or more in a period of only about ten years. The line through Motley had been a secondary line until the mid-1970s, when the number of trains had increased from only a daily local freight train to a combined total of between four and six loaded and empty coal trains per day. These trains were moving to and from a facility at Superior built by a subsidiary of Detroit Edison (an electric-power company) to transfer coal from rail cars to lake freighters, and then movement over the Great Lakes to power plants in Michigan.

In its reports on the three accidents, the NTSB clearly stated the cause it had determined for each one. However, it was necessary for BN's operating management to probe much deeper, as to what brought about or led to the conditions or failures that caused these accidents. We had to look at the conditions under which the operation was being conducted, e.g., the kind of training we were giving to new employees and to those we were hiring who had experience working on other railroads. The kind of evaluation or screening we were giving them when they applied for work was important, as to their aptitude for railroad work, their attitudes and ability to learn, and their willingness and ability to adapt to the "railroad way of life"—irregular hours, being available for work on a 24/7/365 basis, being able to tolerate work in all kind of weather, being able to work without direct "factory-like" supervision, and being able to work as a member of a team (i.e., as a member of a train crew), and whether they had alcohol or drugs in their system.

The quality of supervision and oversight of employees working safety-sensitive positions (mainly conductors, engineers, brakemen, dispatchers, and their supervisors) had to be closely examined. We needed to better determine whether our supervisors were conducting quality efficiency tests as to employees' job knowledge, operating proficiency, general alertness, and whether they needed further training or observation. Were our supervisors at the division level riding on trains with employees assigned to work in their territory? Were supervisors getting out on the railway about 80 percent of the time, and were they able to resist pressure from other departments to give priority to administrative functions, attend meetings, or participate in social or community functions instead of being out on the job? Even with all of the pressures supervisors had on their time, it was important for their bosses to see that they were getting enough rest between derailments or other "crises" that required extended hours of work, and that they were continuing to learn and develop the skills they needed to become effective operating officers.

We had to evaluate whether good decisions had been made in placing some of them on the jobs they held, whether they were up to the demands of overseeing operations in what had become the fastest-growing, highest-density, and most challenging territories any railroad had ever experienced. These supervisors had to be assessed as to which of them were reaching the "burn out" point and needed to be transferred to less demanding positions. In these years, supervisors often were expected to work for many consecutive weeks without a day off. At the same time, we wanted all of our "rising stars" in the company to have the chance to work in this "hot" territory. To become ready or qualified to advance, an aspiring officer needed to have a tour of duty in the territory that had become the foundation on which the company's success would rest for a long time to come.

To say the least, the NTSB's statements were intended to be a strong indictment of the culture on at least some parts of BN, the quality of its leadership, and the operating officers it had in place, from first-line supervisors to the highest level of operating management. Some of the accusations made about supervisory negligence were excessive and had no real, objective basis. It appears the NTSB may have selected a few choice accusations made against the company and its policies by some who had an axe to grind. Those comments were then used as a broad brush of the competency of the management of the Alliance Division.

The NTSB gave no recognition to the fact that thousands of crew starts and train miles were being run safely, day in and day out, by the hundreds of employees who had been hired and trained for train operations over the previous ten to twelve years. Many of these new hires had no previous railroad experience, but they had been given quality training, at the best industry standard of that time. A large number were hired who had prior railroad service. They, too, were given the training required to bring their skills up to the level required to operate 13,000-ton trains safely and efficiently. We were in a time of unprecedented growth, which was being handled very well, overall.

THE DENSITY OF SUPERVISION

As already mentioned, the NTSB was critical of our having reduced the number of first-line supervisors at Edgemont and Gillette. It is interesting to make a comparison of the changes made in the level of staffing of the Alliance Division in the years of heaviest growth in the number of train and engine crews in service. The numbers shown in table 30.1 are taken from the listing of the names and positions of operating and maintenance officers in the operating timetables BN issued from 1978 through 1983:

In 1980, the year in which authority was granted for twelve additional supervisors, three operating officers were based at Gillette and four at Edgemont—two of the "hottest" spots on the division, that were located outside of the Alliance terminal. When staffing was reduced in 1983, two officers were left in Gillette and three in Edgemont. At Alliance, the number of road foremen was reduced from four to two.

The rapid growth in the volume of business, together with the challenge of coaching and leading large numbers of newly hired people within a very short time, had made it essential to increase the number of field supervisors on the Alliance Division. In addition to the increasing number of coal trains being operated, several work

Table 30.1. Density of supervision

	Effective date of timetable	*No. of officers**
Timetable No. 9	September 15, 1974	7
Timetable No. 11	October 26, 1975	13
Timetable No. 18	October 29, 1978	18
Timetable No. 19	October 28, 1979	25
Timetable No. 20	October 26, 1980	37
Timetable No. 21	April 25, 1982	35
Timetable No. 2	October 30, 1983	24
Timetable No. 3	April 29, 1984	23

* Includes the positions of Division Superintendent, Assistant Superintendent–Transportation, Trainmaster, Road Foreman of Engines, Assistant Trainmaster, Chief Dispatcher, and Assistant Superintendent–Administration. Also includes officers assigned to the yard in Alliance.

trains had to be operated virtually every day of the week in order to unload rail, ties, ballast, and other kinds of material for the numerous track, bridge, and signal projects. With the amount of train congestion before CTC was installed, and before enough siding extensions and additional second main track could be put in service, relief crews often had to be called and transported to relieve crews who had run out of time under the Hours of Service Law. As a result, the jobs of local operating supervisors were very demanding, requiring us to have enough officers to be out on the railroad and able to cover the operation on a twenty-four-hour basis throughout the division.

To their credit, BN's senior executives approved the request made by Bill Greenwood, division superintendent, in 1979 to increase the staffing to the number listed in the operating timetable of October 26, 1980 (see table 30.1), an increase of twelve positions. These executives listened, understood, and approved the increases in officer staffing that were being made as business grew in the 1970s. We were blessed with senior-level officers who had worked earlier in their careers as trainmasters, assistant superintendents, and division superintendents. Those who are especially deserving of this kind of recognition were Bob Downing, Norman Lorentszen, Ivan Ethington, John Hertog, and Wayne Arntzsen. It would have been easy for them to have simply said "no" to requests to bolster the officer force. Without that kind of empathy from the senior staff for the very unique, unprecedented challenge we had in running the kind of railroad that was evolving on that part of BN, requests for the additional staffing would likely have been turned down.

It should be noted that increases also were made in the number of supervisors in the roadway maintenance function in those years. We were able to split the territories of some roadmasters and signal supervisors where the workload had become too heavy for one supervisor to handle effectively. Some exempt supervisors also were added to handle the large number of big track gangs we had on the divisions of the Denver and Chicago regions.

Unfortunately, with the pressure to reduce costs starting in 1981, the number of officers on the Alliance Division was cut back. While it certainly cannot be said that the reduction in supervision was what led to train accidents, or any other specific deterioration in the operation, the Alliance Division was the wrong place to make such reductions. The coal corridors on BN had grown to become "big time" operations. The Alliance and Nebraska divisions were handling a higher gross tonnage per mile and a higher density of trains than any other freight railroad in the world, and there was no question this kind of growth would continue for many years to come. It was not a short-lived "shot in the arm." But some of the new senior-level people who had direct authority over maintenance and operations had earned their stripes largely by initiating cost reductions and reducing the capacity of the railroad for their entire career. Managing growth required a new set of skills, and it was difficult for some executives to accept the challenge to "reinvent" themselves.

It took the 1995 merger with the Santa Fe to get the kind of senior operating executives back in place who would recognize what level of staffing was needed, and take action to provide those supervisory resources. Staffing was soon brought back to what it had been in 1980 (as noted in the listing of officers on the part of the new Powder River Division that had previously been named the Alliance Division).[5] It never is safe to assume that people, whether experienced or new on their jobs, can work unsupervised. Even the best of us needs to have a boss.

COMBATING THE SPREAD OF DRUGS AND ALCOHOL IN THE RAILROAD WORKPLACE

With the number of fatalities and injuries in three major accidents, causing millions of dollars of track and equipment damage, and with some employees found to be working under the influence of drugs and alcohol, immediate and drastic steps were required. The problems revealed through these accidents could not be swept aside as isolated incidents. Strong and immediate measures had to be taken to prevent employees from reporting for duty under the influence of drugs or alcohol. This would require that checks be made of employees at the time they reported for duty, which was sure to be controversial and resented by many. The company's employee-assistance program had to be intensified and made better known to employees who were addicted to drugs and alcohol, binge drinkers, or otherwise prone to be violators of Rule G, so they could seek treatment and counseling, rather than hope or expect they would be able to work for a long time until they were caught.

A system of peer referral was needed in which employees could report co-workers they perceived as having a problem of addiction, or coming to work under the influence, to an employee assistance counselor on a confidential basis. Supervisors needed to be better trained on how to evaluate the condition of employees reporting to work, especially on whether they were under the influence of drugs. At the time of its investigation of the accidents at Wiggins and Newcastle, the NTSB found that no employees had ever been referred to the EAP counselor on the Denver Region by another employee. The NTSB noted that it was a voluntary program that could help only those who recognized they needed help and would accept it. This was a somewhat indirect way of saying that far more than a voluntary program was needed to combat what had become a very serious problem for the safety of employees, the railroad company, and the general public who relied on railroads to conduct a safe operation.

To help improve safety, we had to overcome the distractions caused by the style of leadership introduced on BN in the early 1980s, together with large cuts made in employment and officer staffing throughout the railroad. We were pleased that the frequency index for employee injuries had not deteriorated badly in those times, even though the attention to safety and proper work practices was threatened by the distractions of "changing the company." However, these accidents involving train operations showed that all was not well. Clearly, improvement in the frequency ratio for employee injuries was not telling the whole story. There were some serious underlying problems that needed to be handled aggressively and with strong leadership and direction. Action plans for improvement had to be developed quickly and implemented. Regardless of the underlying, root causes that may have brought about a deterioration in safety, action had to be taken.

THE URGENT NEED FOR ACTION

The finding of alcohol and illicit drugs in some of the employees involved in the accidents at Wiggins and Newcastle was of great concern. The use of drugs was becoming a serious problem across the country. Despite the rules of longstanding on railroads that prohibited

5 Operating timetable, Powder River Division, issued in 1996.

the use or possession of alcoholic beverages or narcotics while on duty or subject to duty, the problem had infected the railroad industry as well. We were being told that the young employees we were hiring were thought to be especially good "prospects" by those involved in the sale and delivery of recreational drugs—they were known to be well paid and were showing they had plenty of money by purchasing new cars, pickups, hunting equipment, and houses, so drug dealers knew they would also have plenty to purchase drugs, if desired. Having so many young employees concentrated on the Alliance and Lincoln Divisions was causing the trade to flourish. Detecting whether a person had consumed illicit drugs by outward symptoms or behavior was more difficult than for the consumption of alcohol.

Post-accident testing by analysis of blood and urine samples was started by BN in 1986. Shortly after the 1970 merger, BN had introduced a social counseling program (most often called the EAP or Employee Assistance Program) in which employees who were problem drinkers or drug users could seek counseling and therapy from professionals. This type of program was started on the Great Northern in the early 1950s. With its success, the decision was made to expand it throughout BN soon after the 1970 merger. Referrals could be made by family members, co-workers, or supervisors. Employees who were dismissed from service for violation of Rule G could not be given consideration for reinstatement until they had undergone treatment and a social counselor evaluated them as "a good sobriety risk."

The EAP was viewed by the company, its employees, and the unions representing the operating crafts as a constructive way to deal with the problem of drug and alcohol consumption. However, it could not supplant the need for supervisory oversight, post-accident toxological examination, and the need to know both that employees coming on duty were not under the influence of drugs and alcohol and that they did not have either in their possession while on duty. As the NTSB urged in its report, "A multi-faceted approach to resolving the alcohol and drug issue in railroad operations [was needed]." A much more intensive program of detection and prevention had to be drawn up and implemented without delay.

THE USE OF "SNIFFER DOGS"

With the situation of drug and alcohol abuse being such a serious safety issue for BN, stronger and more immediate steps were needed to stop employees from coming to work under the influence, or carrying alcohol and drugs with them while on company property and on the job. We began to use "sniffer dogs" trained by contractors to detect the presence of drugs being carried by employees in their clothing or in grips or other types of containers they carried with them on the job. The dogs could also detect drugs or drug-associated items in motor vehicles the employees parked on company property while they were on duty. This was a very strong, aggressive approach to the problem. The dogs were used unannounced, at scattered places throughout the system where train crews reported for duty.

Immediately, this brought a strong, negative reaction from many employees and their union representatives. Objections were based mainly on the issue of privacy. Many employees found it offensive, disrespectful, and insulting that the company would subject them to scrutiny by animals, in full view of co-workers, their supervisors, and even the general public. However, virtually all employees were supportive of our efforts to rid the railroad of drugs and alcohol. They disliked having to work with employees who were not fit for duty. Most employees were glad we had established a program in which they could report such employees on a confidential basis, without fear of retaliation, or being labeled a "tattler" or a "company man" who would turn a fellow railroader in. By and large, employees felt that such "voluntary" programs would overcome the problem. An employee could be "rehabilitated" without first having to be caught by a supervisor and dismissed. But we felt this approach alone would not be strong enough to deter not only the problem drinkers or drug abusers, but those who might imbibe only on occasion, and therefore contend they were "not a real problem."

In any event, employees strongly opposed being subjected to searches by the dogs. Union officers filed suit against BN for an order to stop us from continuing the use of the dogs. This issue was debated with intensity among the unions, Labor Relations officers, and operating managers at all levels, from the spring of 1984 when we started to use the dogs, but it lasted only for a few months—when a U.S. district court judge issued a permanent junction against BN prohibiting the use of the drug-sniffing dogs.

BN appealed the decision of the district court. The 9th Circuit Court of Appeals upheld the ruling, stating, "BN's use of sniffer dogs to enforce Rule G concerns 'working conditions' and its primary impact may affect the job security of BN's employees. Therefore, the District Court correctly concluded that the program is a mandatory subject of bargaining."[6] In other words, the use of the dogs was a unilateral change in working conditions that could not be undertaken without a labor agreement.

In its conclusion, the 9th Circuit Court stated, that of the approximately a thousand crew members whose personal effects were checked, the sniffer dogs alerted on the grips—or carry-on bag—of sixty-one employees. Four positive searches ensued. BN presented evidence showing an increase of 26 percent in Rule G violations detected in the five months of the program in which the drug-sniffing dogs were used compared to the first four months of 1984. Accidents and safety-related rule violations decreased by 52 percent. Following that disclosure, the court stated, "We express no opinion as to whether measures such as those imposed by BN in this case could be justified as an exercise of managerial prerogative in the absence of an implied agreement."

Before the ruling of the district court judge was issued, BN had attempted to ameliorate some elements of the program that employees found the most despicable. Before starting a drug search using the dogs, employees were asked to sign a consent form. If they refused, their refusal was noted on the consent form, and the employee was removed from service pending the results of a formal investigation. If consent was given, the search of personal belongings was carried out in a private location. The company officers who witnessed the signing of the consent form were present during the search of personal belongings and the employee's automobile. The employee could request the presence of a fellow employee or a union representative. If drugs or alcohol were found, the employee was removed from service, pending an investigation.

In retrospect, the start of this program using the drug-sniffer dogs may have been put together and started much too rapidly. With employee and union participation, it might have been possible to carry it out on a truly random basis, and in ways that made it less offensive to employees. The need for a more random basis for testing came about through accusations that we were selecting individuals for testing for a multitude of reasons, not necessarily related to our concern of drugs in the work place. That concern was not valid, since the searches we made were concentrated mainly at locations with a high incident of accidents or safety violations.

There is, of course, no certainty that we could have been successful in working out an agreed-upon system of testing with the use of the dogs, without undue delay in getting a program started, or that it would have been watered down so much that it would not have been effective. Even though this program was struck down in the courts, it did at least put employees on notice that we were serious about the problem, and ready and able to take very stern measures toward eradicating drugs and alcohol from safety-sensitive positions—the crews operating trains, switching in yards and those who dispatched trains, and operating supervisors.

IMPOSITION OF RANDOM TESTING

The FRA undertook a major effort to develop regulations to deal with the problem. However, a collision between a Conrail locomotive running "light," i.e., not pulling any cars, and an Amtrak train in the Northeast Corridor in Maryland in January 1987 that resulted in 16 fatalities and 174 injuries had brought the need for federal legislation and FRA rule-making to a head. Testing of both the engineer and brakeman of the Conrail locomotive revealed they had sufficient marijuana in their systems to have been impaired at the time of the accident. The FRA regulations requiring post-accident testing had gone into effect in March 1986. The UTU challenged the new FRA regulations, and its appeal reached the 9th Circuit Court. One year later, in February 1988 the court struck down the requirement for post-accident testing, stating it was far too sweeping, and that testing should be permitted

6 Brotherhood of Locomotive Engineers, Plaintiff-appellee, v. Burlington Northern Railroad Company, Defender-appellant, 838 F.2d 1102 (9th Cir. 1988) U.S. Court of Appeals for the Ninth Circuit—838 F.2d 1102 (9th Cir. 1988).

only if there was "particularized suspicion" that a crew member had been using drugs.

Concern over this accident and the court rulings put great pressure on the FRA, the U.S. Department of Transportation, and the U.S. Congress to enact and implement legislation that would deal much more effectively with the problem of operating crews being under the influence of drugs and alcohol. It culminated in the passage of legislation in 1991. The requirement for random testing was the strongest provision in this legislation. It required 50 percent of "covered" employees (conductors, engineers, dispatchers, and later, signal maintainers) be tested annually. In 1991, the first year of random testing, 0.9 percent tested favorably for drugs. By 1993 the rate decreased to 0.7 percent. A few years later, the FRA allowed railroad companies to reduce the rate of random testing from 50 to 25 percent. Since then, the rate for positive testing has remained at less than one percent.

Beginning in 1990, the rate of injuries and train accidents in the rail industry began to decline sharply in most companies. Not all of that improvement in safety can be attributed to the program of random testing for drugs, but it certainly has been an important part of a very comprehensive effort to accelerate improvement in safety performance for all classes of employees who operate trains and terminals, and who maintain signals, track, and equipment.

A PROGRAM OF PEER INTERVENTION

In the mid- to late 1980s, a program of peer intervention with management support was developed in much of the rail industry, including BN. The new program was named "Operation Red Block" on many railroads, and "Operation Stop" on BN. Through peer-group intervention and confrontation, Operation Stop seeks to prevent the use of alcohol and drugs by employees while on duty or subject to call. The work of the peer group is on a confidential basis. The program is union-initiated and run by the employees, with the support of management. It is intended to combine the traditional values of union fraternalism with a progressive attitude on the part of management, "to enable people to help people." The involvement of committed employees in Operation Stop is recognition that impaired employees contribute a safety hazard to themselves, their co-workers, and the families of all concerned.

Peer-group members try to get troubled employees to get help through the company's Employee Assistance Program. If an impaired employee reports for duty, the peer group is empowered to get him or her out of the workplace without delay, and sent home. If the employee reports to the EAP within five days and follows the treatment, advice, and rehabilitation prescribed by the counselor, and then is evaluated by the counselor as a good sobriety risk, the employee will be allowed to return to work. If he or she refuses to leave the property after being confronted by a fellow employee, a local supervisor will be notified on the spot and the employee will be taken out of service. Operation Stop is judged as highly effective in getting employees off the job before they can jeopardize the safety of the operation, their co-workers, and the general public.

EMPLOYEE ASSISTANCE PROGRAM

As mentioned earlier, a program of assistance by professional counselors was set up by the Great Northern Railway in the 1950s. This was long before FRA regulations required railway companies to make such assistance available to employees as part of an all-out effort to rid the rail industry of the danger of alcohol or drug use. EAP programs have been expanded to cover the needs of family members as well, and to provide counseling on other matters of concern such as family finances, mental health issues, emotional distress, and marital difficulties. Any and all matters are handled on a confidential basis.

With the large investment a railroad company has in its workforce, it is sensible for it to be comprehensive in providing professional assistance to overcome such personal problems, and help bring about job satisfaction and improved work relationships, to recover or improve professional competency. Administering these kinds of programs for keeping drugs and alcohol out of the workplace is very expensive and time-consuming for railroad companies. We would like to say the problem has been overcome, that it is behind us and that the resources we are still using to deter substance abuse could be used in other endeavors. But when one looks at the behavior of many people in our society, we still have exposure to the problem, and it is obvious we still are a long way from completely overcoming it in a safety sensitive industry such as railroading. Having even one person on duty who is impaired is too many.

BECOMING THE BEST IN SAFETY

The initiatives described in this section on safety are part of what has become a very successful effort for improvement of safety on BN, BNSF, and the entire railroad industry. It is especially interesting and rewarding to note the excellent safety record of today's Powder River Division on the BNSF, which includes the territory of the former Alliance and Colorado divisions. In several recent years, the Powder River Division has had the lowest frequency ratio for employee injuries of any division, a far cry from the early to mid-1970s when the Alliance and Colorado divisions were at the bottom of the standings.

Under the leadership of Superintendent Dave Burns, the Colorado Division made remarkable progress in improving safety in only two years. In the April 2017 issue of the *BN Expediter*, a newsletter of a historical society devoted to BN, Dave wrote,

> BN had 17 operating divisions competing for first place in safety. When I arrived on the Colorado Division in August 1979 it was in last place. It was not that the supervisors didn't care, but somehow we were just in the doldrums. Some new energy was needed. Most of the supervisors and I had never finished last, and that became our mantra and focus for the next five months. "We Are NOT Last Place People." We crawled our way up to places by year's end, barely finishing in 15th place.
>
> We experimented with some new ideas, such as more impromptu safety meetings, department heads (including myself) showing up at night time crew briefings, and plain talking up the importance of taking time for safety. We moved up toward the mid-range the next year, but clearly something more was needed to make safety more alive, compelling and personal. Someone proposed having traveling trophies for the best monthly safety performance in the four safety committee areas (Denver, McCook, Cheyenne and Trinidad), broken out into four categories: clerical, train and yard crews, mechanical crews and maintenance crews. The trophies were quite nice, sort of like an Oscar, and the location that won one of them would display it prominently. Pretty soon friendly competition began emerging between the various crafts and locations. . . .
>
> We began holding a safety conference call every Friday afternoon with the four locations participating to report how they had done that week. A lot of hoopla got generated, with taunts between locations. These were actually fun sessions to be in on! Things were looking up. Pride and performance were improving. . . . safety was again becoming a point of personal pride and involvement, and in 1981 the Colorado Division was again in the hunt for first place. . . . The Division didn't end up in first place, but it was not very far off. Heads could and were being held high once again.[7]

Strong and effective efforts were also applied on the Nebraska and Alliance divisions and on the three divisions on the Chicago Region as well in those years. Substantial improvement was accomplished in all departments. Overall, much higher levels of respectability and recognition were gained. Most importantly, more and more employees were able to return home after work in as good condition as they were when they left home on their way to work.

7 Dave Burns, "Colorado Division Days, 1979–81," *BN Expediter* (April 2017): 6–19.

CHAPTER 31

EMPLOYEE REFLECTIONS ON SAFETY

LOOKING BACK AT THE CHALLENGES AND SUCCESSES

• going from frequency ratios of 10.0 or more down to ratios of less than 1.0 on a sustained basis • embedding safety in the culture of the company: "the way we do things here" • an evolution in safety from a mandate of "just get 'er done" to embedding safety into all operating and maintenance practices • making safety a way of life on the railroad •

THIS CHAPTER CONTAINS REFLECTIONS OF several BN people who were employed on the divisions charged with gearing up to handle the enormous work load in upgrading the railroad and moving a heavy volume of traffic while that work was underway. It is interesting and rewarding to hear from those who made their careers on BN reflect on "where we've been and where we are going."

In recent years, many employees have taken the opportunity to evaluate and share their feelings about the career choices they made when they hired out in the 1970s, as well as discuss the skills they have as railroaders and the pride and satisfaction they developed in their profession, their company, and the relationships they built. They see that a good foundation was built for those who follow them: a safety culture and a company with a good future. Overall, they reveal how they helped make BN a safer place to work than it was when they started their railroad careers.

Especially on safety, it is rewarding to hear from them about the excellent performance of today's BNSF Railway. A railroad's safety performance is the strongest and most important indicator of how well its people have done and what kind of shape the railroad is in today, at the time they retired after some twenty-five to forty years of service. Some divisions and work units are achieving frequency ratios of less than one, which no one who worked in the 1970s thought would even be possible. It means that having a goal of zero injuries for large groups of railroad workers over a sustained period is not unrealistic. It has been proved that achieving safety and have high rates of production are not in conflict. When large numbers of new people were being hired for the massive track- and signal-upgrading programs, and many new brakemen were being hired, there was no model or system available for training or work observation on a large scale that would instill safe work methods, correct bad work habits, or otherwise assist employees in taking care of themselves and their fellow workers out on the job. Instead, training was done out on the job through osmosis and informal interaction with what few experienced employees were working at many places in those years.

In the 1970s, it was not uncommon to have frequency ratios in excess of 10 on the divisions with the heaviest work load. This meant that over 10 percent of the employees sustained a reportable injury within a year, a level that had to be reduced. By the late 1970s, managers and employees at the division and shop level were coming up with more structured and organized ways to use the skills and job knowledge of what was often the few experienced employees in a work unit to help turn the situation around. At the same time, managers at all levels came to realize they needed training to better manage safety as a work process, and to develop the leadership skills they needed to effectively build a safety culture—a way of life—as our top priority. The management of basic railroad work had to be more than "get 'er done" and thinking they had to tolerate injuries in the process of trying to maximize production.

For the most part, management at the senior level had not experienced a safety challenge of that depth and breadth in their formative years, and hence, had to be convinced that safety would not come about only by taking tough disciplinary action or simply extoling managers on the front line "to do better." It was vital to have the support of top management for training with the resources needed to correct potentially hazardous workplace conditions and better trained people on how to work safely in the railroad environment. It was necessary that managers at all levels better demonstrate their personal commitment to safety with consistency and determination. We had to learn how to win the hearts and minds of the people.

Such affirmative attitudes toward safety were developed over several years into an enduring commitment throughout the company to the well-being of employees and managers. The results have been outstanding. Several employees and managers who were hired in the early days of the coal boom and are still working and have shared their thoughts and lessons learned as they reflect on the vast improvements made in safety over the years as they were about to begin their final trip or work their last shift:

STATEMENTS ON SAFETY

"I am thankful to have had such a good career that provided good benefits and retirement. Think safety every day so you can return home to your family. Do it by the book. The rules are implemented for your safety."

—*Gary Hudson, Locomotive Engineer, who retired with nearly forty years of injury-free service*

"Don't assume anything. It will get you in trouble. Always be willing to learn and apply what you've learned. Treat people how you want to be treated."

—*Wayne Green, Locomotive Engineer*

"I always told them [while serving as an instructor for Conductors] to keep their head on a swivel. If you look and listen you will work safely. It has been a good life. It's hard to see it coming to an end."

—*Willie Marks, Conductor*

"The company makes it as safe as they can for us. Just stick with it, and you can have a great career. I loved telling people what I did and having them see the finished project. I'm proud to say we had no injuries during my time as Roadmaster."

—*James Mashek, Surfacing Gang Foreman and former Roadmaster*

"Do not take shortcuts. Listen to what your co-workers have to say, especially those with experience. That is the best way to learn."

—*Jim McElwain, Locomotive Engineer*

"There is no room for error in the type of work we do, but it can be done with proper training and equipment. The main thing is being committed to working safely. Our goal is to provide the safest, most efficient, professional electrical crews out there."

—*Jim Hartman, Electrical Supervisor*

"The No. 1 battle out here is fighting complacency. We must always keep that in the back of our minds. Communication is key to fighting complacency."

—*Blane Morse, Conductor, as crews on the Butte Subdivision (this territory includes the operation over Crawford Hill) reached two years of injury-free service*

"Our safety accomplishments are a testament to Alex Adam, Lyle Horton, and Ken Willey [operations supervisors]. They are always there to help, guide and inform employees, whether in the field or otherwise. They take the time to know each employee. This is a source of pride. Safety becomes a culture. New employees follow the lead of experienced employees."

—*Will Hall, Locomotive Engineer (another employee working on the Butte Subdivision)*

"The trick is to learn the most basic way to get things done from the people you work with. When I look back, the people who did things the simplest way were often the people who were never injured. That's because they did what they were supposed to do well."

—*Henry Benjamin, Conductor*

"I am proud of my day-in and day-out dedication to safety. This makes me realize that I do make a difference to the safe movement of trains."

—*Fenton Johnson, Tamper Operator*

"We want people who want to be here, not those that think they have to be. Maintain a positive, wanna-do attitude and a safety-conscious mentality. Things will always come around. It is never as bad as it seems. You make your environment what it is."

—*Brian Chatten, Division Engineer*

"The people and camaraderie you find on the railroad can't be found anyplace else. We take safety seriously and therefore truly watch out for one another like a brother's keeper."

—*Ray Bennett, Water Service Foreman. In an interview, Bennett advised new employees to pay attention to and take advantage of the experienced employees' wisdom and knowledge to avoid making the same mistakes they did.*

"There is no such thing as a small accident on the railroad."

—*Doug Sogn, Conductor*[8]

A REMARKABLE EVOLUTION FROM BN'S EARLY DAYS

Statements such as those listed above are representative of the attitudes that have led to the vast change in employee safety performance that developed from the mid-1970s and on to the present day. A clear indication of how far we have come can be seen in Roger Nelson's statements about the struggles that were faced in the early days to improve the safety and overall work performance in all departments of the division and region organizations. Roger served as a line operating officer and progressed to the level of vice president of Safety in the 1980s. Here is Roger's evaluation of the prevailing safety culture of the early days: "I think the prevailing attitude amongst both the management (at all levels, not on just the divisions) and the employees was just to 'keep from drowning' and 'get 'er done' without regard to good safety practices and processes. Production at any cost."

To bring about a quantum improvement in safety, Roger recalls how BN appointed him to lead a system task force in the early 1990s to determine the best practices the divisions should employ to improve safety. As part of that process, a team of safety professionals from the DuPont Corporation was brought in to apply the systems of leadership and management in safety that had been applied successfully on other railroads and in many other industries. Together with the leadership of retired Air Force general John Chain, a profound improvement in safety came about in the next two years.

From a personal standpoint, a number of thoughts come to mind as to what many of us went through in those early days and how fortunate we were to be "in the right place at the right time" to have those experiences. Part of the effort toward improving morale and building the base needed to improve safety was to get the point across to employees that the company's goals and strategies would benefit of all of its constituencies: owners, investors, customers, employees, and the parts of the general community we touched in one way or another.

We were trying to show concern for the well-being of our people by bringing in large machinery to help clean up the property by picking up years of accumulation of scrap material that was unsightly and, at times, created tripping hazards. We went all out to clean up the trash and spillage in yards and facilities that endangered safety

8 These comments are from employees and managers are contained in various issues of *Powder River Reflections*, a newsletter issued in the early 2000s to BNSF employees and their families.

or at least made it an unpleasant place to work. We rebuilt yard tracks that were in poor condition and improved walkways between and along tracks. We remodeled and upgraded lunch and locker rooms, painted buildings, cleared brush, cut the weeds, and applied chemicals to suppress dust on roads going through or adjacent to working areas in yards. We rebuilt hundreds of grade crossings that were in bad shape and a legitimate source of complaint. Training programs were being set up for both new and experienced employees in all specialties. As a result of such efforts, we made the railroad look like we were in business, we had a future, and that we were not running a junk yard. Most importantly, we were making the railroad a safer place to work.

Having a much better looking (and safer) property, together with the hundreds of new locomotives we were putting in service and the thousands of miles of track we upgraded, was helping employees establish pride in their company. They saw we had the authority, the ability, and the resolve to correct the backlog of conditions of concern to employees, and that BN was committed to building a strong railroad for the future. This really hit home in the lean years in the 1970s, when dividends and executive pay were reduced but yet, the management did not defer or cancel upgrading projects in order to raise or maintain BN's net income in the short term. Employees also learned that the senior management in place in those years consisted of people who knew what railroading was about, and that they spent time out on the railroad to see first hand what was going on. By establishing confidence in these and many other ways, more and more employees were getting on board with the program and the number of "attitude-caused" injuries began to decline.

By 1980 the number of train and switching accidents caused by defective track or equipment also showed a downward trend. The safety record of the divisions on the Chicago and Denver regions was no longer dragging down the record of safety for the entire railroad as it had in earlier years. This was the beginning of a period of remarkable year to year improvement on all measures of performance in safety, that continues to this day.

PART VII

CREATING AND SEIZING NEW OPPORTUNITIES

CHAPTER 32

THE MILWAUKEE ROAD

SHUTDOWN AND BREAKUP

• partnership agreement with the State of South Dakota • BN restoring viable lines to service • opportunity for many Milwaukee Road employees to re-start careers in the rail industry •

AFTER YEARS OF STRUGGLE TO OPERATE and maintain a railroad with declining traffic and track in increasingly poor condition on Milwaukee Road, the bankruptcy court approved abandonment of all lines west of Miles City, Montana, on April 2, 1980. The last train on Milwaukee's West Coast extension departed from Tacoma on March 15, 1980. With that final act, initiatives were quickly undertaken by state authorities, shippers, and BN to acquire parts of Milwaukee's 2,498 route miles that were thought to be viable and of vital interest to users of rail transportation. Over its entire system (including areas east of Miles City), Milwaukee moved to abandon or sell about 7,000 miles of road.

Within a few months, 325 miles of lines in Montana, Idaho, and Washington were sold to BN for $21 million. BN's purchase included the Milwaukee's line over the Cascade Mountains on Snoqualmie Pass, which had much more favorable grades than either of the BN lines over the range. In addition, having a third crossing of the Cascades would provide much more line capacity for BN in the years ahead, when international trade was expected to grow substantially. BN also purchased 119 miles of the Milwaukee's branch lines in central Montana that served some productive grain-growing areas.

PARTNERSHIPS FOR OPERATION OF LINES IN SOUTH DAKOTA AND IOWA

Another buyer of Milwaukee lines at this time was the State of South Dakota, through its purchase of the entire 480 miles of the main line across the state, between the Minnesota–South Dakota state line and Terry, Montana, where the Milwaukee's line connected with BN. The state paid $30.4 million for this line and committed to invest $7.3 million to upgrade it. The bankruptcy trustee had proposed the main line be retained by the Milwaukee as far as Miles City, Montana, under reorganization, but the ICC rejected that part of his proposal. The state also purchased 456 miles of Milwaukee branch lines in eastern South Dakota that became known as the "South Dakota core."

The state's entire purchase was engineered by Governor Bill Janklow, a colorful, aggressive, high-spirited leader who was not hesitant to make decisions and commitments even in the face of political opposition. Janklow quickly moved ahead to complete the purchase and negotiate agreements with BN for operation of the lines the state had acquired and to carry out the maintenance work needed to restore them to a condition satisfactory for the amount of business to be handled. These acquisitions were financed by a temporary increase of one percent in the state sales tax.

Since BN recognized operating benefits and opportunities for developing business on the lines in South

Dakota, BN's president, Richard Grayson, was quick to join hands with the governor in preparing the agreements needed for BN to operate and maintain the lines acquired by the state. It was fortunate that Grayson hit it off well with Janklow and got him to agree that in time, BN would be allowed to acquire ownership of the lines acquired by the state. The deal was in two parts. The first covered the 435 miles of the branch lines in the eastern part of the state. BN contracted to operate and maintain those lines for five years. BN declined the state's offer of a $6.9 million subsidy. Instead, the state would use those funds to rehabilitate the lines to a standard allowing a train speed of 25 miles per hour. When upgraded, the track would be strong enough to safely handle 100-ton capacity cars for hauling grain and fertilizer. Also, BN would offer competitive rates and service for shipping grain by unit train to West Coast destinations.

The second agreement covered operation and maintenance of the Milwaukee's main line across South Dakota and into Montana to a connection with BN at Terry. Starting in April 1982, BN would lease the line for 20 years. Federal funds of $30 million would be committed for upgrading the track to allow train speeds of 40 miles per hour. BN would have an option to purchase the line.

At a celebration of the re-opening of the "core" lines in September 1981, Grayson told the crowd, "It [the agreement between BN and the state] really is a unique system, not necessarily in track layout or the type of service it provides, but in concept. I've been in the railroad business for 40 years, and I can honestly tell you that this state has designed one of the most innovative, realistic and workable rail plans I've seen." It was a real credit to Governor Janklow and Grayson that such satisfactory terms could be worked out so quickly. The contract was renewed in 1986 with a clause allowing BN to buy the "core lines," i.e., the branch lines acquired by the State. In 2005, BNSF acquired ownership of 368 miles of the core for about $40 million.

Rehabilitation work on the main line between Ortonville and Terry was done by BN crews at a cost of $70 million. The Milwaukee Road continued to own and operate only that part of its line east of Ortonville and into the Twin Cities. At the west end, at Terry, the line connected with the BN main line that ran between Fargo, Laurel and Seattle.

About 70 miles of the main line acquired by the State of South Dakota were in Montana. A small part of the line was operated under CTC, but most of it was under ABS (automatic block system) rules. The average distance between sidings used to meet and pass trains was 16 miles between the Minnesota–South Dakota state line and Mobridge, and 13 miles between Mobridge and Terry. West of Mobridge, five of the sidings were less than 6,000 feet in length, making them impractical for meets involving trains typically run with upwards of one hundred or more cars.

The $30 million loan from the FRA for upgrading the track was paid back seventeen years earlier than its maturity date. In addition to handling the movement of coal to a power plant at Big Stone City near the Minnesota–South Dakota state line, BN was successful in setting up unit grain trains to originate on both the core lines and the main line for destinations in the Pacific Northwest. As of this writing, the main line has not been used much as an alternate or overflow route for "through trains" that normally move across North Dakota on the former NP main line. With the FRA loan paid off, the agreement with the State allowed BN to purchase the line for $1.00. That purchase was made in 1990.

Overall, the restructuring and rebuilding of the Milwaukee's lines in South Dakota has been a very successful effort, to the benefit of the shippers, the state and its citizens, and the Milwaukee employees who gained employment with BN. The operation of these lines enhanced BN's revenue base through the additional grain and coal business it developed. The spirit of cooperation among all parties involved in the restructuring of Milwaukee lines in South Dakota made it possible to restore service on a solid footing and over a large part of South Dakota within a short time.

In Iowa, BN agreed to provide service on 93 miles of the Milwaukee's main line running east from Council Bluffs to Bayard. A group of shippers acquired the line in 1983 and raised $9.2 million for purchase and rehabilitation of the track. BN agreed to operate and maintain the line for twenty years and to make the principal and interest payments on the amount borrowed by the shippers' consortium as rent.

LOW-GRADE LINE OVER SNOQUALMIE PASS

In the state of Washington, BN acquired one of the Milwaukee's "crown jewels": its route over the Cascade Mountains between Cedar Falls and Cabin Creek (36 miles). By building on Snoqualmie Pass, the Milwaukee's line had grades that were much less severe than either the GN or NP had in their crossings of the Cascades. Following is a comparison of those grades:

	% GRADE ASCENDING	
	Westbound	*Eastbound*
Milwaukee, via Snoqualmie Pass	0.7	1.7
GN, via Stevens Pass	2.2	2.2
NP, via Stampede Pass	2.2	2.2[1]

In running a heavy freight operation, differences in grade are very significant. To use the newly acquired line over Snoqualmie Pass, BN would have had to build connections with the former NP main line at each end. Construction of those connections would not have been extremely expensive, but the Milwaukee track was in poor to marginal condition and would have required almost complete rebuilding. However, as was the case on all Milwaukee lines I am familiar with, the bridges were in very good condition. A more complete story of what was involved in BN's decision to not shift its traffic to Snoqualmie Pass can be found in chapter 33, "Crossing the Cascades."

It should be noted that although the Milwaukee's line over Snoqualmie Pass had very favorable grades, that was not the case on other parts of the Milwaukee's Pacific Coast Extension, when compared with the grades on BN's preferred route. In Montana, Idaho, and eastern Washington, the Milwaukee's line was built on the following grades:

	% GRADE	
	Westbound	*Eastbound*
Belt Mountains	1.2	1.0
Pipestone Pass	2.0	1.7
St. Paul Pass	1.7	1.7
Saddle Mountains	2.2	1.6

On its preferred route east of the Cascades, BN encountered mountain grades only on Marias Pass, its crossing of the Continental Divide. The maximum grades over Marias Pass were only 1.0 percent westbound and 1.8 percent eastbound. These favorable differences in grades had a very favorable impact on operating expense and provided BN a real competitive advantage.

1 Refer to chapter 33, "Crossing the Cascades," for more detail on the evaluation BN made of its routes over the Cascade Range.

LINES IN MONTANA

In central Montana, BN acquired several Milwaukee branch lines that served grain-growing areas (see map in figure 32.1). The track on these branches was in fair to poor condition, generally laid with 75-, 90-, and 100-pound rail. Train speed was restricted to 10 miles per hour. Substantial upgrading would have been required to bring these lines up to the standard needed to safely and efficiently handle covered hopper cars with the standard gross weight of 263,000 pounds of those years, soon to be followed by a new industry standard of 286,000 pounds. BN agreed to pay $21 million for 94 miles of line in this area:

Lewistown–Moore (jointly owned by Milwaukee–BN)	17.6 miles
Spring Creek Junction–Geraldine (BN embargoed in 1983; donated to State of Montana in 1984)	66.6 miles
Lewistown–Heath (abandoned in 1989)	9.8 miles

The initial cost of upgrading these lines was estimated at $13.7 million. Unlike railroad lines in service in most grain-growing areas, the Geraldine line crossed large coulees, bridged by four long, high steel trestles. Also, there was a 1,391-foot long 85-foot high wood-pile trestle bridge over Spring Creek and a 2,000-foot-long tunnel. Between Geraldine and Denton, there was a grade of 1.5 percent for trains moving in the loaded direction. This grade was far more severe than any other grade that would be encountered in moving grain the entire distance to Portland, if it was routed on the low grade route via Shelby, Whitefish, and the SP&S. But since these lines were in an area of high grain production in most years, BN was willing to acquire them and take on the cost of rehabilitation.[2]

2 The former Great Northern Railway obtained operating rights on 9.2 miles of Milwaukee-owned track between Lewistown and Spring Creek Junction, which allowed abandonment of GN's line between those two points.

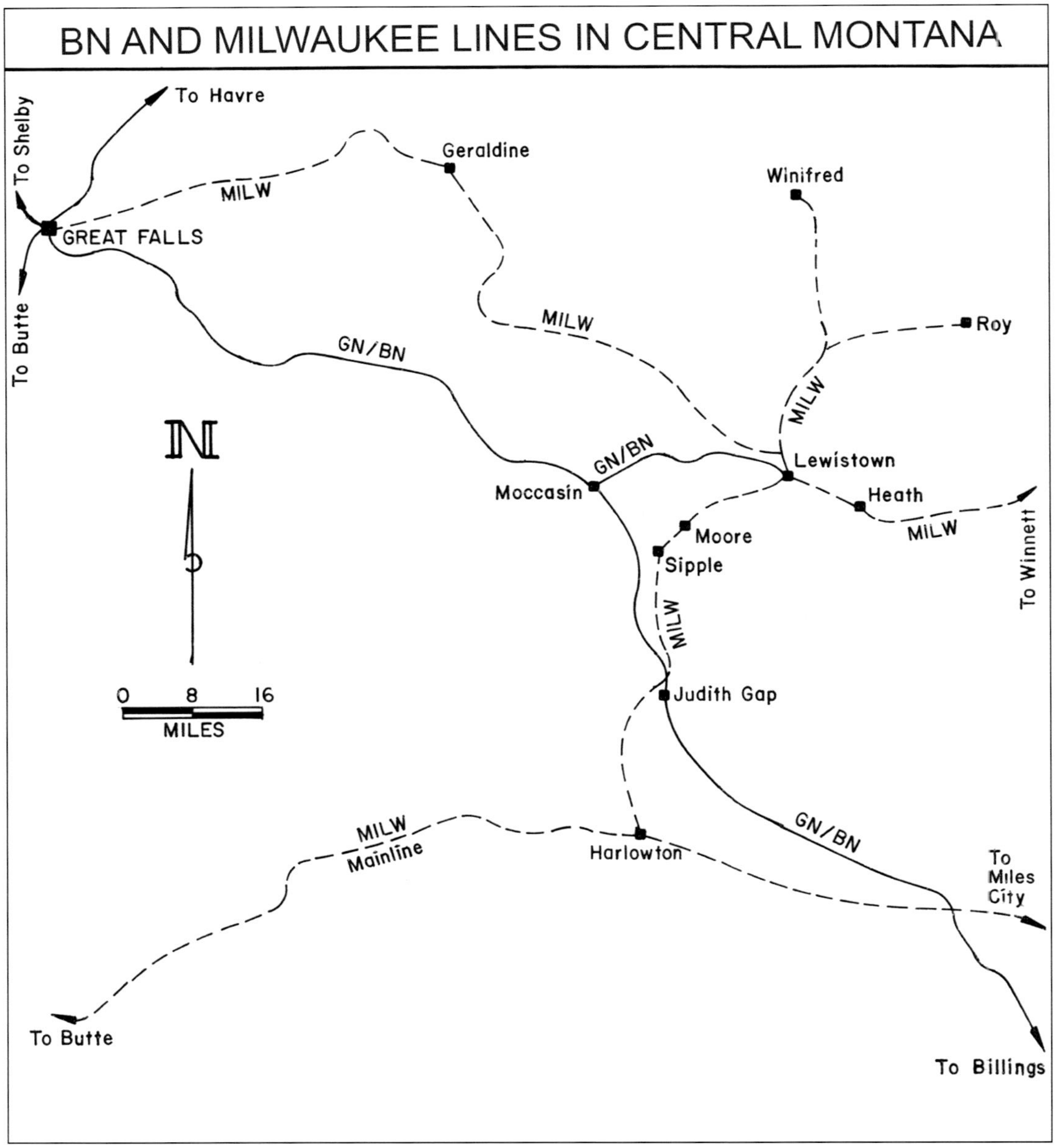
BN AND MILWAUKEE LINES IN CENTRAL MONTANA
To Havre
To Shelby
To Butte
GREAT FALLS
MILW
Geraldine
Winifred
MILW
GN/BN
Roy
MILW
N
GN/BN
Lewistown
Moccasin
Heath
Moore
MILW
Sipple
To Winnett
MILW
0 8 16
MILES
Judith Gap
MILW
Mainline
GN/BN
Harlowton
To
Miles
City
To Butte
To Billings

Figure 32.1.

BN also acquired a 5.75-mile segment between Eastham Junction and Fairfield to serve two grain facilities, including a barley plant owned by Anheuser Busch. Federal rail-freight assistance money administered by the state was used to rehabilitate the track.

BN assumed ownership of the Milwaukee's branch lines in Montana in 1980. Later in the year, when a favorable court ruling was expected on the BN–Frisco merger, Richard Grayson of the Frisco was named president of BN's Transportation Division. Further analysis of the Milwaukee lines BN had just acquired in Montana was conducted under Grayson's direction. It was determined that the cost of rehabilitation of what became known as the "Geraldine Line" would be $30 million, much higher than the original estimate of $13.7 million. In 1983 BN embargoed the Spring Creek Junction–Geraldine line and in August 1984 filed for abandonment.

This action gave rise to a groundswell of protest and general resentment toward BN on the part of grain shippers, their elected representatives, the news media, and Montanans of nearly every walk of life. Statements were made that the land grants the Northern Pacific had received about 130 years earlier obligated BN to provide service forever, even though the value of the land grants had been returned to the government many times over. This assertion was made even though the Geraldine line was built by the Milwaukee and the NP was not involved with it in any way. In deciding to abandon the line rather than spend the $30 million needed to keep it in service to handle only a modest level of business, BN was accused of breaking the agreement it had made to operate and maintain the line. "This is still a state where people feel they can do things on a handshake," argued William J. Fogarty, the head of Montana's Department of Commerce.[3]

The issue of BN's unfilled obligation to keep the Geraldine line in service really came to a head when it was reported in the *Wall Street Journal* that a BN officer allegedly told a reporter, "We reneged. It doesn't pay out. But I don't think any corporation is in a position to dump $30 million just to honor a commitment."[4] Not surprisingly, this statement caused great turmoil to erupt among the parties having a stake in the operation of the line, as well as within BN itself. The problem was resolved in an out-of-court settlement dated September 5, 1984, under which service was restored. BN agreed to turn ownership of the line over to the state and make a cash payment of $11.7 million plus six GP9-type locomotives. From that payment, a trust account of $5 million was set up to finance rehabilitation and operation of the line. Also, the fund provided cash for construction of a locomotive maintenance facility and office in Denton. A new non-profit organization called the Central Montana Railroad (CMR) was set up to lease the line from the state for twenty-five years. In June 1985, after completing some track and bridge maintenance, CMR began service.

In 1988 BN donated its line of 19.6 miles between Moccasin (on its Great Falls–Laurel line) and Spring Creek Junction (nine miles west of Lewistown) to the state. With CMR being able to interchange with BN at a point on BN's main line, BN was able to meet its objective of having a low-cost short-line operator provide service on such light-density branch lines. To reach Lewistown, BN built one mile of new line from Sipple to connect with the right-of-way of a line the Milwaukee had abandoned years before. BN then built four miles of track on the old grade where track had been abandoned in the past, and rebuilt one bridge to the line that ended at Moore. With those connections in place, BN could reach Lewistown and avoid making costly repairs to the mammoth wooden trestle bridge at Spring Creek on the former Milwaukee's Geraldine line.

Twenty-eight years later, the saga of the Geraldine line still had not ended. Further consternation developed when BN set up service to a new high-capacity grain elevator on its main line at Moccasin to which "shuttle service" would be provided. That caused some of the grain shippers and the State of Montana to take BNSF to court, claiming that BNSF unfairly subsidized the private company that built the new elevator by supporting construction of a "loop" track for loading unit trains. Because of the more favorable rates offered to those who shipped grain through the new facility, the amount of grain loaded at elevators on the Geraldine line declined from an average of 1,150 carloads to just over 500 in 2009. Under its contract with CMR, BN initially paid $275 per

3 Bill Richards, "Worried States Enter the Railroad Business to Save Branch Lines," *Wall Street Journal*, September 22, 1983.

4 Richards, "Worried States Enter the Railroad Business."

car CMR delivered to BN. CMR increased the rate to $884 in 2009, and BNSF then stopped making the per-car payments to CMR. In some years, these payments totaled $1 million. A federal court ruled that BNSF had the right to discontinue making this per car payment to CMR. The state has been trying to move the case to a state court, where it expects a favorable ruling will be made for the state.

It is interesting to note that CMR does not charge for the transportation service it provides the grain elevators it serves. In that way, it is hoped that the elevators on the Geraldine line will be able to compete with those BNSF serves on its main line. BNSF has told CMR to publish a tariff rate and charge that rate to its customers in lieu of receiving payments from BNSF.

CMR has been facing another threat to its existence since the spring of 2011, when a raging torrent of water in the Judith River undermined the footing of two of the 120-foot-high support towers of a 2,000-foot-long steel-trestle bridge. As a result, the track on the bridge is severely out of line. The line has been out of service since then, and no means of funding repair costs of $3.5 million has been found as of December 2012, the time of this writing. Twenty-seven years after the state took ownership of the line, train speeds remain authorized for only 10 miles per hour on the entire line.

BN and BNSF have paid dearly for the decision made in 1980 to acquire the Geraldine line. From a business standpoint, one might wonder why that decision was made. It is apparent the initial assessment made of the condition of the track and bridges was inadequate, or that it was ignored or downplayed in favor of political considerations. Also, since the farmers along the line were dependent on rail transportation, BN's decision to acquire the line was intended to help alleviate concerns and accusations that BN had operated as a monopoly since its creation in 1970, and had been taking unfair advantage of farmers and elevator operators. Also, there were some factions in Montana who accused BN of deliberately carrying out unfair practices that put the Milwaukee Road out of business.

It appears BN did everything possible to help the Geraldine line survive. In addition to the payment it made to the bankruptcy trustee to acquire the line, it set up the $5 million trust to fund and support the CMR. In addition, BN built one mile of new track and rehabilitated four additional miles so it could reach Lewistown and connect with the CMR. Only one year later, the segment BN had just spent money on had to be taken out of service and abandoned due to poor subgrade conditions. With the small amount of business moving on that line, it would have been uneconomic to spend the money needed to restore it to service again.

In retrospect, both BN and the agri-business community on the Geraldine line would have been better off if they had faced the economic situation they were in at the time the Milwaukee shut down in 1980, and set up a system for trucking the grain to elevators located on BN's main line. Instead, another chapter on rail history in Montana was written with allegations that the railroad companies were charging exorbitant rates on grain produced in Montana, due to the alleged monopoly they had on transportation. BN was charged with making far too much money at the expense of the farmers. This level of contention continues to arise yet today, even though BNSF provides efficient shuttle service to move Montana's grain to international markets for lower rates than it offered when grain could be moved only on single-car rates.

Allegations that BN never had competition in moving grain out of central Montana are not entirely correct. In the 1970s, before BN established lower rates for 26-car and 52-car rates, about half of the grain was moved by truck to the UP at Butte, or to Lewiston, Idaho, for transfer into barges for movement to Portland or Kalama. The new unit grain train rates were so low that nearly all grain was shifted to BN. The grain growers were relieved of the need to own or hire trucks to make the thousand mile round trip to Lewiston.

TRACKAGE RIGHTS GRANTED MILWAUKEE BY GN AND BN

Over the years, both before and after the 1970 merger, the track on some of the Milwaukee's branch lines deteriorated so badly that it had to seek operating rights on lines owned by BN and its predecessors. For example, the GN gave trackage rights to the Milwaukee so it could continue to serve Choteau, Montana. With these rights, the Milwaukee benefited by being able to run on a high-quality railroad. BN and the GN received no benefit other than the small amount the Milwaukee paid for those trackage rights. It is a good example of what was done by the BN and GN over the years to help keep the Milwaukee in business in several markets, maintaining the kind of competition desired by regulators, shippers, and the elected representatives in Montana.

To enable the Milwaukee to reach its line between Newport and Metaline Falls, Washington, the GN granted operating rights to the Milwaukee on its main line between Spokane and Newport. East of Newport, the line owned by the Milwaukee, with virtually no local business, had the disadvantage of high curvature, a grade of 1.5 percent and crossing rugged terrain over much of its distance. In running on the GN's main line, the Milwaukee gained the benefit of operating on a 60-miles-per-hour piece of railroad. Without these rights, the Milwaukee would not have been able to continue service to a large cement plant on its line at Metaline Falls.

Another example of providing support to the Milwaukee was granting it operating rights it needed to continue to seerve Everett, Washington. Again, this enabled the Milwaukee to abandon its line and still continue to have access to a market. Later, the GN allowed the Milwaukee to extend operation on its main line between Everett and Bellingham. This made it possible for the Milwaukee to discontinue the costly ferry operation it ran between Seattle and Bellingham.

For many years, the Milwaukee benefited greatly from the trackage rights it had on the former NP's line between St. Paul and Duluth. The Milwaukee became the heaviest user of this line, handling more tonnage than even the owning road. It used these rights to become the preferred connection with the DW&P (the Duluth, Winnipeg and Pacific Railway, a U.S. subsidiary of Canadian National) at Superior. The increasing volume of business handled between the Milwaukee and the DW&P was a major factor in the improved earnings the Milwaukee had in the years just before it was acquired by the Soo Line. After the 1970 merger, BN designated the former GN's line as its preferred route between Duluth–Superior and the Twin Cities. That left the Milwaukee as the sole user on nearly all of the NP line. The Milwaukee did not have the money to purchase the line, but continued to use it under the old agreement it had made with the NP many years earlier.

Table 32.1. MILWAUKEE ROAD OPERATING INCOME, 1970–1977

Year	*Operating Income (millions)*
1970	d $7.9
1971	2.6
1972	d 6.8
1973	12.6
1974	8.8
1975	d 23.6
1976	d 8.8
1977	d 29.4

d = deficit

SOURCE: Moody's Transportation Manual

With BN no longer carrying out any tie renewal or surfacing programs on the line, it deteriorated to the point where some speed restrictions of 10 miles per hour had to be placed. In 1987 BN agreed to grant trackage rights to the Milwaukee's successor, the Soo Line, over the former GN line, a high class mainline, free of slow orders. This decision enabled the Soo Line (the new owner of the Milwaukee) to continue to serve Duluth and Superior. Without the rights granted by the NP, the Milwaukee would never have had the opportunity to develop the relationship it had with the DW&P for interchange of traffic. This was yet another example of the northern lines providing the Milwaukee the opportunity to serve markets that the GN or NP could have had for themselves if they had declined the Milwaukee's requests for use of their lines.

Other examples of such cooperation could be cited in Washington, Idaho, and Illinois. All in all, GN, NP, the Burlington, and BN provided considerable opportunity to the Milwaukee to reduce its operating and maintenance costs, by enabling it to abandon hundreds of miles of track in poor to marginal condition, and still retain its customer base. In fact, by being able to operate on much better track, these rights provided much higher competitive capability to the Milwaukee. The comments made by some writers of railroad history that the BN and its predecessors drove the Milwaukee out of business through unfair practices are very biased and inaccurate. To the contrary, they did a great deal to help the Milwaukee stay in business in those areas much longer than would otherwise have been possible. At the end, when the Milwaukee shut down its operations in the western states and BN began serving many of its customers, BN had to assume the cost of providing service on some lines with only a very light density of business. Whatever profit accrued to BN was marginal at best.

CHAPTER 33

CROSSING THE CASCADES

• comparisons of grades and distances •
• issues of maintaining line capacity •

IN COMPLETING THE LAST SEGMENT OF THE GN's transcontinental route, James J. Hill had to compromise on his mandate to build a railroad with the lowest grades. The GN line over the Cascade Mountains was initially built on a grade of 4.0 percent on the west slope and 3.5 percent on the east slope. The line had five switchbacks on the west slope, but seven years after it was opened, a tunnel of 13,813 feet was bored at the summit, allowing the grade to be reduced to 2.2 percent on both sides of the mountain.

The NP's line also was built to a grade of 2.2 percent. James J. Hill could have built the GN on a lower grade if he had decided to cross the Cascades over Snoqualmie Pass. However, because that location was so close to Stampede Pass, where the NP built, he decided against it, in favor of a crossing to the north that would give the GN better access to new territory and new business opportunities in Everett, Bellingham, and Vancouver, British Columbia. When the Milwaukee Road built its West Coast extension several years later, it used Snoqualmie Pass and had the advantage of lower grades (0.7 percent ascending westbound and 1.74 percent eastbound) than either the GN or NP. The UP reached the Pacific Northwest by crossing mountains in eastern Oregon where it operated on grades of 2.2 percent at two locations and 2.0 percent at a third location.

Even after building its first tunnel at the summit of the Cascades in 1900, the GN continued to experience high maintenance and operating costs due to grades of 2.2 percent on both the east and west slopes. Snowsheds totaling 8,401 feet in length had to be built for protection from avalanches. Because of the length of the tunnel, the line had to be electrified for 2.6 miles, which added greatly to the investment cost and required a separate set of motive power.

Hill told Ralph Budd a few years before his death that someday, Budd would have to "fix" this line. Budd took on this challenge after becoming president in 1919 and decided to locate the railroad on a new alignment. However, even with a major line change and a new, much longer tunnel of 7.79 miles, the maximum grade remained at 2.2 percent in both directions. It still was necessary to maintain a manned helper operation.

At the time the GN decided to build the second tunnel, consideration was given to building a much longer tunnel, either 14.5 miles or 17.5 miles in length. With a tunnel of 17.5 miles, the maximum grades could have been reduced to 1.2 percent on both slopes. Having a much lower grade would greatly enhance the efficiency and capacity of the line. Of course, numerous factors had to be analyzed, such as a much higher cost of construction and the need to build a tunnel of this length wide enough at about the mid-point for a siding so opposing trains could meet. Having a single-track segment for nearly 18 miles would have restricted line capacity and offset much of the advantage of having the lower grade.

A LOW-GRADE ALTERNATIVE TO THE CROSSINGS OF THE CASCADES

BN and BNSF have been able to avoid severe grades over the Cascades by using the lower grade line of the SP&S along the Columbia River. However, operation over the former SP&S line makes this route between Spokane and Everett 262 miles longer than the direct route over Stevens Pass.

When the GN's line over the Cascades was completed, Hill asserted it was the only weak and inefficient segment on its entire transcontinental route. Still determined to have a low-grade line all the way to the Pacific, he turned his attention to building a line to Portland along the north bank of the Columbia River. In a speech he delivered in Portland in 1905, Hill announced he would build a line of low grades and slight curvature that would be superior to any other line built west of the Rocky Mountains. This project would be the last link for a railroad of the standard he had established years earlier, and he intended to adhere to until his new rail line was completed to the West Coast. Use of the new line with its minimal grades would overcome the disadvantages of the grades of 2.2 percent over the Cascades. This new line between Spokane and Portland was to be owned in equal shares by the GN and NP. Its potential was not fully realized until after the 1970 merger.

MILWAUKEE'S LOW-GRADE CROSSING

When the Milwaukee shut down its West Coast operation in 1980, BN purchased several of its line segments, including the line over the Cascade Range on Snoqualmie Pass. This gave BN the potential for a much more favorable crossing of the Cascades as well as the additional capacity it might need in the years ahead. Acquiring this line would also prevent the possibility of the UP taking it over to increase its operating capability in new market opportunities that might develop in the future.

In addition to the advantage of operating over a line with lower grades, clearances in the tunnels on the Milwaukee's line were adequate for handling tri-level autorack cars and double-stack container cars. Those types of equipment cannot be moved through the tunnel on the former NP's line over Stampede Pass due to clearance restrictions. We conducted an exhaustive study as to the best locations where connections could be built between the NP and Milwaukee lines, to gain access to the low-grade line over the Cascades. By using the Milwaukee's line, heavier trains could be operated, and we would then have two routes over the Cascades that could handle the rapidly increasing volume of import business moving in double stack containers. Since the restrictive clearances on the NP line limited its use mainly to grain trains, and with the increased capacity we would gain with the Milwaukee line, the line over Stampede Pass would become a candidate for abandonment.

We were prepared to advance this project through the capital project review and approval process for 1982. However, three new and very powerful considerations had intervened since 1980 when the Milwaukee's line was acquired. One was approval of the application of BN and Frisco to merge that brought a new leadership team with a different set of priorities to the railroad. The second was the appointment of Richard M. Bressler as CEO of BNI, who set up a holding-company structure and changed the priorities for capital investment. The third was the deregulation of pricing and the consequent pressure on us to reduce costs, in part by decreasing the amount of track we were maintaining. Also, we were hit with a severe depression in the lumber and forest-products industries in the early 1980s, which greatly reduced traffic originating in the Pacific Northwest. The volume of business declined so much that we were able to move all trains, including the unit grain trains, on the GN route over Stevens Pass. The NP line over Stampede Pass was shut down in 1983.

When BN decided in 1982 to not put the route over Snoqualmie Pass in service, it was turned over to the State of Washington for use as a bike and hiking trail. The agreement between BN and the state provided that BN could serve notice to reacquire control over the line if it was ever needed for railroad service. However, the extent of deterioration of the roadway had become so great that the investment needed to restore it to service would have been formidable and more costly than restoration of the line over Stampede Pass.

RESTORING STAMPEDE PASS TO SERVICE

BNSF's CEO, R. D. Krebs, made a bold decision to put the line over Stampede Pass back in service in 1996. It was a very costly project, amounting to $125 million. In addition to restoring the track, bridges, and tunnels that had been out of service for twelve years, BN had to pay $40 million to a third-party short-line operator to reacquire the 148 miles of that line east of the Stampede Pass, between Kennewick and Cle Elum that he had purchased from BN in 1986. Krebs was roundly criticized by some members of the financial community for making such a large expenditure. He defended his decision on the basis that more capacity was sure to be needed, under the old adage, "Build it and they will come."

The extreme fluctuations in business that have occurred over about the last thirty years show how vulnerable the management of a railroad company is to criticism if it has made investments to expand its capacity. Since the assets a railroad acquires for its infrastructure have very long lives, there can be some merit (in the short run) to the arguments of financial people that it is best during times of heavy volume to just "tough it out" and not react to surges in volume by making investments to expand capacity. However, in looking back over the history of the railroads that formed BN, we are fortunate that such leaders as James J. Hill, Ralph Budd, and John Budd had the courage and foresight to build capacity and efficiency into the GN and SP&S to handle the amount of business they have even in times of economic recession. Had they not made these investments, we would have had great difficulty in meeting the needs our country had to move material and personnel for the war effort, as well as in the economic boom experienced in the Pacific Northwest from the end of the war and into the twenty-first century.

In the period between 2005 and 2008, when the rail system was under pressure to move heavy volumes of imported merchandise, the State of Washington initiated studies of the line of road and terminal capacity of the railroad companies. It was noted that to add significantly to capacity over the Cascades, major projects such as building double track, improving the clearance in the Stampede tunnel, or building a second tunnel of seventeen miles through Stevens Pass to reduce grades to 1.2 percent would require investments that might be far larger than a privately owned railroad company would wish to undertake. Operation through a tunnel of that length might require electrification, depending on whether it would be possible to design a ventilation system adequate for diesel locomotives. Since the state has no desire to add lanes to Interstate 90 or to build an entirely new east-west expressway for trucks, diversion of funds from highway construction to rail projects of that magnitude might become necessary.

CHAPTER 34

EVALUATING THE NON-RAIL SUBSIDIARIES

AIR FREIGHT, TRUCKING, LAND DEVELOPMENT, TELEPHONE, AND AVIATION SERVICES

• BURLINGTON NORTHERN AIRMOTIVE •

• *became the Twin Cities's largest fixed-base operator* •

IN 1968 A NORTHERN PACIFIC SUBSIDIARY, THE Monad Company, acquired a "fixed-base operator" at the Minneapolis–St. Paul International Airport owned by the Peavey Company. Now named Northern Airmotive, the new company soon expanded its services by acquiring two other companies that also provided such services as fuel, hangar storage, line service, and aircraft maintenance for corporate and private aviation. At the time of the merger in 1970, Northern Airmotive was put under BN's subsidiary, the Glacier Park Company.

By 1971 sales had grown to $5 million. Northern Airmotive was said to have 80 percent of the corporate aviation business in the Twin Cities area. Owning such a successful company provided a good "front" to the business community. In 1982 Northern Airmotive was sold to the Van Dusen Company, also a specialist in services to private aircraft, for $1.45 million. As was the case with BNAFI, Northern Airmotive was not part of BN's core business in transportation and the development of its resources, mainly oil and gas.

At the time of the sale, corporate America was leaning toward the retention and focus on only core businesses, and then selling or spinning off its non-core businesses. While Burlington Northern Airmotive required relatively little of management's time, by 1982 it was still believed that the valuable resources of management time and energy could best be applied to a company's largest businesses and those in which the company excelled. In the case of BN, management had so many challenges in running its railroad and resources businesses that it was not considered good to have its attention diverted to "fun" and perhaps more glamorous, small businesses such as Northern Airmotive.

• BURLINGTON NORTHERN LAND DEVELOPMENT CORPORATION (BNLDC) •

• to develop property not needed for rail operating purposes •

BNLDC WAS ESTABLISHED IN 1974 AS A NEW subsidiary to promote development of BN–owned land not needed either for rail or resources activities. In its early years, BNLDC negotiated an interest in a variety of real estate projects, including hotels, office parks, retail facilities, and residential-lot improvements. It even set up a few restaurants known as "Andy's Diner," using retired passenger cars as part of their appeal. In most of its ventures, BNLDC's equity was based on the value of the land it contributed to the project, rather than investing cash, or land plus cash, to get a greater share of the equity and a higher rate of return.

In 1975, BNLDC's first full year of operation, it had operating income of $597,000. In making purchases of land from its parent company, its operating income declined in each subsequent year, down to a loss of $312,000 in 1977 and a gain of only $23,000 in 1978. BN management was not satisfied with BNLDC's performance, but without having surplus funds available for investment in real estate development, it did not see an easy approach to significantly improve results.

Richard Bressler was critical of what he saw as a very conservative, non-aggressive approach in the types of projects BNLDC had undertaken and in the amount of investment made by BNLDC in those projects. He felt BN should be demanding and negotiating for a far greater equity position not limited to the value of the land. It was not long until Bressler brought in a "high-flying" commercial real estate person he had known in California to restructure the development of such projects.

Shortly after Bressler moved into the new holding-company office in Seattle, he called and asked if I would take him on a drive through an industrial park a few miles south of the downtown area that had been built on land once owned by the former NP. Over the previous thirty years, the NP and BN had sold this land in parcels to about fifty businesses that would be using rail service. Those companies built mainly warehouses and distribution centers on the property they acquired from us. Over the years most of them had shifted their business away from the use of rail cars to trucks or rail intermodal service. On the day we made our tour, there were only a handful of cars spotted for loading or unloading at the doors of any of these customers. The rail on some of the tracks was rusted and the tracks were overgrown with weeds and brush. The shift of transport method was not uncommon at the facilities of customers at many locations who had built on land they acquired from railroad companies.

Don Cowles, the Seattle Region's head of industrial development, was with us on our drive through this area. Bressler asked him what level of compensation the railroad had received for the sale and use of its land. Don replied that in most cases, the land had been sold at a relatively low price, on the expectation the railroad would be compensated with new carload business. Bressler clearly stated his dissatisfaction with a policy to sell rather than lease the land. Under a lease rental agreement, we would have been able to increase the rate over time, but once the land was sold, we had given up any such opportunity. Worse than that, our rail service was no longer being used.

Bressler directed there should be no more sales of industrial land, and that whether a potential buyer would be a user of rail service should not be a factor in negotiating the terms for a lease. Bressler was a mild-mannered person, but on this issue, he was very emphatic.

At the end of our drive, Bressler wanted to see the BN–owned land along the waterfront in downtown Seattle where he had been told a hotel was to be built. Bob Ortlip, the head of BNLDC, was with us to explain the parameters of the deal under which we had equity in the project. As generally was the case with such projects, our ownership was to be based on the value of our land as a percent of the cost of the project. Bressler was dissatisfied with that policy. He asserted that with the strong negotiating position we had in the deal, our equity in the project should have been much higher. When Bressler was told BN had not wished to divert cash to investment in non-rail projects, Bressler stated that most such projects would likely give us a far greater return than we were getting from investments being made in the railroad at that time. BNLDC may be an example of too much pressure coming from BN's board and investor interests to begin to develop non-operating land resources before BN could realistically do so, given the limitations of available management to devote time and financial resources in those years.

It wasn't long before restructuring of the management of BNLDC was announced, together with changes in the policies for managing opportunities involving land not being used for operating purposes. A more aggressive approach was taken in such high-potential projects as the hotel on the waterfront in Seattle. BN let it be known to our partners in that project that without the land, it was obvious the hotel could not be built. Besides, with our ownership of property that faced Puget Sound and the Olympic Mountains in the distance, we were bringing one of the world's most valuable commercial properties to the table. The old, traditional policy for managing railroad-owned property was out of another era, and certainly did not fit Bressler's ideas for exploiting the value of the land we owned.

Having yet another subsidiary for managing small, low-income projects was another example of drawing management attention from running the nation's largest railroad system and its extensive resource holdings. Such distractions as railroad-themed restaurants was not the best use of management time and attention.

• BURLINGTON NORTHERN AIR FREIGHT, INC. (BNAFI) •

• a resounding success—became the nation's second-largest air-freight forwarder in its tenth year of operation •

RIGHT FROM ITS START, BURLINGTON NORTHERN was more than a railroad company. It also owned a vast array of assets in forested lands, oil- and gas-producing areas, and mineral rights. In the field of transportation, BN owned a fairly large truck line and had ownership in a pipeline company operating in North Dakota and Minnesota. We owned an aircraft-servicing company based in Minneapolis, and our intermodal freight business was expanding rapidly. We were "more than a railroad."

In the early 1970s, BN's executives and marketing officers began to explore the possibility of establishing an air-freight forwarding company. It was anticipated that synergies could be developed between a new air-freight company and BN's trucking company, and its rapidly growing intermodal service, within the territory served by the railroad company. It was assumed during the planning stage that the company would be based in St. Paul in order to have the advantages of support and synergies from the various BN headquarters functions. Initial plans and regulatory approval filings were prepared on this basis.

Most people of BN were surprised when they learned of plans to go into the air-freight business. Indeed, BN's senior management had made a bold step in announcing plans to start a new company to be called Burlington Northern Air Freight, Inc. (BNAFI). We would be getting into an area of transportation service that would be completely new to us, and having to work with many potential customers having vastly different service requirements than those who used rail service. An equally large difference would be in the kind of equipment needed in moving the customers' business. There were many companies in the air freight business, making it a highly competitive business for a new entrant.

Dave Ylkanen, vice president–Human Resources, was directed to find a person with a record of success in the air-freight business to establish the new company. Dave had been successful in identifying and recruiting many well-qualified people for the Resources Division, as well as for the Finance, Marketing, and Property Management departments. It did not take long for Dave and Norman Lorentzsen to decide to hire Lawrence Rodberg and George Ryan, who held senior positions with Airborne Freight Corporation.

Bob Garland, senior vice president–Finance and Aministration, recalls the early steps BN took in getting the new company established:

> Led by Norman Lorentzsen, BN executives listened carefully to Rodberg and Ryan and revised their plans in accordance with their guidance. While BN headquarters support would be needed, there would be less synergy than previously anticipated. To succeed, it would be necessary to operate nationally and internationally, with stations in most major U.S. cities. [Rodberg and Ryan advised] the air freight forwarder's services would have to be marketed to shippers, not consignees. For best results, the company should be headquartered in one of the nation's largest cities, such as New York, Chicago or Los Angeles. Although it caused some delay in getting regulatory approvals, this willingness to change our thinking was a key factor in BNAFI's great success.[1]

BNAFI began operations on June 15, 1972, with terminals in ten cities and one hundred employees. Its business was to receive shipments, generally of small size, from a large number of customers, consolidate them, and have them shipped on established commercial airlines. BNAFI never acquired its own planes. Local pickup and delivery service was provided with its own employees and with motor vehicles owned by BNAFI. The new company operated terminals for sorting freight by destination and delivery point. At the time of BNAFI's startup, Rodberg predicted it would be among the top ten air freight forwarders, among the three hundred companies already in that business, by the end of 1973, only eighteen months later. That goal was achieved. In its first year, BNAFI also started serving several overseas locations.

In only its second year, BNAFI was already running a profitable operation, and had become the sixth-largest domestic forwarder. By 1976 BNAFI's market share was 45 percent and it was expected to grow to 53 percent by 1985. Among international forwarders, BNAFI ranked in the top ten by 1977. Its employment grew to 914 in 1977, and by 1980, it increased to 1,988.

Bob Garland characterizes the level of oversight BN provided in those times:

> During the 1970s BNAFI's Board of Directors consisted almost entirely of BN executives, along with Larry Rodberg and George Ryan. The BN executives functioned largely as an independent board, providing overall guidance and appraisal of performance. There were few, if any, major disagreements, but rather an approach of understanding what was necessary and supporting BNAFI management in making good decisions. One of these, for example, was the decision not to operate in one profitable foreign market because that wouldn't be possible on an ethical basis. BN people were proud of that decision.[2]

In 1979 BNAFI had pre-tax income of $19.1 million, compared with $8.8 million in 1978. Operating income in 1978 increased 90 percent over 1977. Revenue in 1979 had grown to $236.8 million. BNAFI's senior management attributed this resounding success to the drive that all of the company's people had to provide superior service at a competitive price. They worked by a slogan: "People, not planes, deliver." Another factor was Rodberg's reputation in the industry. Because of it, BNAFI was able to attract the best people. Recognition of the name "Burlington Northern" was said to be an important factor, plus the strong support BN gave to its new subsidiary.

This outstanding rate of growth continued into 1981, making BNAFI the nation's second-largest forwarder of air freight, both in revenue and domestic tonnage. Despite that success and a promising future, the new management under Richard Bressler announced the decision to sell BNAFI early in 1982. The buyer was the Pittston Company, which had interests in coal, fuel distribution, warehousing, truck leasing, and security transportation. It was reported that Pittston bought BNAFI for $177 million in cash.[3]

In announcing the sale, Bressler advised it was difficult to sell a successful company, but that BNAFI had "little interaction with our other businesses."[4] There was also a concern that in becoming such a large air freight

1 Robert Garland, e-mails to author.

2 Robert Garland, e-mails to author.

3 Gordon Donaldson, *Corporate Restructuring*, 117.

4 BN *News*, April 1982.

forwarder, BNAFI would soon face the need to acquire its own planes. With all of the demands for capital to invest in BN's other lines of business, there was no support on the part of the new management for taking on a large investment in aircraft. Instead, the direction was to invest all available capital into the resources side of BN, and less into transportation of any form.

Larry Rodberg left BNAFI a short time after it was taken over by Pittston. The growth and overall success of BNAFI was phenomenal and stood out as a symbol of pride in what had been accomplished in a completely new endeavor. BNAFI serves as a good example of what can be accomplished when a company hires a great leader with expertise in a particular line of business, and then gives that person the authority he or she needs to run it. It also shows that an old-line business such as a railroad company could be successful in starting, owning, and operating a vastly different kind of business. There are some who would argue that a railroad would apply the old railroad-type methods and culture that would stifle the new enterprise and cause it to fail. That certainly did not happen with BNAFI under BN's ownership.

It was a real credit to the BN board and to Menk and Lorentzsen for the support they gave BNAFI and the freedom they gave Rodberg to develop the business. Lorentzsen in particular took great pride in the rapid progress made by BNAFI and in his service on the Board of BNAFI. The only disadvantage in BN owning a company in such a different kind of business was our senior management having to focus on it in addition to the enormous challenge they had in giving direction to the railroad and the Resources Division in those years. Having any "sideline" (although very successful) business to watch over in those times had to be something of a distraction and an additional burden of responsibility for BN's senior management.

• BN TRANSPORT (BNT) •

• an over-the-road trucking company set up to complement rail merchandise freight service •

EACH OF THE THREE LARGE RAILWAYS THAT made up BN owned a truck line. Burlington Truck Lines (BTL) operated in much of the territory of the former CB&Q Railroad as a full-fledged common carrier. BTL handled truckload freight under its own billing, and distributed LCL (less-than-carload) freight between stations that moved under railroad billing. It also provided some intermodal ramping and deramping service for the railroad. Most of BTL's operating certificates were restricted to service that was auxiliary to or supplemental to rail service. BTL was the third-largest truck line, headquartered in Illinois. For the most part, its managers had their roots in the trucking business rather than the railroad.

Northern Pacific Transport (NPT) provided common-carrier service in Montana, Idaho, Washington, and Oregon. It also handled railroad-billed LCL business at several locations on the NP system, as well as intermodal operations in terminals and the unloading of automobiles from multi-level rail cars.

The Great Northern operated a trucking subsidiary called GN Motor Lines, serving stations on GN's railroad lines primarily in Montana, east of Whitefish. It also operated bus service between Great Falls and Havre and between Kalispell and Whitefish, making connections with GN's passenger trains. It served as a motor common carrier of general commodities, but was restricted to service that was auxiliary to or supplemental of rail service.

All three truck lines were set up to handle the delivery and pickup portion of the railroads' LCL business. LCL freight was loaded in boxcars or piggyback trailers, mainly at Chicago and the Twin Cities. The boxcars and trailers were moved to freight houses in such stations as Galesburg, Omaha, St. Joseph, Great Falls, Missoula, Helena, and Spokane, and transferred to the trucking subsidiaries for delivery to local customers and to smaller stations along the railroads' lines.

Not long after the 1970 merger, BN decided to discontinue its remaining LCL service. Without LCL freight to handle, there was no basis for continuing the operation of the GN Motor Lines, and it was shut down. In 1971 the NPT and BTL were merged into a new trucking company named BN Transport, Inc., to be headquartered in Galesburg. Later, BNT moved its headquarters office to Denver. At that time, BNT operated 3,000 pieces of equipment over 17,000 route miles with just over 1,400 employees. It ranked sixty-sixth of the 1,503 Class I motor carriers of general commodities in the United States with gross revenue of $25.6 million. BN's intermodal department was charged with combining the services of the railway with those of the truck line to provide a good service package.

Bob Garland described the relationship between BN and its trucking companies: "In the 1970s guided the trucking company through BNT's Board of Directors which consisted almost entirely of BN executives. BN was supportive and provided overall human resources and finance/accounting oversight, but encouraged the trucking company's management to run the business."[5]

In July 1972 Edward L. McCormick, an experienced executive from the trucking industry, was hired to run BNT. Revenue increased to $30.5 million in 1977, with net operating income of $2.2 million. Good results continued into 1978, with revenue ton-miles increasing by 48 percent over 1977. In those years, BNT's drivers won several awards for safety in competition with drivers working for truck lines that were members of major trucking associations. In January 1978 BNT acquired Hart Motor Express, which had operations in six states, for $9.5 million in cash.

5 Robert Garland, e-mails to author.

In 1984 Michael Lawrence was hired from Schneider National, the nation's largest truckload carrier, to head BNT. Lawrence had served at president of Schneider's National Independent Contractor Group. He held a PhD in Finance and was well known in the trucking industry for his work in mergers and acquisitions. While working at BN, Lawrence established a new trucking company, Burlington Northern Motor Carriers (BNMC) to acquire and operate five truckload carriers. By 1987 BNMC had revenue of $195 million, with 1,892 tractors and 3,354 trailers in service. It became one of the largest such carriers in the United States, only two years after starting its acquisitions program. With nationwide operating rights, the intent of this program of acquisitions and expansion of operations was to gain the economies of scale from operating a large network. Together with Lawrence's success in applying operations research techniques, BNMC became a very successful operation.

BN sold BNMC in 1988 to a group of managers of the truck lines that BN had recently acquired, along with a group of finance companies. The newly formed company was renamed Burlington Motor Carriers. In 1990 the five companies were merged, and soon after that Burlington Motor Carriers declared bankruptcy, allegedly due to "mounting debt."[6]

6 OOIDA vs. Burlington Motor Carriers, Inc. Burlington Northern Annual Reports for 1977 through 1988; Warren B. Powell, "Real-Time Dispatching for Truckload Motor Carriers," 2007, http://thetenneygroup.com; "BN Transport," *BN News,* October, 1972.

• LEMHI TELEPHONE COMPANY •

• generated about $400,000 annually in operating income
• sold to Century Telephone Enterprises in 1981 •

THE NORTHERN PACIFIC BROUGHT TO BN THE Lemhi Telephone Company, a small telephone company that served the area in and around Salmon, Idaho. The lines for telephone service were put into service in the early 1900s by an entrepreneur, W. A. McCutcheon, who also set his sights on building a line of railroad to serve a mining area. Somehow, he managed to interest James J. Hill in building the railroad, even though it was to be located far from any of Hill's interests, including the NP, that Hill controlled at that time. The NP provided technical and engineering support and took control of the new railroad, named the Gilmore and Pittsburgh.

At that time, the NP had visions of extending the branch line it had built to Twin Bridges, Montana, across Bannock Pass and on to Salmon, where it would connect with the Gilmore and Pittsburg. The new line would be the start of an additional transcontinental line across Idaho.

In 1913 the new railroad already was struggling, and the NP wrote off $6 million of debt it had incurred for construction in exchange for full ownership of the line. Ownership of the telephone company came with the railroad. By the 1930s, the mines were depleted and the line was taken out of service. It was abandoned in 1939.

The BN owned and managed the Lemhi Telephone Company until the early 1980s, when it was sold to another independent telephone company in the area. It was one of several non-core businesses BN sold in order to focus on its holdings in transportation and resources. In the years just before the Lemhi Company was sold, it earned operating income of about $400,000, a fairly good return for such a small enterprise.

THE DECISION TO SHED SMALL SUBSIDIARY COMPANIES

As already stated, none of these small subsidiary companies took much day-to-day time of senior BN executives, other than BNAFI, where strategic decisions had to be made on how much further BN should attempt to "grow" the company. The real purpose for selling these companies may have been to show investors and employees that "the new BN" was to be focused entirely on its underdeveloped resource base and on improving the financial performance of its railroad company. Since the small subsidiary companies were a distraction from those two major goals, it was thought best to sell tem.

Further, this was at the beginning of the time in American business history that many large conglomerate-type companies were taking action to reduce their holdings to their core businesses—those in which they felt they had a competitive advantage and the most expertise in managing. To make this possible, they were selling or spinning-off any of their businesses in which they either could not, or chose not to, become the best among their competitors. In the rail industry, this approach was taken by CP Limited, Union Pacific, Norfolk Southern, and CSX as well. A notable exception to this trend for a long time was General Electric, which owned and excelled in its ownership of a widely diverse group of businesses, ranging from financial services to the manufacture of aircraft engines, railroad locomotives, electrical equipment, and computer-based manufacturing systems, among many others.

CHAPTER 35

ELECTRIFICATION

CONSIDERED BUT NOT APPROVED

The gross investment would be about $780 million for 740 miles of line. We are examining electrification because fuel prices have reached the level on which electrification would present an attractive return on investment.

THOMAS J. LAMPHIER, SENIOR VICE PRESIDENT–TRANSPORTATION POLICY AND ANALYSIS, "ELECTRIFICATION: AN ANSWER TO RISING FUEL COSTS," *BN NEWS*, JANUARY 1981

THE RAPID INCREASE IN THE PRICE OF diesel fuel and threats to the ability to maintain an adequate supply of locomotive fuel during the 1970s caused BN to look seriously at electrifying its heavy-tonnage lines. Next to the U.S. Navy, BN was the country's largest user of diesel fuel. A study conducted in 1973 indicated that by electrifying a 1,200-mile section of railroad, BN's cost for the energy to power its locomotives would be reduced from $5 million annually to $1.4 million with electric power. With the large deposits of coal on BN lands, it was thought by some that coal might be traded for electric power, or that power could be generated from coal supplied from mines located on BN lines. BN already had to finance the $2 billion of capital expenditures identified to upgrade its roadway and expand capacity in the next several years. This made it unrealistic for BN to take on an additional project that would cost about $1 million per mile to build the overhead catenary system and for it and electric power companies to jointly finance the construction of new generating capacity.

With electrification, BN would have the advantage of the higher tractive effort and higher adhesion available with electric locomotives. Locomotive maintenance costs would be lower and would enable BN to avoid increasing challenges to reduce emissions from diesel engines. However, there would be significant disadvantages in addition to the capital investment required, among them the need to build separate maintenance facilities for electric locomotives, the cost of maintaining the catenary, the exposure of open wire to ice storms and damage from wind, and the general unsightliness of a catenary structure in the communities and scenic areas along the railroad's lines.

Electric locomotives in freight service were expected to have an economic life of fifty years, and since the heavy movement of low-sulfur coal was anticipated to be only half as long, in the range of twenty to twenty-five years, BN would find itself with a large fleet of electric locomotives with at least half of their economic life remaining. Very likely, there would be no other railroads, at least not in North America, that would want to acquire those electric locomotives, regardless of their age or condition. In returning to diesel-powered locomotives, the catenary would have to be dismantled long before it would be in need of major overhaul or upgrading. Electrification was given very serious consideration by BN's senior staff for some time, and expert advice was sought from several consulting groups before the decision was made in the late 1970s to drop the project from further consideration.

Not long after the change in management in the early 1980s, new financing proposals were presented that would not require BN to take on as large a burden for initial investment as was the case with the proposals considered about ten years earlier. Bob Garland recalled that "these new financing proposals involved leasing virtually all of the electrification system, including electric locomotives, power transmission lines, etc. The leases involved a seemingly lower interest rate that temporarily made the leasing proposal look financially attractive to some of us. However, our new Chairman and CEO, Dick Bressler, who had substantial financial expertise, pointed out that even for such a large and unique project, the correct financial analysis required the use of BN's real (and higher) cost of capital. When this was done the lease-financing proposal was immediately rejected."[1] Together with the mandate to reduce the asset base, and to hunker down and stick to the basic technology, equipment and infrastructure already in place, the new proposals were quickly dismissed.

No other freight railroad in North America has made a move to electrify, even with the much higher earnings of recent years and the strains on capacity that have been experienced on some parts of all railroads. Other than some lines in the former Soviet Union and China and a few other scattered locations outside North America, no high-density freight railroads have ever set up an electrified operation.

1 Robert Garland, e-mails to author, November 2015.

CHAPTER 36

MOVING THE MASSES

SUBURBAN SERVICE

• every day, 65,000 people are taken to and from their jobs safely, at 70 miles per hour, on a high-density line of railroad •

TRANSFORMATION OF THE SERVICE IN THE 1970S

While the service provided by BNSF and its predecessors has been a real success story, the economics of this type of service have never generated a profit, whether a private company operated it or when the operation was completely in the hands of a publicly supported organization such as Metra. Even though it was not a money-making operation, the railroad company had to be sure it was running it safely, efficiently, and at a very high level of reliability. This required daily attention to details, having a well-trained workforce in place with a strong, positive attitude toward customer service, and a commitment from the company to manage the operation to meet combined expectations for freight service, patrons of the suburban service and Amtrak, and governmental agencies that held responsibility for funding and general oversight of suburban passenger service.

Throughout its history, the suburban service has carried a high profile. Failures and deficiencies in any aspect of the operation often resulted in unfavorable publicity. A number of the regular patrons were people of influence in business, government, or politics. The fact that it was a money-losing operation for the railroad company meant little or nothing to patrons if they were late for work or home, if the air conditioning failed, or whenever the behavior of an "undesirable" passenger made their trip unpleasant. Polls conducted by the news media and various agencies over the years consistently found that the patrons of today and years past rated their experiences on BN and CB&Q the highest of any of the suburban rail passenger lines in the Chicago area.

Despite the fact that the operation provides no positive financial gain for the company and it requires a great deal of management attention, the railroad's people have always taken great pride in the service. It is a symbol of a disciplined operation, consistency and "class" that railroad people who are associated with it in some way will rally around. It is not unlike the pride employees had in the premier passenger trains we operated in the pre-Amtrak times such as the *Denver Zephyr, North Coast Limited,* and the *Empire Builder.*

BACKGROUND AND HISTORY ON THE BURDEN OF PROVIDING SERVICE AT A LOSS

In the 1920s and before, when the CB&Q and many other railroads had operating ratios in the 50s and 60s, and made a high return on their invested capital, losses from their suburban passenger operation were not crippling. These losses could be absorbed without causing too much strain on the company's finances. The railroad companies ran it with no public assistance for either capital investment or the operating deficits. In those times, they generated enough cash to be able to pay for the capital expenditures needed for upgrading, modernizing, and expanding the service when needed. After

THE BACKGROUND AND SCOPE OF TODAY'S OPERATION

TODAY'S BNSF OPERATES SUBURBAN PASSENGER SERVICE UNDER CONTRACT WITH A GOVERNMENTAL agency for upwards of 65,000 people (total, inbound and outbound) in the Chicago area each weekday. For many years this has been an impressive operation, highly acclaimed for its record of safety and the quality of service provided. The territory for this operation is BNSF's main line corridor between Union Station in Chicago and Aurora, a distance of thirty-eight miles. Between Cicero and Aurora, this corridor is the artery for BNSF's freight service. At Aurora, this corridor splits, with one main line serving the Twin Cities and the Pacific Northwest, and the other main line leading to Denver, Kansas City, California, and Texas.

The operation for suburban passenger service is conducted on a three-main-track infrastructure, with a fourth main track in place for seven miles at the east end of the corridor. All main tracks are signaled for operation in both directions on each track. Having high-speed crossover switches to permit movement between main tracks an average of every four miles provides operating flexibility on this high-capacity system. Train speeds are set at a maximum of 70 miles per hour for passenger trains and 50 for freight trains, through an area of high-density population.

At the time of this writing, 106 suburban trains are run from Monday through Friday. That number is reduced to 28 trains on Saturdays and 18 trains on Sundays and holidays. BNSF runs between 30 and 50 freight trains per day. That number fluctuates by season, by day of the week, and in line with current business conditions in the sectors of the economy in which BNSF's customers are based. In addition, eight daily Amtrak trains are routed on this line. BNSF personnel handle the dispatching from the network operations center in Fort Worth. The quality of the suburban passenger service provided by BNSF and its predecessor roads, BN and the CB&Q, is credited for much of the growth in population along this corridor. Patronage of the suburban service has increased significantly in the past fifty years. In 1970 about 19,000 passengers were carried on weekdays. By 1980 that number increased to 42,000 and, currently, well over 60,000 people use the service.

having poor earnings in the Depression years, followed by little or no opportunity to modernize the service or carry out heavy maintenance programs during World War II, the railroads lost ground. After the war, they had to invest heavily in dieselization, track renewal, and replacing much of their freight car fleets. In the 1950s and '60s, they had difficulty in achieving an adequate level of earnings due to inflationary pressures and increasing loss of business to competing modes.

By the 1960s, the old model for supporting passenger service had to be changed. Railroad companies, including the CB&Q, could no longer endure losses from providing commuter and intercity passenger service. Fares could not be increased fast enough to keep pace with inflation on wages and materials. Since we were providing a social service rather than a business service in running trains for commuters, a method had to be found to transfer the financial burden to some kind of governmental authority. The time had come for the public and its elected representatives to understand that a public partnership, subsidy, or governmental takeover of these operations had to be established. In the late 1960s, Theodore G. (Ted) Schuster, general attorney for the CB&Q, began to advance the idea of working with the suburban communities to make application for the funds needed to modernize and upgrade the cars and locomotives, and to acquire more equipment to meet the increasing demand for the service.

In his book of recollections, Schuster relates a 1968 meeting of the CB&Q's senior management in which he participated, as a watershed moment in which the company faced an immediate need to deal with the capital overhang in its suburban operation.[1] Robert E. Taylor, chief mechanical officer, advised the senior executives at this meeting of the need to invest $25 million in the near term to upgrade the car and locomotive fleet in order to maintain reliability and quality of service. The immediate and most acute problem was having the air conditioning fail on about one-half of the fleet each day during the weeks of hot, sweltering summer weather. The old Waukesha "engineators" located on each car that generated cool air were simply worn out. Even with heavy maintenance, "the Waukeshas" could not be kept in operation since replacement parts were no longer made. To keep these outdated devices in service, the CB&Q was having to fabricate parts in its own shops.

That was the immediate problem, but Taylor pointed out that in addition to the problems with air conditioning, there was the need to replace the ancient "power cars" that housed the diesel engines used to generate electricity for the passenger cars. Instead of generating heat electrically, the CB&Q relied on old-technology steam boilers located in the locomotives. Having a system using steam for heating the cars was expensive to maintain and it was difficult to regulate and maintain heat for passenger comfort. Also, the locomotives used in commuter service had reached the point where they needed to be rebuilt and upgraded.

It was pointed out in the meeting that the CB&Q had earned only $15 million in net income in 1968. The forecast for earnings in 1969 was only $12 million. Out of those earnings, the CB&Q was expected to pay $12.8 million in dividends to the GN and NP. The amount of cash available for capital expenditures after paying dividends was far too little to pay for the level of heavy track maintenance needed and for other vital improvements to the property to support the company's freight service. Certainly, it was out of the question to invest $25 million (or even $1 million) in improvements to an operation that generated no profit.

A MODEL FOR PUBLIC PARTNERSHIP FOR ACQUIRING AND REBUILDING CARS AND LOCOMOTIVES

William J. Quinn, then president of the CB&Q, directed Schuster to prepare recommendations for new ways of financing the commuter operation. Schuster learned of a new federal grant program under the Urban Mass Transit Administration (UMTA) in which a public body could apply for grants for the upgrading and replacement of rolling stock used by private mass-transit operators. The Illinois Central Railroad had persuaded the communities along its line to form a local mass-transit district, which could apply for the funds needed for investment in equipment. Further, the IC could not afford, nor could it continue to absorb, the operating loses it was enduring in providing commuter service. The transit district applied for the maximum two-thirds funding available to it under the regulations governing such grants. The IC would provide the one-third local match. The equipment acquired would be owned by the transit district and leased to the IC.

BN decided to follow the IC model as the most realistic way available at that time for getting some relief for the capital overhang it faced, and to deal with the annual operating loss of $2 million it was having to endure. To help convince the suburban communities along BN to join together to form a transit district, the question of a source for the one-third local share-matching funds had to be dealt with. Certainly, the CB&Q did not want to put in upwards of $10 million, nor was it realistic to expect the suburbs to agree to form a transit district that would have to impose a tax to raise the money. Schuster discovered a provision in the UMTA regulations that would allow the one-third local share to be an "in-kind donation," rather than being limited to a cash contribution. On this basis, the BN proposed to the suburbs that it would "donate"—transfer ownership of—its entire fleet of ninety-six commuter cars and twenty-one locomotives to the transit district. The district would then assert to UMTA that the local share was represented by the value of the cars and locomotives it had acquired from the BN.

1 *History of the West Suburban Mass Transit District*, self-published.

Before trying to sell the suburbs on the merits of forming a transit district—which would apply for the federal funds needed to modernize the cars and locomotives used in providing a vital service for a high percentage of their residents—the senior management of BN had to be convinced of the advantages of pursuing such a strategy for relief from the burden of ongoing operating losses and investing the massive amount of capital needed to improve and expand that service. Schuster brought this issue to the forefront in the early 1970s, shortly after the BN merger was consummated. At this time, there were no top-level executives on BN who'd had any experience in dealing with the commuter operation and all of the burdens it placed on the Burlington and the six private railways of the Chicago area that provided commuter transportation service. The only exception was L.W. Menk, president of BN, who had spent just one year in Chicago as president of the former Burlington.

The first challenge Schuster faced was to convince BN's management and board to accept the idea of financial assistance from governmental agencies. Railroads had prided themselves by being the epitome of private enterprise that would neither accept nor request any level or form of government aid or other involvement in our affairs. This attitude was in sharp contrast to the airline and trucking industries, which relied heavily on many forms of government support. BN's senior executives were consumed at that time with the many challenging and vital issues and projects involved in getting the newly merged railroad running well. They were not interested in spending time trying to understand enough of Shuster's proposal to make decisions on whether to move forward with it.

At the outset, the position of some senior executives based in St. Paul was to not authorize Schuster and the Chicago Region's mechanical and operating staffs to move ahead with the proposal. It was feared that accepting such federal assistance would give the government the opportunity to erode our "freedom" to operate and manage the Chicago–Aurora corridor of our railway according to our policies, methods, and standards. They expected we would soon begin to lose control of the rights and prerogatives we had as a privately owned railway company. At first, some even branded Schuster as a "socialist" for advocating that we put ourselves in danger of surrendering control of our destiny, losing the independence we needed to run the railroad according to our standards, and being able to maintain our ability to move freight efficiently.

In meeting with the elected representatives and professionals of the suburban governments, some initial reactions were that BN should not be attempting to foist its problems onto the taxpayers and the local government officials elected to represent their interests. However, there also were many forward-looking statesmen in leadership positions in the suburban communities who quickly grasped and favored the concept Schuster was advocating as the best opportunity available to us (and the suburban communities) for maintaining the quality and extent of service their residents needed to get to and from their jobs in downtown Chicago.

By 1972 10 of the 13 suburbs voted to form the West Suburban Mass Transit District (WSMTD). Only three communities, Cicero, Downers Grove and Aurora, decided not to join. The trustees of the district agreed to file for a grant from UMTA to cover acquisition of twenty-five new cars for BN's fleet and modernization of the ninety-four cars and twenty-one locomotives used in suburban passenger service.

At the time of approval of the first grant request, Forester J. Dusell, Director of Suburban Service, issued a communication, "A Partnership Report," summarizing the process and results achieved in modernizing BN's commuter operation:

> This is not a loan but an outright grant to the District (WSMTD) in recognition of a national and local problem that fare box revenues earned by most mass transit systems cannot finance major rolling stock improvements, and that public subsidies are necessary to provide efficient alternatives to highway traffic in urban areas. . . . As the program goes forward, WSMTD will acquire ownership of the entire Burlington Northern fleet, leasing it back to the railroad. Burlington Northern will continue to collect fares, staff and operate trains, and maintain [the] equipment.[2]

2 Forester Dusell, "A Partnership Report," 1972, a one-page handout given to passengers on commuter trains. Dusell was director of Suburban Service for Burlington Northern.

TO COVER OPERATING LOSES

Through the process of grant approval and funding made available by the Regional Transportation Authority (RTA), BN would obtain some relief from what had become an unreasonable and unsustainable burden of operating losses from maintaining service for the commuting public. It was the beginning of a long-lasting, constructive public partnership. To administer public funding for mass transit service, the State of Illinois formed the RTA in 1976. In meetings with the five Chicago-area commuter railroads, BN had taken the lead in working with the state legislature in getting the RTA formed. The RTA was set up as an umbrella organization over financial matters—in effect, a watchdog over operating budgets—to make sure that each of its constituent carriers maintained a certain level of fare receipts as compared to operating expenses. The three operating entities in the Chicago area, the CTA (Chicago Transit Authority), PACE (the suburban bus system), and Metra, were staffed with professional managers and placed under the oversight of the RTA.

BN soon entered into a Purchase of Service Agreement with the RTA. The agreement provided for partial reimbursement of BN's loss in operating and maintaining its suburban services. At that time, the amount of the subsidy was $500,000. During 1976 the RTA granted $7.6 million to BN. When the ICC revised its accounting rules in 1978, increasing the allocation of expenses to passenger operations, the resulting operating loss reported was $11.2 million.[3] Further, if BN operated its commuter trains at or above a threshold level of 90 percent for on-time performance, it would qualify for a modest incentive payment to further offset its operating losses. There was only a three-minute tolerance for late arrival of trains operated in the rush hour and five minutes for non–rush hour trains. The cost recovery through fares was 75 percent on BN. On the other commuter lines in the Chicago area, cost recovery was in the range of 55 to 60 percent. Under the law, Metra was required to increase fares when the rate of cost recovery became less than 55 percent. The first payment made to BN amounted to $38,000.

Ted Schuster's persistent but low-pressure style won the support of BN's senior management team for the strategy he developed for dealing with the capital overhang and the losses incurred by BN for operating the commuter service, both in the short term and in the growth in patronage expected in the future. It was very helpful that the two executives who served as vice president of the Chicago Region in those years, Ivan Ethington and Don King, understood what was at stake and were in position to work diligently in winning over the senior management staff. Ethington's role on issues involving the suburban territory became even more prominent and effective starting in 1972 when he was named vice president–Operations for the entire BN system.

MAINTENANCE AND UPGRADING OF STATION BUILDINGS

Next to getting a solution to the need for additional equipment and upgrading the current fleet, we needed to get some relief from the expense of maintaining the station buildings. In a fairly short time, Ted Schuster convinced the suburbs to assume responsibility for maintenance and upgrading of the station buildings. During the 1970s, while progress was being made on the equipment issues, the Illinois Department of Transportation (IDOT) prepared a program offering financial assistance for the improvement and expansion of stations and parking facilities. BN received a grant of $2 million, to be allocated by BN to the locations of highest need in the thirteen communities it served.

With the requirement that station buildings be kept open during the hours of train service, from about 5:00 A.M. to at least midnight—almost twenty-four hours—vandalism was rampant, even in the "wealthy" suburbs BN served. By law, restrooms had to be provided. Railroad employees were on duty at most stations for only a few hours during the morning rush hour for the sale of tickets, leaving the use and care of these buildings unsupervised most of the time. Railway labor had to be taken from bridge maintenance or work on the large freight houses BN owned in Chicago in order to perform the general maintenance needed to try to keep the station buildings clean and respectable in appearance. Track workers had to be pulled away from their work to maintain platforms and clear snow and ice from parking lots, walkways, and platform areas. While the buildings

3 BN Annual Report for 1978, page 26.

continued to be serviceable, all of them were in need of at least a facelift. Some of these railway-owned facilities were no longer seen as a credit to the community, but rather were becoming an eyesore.

Ted Schuster did a remarkable job of enlisting support and interest from the communities in upgrading and, in some cases, completely redesigning the station buildings, to put them in harmony with the kind of architecture and appearance that was appealing to residents of the area. City employees and volunteers added flower beds, shrubbery, trees, and benches to the station grounds. All of these sites soon became source of pride within each community. Another important part of the program for involving the communities in BN's suburban service was for them to take responsibility for clearing snow and ice from the walkways and station platforms early in the morning. This allowed all of our track-maintenance forces to be out on the track to keep crossover switches functioning during and after snowfalls and freezing rain. The result of these improvement programs for stations and grounds was a better-looking railway property in these high-end communities, as the residents came to recognize the suburban passenger operation we were providing was a social service and not a business responsibility.

Within a few years, the station buildings were rebuilt into show pieces. This successful effort won the hearts and minds of the commuters and the general public, including support from community leaders for the railway company and its place in their community. Local government authorities also stepped up to the plate on projects that would improve the quality and capacity of parking space available for commuters. Overall, this was a very successful effort on the part of IDOT, BN, the communities, and Ted Schuster, without question.

UPGRADING THE TRACK STRUCTURE

Following the issues of equipment, stations, and operating loses, the next challenge pursued by Schuster was the cost of track maintenance and upgrading, including track capacity to handle the demand for additional service. An effort was started to convince the governmental funding agencies that they should provide financial support to maintaining the extent of the infrastructure that was incremental to the suburban passenger service. In theory, that would include capacity equivalent to the third main track we maintained in addition to the two main tracks that would have been adequate if we operated only our freight trains on that corridor. Through that approach, the funding authorities also came to understand the need for our maintaining the ten sets of powered crossovers between main tracks located at intervals of between three to four miles in the 38-mile corridor between Chicago and Aurora.

The first such project was the replacement of the old switch machines on some of the crossovers that were designed to handle 90-pound switch points rather than the 129-, 131-, or 132-pound switch points that were actually in place. Apportionment of the cost between BN and the RTA was worked out for a start on replacement of jointed 131-pound rail that was due for replacement, with 132-pound continuous welded rail. Also, projects for undercutting the road crossings and the track adjacent to station platforms were jointly financed. The old blast-furnace slag ballast and similar kinds of low-quality aggregate had deteriorated and needed to be replaced with high-quality crushed granite rock brought in from sources in Minnesota. All grade crossings were rebuilt. New crossover switches designed for 50 miles per hour were installed at three locations. At two of those locations, the crossovers that were replaced restricted trains to a maximum speed of 35 miles per hour. The third location (at Lisle) was a completely new crossover installation, designed to increase line capacity and give more flexibility to dispatchers and those who were designing new train schedules for additional service that would be needed.

PROTECTING OUR FRANCHISE

Similar to what happened at the time proposals were being developed to modernize and expand the car and locomotive fleet, there was concern on the executive floor in the General Office Building in St. Paul that accepting grants for heavy track work would open the door to governmental control of the operation. It was feared that the length of time in which the morning and afternoon rush hours, when freight operations were curtailed, would be expanded, making it increasingly difficult for us to move our freight trains without undue delay. We held firm to our need to retain control of the operation by continuing to manage the dispatching and scheduling of commuter train service, and in the planning for track maintenance work. In these years, Metra purchased large segments of privately owned lines of other railroad companies that operated commuter service, among them, the Illinois Central, Milwaukee and Rock Island. Fortunately, BN declined an invitation to sell its line, even though the temptation was there to agree to sell and be paid a very large amount of cash. The lines that the Illinois Central, Milwaukee, and Rock Island sold to Metra had far less freight traffic than BN had on its line, making those lines less vital. Apparently, receiving a big windfall of cash was necessary and more important to them at that time than maintaining control of their railroad.

"THE DINKY PARADE": THE ZEAL TO RUN IT WELL

As mentioned at the start of this chapter, running this service required precision execution, day in and day out, by a team of expert employees that included dispatchers, signal maintainers, the local track maintenance (section) crews, locomotive engineers, train crews, car- and locomotive-maintenance personnel, and the local officers responsible for each of these specialties. Because the routines and standards for the operation were well established and consistently adhered to, the operation did not require either micro-managment or almost daily changes in the plan, as happens when consistency in execution is a problem. Instead, everyone involved in the operation knew exactly what was expected. With the experience and team spirit they had, employees were able to handle unexpected, out-of-routine situations such as winter storms, a signal failure, or other type of incident that would cause delay to one or more of the trains.

To the employees, there was nothing particularly amazing about the precision this operation required and the responsibility they had to make it work. It was just the way things had to be done. The challenge and the teamwork required built a real bond among dispatchers, train crews, and maintenance forces. They made it work. It was seldom that intervention by managers at any level in the Operating Department was necessary.

Because the operation was intense, with close headways between trains, an interruption to the routine operation of even one train during the rush hour could have an immediate, cascading effect on what was affectionately called the "dinky parade." There are some who consider the term "dinky" as disparaging or demeaning to such a high-class operation. In reality, it was only a railroad slang expression, "a term of endearment" used in reference to passenger trains that were handling only a few cars. On other railroads, such trains might be called scoots, puddle jumpers, dummies, or plugs.

As mentioned earlier, BN employees manned the suburban trains. Metra furnished the employees on all other commuter lines except for those owned by the Union Pacific. Because all of the runs were assigned rather than manned through a pool, employees had regular jobs with fixed on-duty times and scheduled days off. Even though these jobs generally paid less than through-freight service or most local freight-train assignments, employees who were high on the seniority roster often worked in suburban service, especially as they advanced closer to retirement.

The suburban passenger jobs for conductors and brakemen were not what you would call "real railroad jobs." They served well as a place for old-timers whose legs and knees were getting worn out from years of walking on irregular terrain and getting on and off cars and engines repeatedly while switching cars or making walking inspections of their trains. It also was a reward late in one's career for having had to work irregular hours, out in all kinds of weather, and having had no regular days off for many years of work in through freight service or on the extra board. Nearly all employees who worked in suburban service for any length of time successfully made the transition from the rough-and-tumble culture of freight service to dealing with the general public. It was important for the reputation of the company that the train service employees encountered by the patrons were courteous, pleasant, and professional.

The availability of funding for operating expenses through the RTA provided us the opportunity to establish full-time supervisory positions for the suburban passenger operation. It was a big relief to the trainmaster and road foreman based at Aurora to be relieved of the frequent (often several times a day) questions, suggestions, and directives concerning the "dinkies" they were expected to handle in addition to supervising the freight operation.

It was fascinating to watch the dinky parade in the dispatcher's office located in the division superintendent's office in Freight House 9 in Cicero. The Dispatchers had a large schematic board, about twelve feet by six feet that showed the location of all trains as they moved from one control point to the next, and as they were crossed over from one track to another track. It was an impressive display, with the board lit up like a Christmas tree or the Northern Lights. Some of the dispatchers forbade anyone from entering their "inner sanctum" to talk with them, or even to just watch the show in silence during the rush hour. They did not want to risk distraction or any break in their concentration. The scene of dozens of lights flashing on the CTC board was called a work of art by many who had a chance to watch the activity through the glass wall on one side of the dispatcher's office.

The dispatchers who regularly worked the rush hour were justified in the pride they had in being able to run a precise, complex operation very well, day in day out. After the morning rush hour, they had only a short breather until they had to deal with the many requests of track inspectors, signal maintainers, and maintenance gangs for track time to do their work. With one of the three main tracks usually out of service at scattered locations for maintenance during daylight hours, the dispatcher had to figure out how to coordinate the maintenance and inspection work with the flow of high-priority freight trains operating on tight schedules, moving the intercity passenger trains, plus the off-peak commuter trains that had to stop at every station.

A good way to experience the "thrill" of this operation was to ride the engine of No. 1, the *Denver Zephyr*, which departed Chicago Union Station at 5:00 P.M., right in the heart of the rush hour. No. 1 made no stops between Chicago and Aurora. Dispatchers usually put No. 1 on main track 2, the middle track, all the way. In the trip of about thirty-five minutes to Aurora, upwards of fifteen commuter trains would be seen. The crossover moves made by commuter trains and any freight train still out there during the "dinky parade" made from one main track to another had to be made precisely on schedule to avoid delay to any train. Dispatchers enjoyed the daily challenge of getting No. 1 to Aurora on time, and without delay to any of the "dinkies" that No. 1 either passed or met along the way.

A MAJOR ACCOMPLISHMENT

With the skills Ted Schuster had in forming the strategy and successfully negotiating terms for a revised model for suburban passenger service, BN and the other Chicago-area railroads obtained relief from the costly burden for a social service they could no longer provide without some outside financial support. In its contract with the RTA, BN would be made whole for the operating losses through funding from the RTA, which balanced the financing of capital expenditures to the amount of benefit BN would gain for its freight operation, compared to the suburban passenger operation. The RTA took responsibility for the acquisition and cost of maintaining the cars and locomotives. BN employees continued to operate the trains, maintain the track and signal system, and perform maintenance on the equipment. Their successful efforts in getting the public and its elected representatives to understand that providing suburban passenger service was a social obligation and not a business responsibility saved BN tens of millions of dollars for upgrading and maintaining that service. BN and the public were indeed fortunate that BN had such talent and commitment available in its ranks to handle that challenge.

CHAPTER 37

COAL TERMINAL AT ASTORIA

• desire for a large port facility to prime the local economy •
• potentially another costly upgrade on a long branch line •
• Union Pacific tries to show us up and move in •

IN 1980 THE PORT AUTHORITIES ALONG THE Pacific Coast got wind of the possibility that coal mined in the Powder River Basin might be exported to countries in the Pacific Rim. The demand for attention from BN was heavy, as each port moved quickly to extol the competitive advantages it thought it would have if we were to form a partnership with it in preference to another port. Among the ports maneuvering for our attention was Astoria, a community at the mouth of the Columbia River that had suffered loss of employment for several years from the closure of military installations, forest-product industries, and fish-canning plants.

The railroad line to Astoria was located at the end of a 95-mile branch line that had been maintained only to the standard needed to handle a relatively small amount of business. The track and five movable span bridges would have to be upgraded at considerable expense to handle even the first coal train, if a transfer facility were built on the line. BN did not immediately rise up and embrace the Port of Astoria over the enthusiasm it demonstrated for public funding of a port facility, and for BN to unequivocally state it would commit whatever amount of money would be needed to upgrade its track and bridges to the standard needed to handle heavy-unit trains.

There was no reason for BN to show strong interest in working with Astoria when there were deep-water ports on or close to our main lines along Puget Sound or on the Columbia River that were promoting themselves as well located and with the capability to finance the facilities needed to handle the business. Among those locations were Portland, Longview, Everett, and Cherry Point, near Bellingham. At the Roberts Bank facility near Vancouver, British Columbia, a new, high-capacity coal terminal was already in operation.

The Port of Astoria made clear its dismay with BN's lack of interest through the news media and elected representatives at all levels. In typical Union Pacific fashion, its president, John Kenefick, soon let it be known that the UP stood ready to support Astoria's interest in building a coal port. Although the UP had no operating rights on our line to Astoria, they informed the port and the community that it wouldn't stop them from handling the business. To do that, the UP said it would be willing to purchase the line from us and invest the amount necessary to upgrade it.

That assertion put pressure on us to respond as to whether and how soon we would sell our line to the UP, and thereby remove the issue of adequate rail access from the list of challenges Astoria would have to overcome before the first ship could be loaded with coal. BN's new president, Richard Bressler, responded quickly by inviting Oregon's governor, Vic Atiye, and a large group of government officials to join us on a special train of business cars to be run to Astoria on a Saturday morning in December 1980.

In a car set up to hold the large group, we made presentions on the standards to which the track would have to be upgraded and why. Bressler had already been with BN long enough to understand the dilemma we were facing, because some of our coal rates had not been set high enough to allow a satisfactory return on the capital we had invested to improve the track. We were not about to be stampeded into granting another "missionary" rate that would make Astoria competitive with a port on our main line where such massive upgrading would not be needed. The public officials on the train were able to conclude without our saying so that they should not expect that the UP would set rates that would not give it a satisfactory return on the investment it also would have to make if it acquired our line to Astoria.

Early in 1981, John Hertog, then senior vice president–Coal, advised a committee of the House of Representatives in Oregon that upgrading the Astoria line would cost about $35 million. This estimate included the work required to upgrade fifty bridges on the line. Hertog repeated the statement Richard Bressler had made on several occasions that BN was prepared to upgrade the line. This assertion was supported by the tremendous expenditures and commitments BN had made and fulfilled to handle tremendous tonnages of coal in recent year. However, such an expenditure would be made only if it made economic sense.

BN agreed to work cooperatively with Astoria in developing a detailed plan to upgrade its rail line to move high tonnages of bulk commodities to its port facilities. The port would determine the extent of dredging needed to provide a deep water port, and develop plans for a rail to ship transfer facility. In addition, BN would work with the port to explore business opportunities for increasing employment it might seek other than a coal transfer facility. The port and the community seemed confident that we could be counted on to work cooperatively with them. Bressler made it clear that the movement of coal to Astoria or any other port facility was dependent upon our having commitment from a customer that would make it a good business venture for BN to become involved in.

To facilitate a joint effort on the part of BN, the port and various other government agencies, Bressler enlisted the service of Hollis Dole, a retired executive of Atlantic Richfield. As a geologist, Dole had held a high-level position in the U.S. Department of Interior, and before that, in state agencies in Oregon. Dole had the skills, background, and reputation needed to establish that BN took Astoria's initiatives seriously. Dole's efforts were effective in getting all of the constituencies to work well together. While the work BN had underway with Astoria did not hold as much potential or chance for success as many other business opportunities BN had at that time, the success Bressler demonstrated in handling the challenge from Astoria proved to be a good indication early in his tenure on BN of the skills he had for putting the company in a strong position when its ability to act or to support the interest of its constituents was being challenged.

When the news media and elected representatives reported positively on the relationships we established, and the process for moving forward, the UP seemed to let its interest in acquiring our rail line diminish, at least in the public forum. No large bulk-transfer facilities have been built on the line to Astoria. Several years later, BN sold its Astoria branch to a short-line operator.

General interest in the exporting of the Powder River Basin's low-sulfur, low-BTU coal declined for several years, until about ten years ago, when a few trains were operated into the coal terminal at Roberts Bank. The volume to Roberts Bank has increased to generally two trains daily and rekindled the interest of other ports in building high-capacity rail to ship transfer facilities.

CHAPTER 38

FURTHER ADDITIONS TO ROADWAY CAPACITY

• to handle coal tonnages far greater than anticipated, reaching annual gross tons of from 200 million to 400 million on some line segments • to better handle growth in several other lines of business as well •

THIRD AND FOURTH MAIN TRACKS ON THE GILLETTE–ORIN LINE

By 1994 the new Donkey Creek–Orin line (completed in 1979) that provided access to the new mines opened in the Powder River Basin was handling tonnage at 97 percent of its capacity of about 185 million gross tons per mile. Congestion and inability to move loaded and empty trains to the satisfaction of the mining companies had become a serious problem for both BN and the C&NW, the co-owners of 102 miles of the line. The forecasts prepared by each of the railroads clearly indicated the demand for coal would continue to increase in the next few years. It was obvious that a combined effort was needed to plan far enough ahead to obtain the capital needed to build additional track capacity and to acquire the motive power needed to move the ever-increasing business.

Surprisingly, C&NW's CEO, Robert Schmeige, told *Railway Age* that the problem of congestion and train delay was their: "We were not persuasive enough in convincing others of the need to increase capacity."[1] Apparently Schmiege was saying that he had been unsuccessful in convincing BN, as the co-owner of the line, to make the plans needed to expand capacity and invest the large sums that would be required.

Capturing large tonnages of coal from BN in the first ten years of joint ownership had allowed the C&NW to move from a position of near bankruptcy to one of comparative wealth. With a lower operating ratio, the combined C&NW–UP network had been able to offer lower rates than BN in those years. BN was weakened by the loss of business to the C&NW and by the huge burden of debt it had to bear when the railroad company was separated from the non-rail enterprises BN had owned and spun off to its shareholders. Having to reduce that debt within a few years restricted BN from making capital expenditures of the magnitude needed to expand capacity in the Powder River Basin by the time it was needed.

However, the two railroads were able to reach an agreement in 1994 to build enough additional second main trackage to close up the single-track gaps that remained and to begin building a third main track on the grade on Logan Hill. Both companies acquired large numbers of new locomotives, and for short-term relief, the UP provided twenty-five of its locomotive units to augment BN's fleet. In the following year, BN and the Santa Fe merged to form BNSF, and UP acquired the C&NW. Together, BNSF and UP made the commitments and plans needed to move forward with capacity-expansion projects and to improve their operating capability to handle the unprecedented tonnages offered them.

In the early 2000s the most impressive addition to capacity was the construction of a third main track on 117 miles of the joint line between Donkey Creek and

1 Gus Welty, "C&NW, BN, UP Play Catch-up: Capacity Problems in the Powder River Basin," *Railway Age*, October 1994.

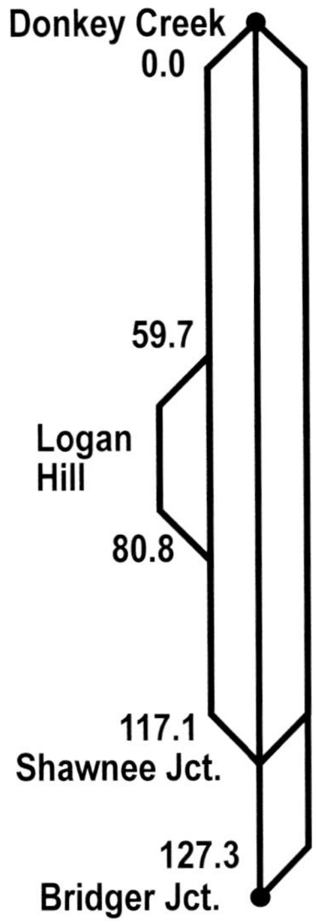

Figure 38.1. Location of second, third, and fourth main tracks on the Donkey Creek–Bridger Junction Line. When BN opened its new Donkey Creek–Bridger Junction line in 1978, it was mainly a single-track railroad. A second main track was soon added for the entire distance. As more and more electric-power companies found they needed to use low-sulphur coal mined in the Powder River Basin, a third main track was built over the entire distance north from Shawnee Junction. The build-up of congestion on the one percent grades on both sides of the Logan Hill required BN and UP to build a fourth main track for 21.1 miles. The 400 million gross tons handled on this line at its peak made it the heaviest and highest density railroad. MIKE BARTENSTEIN AND AMY JO STOCKINGER.

Shawnee Junction. Twenty-two miles of fourth main track were built to add capacity and improve general operating capability on Logan Hill, where congestion often built up due to having twelve consecutive miles of one percent grade.

In the next few years a third main track was built on the entire length of the 117-mile joint line, and a fourth main track of twenty-two miles on Logan Hill. It was necessary to add capacity in order to improve general operating capability on Logan Hill, where congestion often built up due to having five consecutive miles of one percent grade. The gross tonnage moved on the joint line increased to 400 million tons in 2000.

ADDITION OF A SECOND MAIN TRACK ON ALLIANCE–LINCOLN CORRIDOR

The initial plan for expanding capacity on the major coal routes in Wyoming and Nebraska in the mid-1970s provided generally for a "10-10" configuration—to construct segments of two-main-track territory followed by ten miles of single track. With this amount of increased capacity, BN was confident it would have enough capacity for the volume of business anticipated. This concept worked well until the number of trains increased well beyond the projections we worked with when the line-capacity model was run in the mid-1970s. BN then began to build even more miles of second main track by connecting some of the existing ten-mile segments. By 2010 81 percent of the mileage of the Donkey Creek–Alliance segment had two main tracks, 91 percent between Alliance and Ravenna, and 84 percent between Ravenna and Lincoln. BN continued to increase its miles of second main track between Alliance and Lincoln into 2016. On other subdivisions on the Alliance and Nebraska divisions, CTC was installed, additional sidings were built, and existing sidings were extended to about 7,000 feet to provide enough capacity to run trains within the required cycle times.

With the completion of six additional miles of second main track between Milford and Pleasant Dale on the Nebraska Division in 2016, only 2.7 miles (for the single-track bridge and its approaches over the UP main line at Grand Island) of the 128-mile corridor between Lincoln

Figure 38.2. Of the 116-mile Donkey Creek–Bridger Junction line, 112 miles are jointly owned by BN and UP. To provide the capacity to move upwards of 400 million gross tons per year, additional main track had to be built, soon evolving to a three-track configuration. A fourth main track of 21 miles was later built on the one percent grades on both sides of Logan Hill. The track for handling such tonnage was built with the best available technology in rail concrete ties, turnouts, and fastenings and was maintained to the highest standard. CHRIS BURGER.

and Ravenna will remain single track. Between Ravenna and Alliance, only three short segments of single track totaling 22.3 miles remain.

AT GRAND ISLAND, NEBRASKA

With completion of the six miles of second main track between Milford and Pleasant Dale, Nebraska, in 2016, all but a 2.7-mile segment of single track on the bridge over the UP at Grand Island will have been upgraded to a two-main-track operation on the 128 miles between Lincoln and Ravenna. At Grand Island in 1995, BN built a single-track overhead bridge to eliminate crossing the UP at grade, where the two railroads were running a combined total of about a hundred trains per day. In 2013 the 10.3 miles of single track through Grand Island were reduced to 2.7 miles by building an additional main track up to the start of the embankment approaching the bridge that crosses the UP. Since it is evident that the tonnage of coal to be mined and moved out of the Powder River Basin will continue decline, it seems unlikely it will become necessary to close up this short piece of remaining single track or any of the three short remaining segments of single track between Alliance and Ravenna.

LINCOLN–NAPIER

To expand line capacity and reduce operating costs, BN built nine miles of second main track between Saltillo and its yard in Lincoln in 1997 on the corridor used by trains en route to or from Kansas City and beyond. This addition was necessary to eliminate the congestion that occurs when only a single main track is placed adjacent to a terminal such as Lincoln. Trains will tend to "bunch up" when they must reduce speed and stop to change crews and motive power, or to be switched. Also on that line, a new second main track was built on a grade of 0.4 percent over Firth hill, 22 miles southeast of Lincoln. The grade of 0.6 percent on the original main track restricted line capacity and required a third unit (SD40-2

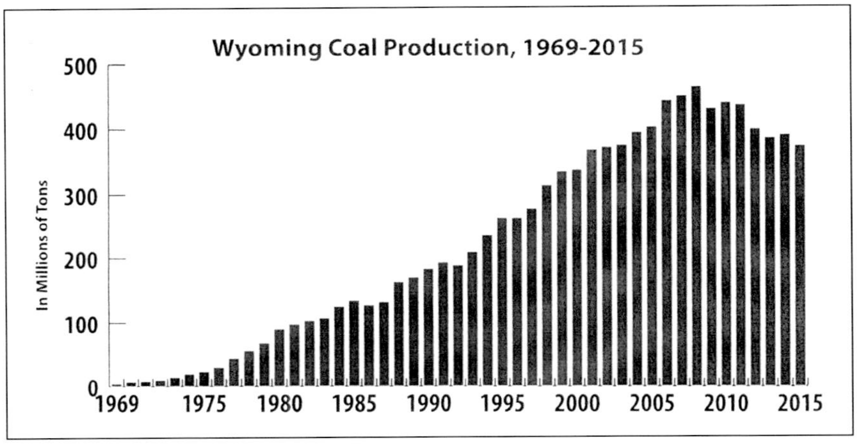

Figure 38.3. The tonnages shown here do not include mines of the Powder River Basin that are located in Montana. The annual tonnage from those mines ranged from about 40 million tons to 45 million tons in the peak years of production in both Wyoming and Montana. WYOMING COAL ASSOCIATION.

or equivalent type) on only the 2.6 miles of 0.6 percent grade out of the 570 miles between Alliance and Kansas City. By retaining the old line, primarily for empty trains, BN gained an additional 7.7 miles of two-main-track territory, thereby increasing line capacity.

Between Lincoln and Napier, empty trains are often run on the alternate route via Pacific Junction instead of on the more direct route through Table Rock. Having this flexibility has added greatly to line capacity between Lincoln, Napier, and Kansas City. However, the alternate route is 25 miles longer, if trains are run between Pacific Junction and Lincoln via Louisville, Nebraska, the most direct route. It is 45 miles longer if trains are run via Omaha instead of Louisville. The track between Napier and Pacific Junction had to be upgraded with 40 miles of second hand-welded rail and 32 miles of new welded rail, crushed-rock ballast, and a heavy program of tie renewals to allow a speed of 49 miles per hour for the empty trains. It is operated under track warrant control (TWC) rules.

LINCOLN–PACIFIC JUNCTION; NORTH KANSAS CITY–NAPIER

In 1977 a 5.4-mile segment of single track was converted to two main tracks between Waverly and Greenwood, Nebraska, a short distance east of Lincoln. Elimination of this restrictive piece of track greatly facilitated the movement of trains between Lincoln and the "three-way" junction at Ashland, which had become the heaviest tonnage line on the Nebraska Division. BNSF has added 12.4 miles of second main track east of Ashland on the Louisville line to increase line capacity on the preferred route between Lincoln and Pacific Junction. Also, the 5.0-mile segment of second main track north (west by railroad direction) of North Kansas City was extended by 4.7 miles.

HIGHER-CAPACITY CARS

As the technology for welding aluminum car bodies improved in quality, aluminum was favored over steel in the construction of new coal cars. With lighter-weight cars built with aluminum, additional tons of coal could be carried in each car, and fewer trains were needed to move a given tonnage. In the early 1980s, the maximum allowable gross weight of loaded cars was increased from 163,000 pounds to 286,000 pounds. Generally, trains are run today with 135 cars and about 20,000 gross tons. The increase in capacity made possible by these improvements in productivity became even more valuable in 1990, when additional restrictions on emissions forced the electric power companies to begin using even more low-sulfur coal mined in the Power River Basin.

ADDITIONAL CAPACITY FOR CAR AND LOCOMOTIVE MAINTENANCE

In addition to major expenditures in track, bridges, and the signal system, BN invested large amounts to expand its locomotive fleet, and for construction of a major locomotive maintenance and servicing facility at Alliance

Figure 38.4. To increase the capacity on its line between Guernsey and Wendover, BNSF carried out the long-awaited plan to "daylight" a 2,480-foot tunnel (as shown on the Alliance Division track charts revised December 31, 1986). Note that the cut was dug wide enough so the Stokes siding could be extended to form 3.1 miles of second main track. It also provided for a road for maintenance vehicles and off-track machinery. MIKE DANNEMAN.

(designed to handle the maintenance of eight hundred units) and new car-maintenance shops at Alliance and Laurel.

IMPROVED CYCLE TIME

The immediate payoff for the large investments made by increasing line capacity and improving its roadway in the 1970s and early 1980s was gaining the capacity needed to handle the rapidly increasing demand for low-sulfur coal. At the same time the efficiency of the operation as represented by reducing the cycle time for unit train equipment owned by a combination of BN, the electric-power companies, and some third-party investors was greatly improved.

Bill Greenwood, division superintendent at Alliance in the early 1980s, reported that cycle time was cut 24 percent from November 1979 to June, 1980, right after the new Donkey Creek–Orin line was opened. The installation of four hundred additional miles of CTC in progress at that time provided additional line capacity by overcoming the limitations of the old system of dispatching by train order authority. In 1980 a writer for *BN News* noted that ninety trains were being operated daily on the Alliance Division, and that sixty-eight of them were hauling coal or returning empty for their next load.[2]

John Hertog, senior vice president–Coal and Taconite, revealed the dramatic improvement in cycle time in the early 1980s in an interview with *Railway Age*. He reported that in August 1982, BN loaded 1,061 coal trains, a record high. John added, "The other side of the coin is that BN could still haul even more coal. During most of last year and this year, we have had thousands of coal cars and locomotives sitting idle. . . . At last count, we had 5,800 shipper and railroad-owned coal cars in storage."[3]

That apparent surplus of equipment made it possible for more power companies to purchase coal mined in Wyoming and Montana without having to invest in still more cars. The number of idled cars and locomotives was soon worked down, as business increased. It should be pointed out that a large number of locomotives that were idled at that time was due to the general economic recession that was affecting other lines of business, and because of significant improvements made in the utilization of locomotives used in other than coal service.

---

2 "Alliance Thrives Amid Tough Challenges," *BN News*, July 1980.

3 "New Record for BN Coal," *Railway Age*, October 11, 1982, page 12.

The work done by BN to build a high-capacity and highly efficient network of coal corridors has made it possible to deliver huge tonnages of coal that is in compliance with EPA standards for emissions, and at very low rates. To comply with those regulations, power companies had to shift a large part of their sourcing for coal from mines in the Midwest and Appalachians to the low-sulfur coal produced in Wyoming and Montana, hundreds of miles to the west. The length of haul for that coal was much greater, and it was vital to the power companies that BN develop a low-cost, high-capacity delivery system to plants scattered in the midwestern and southwestern parts of the country. In time, coal mined in the Powder River Basin was also being shipped to southeastern and northeastern states and the province of Ontario.

In benefitting from low rates for such long hauls, the power companies have been able to sell electricity to their industrial and residential customers at reasonable rates. Even with the low-BTU content and relatively high moisture content of western coal, BN's efficiency has kept the delivered price of coal very low and kept the power companies from having to procure more expensive fuels for power generation.

THE NEED FOR ADDITIONAL CAPACITY IN THE 1990S AND INTO THE EARLY 2000S

With the ever-increasing demand for low-sulfur coal, BN and BNSF continued to provide capital up to 2015 for large projects needed to expand capacity even further. One of these projects (a second main track of six miles between Lincoln and Ravenna) was still underway at the time of this writing in 2016.

A SECOND BRIDGE OVER THE MISSOURI RIVER AT PLATTSMOUTH

With the additional segments of second main track in service between Lincoln and Pacific Junction, Iowa, only 4.8 miles remained, if one included use of the alternate line via Omaha as a second main track. Construction was then started on a second bridge over the Missouri River at Plattsmouth, which included construction of 1.72 miles of additional track. The track constructed over the new bridge was designated the main track, and 1.72 miles of track over the old bridge was officially designated as a siding. In time, the old bridge will be taken out of service and removed, but until then, it serves for operating purposes as an additional segment of second main track.

With the additional segments of second main track in service between Lincoln and Pacific Junction, Iowa, only 4.8 miles of single track remained, if one included the use of the alternate line via Omaha. Construction was then started on a second bridge over the Missouri River at Plattsmouth, including 1.72 miles of additional track. The track constructed over the new bridge was designated the main track, and 1.72 miles of track over the old bridge was officially designated as a siding. In time, the old bridge will be taken out of service and removed, but until then it serves for operating purposes as an additional segment of second main track. Part of the project involved widening the 100-foot-deep cut of over 4,000 feet in length, at the west end of the bridges to construct a second main track. This deep cut was constructed on a line change made in 1976 to reduce curvature from 12 degrees to a maximum of 4 degrees, thereby allowing train speed to be increased from 10 miles per hour to 40. Hopefully, BNSF will soon be able to extend a second main track on the 4.8 miles of single track, to form a combined segment of 78 miles of two main tracks between Lincoln, Pacific Junction, and Balfour, Iowa.

THE AURORA–HASTINGS BRANCH LINE

By upgrading the 27-mile branch line between Hastings and Aurora to main line standards, BN gained the capability of an alternate route for heavy unit trains for seventy-six miles between Lincoln and Aurora. Although the route using the Aurora–Hastings line is forty-seven miles longer than the direct route via Seward, it can be used to great advantage at times of congestion, interruption to traffic for maintenance, accidents, or adverse weather conditions. The portion of the alternate route between Lincoln and Hastings is operated under CTC, and the branch line between Aurora and Hastings is under TWC rules.

MINOT–WILLISTON

In more recent years, BNSF added a significant amount of capacity on its lines in North Dakota by constructing a second main track over the entire distance of 120 miles between Minot and Williston (except for a short segment of single track of 1.2 miles just west of Minot, on the approaches and the large steel-trestle bridge over the Gassman Coulee). CTC has been installed between Fargo and Minot on the alternate route via Grand Forks, and on the former NP main line between Casselton and Huntley, Montana. The driving source for these projects was the greatly increased movement of crude oil, sand for fracking, coal, and export grain.

ON THE TRANSCON, CHICAGO–LOS ANGELES

It would be an understatement to say that the expansion of capacity to get the "Transcon" corridor between Chicago and Los Angeles up to two-main-track capability has been impressive. With the completion of a second large bridge over the Pecos River in 2016, only five miles of single track remained. Upgrading this short distance to two-main-track capability would include construction of a second bridge over the Missouri River just east of Kansas City. Perhaps the most impressive part of this grand project on the Transcon was the construction of five miles of second main track through the rugged Abo Canyon between Belen and Clovis, New Mexico. The Transcon handles from eighty to a hundred trains per day, mainly unit trains of containers loaded with imported consumer goods, UPS business, some export freight, and the business of several large trucking companies, among them J. B. Hunt. Another impressive project was the construction of a third main track of sixteen miles on the heavy grades over Cajon Pass, north of San Bernardino, California.

It has been rewarding and encouraging to see that BNSF has had the financial strength to undertake such large projects to expand the capacity of its network enough to handle the large increases in tonnage it has developed through new opportunities in the marketplace.

OTHER NEW PROJECTS ANNOUNCED OR COMPLETED IN RECENT YEARS TO EXPAND ROADWAY CAPACITY

The section below contains an additional list of many significant projects that have increased capacity and reduced train delay at bottleneck points on the network. With the significant decline in coal and crude oil shipments that started in 2015, fewer projects to increase capacity were initiated in the past two years. Hopefully, BNSF will be able to develop business from new opportunities for growth that will justify new projects that will further increase line and terminal capacity, and overcome new areas of congestion that may develop.

- Construction of 4 miles of second main track east from the yard at North La Crosse, Wisconsin, to eliminate a bottleneck for getting trains through a yard and crew change point.
- Installation of CTC on 264 miles of the double-track line between Savanna, North La Crosse, and Prescott, Wisconsin, to replace operation under ABS signaled in one direction and TWC rules.
- Installation of CTC on 203 miles of double track previously operated under ABS and TWC rules between Coon Creek (10 miles west of Minneapolis) and Dilworth, Minnesota, except for the two segments of existing CTC between Gregory and Philbrook and between Becker and Big Lake.
- Restored 10.5 miles of two-main-track capability between Big Lake and Becker, Minnesota, which had been removed in 1984 in a controversial decision to eliminate the need to relay rail on the westbound main track.
- Construction of 5.3 miles of second main track to eliminate part of the 32 miles of single track between Gregory and Philbrook, Minnesota. When the remaining 26.7 miles of second main track on the latter segment is completed, only the 2.8 miles of single track through Little Falls and over the Mississippi River will remain on the 260-mile line of two main tracks between Northtown (Minneapolis) and Casselton, North Dakota.
- Installation of CTC on the 269-mile line alternate route between Fargo and Surrey (junction 7 miles east of Minot) via Grand Forks.

Figure 38.5. Just over a mile west of the junction of BNSF's northern corridor and a line operated by Montana Rail Link as Sandpoint, Idaho, BNSF's line crosses Lake Pend Oreille on a single-track bridge 4,769 feet in length. Late in 2017, BNSF announced it would revive plans to obtain the necessary permits for construction of a second bridge over the lake. Getting this additional second main track in service will go a long way toward reducing congestion and delay to trains on this vital part of the BNSF system. TOM DANNEMAN.

- Installation of CTC on the 11-mile alternate route (former GN line) through the Twin Cities terminal.
- Construction of new and expanded intermodal terminals at twenty-seven locations, equipping some with logistics facilities and automated gates for reducing delays to trucks delivering or picking up trailers or containers.
- Expanding two-main-track capability with CTC on 68 percent of the high density corridor between Spokane and Sandpoint, Idaho. In 2014 BNSF announced plans to build a second bridge over Lake Pend Oreille, just west of Sandpoint. The new bridge would be over 4,000 feet long, a major structure over one of the Pacific Northwest's most scenic lakes. Shortly after this announcement, a decline in business set in, and the start of construction was set back indefinitely. This was unfortunate because Sandpoint had been a frequent point of congestion—due to the junction of two-main-line corridors at (from Whitefish and Missoula, on today's Montana Rail Link) and having to concentrate so much traffic on a line with long segments of single track—to and from Spokane. It was good to read in April 2017 of BNSF's decision to resume work on the design of the second bridge over the lake. Having it in service should eliminate most of the delays incurred due to congestion caused by the single-track bridge located so close to the junction of two major rail corridors. In 2017 train traffic was running between 50 and 60 trains per day.[4]
- Construction of a fully automated, high-capacity locomotive fueling facility at Hauser, Idaho, 21 miles east of Spokane. Ten locomotive units at a time can be refueled on through trains in only thirty to forty-five minutes. Refueling at older, conventional fueling facilities could delay locomotives and trains for several hours at times. The fuel capacity on many new locomotives is 3,500 gallons, enough for running roughly 1,000 miles, depending on the terrain a train traverses and the gross tonnage in the train the locomotives are handling. Trains refueled at Hauser are able to operate through to Portland, Seattle, or Roberts Bank and return to Hauser without refueling, or east as far as Havre, Montana. Among the advantages of having an efficient fueling facility is to reduce train delays and thereby improve cycle times on unit trains, as well as in improving locomotive utilization.
- Added capacity to the southern route across North Dakota (former NP main line) with the installation of CTC on the 279 miles between Casselton and Dickinson.
- Addition of capacity to the 146-mile line between Spokane and Pasco by increasing the number of miles of second main track, extending sidings, and constructing new sidings. Instead of making further investments to improve the former NP line between Spokane and Pasco, it was hoped by many former BN people that BNSF would decide instead to restore the former SP&S line, with its much lower grades and curvature. Apparently the economics continued to favor additional investment on the former NP line,

4 "BNSF Moves Forward with Plan to Build Second Bridge at Idaho Bottleneck," *Trains Industry Newsletter*, April 19, 2017.

even with its less favorable engineering characteristics.

- Extension of receiving and departure yards at Galesburg, Illinois, and reconstruction of 2.4 miles of third main track between Galesburg and Bishop that had been removed in the mid-1980s.
- Installation of CTC on the 269-mile line alternate route between Fargo and Surrey (junction 7 miles east of Minot) via Grand Forks.
- Installation of CTC on the 11-mile alternate main track route (former GN line) through the Twin Cities terminal.
- Construction of new and expanded intermodal terminals at twenty-seven locations, equipping some with logistics facilities and automated gates for reducing delays to trucks delivering or picking up trailers or containers.
- Construction of an additional set of "universal" crossover switches at Naperville on the three-track main line between Chicago and Aurora.
- Restored several miles of second main track between Seattle and Everett that had been removed in the 1950s and early 1960s, which brought two-main-track capability back to 90 percent of the corridor mileage.
- Constructed 5 miles of second main track between Little Falls and Philbrook, Minnesota, thereby eliminating the part of the 32 miles of single track on the 260-mile line of two main tracks between Northtown (Minneapolis) and Casselton, North Dakota.
- Replaced low-capacity bridges over the Missouri River at Rulo, Nebraska, and Sioux City, Iowa, with new bridges built with the capacity to handle heavy, six-axle locomotives and unit trains with cars loaded to the 286,000-pound limit.
- Upgrading of track and bridges on the entire 330-mile corridor between Willmar, Minnesota, and Ashland, Nebraska, to main-line standards, to handle unit trains of grain and coal on the most direct route between the Twin Cities, Lincoln, and Kansas City.
- Replacement of the old single-track swing span bridge over the St. Croix River at Prescott, Wisconsin, with a new lift bridge and line change that allowed an increase in train speed from 10 to 35 miles per hour.

This summary covered many impressive capacity expansion projects completed since the merger of BN and Santa Fe in 1995. These large expenditures have made it possible for BNSF to handle opportunities for business growth more efficiently and to better meet the expectations of customers for faster, more-reliable service. They have also reduced operating costs as competitive forces continue to hold rates down in the deregulated environment railroads have worked under in the past thirty-five years.

COMMITMENT FOR THE LONG TERM

Other examples of the commitment of BN and BNSF to growth—the construction of long-lived and expensive assets to increase capacity for increasing traffic—could be cited, but this impressive list of "growth capital" projects is a clear indication of confidence in the future of railroad freight transportation. Association with a company of this level of strength and resolve to build infrastructure for the long term should give confidence to shippers in all sectors of the economy, as well as employees, railroad unions, and all levels of government agencies that BNSF has the strength and commitment needed for long-term success in the transportation marketplace.

CONCLUSION, EPILOGUE, AND APPENDIX

CONCLUSION

A LEGACY HAS BEEN BUILT

• railroad operating income reached $980 million in 1984, compared to $278 million in 1980 •
• operating ratio reduced to 78.7 in 1983, the best among Class I railroads for that year •

IT IS FASCINATING TO REFLECT ON THE legacy that evolved through the years of transformation that started in 1981. Cultural changes made the company strong enough to withstand the onslaught of change that became necessary under deregulation and the pressure to improve its return on invested capital. Improving BN's financial and operating performance not only assured the company's survival in changing times, but set a foundation for continuing improvements in business and engineering processes that made BN an industry leader in most areas of operations, maintenance, and innovation. Strong capabilities were built that would give BN the strength and health needed to meet challenges and opportunities in the future.

The spirit and determination of BN people whose roots were in the rail industry, which had already made the company successful, were strong enough for the company to survive and prosper in its second decade, even through the times when new initiatives hitting the company from the outside were moving it in new and different directions. The culture that had been built in BN's first ten years could not be completely destroyed or replaced by a new culture of a much different character that at times was inconsistent with the needs of shippers, employees, and the territory in which BN operated.

Raising the company's financial performance to a high level did not come without having some periods of grief, disruption, and mistakes in judgment that could not easily or quickly be turned around or overcome. Pain was experienced by the thousands of people who lost their jobs as the workforce was rationalized with the introduction of new technology and work methods, when marginal lines were sold or leased, and when some shops and other facilities were shut down. Many employees in train and yard service had to be furloughed when BN was finally able to reduce the size of its train and switching crews.

There were some unfortunate cases of undignified or otherwise improper managerial conduct and style that caught some employees and managers in the cross-fire of cultural changes that occurred in the early to mid-1980s. Some decisions to dispose of or dismantle core assets in those years haunt the company yet today. The decision to abandon the low-grade, superbly engineered line of the former SP&S Railway between Spokane and Pasco stands out as the dominant example of a strategic error in assessing the value of a vital part of the network. The same can be said for some decisions, styles of leadership, and managerial conduct that drove some people of promise out of the company. Nothing can undo the consequences of such decisions.

The strong attributes of BN's franchise made it impossible to set the company back permanently, even though there were a few people in those times who had little faith or optimism for the future of BN or any other company in the rail industry to grow and prosper. However, BN's traffic base and its network served growing segments of the economy that were prone to use rail service. Having a strong work ethic among managers and employees, together with the training and sense of purpose instilled in them, generated a spirit of pride and confidence that drove them to want the company to become stronger and more successful over the long run. BN was fortunate to have a workforce of this caliber. Employees and managers stuck with the company through the tough times, and together we rejoiced in the good times.

In these years of transformation, some outstanding accomplishments were made by BN people in the face of challenges, through their ability to seize opportunities to take advantage of external changes in the transportation market, and to apply some of the company's new strategies into areas that were not anticipated or even thought of at the time they were adopted. For example, with the strategy to reduce year to year capital investments, BN's Engineering and Mechanical departments developed new methods in maintenance and product quality that made it possible to extend the lives of such expensive assets as rail and locomotives. These improvements freed up maintenance capital for investments in technology and investments that produced higher rates of return.

Following is a list of some of the most outstanding achievements of those years:

- Through its drive for innovation in maintenance methods and the application of new technology, BN became a strong leader in the rail industry. Most impressive were the methods developed for extending the service life of the most expensive assets in the company's investment in roadway and equipment.
- Deregulation under the Staggers Act of 1980 provided freedom in the pricing of transportation service, expedited the process of review and decision-making in merger applications, and allowed the sale of marginal, light density lines to third party (non-railroad) operators.
- Decisions and recommendations of PEB 219 led to reductions in the number of employees required on train crews and yard switching crews, and allowed large production track-maintenance gangs to remain intact and work over extended territories.
- Success was achieved in restructuring intermodal service from marginal profitability to a quality high enough to serve new markets, increase volume, and justify capital investment to expand capacity enough to handle it.
- New technology was employed in telecommunications and information processing that allowed local station and office functions and dispatching to be centralized, with a large reduction in force.
- Vast new marketing opportunities were opened through passage of the North American Free Trade Agreement, The Clean Air Act and the granting of Most Favored Nation Status to foreign countries in need of grain produced in BN territory.
- The operation was made much safer by overcoming the causes of employee injuries, and in reducing train and switching accidents by improved maintenance practices, better employee training, development of a spirit of professionalism in employees, and the resolve of management to encourage greater employee involvement in all aspects of safety. Success in safety also made the operation safer for the freight entrusted to BN by its shippers and for the general public.
- A cadre of executives were recruited and developed with the ability and insight needed to operate and take full advantage of business opportunities open to BN in the new deregulated environment.
- Regulators and legislators benefited from BN's success in alleviating the uncertainty surrounding deregulation, through the lower freight rates that resulted from increased competition and the ability BN had to keep its marginal lines in operation by sale to third parties rather than abandonment.

Another great accomplishment was separation of the railroad and the non-rail companies in 1988, which finally removed an issue of long-standing contention of some members of the board and the investment community. Both the railroad and the non-rail companies were no longer subject to holding-company direction in setting their agendas for capital expenditures, or in forming financial objectives and business strategies. They were no longer required to tailor their objectives to support or rely on the agenda of a sister company. The stage was reset for each line of business to succeed or fail within the marketplace in which it operated.

A new team of executives was named by Burlington Northern–Santa Fe (later re-named BNSF) Railway. All but a few of the former Santa Fe's senior level were retained for service in the merged company; almost all of BN's (with the notable exception of Matthew K. Rose) departed. The ensuing change in culture was described to me by an astute observer who stayed with the merged company for many years:

> They [the new team of senior executives] were very business-like, and knew railroading inside and out. They made better decisions, and the railroad became entirely focused on performance for the morning meeting. For the most part, they stopped the anti-union animus and the ill-treatment of employees and junior officers that had been prevalent on BN for too long. After BNSF terminated a few executives involved in personal misconduct, "real" corporate culture change—as distinguished from a flashy Power Point presentation—came about. The result has been a high-performing company held in high regard. Thus, when Warren Buffett went shopping for a railroad, and bought enough stock in each to get a good, deep look at NS, UP and BNSF, he acquired BNSF.

Perhaps the highest level of recognition that could be shown for BNSF's current performance and long term potential has been the decision Warren Buffett made to acquire ownership of the company. Buffett probably could have made an offer to purchase 100 percent of the stock of any of the large North American railroad companies, or a large company in another industry. The fact he chose BNSF clearly indicates he evaluated it overall as the railroad company having the best prospects for the long term. In announcing his decision, Buffett provided the basis for his evaluation as "there's no way rail is going to lose (market) share . . . and I think the rail share of the pie is going to grow. . . . It's a great business in that you know it's going to be here forever. . . . We bought BNSF because it is well-managed.[1]

1 Joe Weisenhal, "Warren Buffett Says He Spent $44 Billion on Burlington Northern to Fulfill a Boyhood Dream," *Business Insider,* December 22, 2009.

When we are all dead and gone, the sun will still shine,
the rain will still fall, and this railroad will run as usual.

JAMES J. HILL, ON THE OCCASION OF A
FRANK TALK TO A GROUP OF EMPLOYEES ON STRIKE AT
THE JACKSON STREET ROUNDHOUSE IN ST. PAUL, MINNESOTA, AUGUST 1880
(ST. PAUL *GLOBE*, AUGUST 23, 1880, QUOTED IN ALBRO MARTIN'S
JAMES J. HILL AND THE OPENING OF THE NORTHWEST, P. 220).

EPILOGUE

RECOLLECTIONS, INSIGHTS, AND KNOWLEDGE TO BE SHARED

BY NORMAN M. LORENTZSEN

AUTHOR'S NOTE: NORMAN LORENTZSEN *has shared his views on a number of the strategies employed and decisions made by his successors in the 1980s. In this chapter, I have included a few of his comments on subjects that have been of particular interest or concern to him as events unfolded at BN after his retirement.*

MERGER WITH THE ST. LOUIS–SAN FRANCISCO RAILROAD (THE FRISCO)

"Bob Downing and I spent five days going over most of the Missouri Pacific with John Lloyd [president] and other officers of the Missouri Pacific. Both of us were very impressed with their operation, the territory they served and the condition of their railroad. . . . They [Missouri Pacific] almost had a lockup with the big refineries and oil producers on the Texas and Louisiana coast that produced substantial revenue. After Downing and I spent a week down there, Downing said Menk wasn't interested in the Missouri Pacific. The MP would have been a far better merger partner than the Frisco, but Menk had in mind only one thing for merger and that was the Frisco. I think Menk was so focused on getting the Frisco merged with BN, and when that was done, getting Grayson into position under Bressler that the merger came about. . . . BN did have talented people who in my mind could have been President. Ivan Ethington was a very good operations man, and then, there was John Hertog, also. Behind those two, the Q [CB&Q or Burlington] had several very good candidates. Worth Smith could also have been included in that group. . . . In a meeting set up to negotiate the price for merger with the Frisco, Grayson, Elliot Stein [Frisco board member] met with Menk, Frank Coyne and I. Agreement was reached on a price the first day we met. Menk had not conferred with any of us before the meeting. Our advisor, when asked about the fairness of Menk's second offer, said it was somewhat high but it should meet Grayson's request and is okay."

LINE SALE AND LEASE TO DENNIS WASHINGTON

"The Sandpoint to Laurel deal [sale of line to Dennis Washington, an entrepreneur from Missoula, who formed Montana Rail Link] creates a situation that with present traffic requiring more trains than the 'guarantee' just enhances Washington's pockets. No consideration [was given] for increased traffic potential and the contract was practically 'iron clad' for Washington. When [Rob] Krebs became the CEO, he made an effort to buy the line back but it could not be done at a price level that was feasible. Washington got a gold plate deal and [there is] no way for BNI to recover at a reasonable the line of railroad at a reasonable cost."

ACQUISITION AND EXPANSION OF PLUM CREEK LUMBER COMPANY

"At merger time Plum Creek Lumber had undertaken improvements that would make it a first-class lumber mill. Its operating profit was on an increasing scale each year. . . . Plum Creek was acquired in 1966 as basically a 'stud mill.' Over a period of about five years, it was transformed into a fully integrated lumber and plywood producer. The plywood was high-quality to medium-density hardboard-plywood made from wood chips and sawdust. Finished lumber from 2 × 4s and up were made. Utilization of almost all parts of a tree including the leaves produced a variety of mulches.

"Most of the timber used by Plum Creek came from our own timber production. Sales were made to other lumber producers and other countries. To replenish forests which had been harvested, we carried on a program of reforestation. Each year up to six million saplings were planted. . . . As a fully integrated company, Plum Creek produced excellent results."

RECRUITING AN "OIL MAN"

"On the matter of a management team, we were lax in not bringing someone in to fill the Resource slot. About two years before I retired I had employed a man who was a Vice President with an oil company in Texas. David Ylkanen had been searching, at my request. I met him [the 'oil man'] once and found him to be a very good prospect. I next asked Menk to come to Denver where he could meet him. Menk liked him and so we hired him. During the reorganization of the early 1980s, he went back to his former employer. Within a short time he was made President, and after that, Chairman. We exchanged notes for several years after he left.

GERALD GRINSTEIN TAKES OVER

"After Grinstein[1] was put in charge, we exchanged some correspondence from time to time. His understanding of the people on the railroad was a complete reversal of his predecessors. I knew him from my time in Seattle. I think Grinstein felt that the turmoil in management was caused by the revolving set of managers. I also sensed that he had respect for BNI people and found them very able. Grinstein closed the swinging doors in management. After almost 10 years of constant change for the people on the railroad, and the treatment senior management rendered to these people, certain things became evident that the labor people, those who did the muscle work, were very unhappy. The injury ratio gave strong evidence that something was wrong. The results on injury expense became very serious. Grinstein recognized this and found the attitudes worse than he thought. He brought in John Chain, eventually moving him to head of safety."

1 Norman is referring to Gerald Grinstein, former head of Western Airlines, who became president and CEO of the BN Railroad in 1989. John Chain was hired as executive vice president–Operations in 1991 after he retired from the U.S. Air Force. Chain had risen to the rank of four-star general in the Strategic Air Command. He also served as executive vice president–Safety, for BN.

APPENDIX

ERUPTION OF MOUNT ST. HELENS

• *railroad operations interrupted by heavy volcanic ash* •
• *BN as owner of land at the summit of the snow-capped mountain peak* •
destruction of timberland owned by BN •

BN's MAIN LINE BETWEEN PORTLAND AND Seattle was located twenty-four miles west of Mount St. Helens. The mountain had been dormant for well over a hundred years when it awakened on March 27, 1980, sending a plume of ash and steam four miles into the air. There was considerable apprehension and uncertainty as to how much more severe future eruptions might be, and what—if anything—could be done to prepare for them. In the next few weeks, the buildup of a 450-foot bulge on the mountain's north side indicated that the mountain might not quietly go back into a stage of dormancy. There was no way for us to project even a broad range of outcomes as to damage or interruption to service that we might sustain.

A series of small eruptions occurred in the next several weeks, and at 8:32 A.M. on May 18, a beautiful Sunday morning, the mountain blew. I had taken over as vice president of the Seattle Region seventeen days earlier, on May 1. On that morning, I was about to walk through the door of Our Lady of Grace Church in Bellevue, intending to attend Sunday Mass before going to the office, when a loud boom shook the heavens. There was no doubt this was "the big one" we had feared. With no hesitation, I drove to the regional office building in downtown Seattle, only about a fifteen-minute drive on a Sunday morning.

The regular corps of operating and maintenance officers who were expected to report on Sunday mornings to check things out were there. Every phone on every desk in the office area was ringing with calls from people in the Operations Control Center in St. Paul, as well as from managers in all departments in the General Office in St. Paul, wondering what was happening, what effect the eruption was having on the railroad, and of course what we were doing about it. Curiosity was great—this was an emergency or threat to the operation far different from the other kinds of disruptions railroads can anticipate and know how to deal with, such as blizzards, floods, and train accidents.

The mountain was spewing ash. At that time, there was no way to know how much of an effect the eruption would have on the railroad or how long it might go on. We were into something that had never been experienced before on any North American railroad, making it impossible to project or estimate how much damage and how long the interruption to service would last. It was not long until the sky was darkened by clouds of volcanic ash as far east as Spokane.

Sam McNaghten, director of Transportation for the Seattle Region at that time, recalls the ash fell the most heavily to the east of the volcano at Sprauge, Ritzville, Lind, and Yakima, up to eight inches in spots. Some train crews had to be tied up at locations where we had no contract for lodging for employees, and they found no rooms were available in any lodging facilities due to the large number of motorists who had to take shelter because of both poor visibility due to the clouds of ash and the damage the ash was doing to their vehicles. The crews of the stranded trains had no choice but to stay in the homes of local residents or BN employees who lived in the area. They chipped in to buy groceries, not knowing how long it might be until they would be able to resume their trips.[1]

Our first concern had to be for the safety of the people out working on the railroad and the passengers on Amtrak trains moving on the line between Portland and Seattle at the time of the eruption. We decided to take the safe course and shut the railroad down on the lines in western and central Washington, as far east as Spokane. Since there was no precedent as to what should be done to protect railroad people and equipment, it was best to get the trains stopped until conditions could be assessed. Already, we had reports from crews on trains east of the mountain of poor visibility and concern about their having to breathe air filled with falling ash. The clouds of ash stirred up by a moving train made breathing conditions and visibility especially bad for crew members riding in cabooses.

The ash-filled air was certain to have an effect on the functioning of locomotives. We got the trains tied up at intermediate terminals and at other locations where the crews could get shelter from the ash. From past practice, it was almost unthinkable to stop operations on a railroad, no matter how bad the weather was, but in this case of so much uncertainty as to how much the ash was affecting the safety of employees and equipment, it was best to take the safe course. It wasn't long before the movement of motor vehicles was severely impaired by the accumulation of ash on streets and highways and air filters getting clogged. A widespread area was immobilized in a very short time.

In its Fact Sheet 036-00, the USGS provided a vivid description of the "cataclysmic eruption":

> Within 15 to 20 seconds of a magnitude 5.1 earthquake at 8:32 A.M., the volcano's bulge and summit slid away in a huge landslide—the largest on earth in recorded history. The landslide depressurized the volcano's magma system, triggering powerful explosions that ripped through the sliding debris. Rocks, ash, volcanic gas, and steam were blasted upward and outward to the north. This lateral blast of hot material accelerated to at least 300 miles per hour, then slowed as the rocks and ash fell to the ground and spread away from the volcano; . . . The blast cloud traveled as far as 17 miles northward from the volcano and the landslide traveled about 14 miles west down the North Fork Toutle River.
>
> The lateral blast produced a column of ash and gas [eruption column] that rose more than 15 miles into the atmosphere in only 15 minutes. Less than an hour later, a second eruption column formed as magma erupted explosively from the new crater . . . Based on the eruption rate of these pyroclastic flows, scientists estimate that the eruption reached its peak between 3:00 and 5:00 P.M. Over the course of the day, prevailing winds blew 520 million tons of ash Eastward across the United States and caused complete darkness in Spokane, Washington, 250 miles from the volcano.
>
> The largest and most destructive lahar [a landslide or mass of volcanic fragments moving down the flanks of a volcano] increased in size as it traveled downstream, destroying bridges and homes and eventually flowing into the Cowlitz River. It reached its maximum size at about midnight in the Cowlitz River, about 50 miles downstream from the volcano.

The eruption lasted for nine hours. Our railroad lines west of the mountain, in the Seattle–Tacoma–Vancouver (Washington) area and across Stevens Pass in the Cascades, were not affected, nor was the former SP&S line along the Columbia River. The main effect of the ash was on our line running through Yakima, Pasco, and Spokane. At the time, there was no way to judge how many hours or days the eruption would last, or the effect it would have, not only on the railroad, but on the lives and property of people, business enterprises, and farm land on which the ash was falling. Even if the eruption would soon stop, how long might it be until the next eruption would occur? Will it be more powerful than the first? For how many days, months, or years might these eruptions continue? Might the railroad have to be taken out of service for a long time? What effect could that have on our revenue and our ability to provide service? Will it be possible for people (including our employees) to

1 Conversation with Sam McNaghten, July 2013.

continue to live and work in the area affected by the huge quantity of ash falling from the eruption? Will farmland being covered by several inches of ash be destroyed?

The biggest and most immediate problem we faced was the enormous flow of water on the Toutle River that was heavily clogged with mud, trees, logs, and other debris flowing downstream toward the Columbia River at an estimated 40 miles per hour. We feared that our 185-foot long double-track bridge over the river fifty-three miles north of Vancouver would be heavily damaged and have to be taken out of service—it was damaged enough from the heavy flow of water, mud and logs tumbling end over end that we had to take the easternmost main track out of service. We kept the other main track in service on a minute-by-minute basis for three days due to the threat that a 200-foot high dam of debris that had built up at Spirit Lake near the volcano might break and cause huge amounts of additional water, mud, and trees to flow at a great speed toward our bridge. To make repairs to the bridge, we had to take out of service for twenty-nine hours. Damage to the bridge amounted to $200,000.

Alex Hasson, trainmaster at Centralia, was one of the first employees to arrive at the bridge. His first observations were reported in the August/September 1980 issue of *BN News:* "By late morning when I arrived at the bridge, the river was up to within two feet of the bridge deck. The river looked to be just about solid mud. Later that afternoon, mud and debris were flowing to the top of the pier in the center span area of the bridge. Then the logs started battering the structure."

Dick Anderson, a member of the local B&B (bridge and building) crew, reported that by late afternoon, "Logs were building up—hitting the bridge. Trees were snapping and cracking like popcorn. The mud was hot and giving off clouds of steam. As the level of debris rose, logs began flying through the superstructure of the bridge, and in some cases clear over it. It looked like an invisible ship was shooting torpedoes through the air over the bridge."[2]

By October, about 25 million cubic yards of mud and debris had been dredged from the Cowlitz River. This was only about half of the amount the Army Corps of Engineers determined would have to be done to restore the river to its normal flow. Until the river channel could be deepened to its full capacity, we had to be concerned about the effect that winter rains and the spring snow melt could have on the railroad.

As many as eighty trains were held in the first three days after the eruption. Ten westbound freight trains were stopped in western Montana for several hours until they could be brought into Spokane. Amtrak service between Seattle and Portland was discontinued until May 20. Amtrak's *Empire Builder* was operating on a tri-weekly basis at that time and resumed service on May 22, three days after the eruption. The greatest difficulty we anticipated in resuming freight operations was having the gritty, fine-grained ash getting into the moving parts of diesel engines and air compressors on locomotives. Air filters quickly became clogged and the ash contaminated the oil lubrication systems. To help prevent damage, air filters were changed every day instead of every three months, thereby preventing the high failure rates being experienced by truckers and motorists.

The effect on motive power was not as severe as had been feared. When we resumed operations east of the Cascade Mountains, trains were restricted to 30 miles per hour, and were stopped every twenty-five miles for inspections until the dust settled down. This precaution was taken because of uncertainty as to the effect the ash would have on car journal bearings, switch machines, and wayside signal equipment. With each passing train, there was less ash left to be stirred up. In a few days, there was no longer a problem of blowing ash on our main lines.

Ballast regulators, track brooms, and jet blowers equipped to remove snow in switches were used to remove as much as six inches of ash from the track. Spraying water on the ash helped settle it into the ballast section. Interestingly, at harvest time a few months later, there were reports of record yields in grain, row crops, and orchards. Apparently, the ash from a volcanic eruption is one of nature's ways of building up the quality and depth of the soil.

At that time, the *Empire Builder* was operating on the former NP line via Yakima between Seattle and Spokane.

2 Jim Verstraete and Kim Forman, "Mt. Saint Helens: A Thundering, Crashing Symphony of Awesome Power," *BN News,* August/September 1980.

The crew on the first westbound Empire Builder made several unscheduled stops to pick up 123 stranded motorists. No fare was charged for their ride on the standing-room-only train. Amtrak and BN offered to run a special train through eastern Washington to pick up more people who could not drive on roads still covered with ash, if the state would reimburse Amtrak for its operating costs. Amazingly, the governor would not accept that offer. On the third day after the eruption, BN responded to an emergency request for additional air filtering masks at Ephrata, Washington, by loading four thousand masks into the caboose of No. 4 at Seattle.

The bridge that carried Interstate 5 over the Toutle River, located adjacent to our railroad bridge, was not damaged, although it was kept out of service for several days. The ash, mud, and debris that flowed from the Toutle River reduced the depth of the channel in the Columbia River from forty to fourteen feet. Thirty-one ocean-going ships were stranded upstream. It took several days to dredge the channel enough to resume shipping on even a restricted basis. The cargo-handling volume of facilities along the river was reduced by 50 percent for a month. The full 360-foot width of the channel was not restored until October. Fifty-seven persons were killed and fifteen were listed as missing (none of them were BN employees) from the effects of the eruption.

The eruption that occurred on May 18 was not the last volcanic activity from Mount St. Helens. Five much smaller and less damaging "explosive episodes" (the term used by the U.S. Geological Survey) occurred from May 25 through October 16. Some ash spewed into the Portland and Seattle areas during these episodes, but the effect of those eruptions on railroad operations was negligible. Of course, those episodes raised questions and concerns as to when or if more major eruptions might occur. The USGS reported that bursts of brief but intense seismic activity continued from October 1980 and on into 1991. Knowing that Mount St. Helens was not yet dormant, and might never be, was at least a little unnerving for people of the Pacific Northwest in all those years.

In addition to owning many miles of railroad in the areas affected by the eruption, BN owned 4,800 acres within sixteen miles of Mount St. Helens. About 23,000 acres of BN's forested lands throughout Washington were damaged, including 640 acres at the summit of the volcano. The eruption reduced the elevation of the mountain by 1,300 feet.

The value of the timber lost on BN's land was estimated at $15 million. Felled timber could be salvaged on only 600 acres. The young Douglas and noble fir trees planted on 5,400 acres of newly forested land were either burned or buried in ash. In November 1981 BN and the U.S. Forest Service agreed to exchange 68 acres of BN land northeast of Mount St. Helens for timber of equal value in the area of Meta Lake. BN's land was sought by the forest service as the site for an interpretative area.

In July 1982 BN agreed to donate the one square mile it owned atop the mountain and in the crater created by the eruption to the federal government for establishment of a historic site. In addition, BN donated 50 acres at Spirit Lake, where a lodge had been operated by Harry R. Truman, the notorious, colorful 83-year-old manager of the lodge who refused to leave even when the threat of an eruption was imminent. The NP had acquired this land, including the top of the mountain, in the land grant of 1864 that was established to help finance the construction of the railroad. Alternate square-mile sections were granted to the NP in a "checkerboard" pattern.

Over the years, much of the land was sold to timber companies, among them the Weyerhaeuser Timber Company. After the eruption, the forest service and BN prepared an agreement for a land trade, which would give BN national forest land elsewhere. In 1982 Congress passed the Mount St. Helens National Volcanic Monument Act, authorizing this exchange of land. In conveying these 691 acres to the federal government, Richard Bressler wrote the following letter to President Ronald Reagan:

May 17, 1982

The Honorable Ronald Reagan
President of the United States
The White House
1600 Pennsylvania Avenue NW
Washington, DC 20500

Dear Mr. President:

Since the eruption of Mount St. Helens two years ago, Burlington Northern has supported the establishment of an interpretative area around the summit. Some of our land ownership in the immediate area of the blast would be a logical part of any such volcanic area or monument.

To assist in the protection of this unique resource, we are pleased to advise you of our intention to donate to the federal government our ownership in the crater itself and the land adjoining Spirit Lake where resort owner Harry Truman's lodge stood. These properties total 690.55 acres and are described legally in the attached statement.

It is our hope that this donation will encourage the careful management of the St. Helens area for the contemplation and enjoyment of future generations.

Sincerely,
(s) Richard Bressler

Richard M. Bressler
Chairman & Chief Executive Officer
Burlington Northern Inc.

In a booklet prepared for BN for this occasion, Alfred Runte, an assistant professor of history at the University of Washinton, Seattle, wrote,

> The presentation is symbolic of that [the] long and remarkable commitment among the western railroads to the establishment, protection and development of national parks and related reserves. For nearly a century, beginning with the creation of Yellowstone National Park in 1872, the parent railroads of Burlington Northern Inc. opened the national parks of the Pacific Northwest to America and the world. To be sure, the dedication of the summit of Mount St. Helens is no exception for Burlington Northern, but, more appropriately simply a reaffirmation of one of its most positive and colorful traditions of corporate philanthropy.[3]

Dr. Runte had written a book and other manuscripts on the role that western railroads had in establishing national parks in the early 1900s, and in promoting travel to them. Bressler enlisted his service in advancing to the National Park Service the idea of acquiring the square mile BN owned at the top of the mountain for a national monument or interpretive center. The state's congressional delegation and the Park Service embraced the idea, and it did not take long for it to come to fruition.

3 Alfred Runte, *Burlington Northern and the Dedication of Mount St. Helens: New Legacy of a Proud Tradition*, 1982.

GLOSSARY

AUTHOR'S NOTE

Contains terminology for both rail and non-rail enterprises owned by Burlington Northern.

ABS (AUTOMATIC BLOCK SYSTEM) Defined in the Consolidated Code of Operating Rules, edition of 1967, as "A series of consecutive blocks governed by block signals, cab signals, or both, actuated by a train or engine, or by certain conditions affecting the use of a block." Although the operation of trains is protected under ABS in a series of wayside signals, trains must still be given movement authority through train orders issued by a dispatcher and by schedules contained in the operating timetable for a specific territory. An ABS system may indicate a broken rail, and if connected to a slide-detector fence, protection to trains from rocks or other material that may foul the track.

AC LOCOMOTIVE Equipped with AC traction motors, thereby not affected by the limitations of the maximum continuous-current ratings or the short time in operating ratings that locomotives equipped with DC traction motors have in service.

AC TRACTION MOTOR First applied to North American railroad freight locomotives in the late 1980s. Has advantage over DC motors by having a higher adhesion rating in the range of 40 percent compared to 20 to 25 percent rating with DC motors, and having no brushes or commutator to maintain. AC refers to alternating current, in which electric current reverses its direction at regular intervals.

ADHESION COEFFICIENT The percent of the weight on the driving wheels of a locomotive that is available for traction. It may be as low as 10 percent with a wet rail condition, to 40 percent on dry, sanded rail, or with AC traction motors.

AFE (AUTHORITY FOR EXPENDITURE) A business form used in the process for review and authorization of projects requiring a capital expenditure. It may include some work that has to be charged to operating expense. May be required for construction, purchase of service or physical change to be made to an existing facility, acquisition or rebuilding of locomotives and cars, or retirement of an asset.

AGREEMENT A contract between the railroad company and the union or unions representing employees of one or more crafts, as to rates of pay, working conditions, handling pay claims and grievances, the scope of work, and many other issues.

ALIGNMENT The location of a line of railroad in terms of its tangents and curvature. It is not defined in terms of the grades on which it is built.

ALLOCATIONS (NO. OF) A provision in merger implementing agreements for train operating crews on some districts of the former GN and NP that allowed employees to "follow their work" when trains they had previously manned were diverted to a newly designated "preferred route" on another former railroad. An example was the allocation of a specified number of GN crews from the Minneapolis–Willmar–Breckenridge line into the Minneapolis–Staples–Dilworth chain-gang pool that operated trains on the newly designated preferred route of the former NP. This provision kept crews from losing a large part of their work when "their" trains were to be diverted to the line of the "other" railroad.

ANODE Copper that was partly refined was cast into anodes for further refining by electrolysis, in the form of slabs. Anodes were shipped by rail from the smelter in Butte, Montana, to a refinery in Black Eagle, Montana, for further refining.

ASSIGNED CREW Employees on assigned train crews report for work according to a schedule or other routine as to days of work, days off, and the time to report for duty.

BAD ORDER A car designated by an inspector as needing repairs before further movement is made.

BALLAST Generally, a crushed hard rock such as granite, trap rock, quartzite, or dolomite placed on the roadbed to help distribute the load imposed by trains, to provide stability to the track structure and good drainage to help maintain good surface and alignment.

BALLAST CLEANING Ballast fouled with mud or other contaminants is excavated from the track and screened to separate any remaining "good" ballast from the mud, and then the cleaned ballast is returned to the track. New ballast will be unloaded to replace the fouled ballast that has been removed.

BENTONITE A soft, plastic, porous rock composed of clay minerals and silica, bentonite is greasy and absorbs large quantities of water, accompanied by an increase in volume of about eight times. Its presence causes great difficulty in track maintenance and quickly contaminates even high-quality ballast.

BLOCKS Groups of cars coupled together for movement to the same destination, junction, or set-out point. A train may be made up with several blocks to reduce the amount of switching or rehandling enroute or at the train's destination. In contrast, an unblocked train will have to be switched at a distant point for delivery to industries, for interchange to another railway, or to connect with another train.

BOARD FOOT The unit of measurement for lumber. Calculated by multiplying thickness (inches) times width (inches) times length (feet) divided by 12.

BRAKEMAN Works under the direction of the train conductor in switching, inspecting cars, making air-brake tests, and coupling and uncoupling cars.

BRIDGE TRAFFIC See OVERHEAD TRAFFIC.

BTU (BRITISH THERMAL UNIT) The amount of heat required to raise the temperature of one pound of water by 1 degree Fahrenheit.

BUFF ACTION Caused by compression forces on couplers and draft gear when slack runs in on cars in a train. Also see DRAFT, the forces "opposite" buff.

CHAIN GANG A group of locomotive engineers, conductors, and brakemen set up to operate freight trains on a "first-in, first-out" basis, with unscheduled hours for going on duty and generally with no assigned days off. Also known as the "pool" on many railroads. Origin of the term "chain gang" is in the nature of the work, with employees not having much freedom to really get away from the job, due to irregularity of hours worked and considerable unpredictability (and short notice) as to when they will be called to go on duty.

CLASSIFICATION Switching cars in a yard according to destination or other category for movement out of the yard on a train or a local industry switching assignment. Groups of cars with a common destination or other status may be called blocks.

CLASS I RAILROAD A railroad with annual revenue in excess of $250 million (in 1991). A regional railroad has annual revenue between $40 million and $250 million, and at least 350 miles of track. Short-line railroads have revenue of less than $40 million.

CLEAR-CUTTING A forestry and logging practice in which most or all trees in an area are uniformly cut down. Removes all trees, regardless of size, in an area in one operation. Used by foresters to create certain types of forest ecosystems and to promote select species to grow in an even-age stand.

CODE LINE A two-wire line running between a CTC control machine and the signals and powdered switches in the field operated by a train dispatcher or control operator. Control codes are sent via the code line to corresponding signals and switches. To avoid the danger of a code line being damaged or torn down by weather or vandalism, as well as the cost of maintaining a pole line with open wire, railroads either buried the code line or installed electri-coding by sending electrical pulses through the rails. (Source: Michael J. Burgett, "The Engineering Basics of CTC," www.ctcparts.com, and "Pole Line to Be Eliminated," *BNSF Whistle Post,* Nebraska Division newsletter, December 2001/January 2002.)

COMPASS (COMPLETE OPERATING MOVEMENT AND PROCESSING SERVICE SYSTEM) Installed by BN in the early 1970s (see chapter 22 in *Burlington Northern: A Great Adventure* for details on what this system was designed to deliver). Among many other capabilities, COMPASS was a system of quality control over freight-car movement on the entire BN system.

COMPENSATION (OF GRADIENT) The easing of gradient on curves to compensate for the additional resistance caused by curvature.

COMPOUND CURVE A continuous curve with two or more curves of different degrees connected without a section of tangent track between those curves.

CONCENTRATOR Centrifugal concentrators rotate to allow heavier and more dense minerals to flow to the outer surface of a bowl, which are then removed for further upgrade.

CONDUCTOR Employee in charge of a train and responsible for giving directions to other employees on the train, the locomotive engineer, and Brakemen.

CONSIST A list of cars and locomotive units in the order in which they stand in a train. Also contains such information as destination of each car, whether the car is loaded or empty, and the commodity it contains.

CONTAINER A large "box" generally built in lengths of 20, 40, or 53 feet, used in common for shipments to be made in one or more modes of transportation, rail, truck, or marine.

CREW CALLER Employee who maintains and inputs data as to the status of train crew members, and initiates calls to them when they are needed for duty or when they are displaced from their position by exercise of seniority by a senior employee.

COMMITMENT A pledge or promise, declaration of an opinion, position, or belief.

CONDUCTOR Employee in charge of a train.

CONTROLLED SIDING A siding within the limits of CTC territory on which a signal indication authorizes use of the siding.

CTC Centralized Traffic Control. A system for governing the movement of trains in which a dispatcher or a control operator under the direction of a dispatcher is authorized by signal indication as opposed to written or verbal authorization. Usually incorporates the remote control of switches with the control of signal indications. (Refer to the railroad's General Code of Operating Rules for a more strict, "official" definition.)

CURRENT OF TRAFFIC The provision for movement of trains in one direction on a main track as specified in the operating rules.

CWR Continuous welded rail. Conventional 39-foot or 80-foot rails welded end to end, thereby eliminating the need for rail joints and their high cost of maintenance.

DEADHEADING Transporting a train crew by train, auto, bus, or other means to a location where their work will begin, or to go off duty.

DIED ON THE ROAD When a train crew has run out of working time under the Hours of Service Law and must be relieved from duty.

DIRECT CURRENT (DC) Electric current that flows in one direction only.

DIRECTIONAL RUNNING The use of each of two somewhat parallel lines for trains moving in one direction only between two common points to gain the capability of a double-track line. With this designation, line capacity is increased and the delays for trains meeting at sidings on a single-track line are eliminated. An example that worked well was between Spokane and Pasco, in which westbound trains ran on the former SP&S line and eastbound trains on the former NP line.

DISPATCHER Employee responsible for directing and authorizing the movement of trains on main tracks.

DISTRIBUTED POWER A locomotive consist set up for remote-control operation in conjunction with locomotive units at the head end of the train. The units operating as distributed power may be placed at the rear of a train or cut into the train at the location that will allow the most efficient train handling for the engineer.

DIVISION SUPERINTENDENT The Operating Department officer in charge of a designated territory referred to as a division. Responsible for all train and terminal operations; on some railways, may also have responsibility for maintenance-of-way and the mechanical (maintenance of equipment) functions. Reports to a general manager.

DRAFT Tension (as opposed to buff or compression) created in couplers when train slack is "out."

DYNAMIC BRAKING A means of braking by using the locomotive's traction motors as power generators, thereby controlling and reducing train speed. The power generated from the traction motors is dissipated through dynamic braking resistors.

ELECTRIC FLASH BUTT WELD A weld of rail ends made by electric welding. Can be made either in the field or in a stationary rail-welding plant.

EMBANKMENT A bank of soil or rock built up from the natural ground surface to bring the roadbed up to the desired grade line.

END-OF-TRAIN TELEMETRY DEVICE Mounted on the trailing coupler of the last car in a train to provide air-brake pressure and indication of motion at the rear of the train (whether moving or stopped) to a device mounted in the cab of the locomotive.

ESCARPMENT A steep slope formed as an effect of faulting or erosion, separating two relatively level areas of differing elevations.

EXTRA BOARD A group of conductors, locomotive engineers, or brakemen set up to fill vacancies created by assigned and "chain gang" employees who are unavailable for work due to vacations, illness, or personal business. Extra-board employees are also used to make up an "extra" crew if no chain gang or assigned crews are available to man a particular train or yard switching crew.

FALSEWORK A temporary structure built during construction of a bridge to hold components or the permanent structure in place until construction has advanced enough to support itself. In the case of the new bridge built over the Missouri River at Rulo, Nebraska, falsework was built adjacent to the piers of the old bridge that would be kept in service for the new bridge. The new truss spans were placed on the falsework by barge cranes and held on the falsework until the contractor was ready to remove the old spans. The new spans were then moved from the falsework onto the piers that had just been cleared. The track was out of service for only forty-eight hours to get the new spans in place.

FIELD WELD A weld made out on the track rather than in a stationery welding plant by a thermite process or electric welding to eliminate joints between rails.

FINAL TERMINAL DELAY (FTYD) A penalty payment made to crews when kept on duty in excess of thirty minutes from their time of arrival at the switch or other location designated at the entrance to the yard until relieved from duty. The exact conditions under which this payment was due varied somewhat among railways. This payment was eliminated when the trip rate bases of pay was adopted.

FIXED BASE OPERATOR Provides such aeronautical services as fueling, general servicing and general maintenance, parking, hangar storage, aircraft rental, and flight instruction.

FREIGHT FORWARDER A company established to consolidate less-than-carload freight shipments into carload lots.

FREQUENCY RATIO Number of employee reportable injuries per 200,000 employee hours worked. As a rule of thumb, it is also the number of injuries per 100 employees.

FROG A steel component in a switch (turnout) placed at the intersection of the two running rails to permit wheels and flanges to move from either rail to cross the other rail, depending on whether the switch points are lined for a "through" (straight) movement or to enable the movement to diverge onto another track. (See also *Railway Ages Comprehensive Railroad Dictionary* or Christopher F. Schulte, *The Dictionary of Railway Track Terms.*)

GED (GENERAL EQUIVALENCY DIPLOMA) A document given to a person who did not complete high school but passed tests on four subjects that show high school–level academic skills.

GENERAL CHAIRMAN Employee elected to represent the interests of employees of a given craft system-wide in contract negotiations and in the appeal of claims, grievances, and disciplinary action issued at a local level, to system officers of the company.

GENERAL MANAGER A middle-level management position in the OperatingDepartment reporting to the vice president–Operations. Generally there are from two to four division superintendents reporting to a general manager.

GRADE (PERCENT OF) The rise or fall of track over a distance of 100 feet. Example: A rise of one foot in 100 feet is a grade of one percent. Generally, grades of 1.0 percent or less are considered light grades, heavy grades between 1.0 and 2.0 percent, and mountain grades 2.0 percent or greater.

GRADE RESISTANCE The resistance to movement on a grade due to gravity, 20 pounds per ton of train weight for each percent of grade.

GROSS TON-MILES The sum of ton-miles handled in a train, made up of the weight of the freight handled plus the empty weight of the cars. It includes the weight of empty cars in the train but does not include the weight of the locomotive.

HELPER A locomotive used to assist a train in ascending a grade when the "primary" locomotive assigned to a train will not produce the amount of tractive effort needed to avoid stalling on a grade, or if the tonnage would cause excessive strain on the drawbars of cars at or near the head end of the train.

HI-RAIL A highway vehicle equipped with retractable flanged wheels that can be placed on a track for inspections or to carry material or machinery needed to assist in maintenance of track, bridges, or signals.

HOLDING COMPANY A business structure allowing a parent firm to control other firms, often outside one's core industry. A holding company does not produce goods or services itself, but enables the ownership to control a number of different companies with benefits from sharing of operating losses and ease of divestiture.

HORIZONTAL DRILLING Directional drilling of an oil well in a horizontal direction rather than vertical. It penetrates a greater length of the oil reservoir and thereby offers significant production improvement over a vertical well. (Source: Summary of Schlumberger Oilfield Glossary, https://www.glossary.oilfield.slb.com/.)

HOURS OF SERVICE A federal law and regulation in place primarily to restrict train crews and yard crews from working in excess of twelve hours on a given tour of duty. Also regulates the amount of time that dispatchers and signal maintainers may work. The full provisions of this law are much more complex than indicated in this summary, but the underlying principle is to limit the number of consecutive hours of work and to provide for a minimum number of hours of rest before going back on duty.

HOSTLER Employee from either engine service or locomotive maintenance who moves locomotives to and from fueling facilities, shop tracks, the locomotive washer, and couples units into consists for outbound trains or switching service.

HUMP YARD A classification yard in which cars are pushed by an engine up an incline ("hump") from which cars roll by gravity when uncoupled to various tracks according to destination, outbound train or other designation. These cars will then be pulled from the opposite end of the classification tracks and moved into tracks that are designated for blocks of cars to be assembled into outbound trains.

HYDRAULIC FRACTURING Creating fractures in rocks and rock formation by injecting a measure of sand and water into the cracks underground to force to open further and allow more oil and gas to flow out of the formation. (Source: https://www.investopedia.com/terms/f/fracking.asp.)

INTERCHANGE The movement (transfer) of cars from one railroad company to another, usually carried out at a common point. May also be handled through a third party or intermediate railroad such as a terminal switching company.

INTERMODAL The movement of freight shipments by a combination of modes including rail, truck, and/or ship, usually in 20-, 40-, or 53-foot containers.

JOINTED RAIL Also known as conventional bolted rail or CB rail. The laying of conventional 39-foot rails end to end, staggered, connected by a steel bar (called a joint bar or angle bar) that fits against the rail and usually secured by four or six track bolts, thereby holding rails in position.

LEVERAGED LEASE A lease agreement partially financed by the lessor through a third-party financial institution. The lending company holds title to the leased asset. (Source: Investopedia.com/dictionary.)

LOCAL CHAIRMAN Employee elected to represent employees of a given craft at a local level in the appeal of time claims, handle grievances, and represent employees at formal investigations (hearings) conducted by the railroad company to determine the facts and responsibility in alleged or possible violations of rules.

LOCOMOTIVE TYPES Types of diesel-electric locomotives produced by the Electro Motive Division of General Motors referred to in the text.

FT Freight locomotives equipped for multiple-unit operation from a single control. Most often, used in two-, three-, or four-unit consists. Rated at 1350 horsepower per unit.

F3, F7 F-type unit upgraded to 1500 horsepower.

F9 F-type unit upgraded to 1750 horsepower.

GP9 Locomotives designated "general purpose" unit, initially built for road switching and local freight service. Soon evolved to use in multiple in "through" freight service. Horsepower evolved from GP5 unit with 1350 horsepower to GP60 with 3800 horsepower.

SD Locomotives designated "special duty," initially intended for heavy drag-type freight service, e.g., to serve mining operations or other operations that will benefit from having six traction motors instead of four as with the F and GP types. Having a higher weight on the driving axles produces higher tractive effort. With the electric current spread over six traction motors, a SD-type locomotive can be operated at a lower minimum continuous speed without danger of overheating the traction motors. In time, the SD-type unit evolved as the mainstay of motive power for heavy-unit train service as well as intermodal and "general merchandise" type trains on most large railroads.

LOW-SULFUR COAL Contains one percent or less sulfur by weight. For air quality standards, contains 0.6 pounds or less sulfur per million BTU.

MAINTENANCE OF EQUIPMENT The function in the Operating Department responsible for the maintenance of cars and locomotives.

MAINTENANCE-OF-WAY AND STRUCTURES The function in the Operating Department for the maintenance of roadway assets, i.e., track, bridges, buildings, and signals.

MANNED HELPER A locomotive consist used to assist heavy trains in getting over grades, controlled by a locomotive engineer.

MASTER LIMITED PARTNERSHIP A type of limited partnership that is publically traded and does not pay taxes from the cash distributions made from its cash flow. Those distributions are taxed when the MLP is sold. Often used by forestry and oil and gas companies due to their having a higher cash flow than taxable income due to high depreciation and other tax deductions. (Source: Investopedia.com/dictionary.)

MILLION GROSS TON-MILES The number of tons of traffic (in millions, including the weight of cars and locomotives plus freight handled) that have passed over a given section of line on an annual basis.

MOVABLE-POINT FROG A frog design with points that will be moved in the same position as the points on a switch. See also FROG.

MU Multiple-unit operation in which two or more locomotive units are coupled to allow control from a single unit.

NON-ABS Non-ABS territory is sometimes referred to as "dark territory," meaning there are no wayside signals in place to protect trains from danger of collision and to warn of unauthorized occupancy of the track by a train or engine, or of switches improperly lined against the movement of a train or to indicate the possibility of a broken rail. In non-ABS territory, crews must protect against following trains by flag protection, unless a manual block system or track warrant control is in place to maintain spacing between trains moving in the same direction.

OPERATOR A position established to issue instructions on the movement of trains per instructions initiated by a dispatcher. In some cases, an operator may operate a machine controlling the position of signals governing train movements, again, under the direction of a dispatcher. The position of operator has largely disappeared due to advances in technology and simplification of rules that allow a dispatcher to communicate instructions directly to the crews of trains rather than by train orders copied and delivered by an operator.

OPERATING DEPARTMENT The department of a railway responsible for the operation of trains and terminals, maintenance of track, bridges, buildings, and signals, as well as cars and locomotives.

OPERATING RATIO The ratio of operating expenses to operating revenue.

OUT-OF-FACE Extended or continuous maintenance work done on a track segment without having to skip some locations not included in the work program. This type of program for tie renewal, replacing rail or track surfacing, is in contrast with spot maintenance work, which covers only short segments of work to be done at a number of disconnected locations.

OVERHEAD TRAFFIC Shipments that are routed on part of the "trip" on an intermediate or "bridge" railroad, i.e., on a railroad that neither originates or terminates those shipments. Overhead or bridge traffic often is very competitive, hence, subject to diversion to another railroad.

PERMANENT BRIDGE Constructed of steel and/or concrete. Programs to replace bridges originally constructed of timber were started by most railways in the 1880s, at least on main lines.

POSITIVE TRAIN CONTROL (PTC) A safety overlay system for train control designed to prevent collisions with other on-track equipment, trains, or cars; to prevent trains from exceeding authorized speeds; and to protect roadway-maintenance workers by enforcing limits of authority and restrictions pertaining to train movement where CTC is in service.

POWDER RIVER BASIN A geologic structural basin in southeast Montana and northeast Wyoming about 120 miles east to west and 200 miles north to south. Supplies about 40 percent of the coal used in generating electricity in the United States. Classified as sub-bituminous containing about 8,500 BTU/pound and a low content of sulfur.

PRESIDENTIAL EMERGENCY BOARD (PEB) A three-member board that may be appointed by the president of the United States under the Railway Labor Act to study and make recommendations for the settlement of contract negotiations between railway companies and unions.

PULL-APARTS The creation of a gap of excess length between two rails, often due to contraction of rails in extremely cold temperatures. Often, the track bolts in one rail end will be sheared as the rails separate and create the gap.

RAIL CREEP Also known as running rail, the longitudinal movement of rail occurring under trains or in temperature fluctuations. Controlled by placement of rail anchors.

RAIL GRINDING Use of a self-propelled, on-track machine to remove irregularities on the surface of rail such as corrugation or to re-profile rail to restore its designed profile following heavy wear from passing trains.

RAIL RUNNING Also known as "rail creep," longitudinal movement of rail due to fluctuations in temperature and forces on rail caused by trains passing over it. Can be mitigated by applying rail anchors under compression to the base of the rail.

RAIL WEIGHT The weight of a three-foot section of new rail.

RAILWAY LABOR ACT A 1926 federal statute recognizing the right of collective bargaining in the railroad and airline industries. It governs such labor-management matters as collective bargaining, mediation, grievance arbitration, and labor protective provisions.

REDUCED CREW CONSIST Operating a train or yard switching crew with fewer employees than what had been a standard crew size (i.e., a conductor or yard crew foreman and two brakemen or two switchmen). The first phase of transition to a reduced crew was to eliminate one brakeman or switchman, followed by elimination of the remaining brakeman or switchman to a "conductor-only" crew. Starting in the early 1960s, the position of fireman was eliminated, leaving only the engineer to run the locomotive.

REGULATOR A track-maintenance machine used to shift ballast and shape the ballast section to the standard level required between ties and on the shoulder with a plow and usually a broom mounted on the machine.

REPORTABLE INJURY Generally, an injury is reportable if the injured employee loses time from work, cannot perform the normal duties of his assignment, or is given medical treatment. Of course, the regulations on reportability are far more complex than this, but these are among the basic factors that determine reportability.

RE RAIL A particular design for rail sections adopted by the American Railroad Engineering Association and widely used on North American railways.

RESISTANCE Refers to resistance to motion of a train due to grade (at 20 pounds per percent of grade), plus the rolling resistance of cars, and the amount due to wind and curvature.

REVENUE TON-MILES The total of ton-miles moved, excluding the weight of the cars. Also does not include ton-miles generated in the movement of company material, e.g., rail, ballast, or locomotive fuel.

ROAD FOREMAN The supervisor of locomotive engineers, also known as the traveling engineer on some railroads.

ROADWAY The entire track section including the roadbed, bridges, culverts, embankments, cuts, and fills.

RULING GRADIENT The grade that limits the maximum tonnage that can be hauled with a given locomotive consist. The ruling grade may not be the maximum grade if that grade is so short that the entire train is not on it at any time, or if the effect of the maximum grade will be offset by the momentum of the train.

RUN-THROUGH An operation that may apply to a train and/or motive power. A run-through train is designed to move "through" from one railroad to another at a junction point or terminal without having to change the power from the inbound train to power owned by the railroad that will be moving it beyond that point.

RUNNING MAINTENANCE Routine periodic maintenance performed on locomotives, often on a mileage or time basis to maintain service reliability and efficiency in fuel consumption. Overhauls and damage repair are performed in heavy repair shops.

SHOULDER The part of the ballast section between the ends of the ties and the toe of the ballast slope.

SHOULDER BALLAST CLEANER A machine used to remove fouled ballast from the shoulders of the track section and run it through a screening process to remove contaminants and then place the cleaned ballast back in the track. Clean ballast will be unloaded to replace the amount of fouled material no longer suitable.

SIDING An auxiliary and usually parallel track used for meeting and overtaking trains.

SKELETONIZED TRACK Condition of track when ballast has been removed from between the ties, awaiting the unloading and tamping of replacement ballast.

SLACK Unrestrained free movement between cars in a train. May be mitigated on passenger trains by the use of "tight lock" couplers.

SLEDDING Use of a machine to raise track out of fouled ballast, which can then be plowed out of the track. While the track is raised, defective ties may be replaced. After track is lowered onto the grade, new ballast may be unloaded and the track raised again to get the standard number of inches of ballast under the ties. Additional ballast is then filled in between ties and broadened out to form the shoulder beyond the ends of the ties. The track is then surfaced by a power tamper. A ballast regulator and broom are used to shape the shoulders and brush out excess ballast from the tops of ties and out onto the shoulder.

SLOW ORDER A temporary speed restriction generally due to maintenance work in progress or when work needed to correct the deficiency has not yet been started.

SPRING SWITCH A hand throw switch designed with a spring mechanism that will allow movement from a diverging route without having to stop to have an employee re-line the switch to its normal position.

STAGGERS ACT Legislation named for Rep. Harley O. Staggers of West Virginia enacted in 1980. Provided for deregulation of railroads, mainly in the area of pricing. It provided greater range for pricing with less regulatory restraint, independence from collective rate-making procedures, and authority for railroads to negotiate contract rates.

STEEL GANG Organized and equipped to lay new or replacement rail. Generally consists of about 75 employees for a large project, or 35 or fewer if the work is limited to a small quantity, such as replacing only curve-worn rail.

SUB-BALLAST Granular material used to separate the roadbed (subgrade) from the ballast section.

SUBGRADE The roadbed that lies below the track, ballast, and subballast.

SUPERELEVATION Often called "banking" of curves in which the outer or high rail on a curve is raised higher than the inner rail to allow trains to move at a designated speed above what would be required without any superelevation.

SUPERINTENDENT A middle-level management position based at a field location responsible for operations and safety on a division and/or terminal. On some railroads, the superintendent also holds responsibility for the maintenance of track, bridges, and buildings, and cars and locomotives, in addition to train and switching operations and overall customer service.

SUSTAINED YIELD The amount of a resource, generally in forested land, that can be harvested without causing depletion. Short-term harvests are limited to allow for longer-term regeneration of the forest from the trees that remain.

SWING-NOSE FROG A frog designed with both a primary power switch machine and a second, separate switch machine to position the switch point. The swing-nose design eliminates the gap over which wheels pass on a standard frog and allows the installation of frogs that will allow higher speeds on the diverging route to be taken. It also requires less welding and grinding than a conventional frog.

SWITCHTENDER An employee assigned to hand operate one or more switches in a limited area to keep trains from having to stop or slow down to a crawl to allow the conductor or brakeman to get off the engine (or caboose) to line those switches.

TACONITE A very hard low-grade iron ore containing about 27 percent iron that must be processed into pellets with iron content of about 65 percent iron for economical use in steel-making. Bentonite clay is used as a binding agent.

TAMPER An on-track machine used to get ballast placed under the ties to bring the surface (smoothness) and alignment to standard.

TERMINAL An operating facility consisting of one or more yards or intermodal transfer facilities. May also include equipment and facilities used for transfer of bulk freight from rail cars to storage or to truck service for delivery. Often defined as the end point for runs made by train crews.

THERMITE WELD Welding of rail ends together with a compound of iron oxide and aluminum powder.

TIE GANG Organized and equipped to replace ties on a production basis. Generally consists of about forty employees and two sets of machinery.

TONNAGE RATING Maximum tonnage to be handled by a given consist of locomotive units. It is based on the tractive effort produced by the locomotive, along with grades on a given territory and the "running time" required per the service schedule or operating plan.

TRACKAGE RIGHTS A contract or agreement for one or more railroads to use the track of an owning railroad. It may provide for a tenant railroad to furnish the crews and motive power and run its own trains, or it may instead pay the owning railroad to move the tenant road's cars in the owner's trains.

TRACTIVE EFFORT The "pulling power" of a locomotive. For a diesel locomotive, it is determined by the weight on the driving axles and the coefficient of adhesion, which will vary from 0.18 for older types of locomotives to 0.40 for the modern types with AC traction motors. The tonnage rating for a locomotive is based on its tractive effort and the resistance to be encountered due to grade, curvature, and the rolling resistance from the cars, as determined by weight, cross-sectional area, and wind velocity.

TR RAIL Refers to "torsion resistant," a rail section designed by the Engineering Department of the CB&Q Railroad for new 115- and 129-pound rail.

THROUGH TRAIN A train operated with no stops or only a minimum number of stops to perform intermediate switching work.

TRAIN BLOCKING Grouping of cars placed in a train according to destination, intermediate point at which they will be set out of the train, or other particular designation intended to help get a train over the road and to speed up the delivery of cars by reducing the requirement to do as much switching enroute.

TRAIN CREW Most often, a freight train crew consists of a conductor and engineer. A brakeman may be included on trains designated to perform "local work," e.g., stopping en route to switch cars at customers' facilities or at yards, or when agreements on staffing require a brakeman be included on the crew of some types of trains.

TRAINMASTER A first-line field supervisor of train operations and/or terminal operations.

TRAIN-MILE RATIO The number of reportable train and switching accidents per million train-miles operated.

TRUST Confidence and reliance on the integrity, strength, and ability of a person or organization. Confident expectation and predictability of the action, behavior, and beliefs of a person or organization. A belief that "we can be counted on to do what we say we will do."

TURNOUT Provides capability for a train or switching operation to move to or from a diverging route.

TWC (TRACK WARRANT CONTROL) TWC replaced the rules governing operation under ABS and non-ABS territory, and by timetable and train order authority, when the technology for radio communication between dispatchers and train crews for movement authority was greatly improved. TWC is in effect on secondary and branch lines (although not in all cases) on which train traffic is lighter than on primary main lines where CTC is in place. In the Union Pacific's rules for TWC, it is defined as "A method to authorize train movements or protect men or machines on a main track within specified limits in a territory designated by timetable. (See the railroad's General Code of Operating Rules, 2017, UPRR.com.)

UNDERCUTTER A track machine that removes ballast generally fouled with dirt and other contaminants to allow replacement with clean ballast.

UNIT TRAIN A train with a fixed consist of cars that is operated intact between origin and destination. The consist is not broken up (i.e., reduced or added to over the entire round trip) except when mechanical defects are found en route, or when some cars are due to be switched out of the train for scheduled maintenance. Unit trains are usually operated per a standard set for the round trip cycle time. The most common applications of the unit train concept are for the movement of bulk commodities such as coal, grain, and fertilizers.

VICE PRESIDENT–OPERATIONS The senior management position responsible for the movement of trains, operation of yards and terminals, and the maintenance functions.

YARD A system or network of tracks usually parallel to each other and connected with each other on both ends to a track called a switching lead. A yard is built within defined limits, used for switching and the classification of cars according to destination, outbound train, or interchange connection.

YARD CREW Employees who classify cars in yard switching facilities according to instructions from a yardmaster or other designated supervisor or employee, and to switch cars to or from customers' facilities. A yard crew consists of a foreman (sometimes called a yard conductor). Depending on local factors, there may be one or two switchmen (sometimes called helpers) on a crew, in addition to the foreman. When remote control equipment is used by the crew, there will be no locomotive engineer assigned to the crew.

YARDMASTER Employee in charge of supervising a freight classification yard or switching facility. Supervises the work of yard switching crews.

REFERENCES CONSULTED

Abbott, James, "Santa Fe Coal-Slurry Damages Seen Reaching $750 Million," *Traffic World,* March 20, 1989.

Abbott, R.A., "Concrete Ties vs. Wood Ties: The Debate Continues," *Railway Track and Structures,* March 1989.

Abramson, Howard and Lawrence Kaufman, "BN Changing Its Reputation as Labor Basher," *Journal of Commerce,* (date not known, but likely to be in late 1990s).

"Actions Achieve Results: New Shop Improvement Committees at Havelock Build Teamwork," *BN News,* April 1985.

"A. C. Breakthrough on BN?" *Railway Age,* March 1993.

"A. Kahn, Pushed U.S. Airline Deregulation," *New York Times,* December 29, 2010.

Adams, John, MD, "Galesburg, Illinois," *The BN Expediter,* April 2010.

Adams, Mikaila, "ConocoPhillips Acquires Burlington Resources for $35.6 Billion: Set to Become Leading Natural Gas Producer in North America," *Oil and Gas Financial Journal,* February 1, 2006.

Adelsberger, Dr. Helmut, "Developments in High-Speed Turnout Design," paper written for Voest-Alpine GmbH, date not specified.

Agreement Between Montana Rail Link and Its Employees Represented by the Brotherhood of Locomotive Engineers, October 1987 (date note specified).

Agreement Between Order of Railway Conductors and Brakemen, Brotherhood of Railroad Trainmen and Switchmen's Union of North America and Burlington Northern, Inc. www.smartunion386.org/agree/68merger.

Agreement for Protection of Employees Who May Be Represented by the Brotherhood of Railroad Trainmen in Event of Approval of Merger and Related Applications Filed by Burlington Northern Inc. in ICC Finance Dockets Nos. 21478, 21479 and 21480.

Allen, John P., Stephen, Eichler, Clifford M. Goldberg, and Louise E. Kier, *Operation: Red Block,* Institute for Human Resources, Inc., Rockville, Maryland, October 1988.

"Alliance, a Boom Town," *BN News,* January 1972.

"Alliance Division: Coal, Youth, Growth," *BN News,* October 1976.

"Alliance Division's Maintenance Complex Combines Rebuilding and Training," *BN News,* July 1980.

"Alliance Terminal Injury-Free for More Than One Year," *Alliance Times-Herald,* September 17, 1998.

"Alliance Thrives Amid Tough Challenges," *BN News,* July 1980.

American Mining Hall of Fame Awards Presentation and Banquet, December 1, 2007, induction of Dennis R. Washington.

"An Assessment of Development and Production Potential of Federal Coal Leases," remarks of R. M. Bressler before the Western Coal Transportation Association, NTIS Order #PB82-149378, December 1981.

Andersen, E. R., "Analysis of Operations of Railways That Have Substantially Reduced the Cost of Construction and Maintenance of Way Work," Committee on Economics of Railway Construction and Maintenance, American Railway Engineering Association, 1970.

Anderson, B. G., "Burlington's Northern New Gillette–Orin Line," American Railway Engineering Association Proceedings, Bulletin 878.

American Railway Engineering Association, Bulletin 678, "Burlington Northern's New Gillette–Orin Line," address by B. G. Anderson, Assistant Vice President–Engineering.

American Railway Engineering and Maintenance of Way Association. 2003. *Practical Guide to Railway Engineering* 2nd Edition.

"Appeal Court Ruling Says BN Can't Derail Union Contracts," *Associated Press,* November 30, 1988.

Appendix E Memorandum of Agreement Between Order of Railway Conductors and Brakemen, Brotherhood of Railroad Trainmen, Switchmen's Union of North America and Burlington Northern, Inc., 1968.

Application Under Sections 1(18) to 1(20) of the Interstate Commerce Act Relating to Construction and Operation of Certain Extensions of Lines of Railroad.

" The Architects of Change: Darius W. Gaskins, Jr.," *Railway Age,* October 1967.

"ARES: Boldly Going Where No Railroad Has Gone Before!," author's collection, date and name of publication not stated.

ARES for Safety and Service, Burlington Northern Railroad, July 1989.

Arkansas Electric Cooperative Corporation—Petition for

Declaratory Order, Surface Transportation Board Decision, Docket No. FD 35305 March 3, 2011.

Armbruster, Kurt, "John M. Budd, One of America's Great Railroad Men," Great Northern Railway Historical Society, Reference Sheet No. 318, December 2003.

Armstrong, Michael N. "Concrete Tie Experience on the Burlington Northern," *Railway Track and Structures,* August 1988.

Asgenmacher, Robert, "The Train That Brings the Coal," *Minneapolis Tribune Picture,* August 7, 1977.

"At Alliance, Young People Predominate," *BN News,* April 1979.

"Attitude Survey Important Step in Changing Culture," *BN News,* August–September 1983.

Austin, Ed. 2018. *Burlington Northern: Oregon.* Scotch Plains, N.J.: Morning Sun Books, Inc.

Austin, Ed, and Tom Dill. 1996. *S.P.&S.: The Spokane, Portland and Seattle Railway.* Edmonds, Washington: Pacific Fast Mail.

"AVP Allan Boyce Explains Coal Rates, BN's Skyrocketing Costs," *BN News,* February 1979.

Awai, Herman Tokuo Kealaula, "Double-Stack Containers: Changing the Image of Intermodalism." Masters Thesis, Naval Postgraduate School, March 1992.

Babcock, Michael W., "Efficiency and Adjustment: The Impact of Railroad Deregulation," <cato.org/pubs/pas/pa033.html>.

Bach, Ashley, "Plum Creek Timber Makes Huge Move on Northwest Forest Conservation," Washington Forest Protection Association, November 13, 2014.

Bachman, Ben. 1987. "Stampede! A Northwest Classic Is Reborn." *RailNews,* October, 1987.

"Bakken Oil and the BNSF."2015. *The BN Expediter,* July, 2015.

Baldwin, William, "This Is Deregulation?" *Forbes,* October 27, 1980.

"Banks Will Finance C&NW Coal Line," *Railway Age,* December 28, 1981.

Barnes, David, "Shippers Urge Senate Panel to Reregulate Railroads," *Traffic World,* December 15, 1997.

Bauer, Edward L., Jr., "BN Explores Car, Locomotive Needs," *Modern Railroads,* November 1989.

Baugh, Odin. 2005. *John Frank Stevens: American Trailblazer.* Spokane: The Arthur H. Clark Company.

Bean, Radford, "Roberts Bank and the Railroads," *Railroads Illustrated,* March 2012.

Bechtold, Timothy Matthew. "Now v. Forever: The Conflict Between Business and Forestry in the Management of Plum Creek Timberlands in Montana." University of Montana ScholarWorks, 1992.

"Becoming No. 1: An Interview with Chairman and CEO Walter A. Drexel. "*BN News,* July 1984.

Bell, Wendell A., communication with author, 2014-2018.

Belmont Tunnel (Nebraska) <wikivisually.com/wiki/Belmont Tunnel_(Nebraska)>.

Berger, Jay, "BN Reopens Milwaukee Track," *BN News,* December 1980.

Berman, Phyllis and Roula Khalaf, "Sweet-Talking the Board," *Forbes,* March 15, 1993.

"'Best Ever' Job Protection Agreements Signed," *Burlington Bulletin,* January–February–March 1968.

"Betterment Committee: A Positive Influence," *Burlington Northern St. Cloud News and Views,* April 1985.

"Bill, Wyoming," *Trains,* September 1992.

Birkholz, Paul, with Al Krug, "Burlington Northern Fuel Tenders," <mtnwestrail.com/wyoming/BNft>

"Bizjet Biz at BN," *BN News,* July 1971.

Black, Jo Dee, "Asian Demand Driving Increase in Coal Train Traffic Through Area," *Great Falls Tribune,* March 13, 2011.

"Black Thunder: Facing the Competition on Hauling Powder River Basin Coal with a Firm Self-confidence," *BN News,* November 1985.

Blaha, John, correspondence with the author, various dates in 2013.

Blaszak, Michael W., "Free to Compete," *Trains,* October 2010.

Bleizeffer, Dustin, "Railroads Play Coal Catch-up," *Casper Star-Tribune,* March 18, 2006.

"BNAFI Sold," *BN News,* May, June, 1982.

"BNAFI to Be Sold," *BN News,* April 1982.

"BN Air Freight Climbs to No. 3 Spot in Industry," *BN News,* February/March 1978.

"BN Airmotive Ranks Near Top in National Survey," July 1980.

"BN and Utility Sign 15-Year Pact to Move Powder River Coal," *Traffic World,* November 7, 1983.

"BN Asks Court to Order Mediation in Labor Dispute," *Traffic World,* January 27, 1991.

"BN: A Turnout 'First.'" 1987, *Railway Age,* May 1987.

"The BN At 10: 'The Amazing Thing Was, It Worked," *Railway Age,* February 25, 1980.

"BN Backs Off on Plan to Auction Grain Cars," *Traffic World,* February 14, 1983.

"BN Begins Drug Tests," *Associated Press,* January 18, 1990.

"BN: Big Bucks for C&S [communications and signals]," *Railway Age,* February 1984.

"BN: Big Switch at Cicero," *Railway Age,* January 1983.

"BN Brings Futures Contracts into the Railroad Business," *Traffic World,* January 18, 1988.

"BN Chairman Accuses Texas Utility Firm of Using Political Pressures in Coal Haul Rates," *BN News,* July 1978.

"BN Considers Move of Some St. Paul Staff," *Mgr.,* December 14, 1983.

"BN Consolidates Repair Operations," *Railway Age,"* June 1992.

"BN Denies Role in Milwaukee Fall," *Railway Age,* April 28, 1980.

"BN Dismisses Dispatcher," *BN News,* October 1984.

"BN Elects Bressler of Arco to President and CEO Posts," BN press release, May 19, 1980.

"BN Fights Drug Dog Injunction," *Associated Press,* October 10, 1984.
"BN, Frisco Join Forces," *BN News,* special edition, January 1981.
"BN, Frisco Win the ICC's Blessing," *Railway Age,* April 28, 1980.
"BN, GE Begin Electrification Study," *Railway Age.*
"BN—Getting a Jump on Tomorrow," *Railway Track and Structures,* September 1983.
"BN Increases Safety and Reduces Costs: A Concrete Example," *BN Technical Bulletin,* July 1988.
"BN Installs Swing-Nose Frog in Nebraska." *Railway Age,* June 1986.
"BN Keeps On Track with Locomotive-Borne Lubrication," *BN Technical Bulletin,* May 1988.
"BNL Development Converts Property to Income," *BN News,* March 1979.
"BN, Montana Reach Accord," *BN News,* October 1984.
"BN News Interview: N. M. Lorentzsen," *BN News,* July 1975
"BN News Interview: Richard M. Bressler," *BN News,* March 1981.
"BN News Interview: Richard C. Grayson," *BN News,* February 1981.
"BN Offshoot to Run Hi-Line," *Billings Gazette,* November 28, 1987.
"BN Oil Refinery," *BN News,* October 1975.
"BN Operates Rail System for South Dakota," *BN News,* August/September 1981.
"BN Pays Milwaukee Road $21 Million for 383 Route Miles," *See-Port News,* April 1981.
"BN Plans $50 Million Alliance Expansion," *BN News,* September/October 1977.
"BN Plans to Offer $100 Million in Preferred Stock," *BN News,* June 1977.
"BN Rated No. 1 by Chicago Commuters," *BN News,* March 1981.
"BN 'Rubber Room' Lawsuit to Resume," *Spokesman Review,* December 6, 1988.
"BN Sets New Safety Mark in '83," *BN News,* March 1984.
"BN Sets Up Its Own R&D Program," *Railway Age,* February 8, 1982.
"BN Studies Structure, Location," *BN News,* July 1982.
"BN Switches Off On Electrification."
"BN's First 10 Years: Highlights of the Decade from Past BN News," *BN News,* March 1980.
"BN's Grinstein: Charting a Steady Course," *Railway Age,* January 1991.
"BN's Operations Department Has Moved South," *BN News,* July 1983.
"BN's 'People Trains' Seek Federal Grant," *BN News,* October 1970.
"BN's Plans for Galesburg," *BN News,* April 1983.
"BN Provides a Fast Track for Innovation." 1989. *Railway Track and Structures,* December, 1989.
"BN Puts Line Up for Sale," *The Montana Standard,* November 26, 1986.
BN Railroad, "An Open Letter to BN Railroaders," *Livingston Enterprise,* October 27, 1987.
"BN Rated No. 1 by Chicago Commuters," *BN News,* March 1981.
"BN Realigns Top Operating Staff," *Railway Age,* October 1992.
"BN Rejects ICC Price on Wyoming Joint Line," *Traffic World,* November 15, 1982.
"BN Retracts from Proposed Kansas City–Northern Line," *BN News,* March 1981.
"BN 'Rubber Room' Lawsuit to Resume," *Seattle Times.*
"BN Runs New Expediter in Chicago–Minnesota Lane," *Traffic World,* October 13, 1986.
"BN, SD Celebrate Core System Opening," *BN News,* November 1981.
"BN Seeks Coal Talks with Utilities," *Railway Age,* October 26, 1981.
"BN Sets Price for Powder River Basin Line," *Mgr.* July 21, 1982.
"BN Sets New Safety Mark in '83," *BN News.*
"BN Sets Up Pilot Projects to Test Hub Terminal Concept," *Mgr.* September 23, 1982.
"BN Shops: Cutting Costs—Not Quality," *Railway Age,* October 26, 1982.
"BN Studies Structure, Location," *BN News.*
"BN Suburban Operations Win Transportation Award," *Chicago Region News,* August/September/October 1978.
"BN Sues Engineer, Brakeman Over Wreck," *Livingston Enterprise,* April 25, 1984.
"BN Suggests a BYOM Party," *Railway Age,* October 26, 1981.
"BN 'Swats' Track Maintenance Chores," *Railway Track and Structures,* October 1987.
"BNT Takes First Place—Ten Times," *BN News,* December 1980.
"BN Takes $435 Million Charge Against Operating Income in Quarter," *Traffic World,* July 1, 1991.
BN TEAM Technical Bulletin:
Acoustic Bearing Detection, March 1989
BN Increases Safety and Reduces Costs: A Concrete Example, July 1988
High-Speed Turnouts, September 1990
In- Place Tie Treatment, October 1991
Locomotive Analysis and Reporting System (LARS), July 1991
Rail Grinding, August 1989
Rehabilitated Welded Rail, January 1991
Swing Nose Frogs, October 1988
Track Surface Management, July 1990
"BN Tests Natural Gas as Locomotive Fuel," *BN News,* November 1985.
"BN: The Measure of Good Management," *Railway Age,* February 28, 1972.
"BN Trains Running Over 140 Miles of Milwaukee Road," *See-Port News,* May 1980.
"BN: Up to the Sky," *Progressive Railroading,* 1987.
"BN's Bid to Scrap Merger Conditions Meets Opposition from Competitors," *Traffic World,* September 14, 1981.
"BN's Expediter: A Pioneer in the Intermodal Industry," *BN News,* July–August 1986.

"BN's Plans for Galesburg," *BN News,* April 1983.
"BNSF Bridge 3.8 over Missouri River," AREMA (American Railway Engineering and Maintenance Association), 2018.
"BNSF Completes Triple-Tracking of Joint Line," railwayage.com/ breaking_news.shtml#Feature.
"BNSF Employees Celebrate Orin Line's 30-Year Anniversary," <rtands.com/index.php/news/BNsf-employees-celebrate-orin-lines-30-year-anniv>
"BNSF Moves Forward with Plan to Build Second Bridge at Idaho Bottleneck," *Trains Industry Newsletter,* April 19, 2017.
BNSF Railway Statement on STB Coal Dust Decision, bnsf.com/ customers/what-can-i-ship/coal/coal-dust.
"BNSF Reopens Stampede Pass," *Railway Age,* January 1997.
"BNSF Strikes Deal to Buy 'Core Lines' from South Dakota," *Trains,* August 2005.
"BNSF: 'That Big Berkshire Hathaway Railroad Deal." 2016. *Bloomberg,"*November 11, 2016.
"BNSF to Move Coal That Will Power New IGCC Plants in Japan," *Progressive Railroading,* January 17, 2018.
Borchersen-Kelo, Sarah. 2014. "Plum Creek Timber Harvesting Opportunities Across Its Portfolio," *Reit News,* October 32, 2014.
"Breezy Point and Beyond," *CTC Board,* April 1991.
Brehm, Kyle, "The Montana Rail Link Story," *Railfan and Railroad,* April 1990.
"Bressler Named BN Chief," *BN News,* July 1980.
"Bressler: Railroad (is) 'Crown Jewel' of BNI," *Mgr.,* April 1982.
Bressler, Richard, Letter to employees, December, 1980.
Bressler, Richard, transcript of speech delivered to the Western Coal Transportation Association, September 10, 1980.
Bressler, Richard M., "Operating Trains, After All, Is a Business," *Trains,* August 1982.
Bressler, R. M., Testimony before a Senate Subcommittee, reported in *Mgr.* April 1982.
Briggeman, Kim, "Towing the Line 20 Years After Montana Rail Link Took Over Track Owned by Burlington Northern Things Have Settled Down," *Missoulian,* October 7, 2007.
"Bring Money, 'BN Tells Would Be Competitors,'" *Traffic World,* October 19, 1981.
Brohaugh, R. G., "The Gellette – Orin Line, One Year Later," American Railway Engineering Association, *Bulletin 683.*
Brotherhood of Locomotive Engineers, Plaintiff—appellee, v. Burlington Northern Railroad Company, Defender-appellant, 838 F.2d 1102 (9th Cir. 1988).
Brotherhood of Locomotive Engineers v. Burlington Northern Railroad Company, Court of Appeals for the Ninth Circuit, Case No. 85-4138.
Brown, Douglas John, "STB Backs BNSF on Coal Dust Issue," *Railway Age,* December 17, 2013.
Brown, Matthew, "King Coal: Despite Concerns About Climate Change, A Batch of New Plants Confirms the Reign of Coal Is Far From Over," *Minneapolis Star-Tribune,* August 20, 2010.
Brownlee, James H., "Protecting an Asset" (rail), *Modern Railroads,* March 1985.
Bryan, Frank W., "Computers in the Cab," *Trains,* June 1990.
Buchsbaum, Lee, "A Dragon They Just Can't Kill," *Coal Age,* July 2005.
Buchsbaum, Lee, "BNSF: We Won't Pay for Dust Fix," *Trains,* December 2007.
Budd, Ralph, "Northern Rail Lines Across the Divide," *Civil Engineering,* April 1940.
Buekett, John, Derek Firth and John R. Surtees, "Concrete Ties in Modern Track,"*Railway Track and Structures,* August 1987.
Buhayar, Noah, "Buffett Said He Paid a Lot. $15 Billion Later, BNSF Is a Cash Machine. 'He Stole It.'" *Bloomberg News,* November 10, 2014.
"Buffett Buying Burlington Northern Railroad," Associated Press, November 3, 2009.
"Buffett: BNSF Buy 'Even Better Than I Expected,'" *Railway Age,* April 2011."
Burgett, Michael J. "The Engineering Basics of CTC," ctcparts.com.
Burke, Jack, "Northern Tier Agreement with UTU 'Overwhelmingly' Approved by Members," *Traffic World,* May 24, 1993.
Burke, Jack, "Burlington Northern, Soo Line Settle Track Rights Case Out of Court," *Traffic World,* February 7, 1994.
Burke, Jack, "Burlington Will Buy General Motors AC Locomotives for $675 Million," *Traffic World,* March 22, 1993.
Burke, Jack, "Management Shake-up at Burlington Northern Ousts Two Veterans; DHL, Frito-Lay Execs In," *Traffic World,* June 6, 1994.
Burke, Jack, "Rings, Radios, Re-enactments Irk BN Workers; Labor Relations Strained Over Series of Issues," *Traffic World,* February 14, 1994.
Burke, Jack, "Is BN Back? Strong Fourth Quarter, Cost Reductions May Signal Blue Skies, Black Ink Ahead," *Traffic World,* February 15, 1993.
"Burlington Begins Study of Whether to Move Corporate Headquarters," *Traffic World,* June 28, 1982.
Burlington, Great Northern, Northern Pacific Merger: ICC Finance Docket 21478-21480.
Burlington Northern Air Freight 1979 Annual Report.
"Burlington Northern: An Elephant by the Tail." *Forbes,* October 30, 1978.
"Burlington Northern Asks Conditions on North Western's Powder River Line," *Traffic World,* December 9, 1985.
Burlington Northern Railroad: Back on Track, Harvard Business School Case 9-396-214 prepared by Carin Knoop, March 20, 1996.
Burlington Northern Railroad Company, Plaintiff—Appellant, v. United Transportation Union, et al., Defendants—Appellees.

Brotherhood of Locomotive Engineers, Plaintiff—Appellee, v. Winona Bridge Railway Company, Defendant—Appellant.

Burlington Northern Railroad Company v. United Transportation Union a Jw Jg We Railway Labor Executives' Association 848 F. 2d 856, decided May 31, 1988.

Burlington Northern Railroad Company v. United Transportation Union, Brotherhood of Locomotive Engineers v. Winona Bridge Railway Company, United States Court of Appeals, Seventh Circuit, Decided November 18, 1988, and 851 F.2d 1056, M.M. Winter, Petitioner, v. Interstate Commerce Commission and United States of America, Respondents.

"Burlington Northern, EMD Ink 2nd Loco Upkeep Deal," *Traffic World,* July 31, 1989.

"Burlington Northern Expands Cicero Yard, Makes It Intermodal Facility," *Traffic World,* January 10, 1983.

"Burlington Northern Given Good Marks on FRA Safety Inspection," *Traffic World,* May 20, 1985.

Burlington Northern, Inc., Annual Reports, 1969–94.

Burlington Northern, Inc. common stock history—BNSF Railway www.bnsf.com/about/bnsf/financial-information/pdf/bn_history.pdf

Burlington Northern, Inc., et al., Petitioners, v. The United States of America and Interstate Commerce Commission, Respondents San Antonio, Texas, Acting by and Through Its City Public Service Board, Invervenor-Respondent. *No. 76-1899.* United States Court of Appeals, Eighty Circuit. Decided March 29, 1977.

Burlington Northern, Inc., Notice of Annual Meeting of Shareholders to Be Held April 20, 1995, dated March 17, 1995.

Burlington Northern Annual Report to Employees, 1974 and 1978.

Burlington Northern Bankers Tour, September 24–27, 1979 (notebook containing engineering and operating data, maps and transcripts of presentations to be made on an inspection trip).

Burlington Northern Financial Analysists Presentations, February 18, 1976, August, 1979, and August, 1981.

Burlington Northern Institutional Lenders Tour, September 18-21, 1978 (notebook containing engineering and operating data, maps and transcripts of presentations to be made on an inspection trip).

Burlington Northern Company, Appellee, v. United Transportation Union, Appellant, Fred A. Hardin, et al. Appeal from the United States District Court for the Western District of Missouri, *No. 87-2581.* Filed: May 31, 1988.

Burlington Northern Railroad. <en.wikipedia.org/wiki/Talk%3ABurlington-Northern-Railroad/temp>.

"Burlington Northern Railroad Unit Names Gen. Chain to Post," *Wall Street Journal,* December 5, 1990.

"Burlington Northern Sells Truck Subsidiary," *Traffic World,* Auguat 15, 1988.

"Burlington Northern Spared No Expense in Hiring New Chief," *Wall Street Journal,* May 4, 1981.

"Burlington Northern Splits Operations in 2: Non-Transport Units Isolated, to Be Spun Off," *Associated Press,* June 3, 1988.

"Burlington Northern Takes a Look South." 1970. *Railway Age,* May 25, 1970.

"Burlington Northern: The ARES Decision," Center for Digital Economic Research, Sloan School of Business, Working Paper, IS-93-18.

Burlington Northern: The ARES Decision (A) and (B), Harvard Business School Cases 9-191-122 and 9-191-123, February 21, 1991.

"Burlington Northern's Ditching Program," BN *Technical Bulletin,* May 1989.

"Burlington Northern's Fight to Repel Invaders," *Business Week,* November 3, 1980.

"Burlington Northern's Tamping Technology," BN *Technical Bulletin,* February 1989.

"Burlington Resources Shifting Its Focus," *Seattle Times,* March 2, 1993.

"Burlington Resources, Inc. History," <fundinguniverse.com/company-histories/burlington-resources-inc-history/>.

Burlington Resources Inc., Prospectus, Proposed Merger with ConocoPhillips, February 24, 2006.

Burlington Resources Inc., Prospectus, Sale of 20,000,000 Shares of Common Stock, July 7, 1988.

Burlington Resources, Inc., Information Statement Concerning the Distribution of Approximately 87% of the Outstanding Shares of Burlington Resources, Inc., by Burlington Northern, Inc., November 14, 1988.

"Burlington Resources Shifting Its Focus," *Bloomberg Business News,* March 2, 1993.

"Burlington Spinoff About to Happen," *Seattle Times,* December 5, 1991.

Burns, Alan, "Under a Big Sky," CTC *Board,* December 1989.

Burns, David H., "BN Chicago Region in the Early Days 1970–72," BN *Expediter,* January 2014.

Burns, David H. 2017. "Colorado Division Days 1979–81." *The* BN *Expediter,* April, 2017.

Burns, David H., "Deregulation and the Rise of Intermodalism," October 2012.

Burns, David H. 2013. "M-Day on the Dakota Division," *The* BN *Expediter,* July, 2013.

Burns, David R., "M/W Cost Components: Part I—Surfacing," *Railway Track and Structures,* April 1987.

Burns, James B. 1998. *Railroad Mergers and the Language of Unification.* Westport, Conn.: Quorum Books.

Burton, R. C., Jr. "Financing a Railroad," September 1979.

Busse, Meghan R. and Nathanial O. Keohane, "Market Effects of Environmental Regulation: Coal, Railroads and the 1990 Clean Air Act," University of California Energy Institute, September 2004.

Button, John J., Statement Before the Federal Railroad Administration on Control of Alcohol and Drugs in Railroad Operations, September 2, 1983.

Byrne, Don, "Rail Union Head Attacks Safety Board for Seeking 'No-Drinking' Regulation," *Traffic World*, May 14, 1984.

"Cabooseless Operation . . . Safer, Money Saver," *Progressive Railroading*, September 1987.

Callahan, Lynn Casey, "Alliance Thrives Amid Tough Challenges," BN *News*, July 1980.

Callahan, Lynn Casey, "BN Airmotive Takes Off As Leader in 'FBO' Business," BN *News*, November 1979.

Callahan, Lynn Casey, "BN Commuters Leave Car Keys at Home, Still Get to Chicago," BN *News*, February 1980.

Callihan, Lynn Casey, "Coal Makes the Difference at Guernsey," BN *News*, May/June 1980.

Callihan, Lynn Casey, "On the Playing Field: Deregulation Gets Railroads Off the Bench and Into the Game," BN *News*, January 1982.

Cama, Timothy, "Toxic Air Pollution Has Dropped Dramatically, EPA Tells Congress," *The Hill*, August 21, 2014.

Camp, Janice, "The Problem Center: Employee Assistance Expands," BN *News*, August/September 1982.

"C&NW and BN Still Don't Agree," *Railway Age*, November 8, 1982.

"C&NW—Going for a Bundle from FRA," *Railway Age*, December 26, 1977.

"C&NW Seeks Access to More BN Traffic," *Railway Age*, February 1985.

"C&S Engineering Closes a Busy Year," *Denver Region News*, December 1980.

"C&S Merger Plan Outlined," BN *News*, November 1981.

"Can Acoustic Detectors Reduce Bearing Failures?" *Railway Age*, October 1988.

Cantrell, Anne, "Q&A with Jerry Grinstein." www.montana.edu/news/15781/jerry-grinstein-montana-state.

Carr, John, *Western Coal: 2005 Compendium of Western Coal Mines, Electric Utilities and the BNSF and UP Trans That Serve Them*, 2006. Duncanville, Texas, Carr Tracks.

"The Carrot Instead of the Stick: One Division's Experiment in Discipline," BN *News*, Fall 1989.

"Cascade Tunnel Ventilation, dslweb.nwnexus.com/tawhite/CASCADE%20TUNNEL

Caughey, Peter, "Railroad Gives Livingston $1 Million Aid Package," *Boseman Daily Chronicle*, May 7, 1986.

Cawthorne, David M., "BN Places Non-Rail Holdings in Separate Corporate Unit," *Traffic World*, June 6, 1988.

Cawthorne, David M., "BN Proposes Major Overhaul in Work Rules, Pay Practices," *Traffic World*, June 22, 1987.

Cawthorne, David M., "BN Rail to Have Far More Debt After Restructuring Finished," *Traffic World*, June 18, 1988.June 18, 1988.

Cawthorne, David M., "BN Seeks Final ICC Approval of Transport Certificates Program," *Traffic World*, May 27, 1991.

Cawthorne, David M., "Burlington Northern Gets Final OK for Freight Car Futures Program," *Traffic World*, February 3, 1992.

Cawthorne, David M., "Future of Winona Bridge Plan Doubtful After Court Ruling," *Traffic World*, June 20, 1988.

Cawthorne, David M., "ICC May Collide with Congress over Line Sale Labor Protection," *Traffic World*, September 14, 1987.

Cawthorne, David M., "U.S. Supreme Court Likely to Review Rail Line Sales," *Traffic World*, June 6, 1988.

Celis, William III, "New Burlington Northern Unit to Offer Shares," *The Wall Street Journal*, June 3, 1988.

Chesser, Al (president of United Transportation Union), *Project Seventies, 1970.*

"Chicago Accounting Dept. Moves to General Office," BN *News*, November 1970.

Chicago, Burlington and Quincey Railroad Co., *Annual Reports, 1960–1968.*

Chicago, Milwaukee, St. Paul and Pacific Railroad Company, Petitioner, v. United States of America and Interstate Commerce Commission, Respondents. 585 F.2d 254, No. 77-1453. October 4, 1978.

"Chicago's People Trains," BN *News*, July 1970.

Christensen, Jack, "Arthur Fiedler, 1927–2011," *The Mainstreeter*, Summer 2012.

Christensen, Kathryn, and Richard D. James, "Volcano's Continuing Eruption Damages Lane, Stifles Commerce in the Northwest," *Wall Street Journal*, May 20, 1980.

"Chronology of the Northern Pacific and Related Land Grant Railroads," compiled by George Draffan, July 24, 2001.

Circular, $60,000,000 Burlington Northern, Inc., Consolidated Mortgage 8.60% Bonds, Series D, Due 1999.

Citizens' Alliance to Save the Southline, letter to U.S. Senator Max Baucus, April 7, 1987.

"Citizens of Alliance Comment on Effects of BN's Expansion Plans," BN *News*.

Clark, Milt, operations in Montana and Washington (Milwaukee Road), correspondence with the author.

Clark, Milt, "The Milwaukee Road's Seattle Connection," *The Milwaukee Roader*, Third Quarter 2009.

"Clean Coal Project in Texas Wins $450mn in Federal Help," *Power Engineering*, September 2009.

Cliff, Daniel F. 1988. "Business People; Burlington Northern Names 2 Executives," *New York Times*, October 21, 1988.

"CNW Earns $43 Million After $27 Million Loss," *Traffic World*, February 16, 1987.

"CNW Unit Buys Interest in BN 10-Mile Coal Line," *Traffic World*, January 5, 1987.

"Coal Boom: Area Set for Another Boom by 1990," *The News-Record* (Gillette, Wyo.), December 14, 1981.

"Coal Car Repair Shop Opens at Laurel," BN *News*, June 1977.

Coal in Montana-Montana State Legislature <leg.mt.gov/content/publications/Environmental/2004deq.../coal_text.pdf>.

"Coal Line Upgrading, Fremont, Nebraska to Shawnee, Wyoming," *North Western Lines,* Summer 2004.

"Coal Makes the Difference at Guernsey," *BN News,* May/June 1980.

"Coal Mining in Powder River," <coaldiver.org/coal-diver/Powder-River?>.

Coal Rates Guidelines, 1 ICC 2nd 520 (1985).

"Coal Shippers Are Pulling Together on Policy for Railroad Freight Rates," *Traffic World,* May 30, 1982.

"Coal Transportation Issues," U.S. Energy Information Administration, www.eia.gov/oiaf/aeo/otheranalysis/cti.

"Coal Use Expected to Increase in U.S. by 2025," *BNSF Today,* January 2, 2004.

"Col. Crown Calls Frisco Good Investment," *Chicago Tribune,* February 19, 1967.

"Collective Bargaining Under the Railway Labor Act," *The Locomotive Engineer,* May 18, 1984.

"Coming of Age," *BN News,* September-October 1986.

"Common Stock Dividends Resumed," *BN Westviews,* January/February 1976.

"Communications Division: Vital to BN Operations," *BN News,* November 1975.

"Commuter Service Moves 46,000 Daily," *BN News,* September 1976.

"Commuter Trains: Passengers Rate BN's Suburban Services Best in Chicago," *BN News,* July 1970.

"Company Meets Taconite Challenge," October 1976.

"Company Omits Dividend," *BN News,* September 1975.

"Company Reduces Dividend," *BN News,* October 1970.

"COMPASS Points the Way," from author's collection; date and name of publication not names.

"Competition Begins in Basin," *BN News,* October 1984.

"Competition Comes to Powder River," *Railway Age,* October 1984.

"The Computer Age Comes to Southern Pacific," *Southern Pacific Bulletin,* December 1967.

"Computerizing Track Warrants," *BN Lakes Division Monthly Report,* no date shown.

"Concrete Tie Turnouts Emerge." *Progressive Railroading,* October 1989.

Conference of BN Executives in March 1983, excerpts quoted in *BN News,* May/June 1983.

The Consolidated Code of Operating Rules, Edition of 1967.

"Construction at Mandan and Sioux City Helps BN Handle Rail Traffic," *BN News,* August/September 1980.

"Construction Update: Getting Ready to Run," Union Pacific *InfoNews,* March 1984.

"Conversation with the CEO," *BN News,* November 1990.

Conway, Chuch, "Powder River Coal," CTC *Board,* April 1991.

Cook, James, "All Alone by the Telephone," *Forbes,* November 16, 1987 (Richard M. Bressler quoted).

Cook, James, "The Turning Point," *Forbes,* September 24, 1984.

Corbin, Steven B., and Harry W. Zanville, "Why Would Anyone Want to Try to Teach a Course About the Rail Industry and How Would They Do It?" *Journal of Transportation Law, Logistics and Policy.*

Corr, O. Casey, "The Chairman: BN's Bressler Is One Tough Boss – And a Puzzle," *Seattle Post-Intelligencer,* March 22, 1988.

"The Cost Effectiveness of America's Freight Railroads," AAR position paper, May 2014.

"Costly Line Change Pays Off for NP," *Railway Age,* December 13, 1965.

"Court Says Railroad Workers Can Engage in Secondary Picketing," *Associated Press,* April 28, 1987.

Coyne, Frank H., remarks at Burlington Northern–held Seminar on Grain Transportation in 1980.

"Crawford Hill Line Change Completed," *Mgr.,* July 21, 1982.

"(1980) Crew Consist Agreement Between Burlington Northern Railroad and the United Transportation Union" utu324.com/93_crew_consist.

Crew Consist Agreement Between Burlington Northern Railroad and Its Employees Represented by United Transportation Union Effective November 1, 1993.

"Crew Consist Agreement Between Burlington Northern Railroad and its Employees Represented by United Transportation Union Effective May 20, 1993.

"Crew Consist Agreement Signed," *BN News,* October 1984.

Cross, B. B., "Alfred E. Kahn: The Life and Death of the Father of De-regulation," Associated Content, 2011.

Cuff, Daniel F. "Burlington Northern Names 2 Executives," *New York Times,* October 21, 1988.

Currie, Earl J. 2007. *James J. Hill's Legacy to Railway Operations.* Self-published.

Currie, Earl J. 2015. *Building Burlington Northern: The Lorentzsen Years, 1970–1980.* Self-published.

Currie, Earl J. 2010. *BN-Frisco: A Tough Merger.* Self-published.

Currie, Earl J. 2010. *Nebraska Division: Challenge and Reward, 1975–1977.* Sefl-published.

Currie, Earl J. 2011. *Robert W. Downing: One of the Best and Brightest.* Self-published.

Currie, Earl J., Statement Before the Federal Railroad Administration on Control of Alcohol and Drug Use in Railroad Operations, August 2, 1984.

"Customer Service: It's Everybody's Job," *BN News,* Spring 1987.

"The Customer: What BN Is Doing to Win Them and Keep Them," *BN News,* November 1983.

"Cutover Seen as Significant Change by Burlington Northern," *The Plattsmouth Journal,* December 2, 1976.

Danneman, Mike, "Coal and Curves," CTC *Board Railroads Illustrated,"* December 2004.

Danneman, Mike and Dave Gayer. 2010. *Montana Rail Link.* Kansas City: White River Productions.

Darius W. Gaskins, Jr. www.zoominfo.com/people/Gaskins_Darius_79175318.asps.

"Dave Crooker, Resources Division Silviculturist, Uses His Knowledge to Help Forest Renew Itself," *BN News,* November 1978.

Davis, David D ."Evaluation of Load Environment of Flange-bearing Frogs," *Railway Track and Structures,* July 2013.

DeBoer, David J. 1992. *Piggyback and Containers: A History of Rail Intermodal on America's Steel Highway.* San Marino, Calif.: Golden West Books.

DeBoer, Dave, "Stacking the Deck," *Trains,* November 2011.

"Dedication and Determination," *Powder River Reflection,* October 2009.

"A Definition of Corporate Culture," *BN News,* March 1985.

Del Grosse, Robert C. 1991. *Burlington Northern: Trackside Guide.* Bonners Ferry: Great Northern Pacific Publications.

Del Grosso, Robert C. 1994. *Burlington Northern: Railroad Giant of the Pacific Northwest.* Bonners Ferry: Selkirk Press.

Del Grosso, Robert C. 2014. *Burlington Northern Railroad: Historical Review 1970 – 1995.* Halifax, Penn.: Withers Publishing.

"Deliveries of Coal from the Powder River Basin: Events and Trends 2005–2007," U.S. Department of Energy, October 2007.

Dennis Washington, Hawassa Online. www.hawassaonline.com/biography_detail.php?id=18&type=entrepreneurs>.

Dennis R. Washington, 2007 Inductee into American Mining Hall of Fame, quoted in "Mining Foundation of the Southwest."

"Depreciation Accounting for Track Structure," *BN document,* Effective January 1, 1983.

Derailment of Extra 5701 East at Sheridan, Wyoming, March 28, 1971, National Transportation Safety Board Report Number: NTSB-RAR-72-4, April 26, 1972.

"Deregulation: Terms, Questions, Constraints," Burlington Northern Technical Training, 1980.

"Deregulation: What Happen Next?" *Railway Age,* October 27, 1980.

DeRouin, Edward M., "Land of the Burlingtons, Part II, Building on the Foundation Laid by CB&Q," *Passenger Train Journal,* January 1989.

"Differential Pricing: Efficient and Necessary," Association of American Railroads Policy and Economics Department, July 2006.

DiMichael, Nicholas J., "Living with Stand-Alone Costs: The OPPD Decision," *Traffic World,* January 5, 1987.

Ditmeyer, Steven R., "Burlington Northern and Technology," letter to *Trains,* January 2015.

Ditmeyer, Steven R. and Edward L. Butt, "S&C (Signals and Communications) Projects Focus on Service, Safety," *Modern Railroads,* November 1989.

"Division Bids Farewell to Don Maze," *Pride of the Northwest,* March/April 2003.

"Doctors Plan Gillette Practice," *The News-Record* (Gillette, Wyo.), December 31, 1975.

Dodge, John, "Positive Train Control Ran Successfully in Years-Long Burlington Northern Railroad Trial," *Design News,* October 21, 2008.

Doerr, Norman M., "Burlington Northern Railroad Merger from a Non-Operating Department Perspective," 2015.

Donaldson, Gordon. 1994. *Corporate Restructuring: Managing the Change Process from Within.* Boston: Harvard Business School Press.

Dorin, Patrick C., and Robert C. Del Grosso. 1995. *Burlington Northern Railroad: Coal Hauler and Coal Country Trackside Guide.* Great Northern Pacific Publications.

Downey, Mark, "Crew, Seattle Dispatcher Misunderstood Clearance," *Great Falls Tribune,* September 3, 1991.

"Downing Recounts Great Northern, Burlington Northern Merger Days," *Vingage Rails,* Winter 1996.

Downing, Robert W., Annual Luncheon Address, American Railway Engineering Association, Bulletin 648.

Draffan, George, "Annotated Bibliography on Railroad Land Grants," <www.landgrant.org/biblio>.

Draffan, George, "Chronology of the Northern Pacific and Related Land Grant Railroads," Endgameame.org, July 24, 2001.

Drajem, Mark, "EPA Final Rule for Coal Plants Deemed 'Unfortunate' by Industry," Bloomberg, December 19, 2011.

Drexel, Walter A., "TEAMWORK: Management, Labor Must Unite at BN," presentation to company officers, *BN News,* May/June 1983.

"Drugs: Risky Business," *BN News,* October 1985.

Dunwiddie, Paul, "Derailed: Auburn's 'Grand Ol' Lady' About To Make It a Widower," *Daily Globe News,* September 10, 1981.

Dusell, Forester, "A Partnership Report," 1972 (a one-page handout given to passengers on commuter trains).

Eakin, B. Kelly, and Mark E. Meitzen, "Opinion: After 30 Years, Railroad Deregulation Continue to Deliver," <aolnews.com/opinion/article/opinion-after-30-years-railroad-deregulation j-con>.

Eakin, B. Kelly, A. Thomas Bozzo, Mark E. Meitzen and Philip E. Schoech, "Railroad Performance Under the Staggers Act," *Regulation,* Winter 2010–2011.

"Economists: Rereg Would Imperil Productivity Gains," *Railway Age,* November 9, 2010.

"EEOC, Burlington Reach $10 Million Settlement in Discrimination Suit," *Traffic World,* November 21, 1983.

"Effectively Competing: The Product Has Improved," *BN News,* June 1985.

Eisthen, Bob, "Union Pacific Builds for the Future," *CTC Board Railroads Illustrated,"* May 1989.

Ekey, Robert, "BN Ponders Its Future in Livingston," *Billings Gazette,* October 27, 1986.

Ekey, Robert, "Railroad Claims Law Will Double Its Taxes," *Billings Gazette,* October 27, 1985.

Ekey, Robert and Paul J. Holley, "State Off Track, BN Says," *Billings Gazette,* October 27, 1985.

"Electrification: An Answer to Rising Fuel Costs," *BN News,* January 1981.

"Electronic Search Simplifies Diesel Problem Diagnonis," *BN News,* January 1979.

Ellig, Tracy, "Grain Byer Gene Thayer Grows a Future for Bobcat Athletics," *Mountains and Minds Magazine,* Fall 2007. Press release issued by Montana State University, 2007.

"EMD Takes Over Former BN Shop," *Railway Age,"* March 1989.

"Employee Opinion Survey: 2,419 Managers Speak Out," *Mgr.,* April 18, 1984.

"Employee Opinion Survey Report," *BN News,* March 1984.

Employee Protection Agreement Between Burlington Northern Railroad Company and Brotherhood of Locomotive Engineers, July 18, 1985.

"The End of the Line?" (for cabooses), *BN News,* May 1985.

"The End of the Line: Why BN Sheds Unprofitable Lines," *BN News,* July 1983.

"Energy Boom Will Double Gillette's Population by '78," *Rapid City Journal,* May 5, 1974.

"Energy: Frequently Asked Questions," <uprr.customers/energy/sprb/faq.shtml>.

Energy Transportation Systems, Inc. <www.engagingnews.us/select/Energy-Transportation-Systems-Inc.>.

Engineering Division Data Book. Burlington Northern, December 31, 1979.

"Engineer Is Indicted on 16 Counts of Manslaughter in Amtrak Crash," *New York Times,* May 5, 1987.

"Environment and Economics: The Need for Balance," *BN News,* July 1980.

Enzi, Michael B., *Gillette History (The 1970's),* Wy. V-File, October 1, 1976.

"Equal Employment Opportunity: Two Decades of Progress," *BN News,* Fall 1989.

Etheridge, A. Charles, "BNAFI-Chicago Was a Gamble—But It Proved to Be a Sure Thing," *BN News,* December 1978.

Etheridge, A. Charles, "BN Investment in Minerals Good for Country and Company," *BN News,* October 1980.

"ETSI's Coal Slurry Pipeline' Nothing New'" *Gillette News – Record,* June 5, 1975.

"ETSI Pipeline Project v. Burlington Northern, Inc. (U.S. District Court, Eastern District of Texas)" <furth.com/historical>

"The ETSI Settlement Took $108.5 Million . . . ," *Burlington Northern Railroad News Update,* February 1989.

Ettorre, John J., "Rails Cautiously Pursue Testing Despite Drug, Alcohol Rule Suits," *Traffic World,* June 16, 1986.

EuDaly, Kevin. 2004. "Coal." *North Western Lines,* Summer 2004.

"The Energy Crisis and Wyoming Coal." Burlington Northern, 1979.

"The ETSI Settlement Took $108.5 Million . . . ," *Burlington Northern Railroad News Update,"* February 1989.

The Facts About Air Quality and Coal-Fired Power Plants. <instituteforenergyresearch.org>.

Farney, Dennis, "Unkindest Cut? Timber Firm Stirs Ire Felling Forests Faster Than They Regenerate," *Wall Street Journal,* June 18, 1990.

"Fast On/Off Equipment Buys Tie Gangs Track Time," *Railway Track and Structures,* October 1989.

Feurer, Keith, "Look Who Came Out on Top," *North Western Lines,* Summer 2004.

Field, David, "Shippers' Agents Debate Linertrain; Opportunity, Threat to Future Seen," *Traffic World,* June 10, 1985.

"First Quarter Random Drug Testing Results Tallied," *Burlington Northern Railroad Inside,"* May 1990.

Forman, Kim, quoted in "1970 News" in <Wikipedia.org/wiki/Talk%3ABurlington_Northern_Railroad/temp>.

Forman, Kim, "BN Timber and Land Division Manages Resources with Eye to Needs of Future Generations," *BN News,* August 1977.

"Final Run for Sogn Patriarch," *Powder River Reflection,* 3rd ed., 2011.

"Fort Worth Move Completed," *BN News,* October 1984.

"Fort Worth Relocation," *Mgr.,* June 20, 1984.

Fox, Wesley, *Powder River Coal and the BN's Denver Division,* Arvada, Colo.: Fox Publications, 1999.

Frailey, Fred W., "A Different Way to Run a Railroad," *Trains,* October 2013.

Frailey, Fred W., "Powder River 'Blowout' Sends BNSF, UP Reeling," *Trans,* September 2005.

Frailey, Fred W. 1989. "Powder River Country: America's Last Rail Frontier," *Trains,* November, 1989.

Frailey, Fred W. 2010. "Powder River Stories: Five Moments That Made a Difference in the Life of North America's Busiest Coal Railroad." *Trains,* April 2010.

Fram, Alan, "Drug, Alcohol Use Widespread in Rail Industry, Accident Crewmen Say," *Associated Press,* February 25, 1988.

Frank Christopherson, Locomotive Engineer, Leader and Volunteer, an oral history conducted by Tom Gannon and Tim Schandel, compiled by Earl J. Currie, December 2011.

"FRA Orders Safety Audit of Burlington Northern," *Traffic World,* August 27, 1984.

Fredrix, Emily, "Officials Sign Documents to Close Sale of Core Rail Line," Associated Press, December 17, 2005.

"Freight Railroads: Industry Health Has Improved, But Concerns About Competition and Capacity Should Be Addrressed," United States Government Accountability Office, October 2006.

French, Peter. "U.S. Railroad Safety Statistics and Trends, 1980–2010," Association of American Railroads, May 17, 2011.

Friedlaender, Ann F., Ernst R. Berndt, and Gerard McCullough. "Governance Structure, Managerial Characteristics and Firm Performance in the Deregulated Rail Industry," *Brookings Papers on Economic Activity. Microeconomics,* Vol. 1992. www.jstor.org/stable/2534763.

"Frisco's Good Connections, Confidence Help Maintain High Level of Service," *BN News,* May 1978.

"Frisco Vice Presidents Appointed to BN Posts," BN press release, May 19, 1980.

"Frogs: More Than What Meets the Eye." 1991. *Railway Track and Structures,* September, 1991.

"From the Desk of Jerry Grinstein: A New CEO's Perspective," *Mgr.* First Quarter, 1989.

"Frontiersmen of the Powder River Basin," *TrainsTalk,* September 25, 2009.

Fruin, Jerry and Robert Crnkovich, "Western Coal Transportation Rates for Minnesota Users," Staff Paper P78-3, Department of Agricultural and Applied Economics, University of Minnesota, February 1978.

Gaertner, John T. 1990. *North Bank Road: The Spokane, Portland and Seattle Railway.* Pullman: Washington State University Press.

Gaertner, John, "The Twin Cities Joint Terminal," *The Mainstreeter,* Spring 2009.

"Galesburg Gears for Growth," *Railway Age,* April 1985.

"Galesburg Yard Dedicated," *BN News,* October 1984.

Gallagher, John, "Reconsider This: Some Ex-Railroaders Question Benefit of a Scheduled Railroad," *Traffic World,* July 12, 1999.

Gallagher, John, "UP Eating BNSF's Lunch," *Traffic World,* July 19, 1999.

Gardner, A. Dudley, and Verla R. Flores. *Forgotten Frontier: A History of Wyoming Coal Mining.* Boulder, Colo.: Westview Press.

Gallamore, Robert E. and John R. Meyer. 2014. *American Railroads: Decline and Renaissance in the Twentieth Century.* Cambridge, Mass., and London: Harvard University Press.

Gaskins, Darius W., "Regulation of Freight Railroads in the Modern Era: 1970–2010," *Review of Network Economics,* December 2008.

Gayer, Dave and Mike Danneman, "Montana Rail Link Turns 20," *Railroads Illustrated,* November 2017.

"Gerald Grinstein Speaks to BN Union Leaders," *Mgr.* Fourth Quarter, 1988.

"Gerald Grinstein Succeeded Darius Gaskins . . . ," *Burlington Northern Railroad News Update,* February 1989.

"George Lamphier: Super Gandy," *BN News,* April 1980.

Gerking, Shelby, and Stephen F. Hamilton, "What Explains the Increased Utilization of Powder River Basin Coal in Electric Power Generation?" *American Journal of Agricultural Economics,* Vol. 90, Issue 4, November 1, 2008.

Gibson, Paul, "A Railroad for the Long Haul," *Forbes,* April 27, 1981.

Gillespie, M.E., "Housing Lack Stymies Boom," *The News-Record* (Gillette, Wyo.), October 31, 1974.

Gilpin, Kenneth H., and Eric Schmitt. "Business People: Burlington Northern Promotes 2 Executives," *New York Times,* December 18, 1985.

Gibson, Paul. 1981. "A Railroad for the Long Haul." *Forbes,* April 27, 1981.

Glavin, William E. 1989. "BN Becomes Roadway Innovator," *Progressive Railroading,* March 1989.

Glavin, William E. 1991. "Quality Now Railroads 'Religion,'" *Progressive Railroading,* March 1991.

Glischinski, Steve. 1992. *Burlington Northern and Its Heritage.* Andover, N.J.: Andover Junction Publications.

Glischinski, Steve. "Crawford Hill: Mountain Railroading in Nebraska?" *CTC Board Railroads Illustrated,* July 1999.

Glischinski, Steve, "Main Street of Big Sky Country," *Trains,* April 1993.

Glischinski, Steve. "The Train That Started It All," *Trains,* March 2011.

Gohmann, John W. 1984. *The Railway Labor Act Primer.* Chicago: Gohmann and Associates, Inc.

Golden, Erin. "High-tech Derailment Defense," Omaha *World – Herald,* 2012.

"A Good Start . . . A Lot Left To Do," *Railway Age,* February 22, 1971.

"Got a Question? Cut Through the Red Tape: DIAL BOSS," *BN News,* January 1973.

"Gov. Rounds and BNSF Announce Settlement on South Dakota ' s Core Railroad Line," *BNSF Today,* May 2, 2005.

Graham-White, Shean, "BN's SD70MAC," *CTC Board Railroads Illustrated,* November 2004.

Grande, Walter R. 1992. *The Northwest's Own Railway: Spokane, Portland and Seattle Railway and Its Subsidiaries.* Portland, Ore.: Grande Press.

Grant, H. Roger. 1996. *The North Western: A History of the Chicago and North Western Railway System.* DeKalb: Northern Illinois University Press.

"The Grapevine: Is it Really the Root of Unfounded Rumors?" *BN News, April 1985.*

Gratitude—Stewardship—Opportunity: 25 Years of Plum Creek, 2014. Publication by Plum Creek, LLC.

Gray, Kristy, "Explosion in Gillette," *Casper Star-Tribune,* June 27, 2007.

"Grayson: BN in Rail Business to Stay," *BN News,* April 1982.

"Grayson Named to New Post, Drexel New Rail President," *BN News,* March 1982.

Grayson, Richard G., Sr., <www.ancestry.com/boards/localities.northam.usa.states.missouri.counties.crawford/950/mb.ashx>.

"Grayson to Competitors: 'Welcome, But Bring Money.'" *BN News.*

"Grayson to Leave Frisco RR for New Post at BN Jan. 1," BN press release November 14, 1980.

Great Northern Pacific & Burlington Lines, Inc., letter to all employees, September 29, 1967.

Great Northern Pacific & Burlington Lines, Inc.—Merger, Etc.—Great Northern Railway Company, et al, Interstate Commerce Commission, Finance Docket No. 21478.

Great Northern Pacific & Burlington Lines, Inc., Merger, Etc.,

Applicants' Petition for Reconsideration, Finance Docket Nos. 21478, 21479 and 21480, July 27, 1966.

Great Northern Pacific & Burlington Lines Inc.—Merger—Great Northern Ry., et al., 348 ICC 821, 829 (1977).

Great Northern Railway Co., *Annual Reports, 1960–1968.*

"Grinstein Succeeds Bressler as Chairman of BN's Board." 1990. *Traffic World,* October 22, 1990.

"Growing the Company: A Labor Relations View," *BN News,* August–September 1985.

Gruber, John. "Huge Chance, Big Payoff," *Trains* web exclusive, February 19, 2010.

Grunwald, Michael, "Back on Tracks," *Time,"* July 9, 2012.

"Guernsey Tunnel No. 2 Loses Its Top," *Alliance Times-Herald,* September 17, 1998.

Guillen, Tomas, "Killing Time in 'Rubber Room': Surplus Workers Are Idle, But Paid," *Seattle Times,* November 30, 1986.

Hackett, Jason, "Burlington Northern Complex Houses Operations," *Alliance Times-Herald,* September 21, 1995.

Haeg, Larry. 2013. *Harriman vs. Hill: Wall Street's Great Railroad War.* Minneapolis: University of Minnesota Press.

Hage, Dave, "BN's Court Defeat Won't End Labor-Cost Battles," *Minneapolis Star-Tirbune,* November 29, 1988.

Haines, Henry S., *Efficient Railway Operation,* New York: Macmillian, 1919.

Haines, Joan, "BN Closure No Shock to Man Who Fought Railroad Merger," *Bozeman Daily Chronical,* November 7, 1985.

Haines, Joan, "BN, Labor Split on Court Drug Testing," *Bozeman Daily Chronical,* February 2, 1988.

Haines, Joan, "Judge Says Winona Can't Start," *Bozeman Daily Chronical,* June 10, 1988.

Haines, Joan, "Unions Disagree with Railroads on Winona Cost," *Bozeman Daily Chronical,* April 21, 1988.

Haines, Leslie, "Former Burlington Executives Discuss Management," *Oil and Gas Investor,* October 1, 2014.

Hamberger, Edward R., "The Anniversary of Our American Success Story," <huffingtonpost.com/Edward-r-hamberger/the-anniversary-of-our-am_b_75626>.

Hansen, Peter A., 2016. "Coal: A Twisted Future," *Trains,* March 2016.

Harball, Elizabeth and Brittany Patterson, "Coal's Western Stronghold Faces Precarious Future," <www.eenews.net/stories/106003534/>.

Harmen, Robert R., "Pueblo Junction, Colorado," *Trains,* November 1992.

"Havelock Wheel Shop Opens Soon," *BN News,* October 1976.

Hayes, Thomas C. "Taking Control At Burlington," *New York Times,* April 16, 1982.

Head-End Collision of Nine Burlington Northern Locomotive Units with a Standing Freight Train, Angora, Nebraska, February 16, 1980. National Transportation Safety Board Report No. NTSB-RAR-80-7.

Head-on Collision Between Burlington Northern Railroad Freight Trains 602 and 603 Near Ledger, Montana, on August 30, 1991, National Transportation Safety Board Report NTSB/RAR-93/01, May 25, 1993.

Head-on Collision of Burlington Northern Railroad Company Freight Trains Extra 6311 West and Extra 6575 East Near Westminster, Colorado, August 2, 1985. National Transportation Safety Board Railroad Accident Report NTSB/RAR-86/02.

Head-on Collision of Burlington Northern Railroad Company Freight Trains Extra 6760 West and Extra 7907 East Near Motley, Minnesota, June 14, 1984, National Transportation Safety Board Report No. RAR-85/06.

Healey, Judith Koll. 1998. *Frederick Weyerhaeuser and the American West.* Reprinted from William Stafford, "The Way It Is." St. Paul: Minnesota Historical Society Press.

Healy, Kent T. *The Effects of Scale in the Railroad Industry,* Yale University, 1961.

"Heavy Haul Balances the Conflicts," *Progressive Railroading,* July 1991.

Hein, Rebecca. 2014. "Campell County, Wyoming," WhoHistory.org.

Helge, Doris, "Employee Motivation: Rip Off the BandAids," www.selfgrowth.com/articles/Employee_Motivation_-_Rip_OFF_The_BandAids.

Henderson, Dean, "Burlington Northern: On the Wrong Track," www.multinationalmonitor.org/hyper/issues/1993/03/mm0393_11.

"Henry Crown and Company," www.answers.com/topic/henry-crown-and-company.

Hertog, John H. "Railroads as a Coal Transportation System," International Right of Way Association, August 1982.

Hertog, John H. "Remarks of John H. Hertog, Vice President–Operations Before Annual Executive Seminar," Electro-Motive Division, General Motors Corp., May 4, 1977.

Hertog, John H. "Remarks of John H. Hertog, Vice President, Operations, Burlington Northern, Inc., Financial Analysts Trip, September 27, 1977.

Hertog, J. H. "Coal Presentation," Western Coal Transportation Association, May 4, 1976.

Hidy, Ralph W., Muriel E. Hidy, and Roy V. Scott with Don L. Hofsommer. 1988. *The Great Northern Railway: A History.* Boston: Harvard Business School Press.

"High-Speed Turnouts," *BN Technical Bulletin,* September 1990.

Hillard, John, correspondence with the author, 2013.

Hill, James J. 1910. *Highways of Progress.* New York: Doubleday, Page and Company.

Hill, James J., letter to stockholders upon retiring from Chairmanship of the Board of Directors, Great Northern Railway Company, July 1, 1912.

Hill, James J., on the occasion of a frank talk to a group of employees on strike at the Jackson Street Roundhouse in St. Paul, Minnesota, August 1880, *St. Paul Globe,* August 23, 1880, quoted in Albro Martin's *James J. Hill and the Opening of the Northwest.*

History of Plum Creek, nhcs.wikispaces.com/History+of+Plum+Creek.

"Historical Background Information: Major Burlington Northern Predecessor Companies," Burlington Northern Railroad, 1981.

History of the Clean Air Act, <www.epa.gov/air/caa/caa_history>.

"History of TOPS," www.trainweb.org/rews/tops/history.

"HL&P, Railroad Settle Coal Transport Suit," Associated Press, November 30, 1988.

Hofsommer, Don L., "Hill's Dream Realized: The Burlington Northern's Eight-Decade Gestation," *Pacific Northwest Quarterly,* October 1988.

Hofsommer, Don L., "Robert W. Downing: A Life Worth Remembering," *Railroad History,* Fall–Winter 2010.

Hofsommer, Don L., "What It Takes: Portraits of Three Successful Managers," *Railroad History,* Fall–Winter 2002.

Holding, Brian. "Railroaders View Conditions at Galesburg BN Yards," Galesburg *Register-Mail,* August 29, 1974.

Holley, Paul J., "Labor Unions Dispute BN Spinoffs," *Billings Gazette,* December 28, 1986.

Holley, Paul J. and Jim Ludwick, "Railroad Deal Expands to Huntley," *Billings Gazette,* July 24, 1987.

Hon, D. V., "The Rising Cost of Car Maintenance," *Progressive Railroading,* February 1978.

"House Units Shelve Bill to Let Pipelines Carry Coal Slurry," *The Wall Street Journal,* June 28, 1977.

"How BN Manages M/W," *Railway Age,* July 1990.

"How BN Put the Pieces Together," *Railway Age,* March 29, 1976.

"How Milwaukee's New Train Speeds Freight," *Railway Age,* November 25, 1963.

"How Mr. Henry Crown Derailed the Rock Island," 1979. *Executive Intelligence Review,* October 2–8, 1979.

"Hub Program Successful, Expanding," *BN News,* July 1983.

Hwang Suein L., "Loss Is Expected by Burlington Northern Inc." *Wall Street Journal,* June 24, 1991.

Hwang, Suein L., "Stock of Burlington Northern Declines on Write-Off Plans," *Wall Street Journal,* June 28, 1991.

"IBM 360 Computer Is Newest Addition to GN's Data Processing Department," *Talking It Over,* March 1968.

"ICC Approves C&NW Plan to Haul Coal Out of Powder River Basin," *Traffic World,* August 3, 1981.

"ICC Proposes Coal Rate Standards Aimed at Adequate Rail Revenues," *Traffic World,* February 26, 1983.

"ICC Releases Decision Outlining Rationale of Coal Rate Guidelines," *Traffic World,* September9, 1985.

"ICC Removes Conditions Imposed on 1967 Merger of BN's Predecessors," *Traffic World,* March 30, 1987.

"Images for GAO Report on Coal Rates 2005," a series of graphs showing trends in coal rates and other aspects of coal usage.

Implementing Agreement No. 1 (1970) Between Burlington Northern Inc. 1 (Formerly the Great Northern Pacific & Burlington Lines, Inc. 1) and Its Employees Represented by The Brotherhood of Locomotive Engineers.

Implementing Agreement No. 5 Between Burlington Northern, Inc. and Its Employees Represented by United Transportation Union, October 15, 1971.

"Improving Crosstie Materials and Design," *Railway Track and Structures,* September 1991.

"Industry Seeks Smaller Train Crews," *BN News,* July 1983.

"The Information Evolution: Computers and the Systems They Process Assume a Greater Importance at Burlington Northern," *BN News,* August/September 1985.

Information Statement Covering the Distribution of Approximately 87% of the Outstanding Shares of Burlington Resources, Inc., November 14, 1988.

Ingles, J. David, "Burlington Northern: Window to the Future? Dedicated to exploring alternatives to diesel fuel," *Trains,* November 1983.

"Injuries, Accidents Down in 1982," *BN News,* August-September 1982.

"In Memoriam: Bob Binger, *WMCA Camp Widjiwagan.*

"In Memoriam: Robert Downing, the Driving Force Behind the Burlington Northern Railroad Merger," *Progressive Railroading,* August 6, 2010.

"In Memoriam: Two Former Top Execs Who Helped Shape the Class I Landscape," *Progressive Railroading,* September 2010.

Inmon, Cliff, data on line changes constructed on Colorado and Southern Railway addressed to author, July 27, 2014.

"In Search of Quality," *BN News,* August/September 1983.

"Intermodal Piggybacking Key to Railroading's Future," *BN News,* October 1980.

"Innovative Intermodal . . . A Matter of Attitude,' *Progressive Railroading,* November 1986.

International Heavy Haul Association. 2001. *Guidelines to Best Practices for Heavy Haul Railway Operations: Wheel and Rail Interface Issues.* Virginia Beach, Va.: International Heavy Haul Association.

Interstate Commerce Commission, "ICC Authorizes Merger of Northern Lines Railroads," November 30, 1967.

An Interview with Al Egbers, "Across the Bargaining Table," *BN News,* April 1984.

An Interview with Chairman and CEO Walter A. Drexel, "Becoming No. 1," *BN News,* July 1984.

An Interview with D. W. Gaskins, "The Long View," *BN News,* December 1982.

An Interview with D. W. Gaskins, *BN News,* January/February 1986.

An Interview with D. W. Gaskins, "Marketing in a Challenging Environment," *BN News,* November 1984.

An Interview with D. W. Gaskins, Jr., "Together We Have Ironed Out Most of the Problems, *BN News,* January/February 1986.

An Interview with Eli Wackenstein, *BN News,* August/September 1985.

An Interview with Gerald Grinstein, Charting a Steady Course, *Railway Age,* January 1, 1991. Interviewed by Gus Welty

An Interview with Jim Dagnon, Working Across the Table, *BN News,* Spring 1988.

An Interview with John Hertog, *BN News,* November 1985.

An Interview with Raymond D. Burton, Jr. (name of interviewer not given), Railroad Executive Oral History Program for The John W. Barriger III National Railroad Library, December 2000.

An Interview with Richard M. Bressler, Chairman, President and Chief Executive Officer, Burlington Northern, Inc., June 15, 1984, conducted by John F. Kawa, First Vice President, Dean Whitter Reynolds, Inc.

An Interview with Robert Downing by Professor Donald Hofsommer, Railroad Executive Oral History Program #3, John W. Barriger III National Railroad Library, January 12, 2000.

An Interview with Robert D. Krebs by Professor Donald Hofsommer at Lake Forest, Ill., Railroad Executive Oral History Program, John W. Barriger III National Railroad Library, June 7, 2008.

An Interview with Thomas J. Lamphier by Professor Donald Hofsommer, Railroad Executive Oral History Program, John W. Barriger III National Railroad Library, University of Missouri-St. Louis.

An Interview with Tom Matthews, "Building Teamwork," *BN News,* March 1984.

An Interview with the Top Rail Officers (Richard Grayson and Walter Drexel), "What's in Store," *BN News,* May/June 1982.

An Interview with William Quinn by John W. Barriger IV and Paul Cruikshank, John W. Barriger III National Railroad Library, St. Louis Mercantile Library, University of Missouri–St. Louis.

An Interview with Worthington Smith by John W. Barriger IV, Railroad Executive Oral History Interview, John W. Barriger III National Railroad Library, July 31 and August 1, 2001.

"In the Last Half of '70, We Really Got Rolling," Interview with Louis W. Menk, *Railway Age,* February 22, 1971.

"Investing in the Future: 1984 Track Program Sharpens BN's Competitive Edge," *BN News,* April 1984.

"Is Clear-cutting Bad? How About Select Cutting?" The Pennsylvania Forestry Association, <www.paforestry.org/is-clear-cutting/bad/how/about/select/c...>.

"Issues and Comments: Addressing Employee Concerns," *BN News,* March 1985.

"I've Been Working on the Railway," *BN News,* September 1974.

"Jackson Finds New Home in Newcastle," *Powder River Reflection.*

Jamison, Michael, "Plum Creek to Close Pablo Mill," *Missoulian,* April 28, 2009.

Jenkins, Bess, "Mountains (of Paper) Waiting in Burlington Northern Inc, Merger," *Sunday Journal and Star,* February 8, 1970.

Jensen, Derrick, and George Draffan with John Osborn, M.D. 1995. *Railroads and Clearcuts: Legacy of Congress's 1864 Northern Pacific Railroad Land Grant.* Spokane: Inland Empire Public Lands Council.

"Jimmy Little and Art Mattila Cleared of Motley Accident Charges," *Straight Track,* Inter Craft Association of Minnesota Newsletter, August 1984.

Johnson, Gregory S., "BN Rail Begins Selling Grain Transport Futures," *Journal of Commerce,* January 13, 1988.

Johnson, Stephen S., "A Tycoon in the Old Mold," *Forbes,* May 20, 1996.

Jones, Todd, "Milwaukee Road in the '70's: What Really Happened?" <www.trainweb.org/milwaukee/article>.

Joplin, William N. 1990. "Burlington Northern Railroad: A Centennial Review," pamphlet prepared by BN's Corporate Communications Department.

"Jury Awards ETSI $345 Million in Slurry Suit," Associated Press, November 10, 1989.

"Justice Clears BN in Milwaukee Case," *Railway Age,* April 26, 1982.

Kalbach, John, "Crossing a Creek in Style," *Trains,* March 1984.

Kametz, Tom, "A Layman's Analysis of Plum Creek Timber," seekingalpha.com/article/507561-a-laymans-analysis-of-plum-creek-timber.

Karr, Albert R., "Coal-Slurry Pipelines Face Key Hurdle This Week in Fight for Eminent Domain," *Wall Street Journal,* May 18, 1976.

Karr, Albert R., "Nation's Railroads to Seek Big Reduction in Federal Regulation of Their Industry," *Wall Street Journal,* March 7, 1979.

Katzenbach, Jon R. and Douglas K. Smith. 2002. *The Wisdom of Teams.* New York: HarperCollins.

Kaufman, Jonathan, "Burlington Northern Taps Arco Executive as President and Chief, *Wall Street Journal,* May 20, 1980.

Kaufman, Larry, "BN Chief Executive Apologizes for Crew-Calling Snafus," *Journal of Commerce,* December 15, 1993.

Kaufman, Larry, "Focus on Bottom Line Drove BN to Abandon 'Sun Belt Strategy,'" *Journal of Commerce,* February 23, 1994.

Kaufman, Larry, "Old Union Foe of BN Bows Out in Severance Deal," *The Journal of Commerce,* July 14, 1893.

Kaufman, Lawrence H., "Air Force General to Join Burlington Northern," *Journal of Commerce,* December 7, 1990.

Kaufman, Lawrence H., "BN Seeks Talks with UTU on Northern Tier Crew Sizes," *Journal of Commerce,* March 12, 1992.

Kaufman, Lawrence H., "'Duopoly' Grates on Grain Shippers," *Railway Age,* May 1999.

Kaufman, Lawrence H., "Focus on Bottom Line Drove BN to Abandon 'Sun Belt Strategy,'" *The Journal of Commerce,* February 23, 1994.

Kaufman, Lawrence H. 2005. *Leaders Count: The Story of BNSF Railway.* Austin, Texas: Texas Monthly Custom Publishing.

Keeney, Kathleen R., and Allen R. Wastler, "Winona Transaction Mishandled, ICC Official, Rail Labor Claim," *Traffic World,* December 14, 1987.

Keeney, Kathleen R., "Picketing, Taxation Top List of High Court Transport Acts," *Traffic World,* July 6, 1987.

Keeney, Kathleen R., "Senators Seek Investigation of BN Line Sale in Montana," *Traffic World,* October 25, 1987.

Kelly, Bruce E., "BNSF Greenlights Second Idaho Bridge," *Railway Age,* May 2017.

Kelly, Bruce E., "BNSF Plans Second Bridge over Idaho Chokepoint," web.mail.comcast.net/zimbra/h/printmessage?id=231240&tz=...

Kelly, Bruce, "Stampede Pass Comes Back to Life," *Trains,* January 1997.

Kelly, Bruce E., 2014. "The Crude Oil Challenge," *Railway Age,* February, 2014.

Kelly, Bruce E., "Three-sided Traffic Solution," *Railway Age,* November 2012.

Kipling, Rudyard, "The Sons of Martha," www.online-literature.com.

Kirby, Jeff, letter re elimination of EMD-assigned jobs and elimination of EMD supervisory roles, *Glendive Diesel Shop* (newsletter), February 2011.

Klauser, P. E. "Assessing the Benefits of Tangential-Geometry Turnouts," *Railway Track and Structures,* January 1991.

Klein, Maury. 2011. *Union Pacific: The Reconfiguration: America's Greatest Railroad from 1969 to the Present.* Oxford University Press.

Klinger, Sue, "Alliance Division's Maintenance Complex," *BN News.*

Klobuchar, Jim, "A Railway Threatens to Leave," *Minneapolis Star,* April 7, 1978.

Knutson, Rick and Karl Rasmussen, "Dispatching BN's Dakota Division," *Trains,* October 1992.

Kochan, Thomas A., "A Jobs Compact for America's Future," *Harvard Business Review,* March 2012.

Kohrs, ElDean V., 1974. "Social Consequences of Boom Growth in Wyoming," paper presented at the Rocky Mountain American Association of the Advancement of Science Meeting, April 24–26, 1974; Laramie, Wyoming.

Kolpach, Dave, "BNSF President Says Company Will Improve Service," Associated Press, January 9, 2004.

Kolstad, Toby, "Next Game Changer: The Containerization of Domestic Intermodal Traffic," *Progressive Railroading,* May 2012.

Kroll, Luisa, "Billionaire Highway Man: Life Lessons Dennis Washington Learned When He Was 25," *ForbesLife,* June, 2013.

Kursar, Robert J., "BN President Says Political Enmity Between Rails, Truckers Is Waning," *Traffic World,* March 17, 1986.

Kursar, Robert J., "Rail 'Renaissance' Still Unfolding, Shippers Told by Industry Leaders," *Traffic World,* May 20, 1985.

Kursar, Robert J., "Rail Secondary Picketing Upheld by Supreme Court," *Traffic World,* May 4, 1987.

"Labor Loses in Attempt to Halt FRA Drug Rules," *Traffic World,* December 9, 1985.

Lalonde, James E., "Paid to Do Nothing—Suit Says BN Broke Promise to Workers," *Seattle Times,* December 5, 1988.

Lamphier, George K., track inspection and evaluation reports for BN system, 1970–1981, Northern Pacific Railway Historical Association archives.

Lamphier, Thomas J., "Track Building No Job for Amateurs; Each Component Has Role in Final Product," *BN News,* April 1978.

Lane, Polly, "Burlington Chairman Named," *Seattle Times,* October 11, 1990.

Lang, A. Scheffer, "Electrification: A Dissenting View," *Railway Age,* January 12, 1961.

Lasher, Steve, "'Booming' in Modern Times," *Classic Trains,* Spring 2017.

"Larson Leaves BN Truck Lines After Leveraged Buyout Fails," *Traffic World,* March 21, 1988.

Larsen, Michael E., "Extension of Second Main Line on C&NW Western Coal," Proceedings of the 104th Annual Conference of the Roadmasters and Maintenance of Way Association of America, September 21–23, 1992.

Lavallee, Omer. 1998. *Van Horne's Road.* Toronto: Railfare Enterprises Limited.

Leachman, Rob. 1998. *Northwest Passage.* Mukilteo, Wash.: Hundman Publishing Company.

Lee, Peter M. "Consolidation of Great Northern Pacific and Burlington Lines, Inc." October 2012.

Lenzen, Mike. 1997. "A C&NW Coal Line Story." *North Western Lines,* Summer 1997.

"Les Vaughan Ends BN Social Counseling Career" *BN News,* June 1978.

Levine, Jonathan B., "Will a Takeover Derail Burlington Northern's Makeover?" *Business Week,* August 3, 1987.

Lewis, Eugene M. 2005. *12,000 Days on the North Western Line.* Chicago and North Western Historical Society.

Lindblom, Mike, "Feds Give $16M for Slide Control by Rail Tracks," *Seattle Times,* September 21, 2011.

Lindeman, Eric D., "Burlington Northern Truck Unit Moves Ahead on Strategic Plan," *Traffic World,* April 29, 1985.

Lindquist, John, "Burlington Northern in Good Shape," *Associated Press,* May 18, 1972.

Linn, Linda, "Feds Oppose Slurry Plan," *Billings Gazette,* August 2, 1977.

"Livingston, Mont., Likes BN—And Shows It Annually," *Railway Age.*

"Livingston Shows Appreciation of BN," *BN News,* July 1977.

"Locomotive 'Power-by-the-Hour' Largely Stalled at the Station," *Traffic World,* July 27, 1991.

"Logs to Lumber," *BN News,* January 1971.

Loidolt, Jared, presentation at the University of Wisconsin – Superior, April 2012.

"The Long and Winding Road: Unraveling the Lengthy, Complicated Bargaining Process," *BN News,* April 1984.

"Long – Standing Rate Fight May Be Over After City Pays BN, SP $26 Million," *Traffic World,* January 28, 1985.

"Lorentzsen: 'Gamesmanship' Not His Style," *BN News,* January 1978.

"Lorentzsen of the BN," *Inside Story International—Stanley Corporation,* Winter 1978–1979.

"Lorentzsen Reflects on New CEO Role," *BN News,* October 1978.

Lorsch, Jay W. 1989. *Pawns or Potentates: The Reality of America's Corporate Boards.* Boston: Harvard Business School Press.

Loving, Rush, Jr., "The Merger That Worked," *Trains,* June 2016.

LSU College of Engineering, "Reflections of Donald W. Clayton, "Hall of Distinction Class of 1992–1993.

Lustig, David, "AC vs. DC: What's the Difference?" *Trains,* May 2010.

Lustig, David, "Catching Trouble Before the Fact," *Trains,* November 2005.

Lutch, Russell H., Devin K. Harris and Theresa M. Ahlborn, "Causes and Preventative Methods for Rail Seat Abrasion in North America's Railroads," American Railway Engineering Association, October 2014.

Machalaba, Daniel, "Burlington Northern Shows Risks of Hiring an Outsider as CEO." *The Wall Street Journal,* April 6, 1993.

Machalaba, Daniel, "Burlington Names Grinstein to Head Its Railroad Unit," *The Wall Street Journal,* January 20, 1989.

Machalaba, Daniel, "Burlington Says Two Executives Leave Rail Firm," *The Wall Street Journal,* June 2, 1994.

Machalaba, Daniel, "Railroads Confront Unions on Crew Size," *The Wall Street Journal,* November 23, 1987.

Malone, Frank, "C&NW: Flying High as Rival Roads Founder," *Railway Age,* July 28, 1980.

Malone, Frank, "Why a Federal Court Said Yes," *Railway Age,* December 2, 1968.

Malone, Michael P. 1996. *James J. Hill Empire Builder of the Northwest.* Norman and London: University of Oklahoma Press.

Mannello, Timothy A., "Problem Drinking Among Railroad Workers: Extent, Impact and Solutions," University Research Corporation, Washington, DC.

Marshall, Evelyn T., "Mary and Martha: Faithful Sisters, Devoted Disciples," *Ensign,* January 1987.

Martin, Albro. 1976. *James J. Hill and the Opening of the Northwest.* New York: Oxford University Press.

Martin, Jack, "Electrification One Answer to Rising Fuel Costs," *BN News,* January 1981.

Martin, Jack, "116-Mile Rail Line Nearing Completion in Central Wyoming," *BN News,* July 1979.

Martin, Jack, "Zestful, Zealous Don Zeiss Zooms in on Problems as Alliance Project Construction Director," *BN News.*

Martin, Mike, "The Yellowstone Division Story: From 1973 Through 1980," *BN Expediter,* October 2011.

Matzenbach, Jon R. 1993. *The Wisdom of Teams.* Harper Collins 1993.

"Maze Heads Northwest," *Nebraska Division Whistle Post,* December 2001/January 2002.

McCarty Farms, Inc. v. Burlington Northern, Inc., 787 F. Supp. 937 (decided Montana 1992).

McCue, Dan, "Intermodal: A New Level of Reliability," *World Trade WT100,* January 3, 2012.

McDonnell, Greg. 2008. *Locomotives: The Modern Diesel and Electric Reference.* Erie, Ontario, Canada: Boston Mills Press.

McFarlen, G. L., presentation, "Burlington Northern and Western Coal," to the Montana Water Development Association, September 27, 1976.

"McGovern: Federal Loans for UP/C&NW Unacceptable," *BN News,* October 1980.

McKay, Floyd, "How Great Corporate Power Shadows Gregoire on Coal Shipments to China," *Crosscut,* January 7, 2011.

McPhee, John, "Coal Train—I and II," *New Yorker,* October 3 and October 10, 2005.

McPhee, John. 2006. *Uncommon Carriers.* New York: Farrar, Straus and Giroux.

"Meet CAPMAC: A Sophisticated Computer That Helps BN Make the Most of Its Locomotive Fleet," *BN News,* October 1983.

"Meeting an M/W Challenge—Burlington Northern," *Railway Age,* June, 1991.

Memorandum of Agreement Between BNSF Railway and Brotherhood of Railway Carmen Division/TCIU and International Association of Machinists and Aerospace Workers and International Brotherhood of Electrical Workers/System Council No. 16, October 12, 2010.

Memorandum of Agreement Between Burlington Northern Railroad and the United Transportation Union, May 20, 1993, Article I, Crew Consist.

"Memorable Moment in Time," *Powder River Reflection,* December 2009.

"Memories of Merger Day—and the Days After," *Mainstreeter,* Summer 2010.

"Menk Happy with BN's 'First Hundred Days,'" *Railway Age,* July 13, 1970.

Menk, Louis W., *A Railroad Man Looks At America; Excerpts from the Speeches of Louis W. Menk.* No place: privately published, n.d. [circa 1974].

Menk, Louis W., Remarks Before the Committee on Interior and Insular Affairs, U.S. House of Representatives, November 7, 1975.

"Merger History," *BN News,* March 3, 1970.

"Merger Memories, Part 3: The View from the West End," *Mainstreeter,* Winter 2010.

Merger Protective Agreement and Implementing Agreement No. 1 and Implementing Agreement No. 2 for Employees of Burlington Northern, Inc. Represented by Brotherhood of Locomotive Engineers.

"A Merger That Started on the Right Track," *Business Week,* June 12, 1971.

"Merle, W. Geiger, Jr.," *BLET Journal,* Winter 2010.

Merrild Augspurger et al., Appellants, v. Brotherhood of Locomotive Engineers, Appellee. 510 F.2d 853 No. 74-1363. February 4, 1975.

"A Message to All Employees from Burlington Northern's Top Officers," *BN News,* March 3, 1970.

"Method for Computation of Frequency and Severity Rates for Industrial Injuries and Classification of Industrial Accident?" <wiki.asnswers.com/Q/Method_for_computation_of_frequency_and_severity_rates_fo . . .>.

"Metra: BNSF Line Puts on Daily Parades," *Railway,* Fall 2010.

Mickelson, Sig. 1993. *The Northern Pacific Railroad and the Selling of the West.* Sioux Falls, S.D.: The Center for Western Studies.

Middleton, William D. 1999. *Landmarks on the Iron Road: Two Centuries of North American Railroad Engineering.* Bloomington, Ind., and Indianapolis: Indiana University Press.

"Milwaukee Asks Inclusion in BN Merger," *BN News,* April 1973.

Miotek, Bill, "BN's Chicago Commuter Operations," *The BN Expediter,* January 1999.

M. M. Winter, Petitioner, v. Interstate Commerce Commission and United States of America, Respondents. No. 88-1250. United States Court of Appeals, Eighth Circuit. Decided July 12, 1988.

Moin, Ebrahim, "The Current Status of Field Welding of Rail," *Railway Track and Structures,* October 1988.

"Montana Line Up for Sale by Burlington Northern," *Minneapolis Tribune,* November 27, 1986.

Moody's Transportation Manual, annual issues 1965–95.

Morgan, David P., "Burlington Northern: A Railroad Worth Waiting for," Burlington Northern advertising supplement, 1970.

Morgan, David P., "Farewell, CB&Q, GN, NP and SP&S; Hello, BN," *Trains,* June 1970.

Morrell, Peter, "Airlines Within Airlines: An Analysis of U.S. Network Airline Responses to Low Cost Carriers," *Journal of Air Transport Management,* September 2005.

"Mount St. Helens—From the 1980 Eruption to 2000," U.S. Geological Survey Fact Sheet 036-00.

Muchnic, Suzanne, *Norton Simon and the Pursuit of Culture: Odd Man In,* Berkeley: University of California Press, 1998.

Murray, David. "Back on Track: State and Feds Give $4 Million to Fix Railroad Trestle," *Great Falls Tribune,* May 31, 2013.

Murray, David. 2014. "Right on Track: Flood-damaged Trestle Set for Repair," *Great Falls Tribune,* February 13, 2014.

Murray, Tom. 2005. *The Milwaukee Road.* St. Paul: MBI Publishing, 2005.

Myers, Edward T., "GN Sleds Ballast Under Track," *Modern Railroads,* June 1964.

Nagarajan, Ravi, "Buffet's Plans for Burlington Northeren May Involve Rapid Expansion," *Seeking Alpha,* January 26, 2010.

"Natural Resources: A Proper Balance," *BN News,* November 1974.

Neal, Roger, "Why Merge If You Can Share?" *Forbes,* May 20, 1985.

"Nebraska Division Develops Programs to Make Working on Railroad Safer for Track Employees," *BN News,* June 1978.

"The Neighborhood Store: Materials Stores Give Better, Less – Costly Service," *BN News,* May/June 1983.

Nelson, Roger H., Letter to Earl J. Currie, July 25, 2012.

"New BN Grain Train Operations to Benefit Shippers," *BN News,* August/September 1980.

"New BN President Richard Bressler Sees Exciting, Challenging Future," *BN News,* August/September 1980.

"New Drug and Alcohol Program Initiated," *BN News,* November 1984.

"New EPA Rules to Devastate Coal Industry," <www.scam.com/showthread.php?t=140153>.

"New Record for BN Coal," *Railway Age,* October 11, 1982.

"New Strategy for Labor," *Railway Age,* June 1991

"New Technology to Find Problems Before They Occur," *Powder River Reflections,* November–December 2000.

Nickerson, Gregory, "Clean Power Plan May Cut Wyoming Coal Revenue 31–63 Percent," <wyofile.com/clean-power-plan-may-cut-mining-coal-revenue-by-46-percent>.

Nisselius, Jack, "Campbell County Ushers in Coal Age," *News-Record* (Gillette, Wyo.), December 23, 1976.

Nixon, Ron. 2015. "Rail Industry Had Safety Technology Decades Ago," *The New York Times,* November 3, 2015.

"NMB Rules That BN Is One Company, Not 11. Will Unions Agree?" *Railway Age,* June 1991.

"No Appeal on C&NW Ruling," *BN News,* November 1981.

Norman, James R., "Divide and Prosper," *Forbes,* March 30, 1992.

Norman M. Lorentzsen, Narrator, James E. Fogerty, Inverviewer. Interviewed on August 16 and September 23, 2005, at the Minnesota Historical Society, St. Paul, Minnesota

"Northern Lines Merger Approved," *Railway Age,* February 2/9, 1970.

Norton Simon Biography, <www.nortonsimon.org/norton-simmon-biography>.

Norton Simon, letter to BN shareholders following annual meeting of shareholders held in 1974.

"Norton Simon Quits BN Board Position," *St. Paul Sunday Pioneer Press,* January 27, 1974.

North, Irene, "Inside Nebraska's Only Rail Tunnel the Belmont Tunnel," *Scottsbluff, Nebr., Star Herald,* May 3, 1982.

"North Western Gets Ready to Absorb and Expand," *Railway Age,* May 1983.

Northern Pacific Railway Co., *Annual Reports, 1960–1968.*

"No We're Not Moving," *Mgr.,* April 1982.

O'Brien, Gerard, "Tech a Family Tradition," *The Montana Standard,* <www.mtech.edu/alumni/Profiles/dyk.php>.

Odden, Anne S., "The Powder River Basin, Chapter 1: The Coming Conflict," Research Note, Dean Witter Reynolds, Inc., June 21, 1983.

"Oil, Timber, Coal, Minerals Loom Big in BN's Future," *Railway Age,* February 22, 1971.

"The Old Order Changeth, Yielding Place to New," *BN News,* March 3, 1970.

Olson, John, "Early Burlington Northern Fuel Tenders," <jimsjunction.com/sidetrack/st02/ftl>.

"$175 Million Settlement in BN Antitrust Lawsuit," *Traffic World,* December 12, 1988.

O'Neil, Martha, "Does BN Want Out of Railroading?" *BN News,* October 1981.

OOIDA vs, Burlington Motor Carriers, Inc.

O'Reilly, Joseph, "Rail Intermodal: Where Rail Meets Road," *Inbound Logistics,* October 2012.

"Osage Refinery," *BN News,* March 1976.

"Osage Refinery in Production, Among Cleanest, *BN News,* May 1977.

Oslund, John J., "BN Railroad Receives Approval to Operate Subsidiary Railway," *Minneapolis Star-Tribune,* December 2, 1987.

Oslund, John J., "Different Rulings Could Send 'Short Rails' to High Court," *Minneapolis Star-Tribune,* June 1, 1988.

"Over the Goal Line," *BN News,* January 1983.

Overton, Richard C. 1965. *Burlington Route: A History of the Burlington Lines.* New York: Reprint by Alfred A. Knopf, Inc.

Overton, Richard C. 1953. *Gulf to Rockies: The Heritage of the Fort Worth and Denver-Colorado and Southern Railways,1861-1898.* Austin: University of Texas Press.

"Pace of Litigation Speeds Up in BN Coal Contract Rate Disputes," *Traffic World,* August 2, 1982.

Page, Paul, "Intermodal's Switching Perceptions," *Traffic World,"* June 7, 2004.

Palley, Joel, "Freight Railroads Background," Office of Rail Policy and Development, Federal Railroad Administration, March 2012.

Palmeri, Christopher, "Serving Two (Station) Masters," *Business Week,* July 24, 2006.

Park, Donald K. II, "The Hastings Rail Relocation Project," *The Streamliner,* Vol. 16 No. 2.

Park, Donald K. II. 1990. *Powder River Coal: A Guide to Facilities and Operations.* Fort Collins, Colo.: PARKRAIL.

Partlow, Bob, and Barbara Winslow, "Coal May Be Sent to Cherry Point," *Bellingham Herald,* December 30, 1980.

Patterson, Brittany, "Creating a New Future in Wyoming's Biggest Coal Town," *EE News,* April 12, 2016.

Patterson, Steve, "A Route Caught in Traffic," *Trains,* April 1999.

"People, Not Planes, Deliver" *Traffic World,* May 11, 1981.

Peterson, Chris, "Coal Creek: More Tax Base But More Services," *News-Record* (Gillette, Wyo.), April 27, 1978.

"Pertinent Personnel." 1980. *Trains,* August, 1980.

Petersen, Jim, "Burlington Northern Rolls into the South," *Oregon and Washington Industrialist,* March/April 1981.

Petery, Andras R., Investment Perspectives Excerpt, Burlington Northern, September 14, 1981.

"Petroleum Important in BN's Resource Program," *BN News,* June 1977.

Phillips, Don, "Bob Downing Deserves His Place in History Books," *Trains,* January 2011.

Phillips, J. A. III, "From A to Z with Warren McGee," *Mainstreeter,* Winter 1999.

Piller, Dan, "BN Inc. Returns to Railroading," *Modern Railroads,* November 1989.

Pitts, Jerry, "The BN Fuel Tender Story," *The BN Expediter,* October 1993.

Ploss, Thomas H. 1991. *The Nation Pays Again: The Demise of the Milwaukee Road, 1928–1986.* Thomas H. Ploss, 1991.

Plough, Bob, "From the Foothills to No Man's Land: BNSF's Colorado to Texas Coal Routes," *Railroads Illustrated,* May 2012.

Plous, F. K., Jr., "BN's Extraordinary Expediters," *Railway Age,* November 1987.

"Plum Creek History," <plumcreek.com/about/history>.

"Plum Creek Timber Company, Inc.—Company Profile, Information, Business Description, History, Background Information on Plum Creek Timber Company, Inc." <referenceforbusiness.com/history2/35/Plum-Creek-Timber-Company-Inc>.

"Plum Creek Timber Announces Montana Plant Closures," *Associated Press,* June 5, 2009.

Plum Creek: Timber Conversion with Emphasis on Efficiency," *BN News,* August/September 1980.

Plume, Janet, "BN, UP Look to Liquified Natural Gas As Alternative Locomotive Fuel," *Traffic World,* May 17, 1993.

"Pole Line to Be Eliminated," *Whistle Post,* December 2001/January 2002.

"Pooling of Grain Cars, Elimination of Private Ownership Eyed by BN," *Traffic World,* January 3, 1983.

Poplawski, Dave, "Locomotive Chronicles: 1986, Part I," *The BN Expediter,* October 2012.

"Portable Rewelder Cuts Costs," *Progressive Railroading,* November 1990.

"Positive Train Control Ran Successfully in Years-Long Burlington Northern Railroad Trial," *DesignNews,* October 21, 2008.

Potarf, E. L., "Statement," Management-Labor Conference, St. Paul, October 27, 1960.

Powder River Basin, <www.sourcewatch.org/index.php?title=Powder_River_Basin>.

"Powder River Basin Coal Production." 2016. Bureau of Land Management, May 6, 2016.

Powder River Basin Coal Resource and Cost Study Prepared for Xcel Energy by John T. Boyd Company, Report No. 3155.001, September 2011.

"Powder River 'Blowout' Sends BNSF, UP Reeling," *Trains,* September 2005.

"Powder River Country: America's Last Rail Frontier." 1989. *Trains,* November, 1989.

Powell, Warren B., "Real-Time Dispatching for Truckload Motor Carriers," 2007, http://thetenneygroup.com "BN Transport," *BN News,* October 1972.

Powers, Bob P. E., and Ron Poulsen, "Stampede Pass Reopens," American Railway Engineering Association, Bulletin 61.

"Preventive Maintenance Keeps BN Coal Cars Rolling," *Railway Age,* October 9, 1978.

Price, Donna, "Merry Rachetts: A Strong Voice for Unionism," *Alliance Times-Herald,* September 23, 1993.

"Production Tie Renewal vs. Quick-Removal Operations," *Railway Track and Structures,* October 1991.

"Productivity: From a Union View," *BN News,* October 1983.

Projected Retirements of Coal-Fired Power Plants, U.S. Energy Information Administration, July 31, 2012.

"Project Tames Curves in Canyon", *BN News,* October 1984.

"Project Yellow," *The Mixed Train,* September 1984.

"A Proper Balance: Natural Resources," *BN News,* September 1974.

Proposed Revisions to AFE Accounting Procedures for Ratable Depreciation on Property Accounts (including track structures), discussion draft, 49 CFR 1201, Docket No. 36988.

Pulliam, John R., "Galesburg BNSF Yards Poised for Growth," *The Register-Mail,* October 20, 2008.

"Putting Advanced Turnouts to the Test," *Railway Track and Structures,* March 1991.

Pyle, Joseph Gilpin. 1936. *The Life of James J. Hill.* New York. Peter Smith.

"Quarterly Coal Production Lowest Since the Early 1980s." 2016. U.S. Energy Information Administration, June 10, 2016.

"A Rail Giant Is Born," *Railway Age,* March 30, 1970.

"Rail Grinding," *BN Technical Bulletin,* August 1989.

"Rail Link Reveals Data on BN Deal," *Journal of Commerce,* November 17, 1987.

Rail Transportation of Coal to Power Plants: Reliability Issues, Every CRS Report, September 26, 2007.

Railroad Accidents Report, Head-on Collision of Burlington Northern Railroad Freight Trains Extra 6714 West and Extra 7820 East, Wiggins, Colorado, April 13, 1984 and Rear-end Collision of Burlington Northern Railroad Freight Trains Extra 7843 East and Extra ATSF 8112 East Near Newcastle, Wyoming, April 22, 1984, NTSB Report No. NTSB/RAR-85/04 (note NTSB made this a combined report, covering both accidents).

"Railroad Asks Damages Against Union," *Gillette News-Record,* July 16, 1975.

"Railroad Regulation—Shipper Experiences and Current Issues in ICC Regulation of Rail Rates," United States General Accounting Office, Report to the Chairman, Subcommittee on Oversight and Investigations, Committee on Energy and Commerce, House of Representatives, September 1987.

"Railroads Enhancing Turnouts," *Progressive Railroading,* December 1991.

"Railroads: Safer Than Most Other Industries," <www.montanarail.com/images/safer-than-most-industries.jpg>.

"Railroads Progress Report, Burlington Northern," Morgan Stanley Investment Research, December 20, 1984.

"A Railtown Booms," *Fortune,* August 25, 1980.

Ramsey, Bruce, "BN Shuns Ideas of Nuclear Foes," *Seattle Post-Intellingencer,* April 4, 1987.

"RAND Corp. Study Says Railroad Capacity Is Public Concern," <www.rtands.com/breaking_news.shtml#Feature3-8-21>.

"Rankings: Coal Production, 2014, Montana" U.S. Energy Information Administration.

"Rapid Response Ready for Orin Work," *Alliance Mechanical Employee Newsletter,* second quarter 2005.

Rattner, Steven. 1977. "The Battle for Western Coal," *New York Times,* January 1, 1977.

Rebello-Rees, Kathy, "Coal Boom Heating Up the West," *USA Today, January 26, 1983.*

"The Rebirth of Stampede Pass," *Railway,* November/December 1996.

"Reconstructive Surgery: BN's Laurel Yard Undergoes a Face-Lift," *BN News,* September 1984.

"Recovering Alcoholics Help Co-workers—Treatment Program 80% Successful," *BN News,* October 1980.

"Refund of $40 Million to San Antonio from BN, SP Ordered by ICC," *Traffic World,* April 21, 1986.

"Regulation of Freight Railroads in the Modern Era: 1970–2010," *Review of Network Economics,* December 2008.

Remarks of Thomas J. Lamphier, President, Transportations Division, Burlington Northern, Inc., Financial Analysts Trip, September 27, 1977.

Remarks to Security Analysts by Walter A. Drexel, September 29, 1982.

"Removing-All-Doubt Department." *Trains,* 1967.

Report to the President by Emergency Board No. 219, January 15, 1991.

Responsibilities of Railroads and Employees, 49 CFR 219.203.

"Retired Railroad Employee Calls BN 'Corporate Terrorists,'" 1983. *Star-Tribune of the Twin Cities,* March 31, 1983.

Rhodes, Michael. 2003. *North American Railyards.* St. Paul: MRI Publishing Company.

Richards, Bill, "How Dennis Washington Won a Beaut of a Gamble on His Butte Copper Mine," *The Wall Street Journal,* May 3, 1988.

Richards, Bill, "Worried States Enter the Railroad Business to Save Branch Lines," *The Wall Street Journal,"* September 22, 1983.

Riley, John H., Testimony Before the Committee on the Judiciary United States Senate, March 4, 1986.

Roberts, Phil, *A New History of Wyoming*, <uwacadweb.uwyo.edu/robertshistory/New_History_of_Wyoming_chapter_19>.

Robl, Ernest H., "The Powder River Basin: A Guide to America's Power Railroading Base," second edition, self-published, 2000.

Robl, Ernest H., "Powder River Country," *Railfan and Railroad*, March 2002.

Robl, Ernest H., "Stampede Pass Revival," *Pacific RAILNEWS*, October 1996.

Rockwell ARES: Advanced Railroad Electronics System, brochure prepared by Rockwell International in 1983.

Rodgers, David H., 2006, "The Permanent Legacy of Expo '74: An Insider's Story of How Spokane Acquired Riverfront Park, The Opera House and the Convention Center," *The Pacific Northwesterner*, Volume 50, Issue 2, October, 2006.

Rosenfeld, Ira, "Burlington Northern and Unions Dance, But It's Not Clear Which Is Leading," *Traffic World*, December 11, 1989.

Rosenfeld, Ira, "Burlington Northern, Labor Union Reach Tentative Acord on Crew Size," *Traffic World*, September 9, 1991.

Rosenfeld, Ira, "BN to Rely More on COTS Program As Part of Its Strategy for the Future," *Traffic World*, October 29, 1990.

Rosenfeld, Ira, "Holes in C&NW Buy-Out Blanket Sending Shivers Through Analysts," *Traffic World*, April 9, 1990.

Rosenfeld, Ira, "Locomotive 'Power by the Hour' Largely Stalled," *Traffic World*, July 22, 1991.

Rosenfeld, Ira, "NMB Decertifies Union Negotiators, Handing BN Big Victory over Labor," *Traffic World*, April 29, 1991.

Rosenfeld, Ira, "Rail Labor Leaders Feeling Wrath as Member Backlash Claims First Victim," *Traffic World*, July 29, 1991.

Rosenfeld, Ira, "Rail Labor Takes Uncle Sam to Court Over Law Ending April Rail Strike," *Traffic World*, August 5, 1991.

Rosenfeld, Ira, "Railroad Stocks Claiming Higher Despite Recession-Hit Earnings in Quarter," *Traffic World*, July 29, 1981.

Rosenfeld, Ira, "SP Names Tough Union Negotiator to Key Labor-Relations Position," *Traffic World*, March 4, 1991.

Rosenfeld, Ira, "Santa Fe Settles ETSI Suit, Agrees to Pay $350 Million by 1997," *Traffic World*, April 30, 1990.

Rosenfeld, Ira, "3,500 Burlington Northern Workers Boycott National Rail Labor Talks," *Traffic World*, April 15, 1991.

Ruff, Joe, "Why Buy Burlington?" *Omaha World-Herald*, January 31, 2010.

Rung, Albert M., Remarks at Isaac Walton League Annual Dinner, Lincoln, Nebr., December 23, 1975.

Runte, Alfred, *Burlington Northern and the Dedication of Mount St. Helens: New Legacy of a Proud Tradition*, 1982.

Sachar, Laura, "Rail Stripper," *Financial World*, January 10, 1989.

"A Safer Work Environment," *BN News*, December 1984.

"Safety Issues: FRA Gives BN a Whitewash," *Labor*, July 17, 1985.

Salpukas, Agis, "Burlington Northern's Spinoff Plan," *The New York Times*, June 3, 1986.

Sanders, Dale. 2002. *The Northern Pacific*. Mukilteo, Wash.: Hundman Publishing Company.

Sanzillo, Tom, "PRB Coal Fast Becoming a Stranded Asset," *High Country News*, August 2, 2015.

Sartore, D. V., "BN's Taconite Transfer and Storage Facility at Superior, Wisconsin," *Bulletin 653—American Railway Engineering Association*.

Sauer, Stacy J., "An Overview of Burlington Northern's Advanced Turnout Designs Including Recommendations for Future Turnout Technology," Association of American Railroads Advanced Turnout Evaluation Program, January 17, 1991.

Sauer, Stacy J., "Tackling the Turnout Problem," *Railway Age*, March, 1991.

Saunders, Richard, Jr. 2003. *Main Lines: Rebirth of the North American Railroads, 1970–2002*. DeKalb: Northern Illinois University Press.

Scates, Shelby, "Town Gets Derailed," Seattle *Post-Intelligencer*, March 1, 1984.

Schmeling, Richard L., "BNSF Construction Update," *The Diamond Newsletter*, 2016.

Schmollinger, Steve, "Public/Private Cooperation Means Upgrades for BNSF's Ottumwa Subdivision," http://trn.trains.com/Interactive/Web%20Exclusives/2011/01/Incoming%20improvements.

Schneider, Lewis M., Peter F. Rousselot, Paul L. Joffe and George W. Mayo, Jr., "Rail Service Contracts—The New Frontier," *Traffic World*, August 3, 1981.

Schneider, Paul D. 1993. *Burlington Northern Diesel Locomotives: Three Decades of BN Power*. Waukesha, Wisc.: Kalmbach Publishing Company.

Schulz, John D., "BN Truck Subsidiary Buy-out by Investor Group Completed," *Traffic World*, September 5, 1988.

Schuster, T. G. 2016. *History of the West Suburban Mass Transit District*. Compiled and self-published by Earl J. Currie.

Scribbins, Jim. 2001. *The Milwaukee Road: 1928 – 1985*. Forest Park, Ill.: Heimburger House Publishing Company.

Securities and Exchange Commission, Form 10-K, Burlington Northern, Inc., December 31, 1980.

"Segment of Third Main Line Opens," *UP Online*, January 8, 1998.

Senate Bill 315 Rail Freight Competition Study, prepared by R. L. Banks and Associates for the Governor's (Montana) Office of Economic Opportunity, 2004.

Senior, Jeannie, "Becky McMahon Makes Way in BN Train World," Correspondent, *The Oregonian*, quoted in *BN News*, June 1978.

Shaffer, David, "Utilities to BNSF: More Coal," *Star Tribune*, August 5, 2014.

Shaffer, Frank E., "Burlington Northern Off to a Smooth Start," *Modern Railroads*, May 1970.

Shedd, Tom, "Burlington Northern: Aggressive, Innovator – and Thoroughly Non-Traditional," *Modern Railroads,* November 1986.

Shedd, Tom, "In MoW, BN Seeks Long-Term Solutions," *Modern Railroads,* April 1991.

Shedd, Tom, "MoW Trends at BN: The Sky's the Limit," *Modern Railroads,* March 1991.

Shine, Joseph W. 1991. *Burlington Northern Into the 90's: Motive Power Pictorial.* La Mirada, Calif.: Four Ways West Publications.

"(Shop) Closings Announced," *BN News,* January/February 1986.

"Shop Craft Unions Signed an Agreement with BNRR . . . ," *Burlington Northern Railroad News Update,* October 1987.

"Shops: Less Can Be More—Railroad Repair Facilities," *Railway Age,* March 1990.

Shands, Tom, "BN Sells Southern Line to Missoula Entrepreneur," *Livingston Enterprise,* July 23, 1987.

Sheet Metal Workers' International Association, Appellant, v. Burlington Northern Railroad Company, Appellee, 893 F.2d 199, 1990.

Shuster, Rep. Bill, "Rail Re-regulation May Be Catastrophic Public Policy," *The Hill,* March 11, 2010.

Shuster, Rep. Bill, "Shuster: Don't Regulate Freight Rail System," <rollcall.com/features/Transportation_Energy/tande/47012-1.html>.

"Signal Group Marks Ten Years, Zero Injuries," *Northern Light.*

"Sky Eyes: BN Becomes the First Railroad in the United States to Test Space-age Technology in Its Dispatching Operations by Using Satellites to Track Trains," *BN News,* March 1985.

Sloane, Donald, "BUSINESS PEOPLE; Burlington Names a Chief Executive," February 17, 1982.

Smalley, E.V. 1883. *History of the Northern Pacific Railroad.* Reprinted by David S. Coster in 2002.

"SMART-TD Members Reject One-Man Crew Agreement with BNSF," *Progressive Railroading,* September 12, 2014.

Smith, Jeffery, "Sensory Deprivation on the High Plains," *High Country News,* www.hen.ord/issues/105/3285/print_view.

Smith, Rebecca, "The Coal Age Nears Its End," *Wall Street Journal,* December 23, 2011.

Smith, Rebecca and Cameron McWhirter, "Mississippi Plant Shows the Cost of 'Clean Coal,'" *Wall Street Journal,* October 14, 2013.

Snider, Joe, "The Denver Railroad Scene," *The BN Expediter,* April 2006.

"Sniffer Dog Case Feb. 15," *Mgr.* January 30, 1985.

Soendker, Sandi, "Burlington Motor Carriers Files for Voluntary Reorganization Under Chapter 11," <ooida.com/issues&actions/Judicial/Burlington/Burlingtonbankrupt.shtml>.

Sol, Michael, "The Milwaukee Road's Demise, Notes from Michael Sol," <online.fliphtml5.com/trun/ahvm>.

Solomon, Brian. 2000. *The American Diesel Locomotive.* Osceola, Wisc.: MBI Publishing Company.

Solomon, Brian. 2005. *Burlington Northern Santa Fe Railway.* St. Paul: MBI Publishing Company.

Solomon, Brian. 2007. *Intermodal Railroading.* St. Paul: MBI Publishing Company.

Solomon, Brian. 2001. *Railway Maintenance: The Men and the Machines That Keep the Railroads Running.* St. Paul: MBI Publishing.

Solomon, Brian, and Patrick Yough. 2009. *Coal Trains: The History of Railroading and Coal in the United States."* Minneapolis: MBI Publishing Co.

"South Dakota Completes Track Sale," *BN News,* August/September 1982.

Southern Pacific Transportation Company, et al., v. San Antonio, Texas, Acting by an Through Its City Service Board, 748 F.2d 266, 1984.

"Speaking Out: Employees Voice Opinions on Survey Results," *BN News,* April 1984.

"Special Bridge Designs Win Approval for a BN Line Change," *Railway Age,* March 8, 1971.

Speroff, Leon, M.D. 2007. *The Deschutes River Railroad War.* Portland: Arnica Publishing.

Sprau, Dave, Milwaukee lines in Washington, correspondence with the author.

"Staggers Act Handcuffs U.S. Grain in World Markets, Gargill Says," *Traffic World,* December 6, 1982.

"The Staggers Act: Under Attack; New Threats Surface to Reimpose Old Constraints," *BN News,* October 1984.

Staggers, Dr. Margaret, "Staggers Act Saved Railroads," *Charleston Gazette,* October 4, 2010.

Stagl, Jeff. 2006. "What Will It Take for the Powder River Basin's 20 Mines to Meet the Nation's Insatiable Energy Needs? *Progressive Railroading,* August, 2016.

Staroski, Nick, PE. 2013. "Design Challenges of BNSF Bridge 3.8 Over the Missouri River Near Plattsmouth," American Railway Engineering and Maintenance Association, 2013.

Statement by N. S. Westergard, Vice President and General Manager, SP&S Railway, Management-Labor Conference, St. Paul, Minn., October 27, 1960.

Stephens, Bill, "Union Pacific Sees Coal Traffic Holding Steady," *Trans Industry Newsletter,* June 8, 2017.

Stephens, Bill, "Why Coal's Rebound Might Be Just a Bounce Down the Stairs, *Trains Industry Newsletter,* September 19, 2017.

Stern, Richard L., "Denny's Always the Low-Cost Producer," *Forbes,* May 15, 1989.

Stack, Don (compiled by), "Western Railroad Properties, Inc. (WRPI), <utahrails.net/up/wrpi.php>.

"Straight Bids Division Farewell," *Powder River Reflection,* 4th Space ed., 2012.

Strack, Don, "Western Railroad Properties, Inc. (WRPI)," <utahrails.net/up/wrpi.php>.

Strauss, John F. Ph.D. 1998. *The Burlington Northern: An Operational Chronology 1970–1995.* West Bend, Wisc.: Friends of Burlington Northern Railroad.

"STB Denies AAR's Petition to Consider Indirect Competition as a Coal Rate Factor," *Progressive Railroading Daily News,* March 21, 2013.

"STB Proposes New Standards to Railroad Rates for Nonj-Coal Shippers," *infor@thompsonhine.com,* August 18, 2006.

Stern, Richard L., "Denny's Always the Low-Cost Producer," *Forbes,* May 15, 1989.

"Steve Straight of Alliance," *Powder River Reflection,* October 2009.

Stone, Jeffrey B., Wertheim Schroder report on Burlington Northern, Inc., June 1, 1987.

Stucke, John, "Montana Rail Link Wins National Safety Award," *The Missoulian,* May 21, 1999.

"Study Says Gillette Will Adjust to Coal Development," *The News-Record,* September 12, 1974.

"Study Team Lists Benefits of BN-Frisco Merger Plan," *BN News,* February/March 1978.

"Suburban Equipment Grand Is Announced," *Chicago Region News,* March/April 1972.

Sullivan, John L., "Engineering Expedites Third Main Line," *UP Online,* September 2, 1998.

Sullivan, Patricia, "Robert Harris; Helped Push D.C. Home Rule," *Washington Post,* October 7, 2007.

Summary of Proceedings, 1985 Burlington Northern Energy Seminar.

"Summary of the Clean Air Act," 42 U.S.C. 7401 et seq. (1970).

Summary of Proposed Labor Agreements, Burlington Northern Railroad, June 1987.

"'Super System' for Ballast Undercutting/Cleaning," *Railway Track and Structures,* October 1987.

"A Superior Coal Facility," *BN News,* May 1976.

"Survey to Tell More Than How 'Happy' We Are," *Mgr.,* third quarter 1985.

Swenson, Ty, "Port Completes $52 Million E. Marginal Way Grade Separation: Expected to Improve Freight Movement, Ease Gridlock," *West Seattle Herald,* April 12, 2012.

"Swing Nose Frogs," *BN Technical Bulletin,* October 1988.

"Swing-Nose Frogs, Tangential Geometry Extend Turnout Life," *Progressive Railroading,* August 1990.

"Switch 'Em Once and Go" *Modern Railroads,* October 1973.

"Tab for Signing Bonuses at BN Put at $11.6 Million and Counting," *Traffic World,* June 24, 1991.

"Taconite Facility Dedicated at Superior," *BN News,* October 1977.

"Taming the Curves: Crawford Line Changes Completed," *BN News,* August–September 1982.

Tarbox, Gary, "Robert W. Downing, 1913–2010," *The Mainstreeter,* Fall 2010.

Taylor, Jeremy. 1997. *Powder River Coal Trains.* Telford, Penn.: Silver Brook Junction Publishing.

"Teamwork: Management, Labor Must Unite at BN," *BN News,* May/June 1983.

"Technology Overtakes the Caboose," <www.uprr.com/aboutup/history/caboose/caboo02.shtml>.

"Tenders Return," *BN News,* August–September 1983.

Ten Year Accident-Incident Overview by Railroad, Montana Rail Link, Federal Railroad Administration Office of Safety Analysis, 1998–2006.

"The Land Bridge: Myth or Method?" *Railway Age,* July 7, 1969.

"The Truck Question: Radial Or Not?" *Trains,* May 2007.

"Three Are Killed in Minnesota Head-on Collision," *Mgs.,* June 20, 1984.

"Three Railroads Join Forces to Rediscover Northwest Passage." 1990. *Traffic World,* July 30, 1990.

"Timber and Western Lands: 'A Keen Sense of Awareness Guides Their Land Management Objectives,'" *BN News,* November 1970.

"Tipping the Scales: BN's Coal Contracts Outweigh the Competition's," *BN News,* September-October 1986.

"Track Work" (to tie gangs from Montana sent to work on lines in Illinois), *BN News,* December 1974.

"Tractors Speed Up Car Inspections," *BN News,* April 1982.

"Train Accidents Claim Lives of Seven Employees," *BN News,* June 1984.

"Trainmaster: Attitude More Important Than Age," *BN News,* February 1982.

"Treatment Program 80% Successful," *BN News,* October 1980.

"Trucking Subsidiaries Sold," *BN News.*

"Tulsa Yard Betterments Circa 1974–1976," *Frisco All Aboard,* January 18, 2007.

Turley, Mike, "Personal Railroad History Page," <bearstoc.com/MRL/hist/career>.

Turney, D. E., "Advantages of #132 RE as a Heavy-Duty Rail Section," *Bulletin 711-American Railway Engineering Association.*

"Turnout Technology Takes a New Direction." 1990. *Railway Track and Structures,* July, 1990.

Tutumluer, Erol, William (Zach) Dombrow and Hai Huang, "Effect of Coal Dust on Railroad Ballast Strength and Stability," Railroad Engineering Program, University of Illinois, October 10, 2008.

Tuzik, Robert E., "Fast-on, Fast-off Machines," *Railway Age,* September 1991.

"12,000 Jobs in Jeopardy Railroad Says," *Chicago Tribune,* June 17, 1987.

"Two Railroads Assail Critics of Montana Track Transfer," *Journal of Commerce,* November 6, 1987.

Udland, Myles, "Warren Buffett Made a Deal in 2009 That Was So Good You Could Say He Stole It," *Business Insider,* November 12, 2014.

"Understanding the Clean Air Act," <epa.gov/air/peg/understand>.

"Union Leader Assails U.S. Justice Dept. Action in Northern Lines Merger Case." 1968. *Talking It Over,* June, 1968.

"Union Opposes Rail Sale Despite Signing Contract," *Livingston (Mont.) Enterprise,* September 15, 1987.
"Union Pacific Marks Silver Anniversary of Its First Southern Powder River Basin Coal Train, <uprr.com/newsinfo/releases/service/2009/0817_silver.shtml?print>.
"Union Pacific Moves Its 200,000th Loaded Coal Train from Wyoming's Southern Powder River Basis, <uprr.som/newsinfo/relesases/service/2009/0520_200000-coal.shtml>.
Union Pacific Railroad North Platte Area Timetable #1, October 25, 1998.
"Unions Win Fight to Stop New BN Line," *Associated Press,* June 11, 1988.
"Unit Train Car Shop," *Progressive Railroading,* September 1977.
United States, Appellant, v. Interstate Commerce Commission et al. Charles E. Brundage et al., Appellants, v. United States et al. City of Auburn, Appellant, v. United States et al. Livingston Anti-Merger Committee, Appellant, v. Interstate Commerce Commission 396 U.S. 491 (90 SCt 708, 24 L.Ed.2d 700), February 2, 1970.
United States Code, Section 10901 (e) of Title 49
United States v. ICC 396 U.S. 491(1970).
"Unprofitable Truck Lines Sold by BN's Parent Firm," *Traffic World,* September 3, 1984.
"UP, BNSF Announce Southern Powder River Basin Joint Line $100 Million Capacity Expansion Plan," <uprr.com/newsinfo/releases/capital_investment/2006/0508_sprb.shtml>, June 12, 2010.
U. S. Energy Information Administration, "Coal Transportation Issues," 2007.
"Use of Satellites Signals New Era in Train Control," *BN News,* Winter 1987.
Vance, Catherine A., "Secondary Picketing In Railway Labor Disputes: A Right Preserved Under the Norris-LaGuardia Act," *Fordham Law Review,* Volume 55, Issue 2
"Vandalism Mars Takeover of Lines in Two States by Montana Rail Link, Inc.," *Traffic World,* November 9, 1987.
Van Hattem, Matt, "Sweeping Aside a Dusty Problem," *Trains,* November 2007.
Van Hattem, Matt, "Wyoming Coal Line Expansion," *Trains.*
Vantuono, William C., "How Staggers 'Saved the Freight Railroad Industry from Socialism,'" *Railway Age,* November 2005.
Vantuono, William C., "Maximizing Productivity in 'The Heart of Coal,'" *Railway Age,* August 2012.
Vantuono, William C., "Regional Railroad of the Year: Montana Rail Link," *Railway Age,* April 2013.
Vartabedian, Ralph, "Bressler: Engineer on BN's Train Out of St. Paul," *The Minneapolis Star, April 1, 1981.*
Vartabedian, Ralph, "Bressler Has BN Making Tracks," *Minneapolis Star,* April 1, 1981.
Verstraete, Jim and Kim Forman, "Mt. Saint Helen's: A Thundering, Crashing Symphony of Awesome Power," *BN News,* August/September 1980.
Vietor, Richard H. K. 1994. *Contrived Competition: Regulation and Deregulation in America.* Cambridge, Mass., and London: Belknap Press of Harvard University Press.
"Volcano Damage Limited," *BN Westwords,* June 1980.
Voorhees, Josh, "Railroads, Utilities Clash Over Dust from Coal Trains," *EE News,* January 25, 2010.
"Walking Away From Clean Coal." 2015. *Bloomberg,* February 16–February 22, 2015.
"Walter Drexel: An Interview with the New President," *BN News,* April 1982.
"The Washington Companies—Company Profile, Information, Business Description, History, Background Information on the Washington Companies," <referenceforbusiness.com/history2/47/The-Washington-Companies>.
"Washington Star Exposes Coal Slurry Tactics, Sees Conflict of Interest Issue," *Burlington Northern Grass Roots Report,* November 1975.
Wastler, Allen R., "BN Hopes That Class III Railroads Will Develop Traffic for Main Line," *Traffic World,* October 27, 1986.
Wastler, Allen R. and Kathleen R. Keeney, "Labor Feathers Ruffled over BN Subsidiary Move," *Traffic World,* December 7, 1967.
Wastler, Allen R., "Peer Drug Intervention Effective, Riley Says, But Drug Tests Needed," *Traffic World.*
Wastler, Allen r., "Transport Labor Unions Attack Random Drug, Alcohol Testing," *Traffic World,* November 9, 1987.
"Wayside Wheel Inspection," www.dapcondt.com/?page_id=101.
Webb, H. G., "Advantages of 136/# RE Rail as a Heavy Duty Rail Section," *Bulleton 711—American Railway Engineering Association.*
Weinstein, William W., Philip, S. Babcock IV and Frank Leong, "Safety Analysis of ARES," Charles Stark Draper Laboratory, Inc., October 1987.
Welty, Gus, "BN America: Quality Counts," *Railway Age,* November 1991.
Welty, Gus, "BN and ARES: 'Control' in a New Dimension," *Railway Age,* May 1988.
Welty, Gus, "BN Confronts That Old Problem: Too Many Unions," October 1987.
Welty, Gus, "BN Employees Help Make the Merger Work," *Railway Age,* July 27, 1970.
Welty, Gus, "BN/Frisco: A Good Fit of Properties and Personalities," *Railway Age,* January 23, 1981.
Welty, Gus, "BN Gets Flexibility—And a 'Spirit of Cooperation,'" *Railway Age,* December 14, 1970.
Welty, Gus, "BN Maps Power Strategies," *Railway Age,* October 1989.
Welty, Gus, "BN Objects to Lines on Labor Column," *Railway Age,* September 1993.
Welty, Gus. 1977. "For Burlington Northern, It's Coal—And Whole Lot More." *Railway Age,* December 28, 1977.
Welty, Gus, "BN America: Quality Counts—Burlington Northern's Domestic Container Business," *Railway Age,* November 1991.

Welty, Gus. "BN—High-Tech Training," *Railway Age, July 1989.*

Welty, Gus. "BN's New Alliance Shop: Big, Capable, Expandable," *Railway Age,* August 3, 1979.

Welty, Gus. "BN's New Control Center: 22,000 Miles Under One Roof," *Railway Age,* June 1995.

Welty, Gus, "C&NW, BN, UP Play Catch-up: Capacity Problems in the Powder River Basin," *Railway Age,* October 1994.

Welty, Gus, "Crew Consist: The New Pacts Are Paying Off," *Railway Age,* March 31, 1980.

Welty, Gus, "From BN to Its Employees: 250 Questions," *Railway Age,* April 1984.

Welty, Gus., "What's So Good About Holding Companies?" reprint from *Railway Age* in *BN News,* July 1981.

Welty, Gus, "Is All of This BN-Bashing Really Necessary? Burlington Northern Railroad Co. CEO Jerry Grinstein's Management," *Railway Age,* May 1993.

Welty, Gus, "Look, I've Got a Problem," story from *Railway Age* quoted in *BN News,* November 1973.

Welty, Gus, "Management, Labor, Philosophies and 'A Major Thrust,'" *Railway Age,* June 1983.

Welty, Gus, "'Preventive' Payoff Is Big," *Railway Age,* June 1990.

Welty, Gus. "The BN at 10: 'The Amazing Thing Was, It Worked,'" *Railway Age,* February 25, 1980.

Welty, Gus, "The Era of the Giants," *Railway Age,* Fegruary 23, 1981.

Welty, Gus, "The Strange Case of the BN and the UTU," *Railway Age,* April 1992.

Welty, Gus, "Tracking Heavy-Car Impact," *Railway Age,* March 1989.

Welty, Gus, "Two Accidents That Didn't Have to Happen," *Railway Age,* August 1985.

Welty, Gus. 1989. "What's New in Turnouts," *Railway Age,* April, 1989.

Wendt, Darrell, "Bridging the 'Mighty Mo,'" *Railroads Illustrated,* April 2013.

Wermiel, Stephen, "High Court to Decide Whether Railroads Must Negotiate with Workers Over Sales," *Wall Street Journal,* November 29, 1988.

Wernick, Robert, "Norton Simon's Zeal for the Best and Its Results," *Smithsonian,* September 1979.

Wesselmann, Carl H., "Ray Burton: Piggyback Leadeer/Corporate Healer," *Modern Railroads,* January 1986.

Wesselmann, Carl, "The Case for Concrete Tie Turnouts," *Modern Railroads,* October 1987.

"Western Coal to Meet Energy Crisis," *BN News,* April 1973.

"Western Railroad Properties, Inc. (WRPI)," <utahrails.net/up/wrpi.php>.

"Weyerhaeuser Is Buying Plum Creek for $8.4B to Form Timber Giant," *Seattle Times,* November 9, 2015.

"What Price Railroad Safety?" *Baseline,* <www.baselinemag.com/c/a/Projects-Management/What-Price-Railroad-Safety>.

"What the Merger Taught BN About Its Employees," *Railway Age,* July 14, 1975.

Wiedrich, Bob, "12,000 Jobs in Danger, Railroad Tells Workers," *Chicago Tribune,* June 26, 1987.

Wiedrich, Bob, 1989. "Power-by-the-Hour: A Rail Success Story," *Chicago Tribune,* April 16, 1989.

Wiedrich, Bob, "Railroad Women Write a New Saga," *Chicago Tribune,*

Wiedrick, Bob, "She's a Railroader—Simple as That," *Chicago Tribune,* re-published in the *Alliance Times-Herald,* March 5, 1977.

"Will Crews Really Benefit from UTU's Crew Consist Fight?" *Railway Age,* September 1991.

"Will a Takeover Derail Burlington Northern's Makeover?" *Business Week,* August 3, 1987.

Will, George F., "China Has Seen the Future, and It Is Coal," *Washington Post,* December 30, 2010.

Williams, Winston, "Burlington Road Limps Faster," *The New York Times,* February 12, 1978.

Wilner, Frank N., "Coal Shippers in Revolt," *Railway Age,* March 1999.

Wilner, Frank N., "STB Expert: Consider PTC's Business Benefits," *Railway Age,* November 2008.

Wilner, Frank N., *Understanding the Railway Labor Act,* Omaha: Simmons-Boardman Books, Inc., 2009.

Wilner, Frank N., "When You Get a Good Deal, Take It," *Railway Age,* July 28, 2014.

"With BN Unit Grain Trains, Rates Reduced 5-15% from Single Car Rates," *Traffic World,* August 24, 1981.

Withers, Paul K., "Oakway SD60s," *Diesel Era,* vol. 7, no. 4.

Wong, Brad, "Transportation Officials Seek Solution to Bottlenecks on Rails," *Seattle Post-Intelligencer,* April 18, 2005.

Wood, Charles R. 1968. *The Northern Pacific: Main Street of the Northwest."* New York: Bonanza Books.

Wood, Charles and Dorothy. 1974. *Spokane, Portland and Seattle Railway.* Seattle: Superior Publishing Company.

Wood, Charles, and Dorothy, 1978. *The Great Northern Railway: A Pictorial Study by Charles and Dorothy Wood.*

"Working: Maintainer Puts Training to Work," *BN News,* January 1983.

"Working the Line," *BN News,* May/June 1985.

"Working Women: The Challenges of the Workplace," *BN News,* November 1985.

Woxland, M. O., "New Facilities for Increased Traffic at Alliance," American Railway Engineering Association, Bulletin 678.

Wright, Robert A. "The Way West Looks Bright for Merged Railway," *The New York Times,* March 25, 1973.

"WRPI Buys into BN Coal Line," *Railway Age,* February 1987.

Wyer, Dick and Co., *Burlington—Great Northern—Northern Pacific—SS&S Consolidation Study,* Study I, II, III, VI, X, X-L, X-F and XI, Common Points, Duplicate Lines, Car Load

Freight—Shortest or Most Economical Joint Routes, General Repair Facilities—Diesel Locomotives, General Repair Facilities—Freight Train Cars.

"Wyoming Coal Line Expansion," *Trains,* November 2008.

Wyoming Coal Production, 1969–2015. <wyomingmining.org>.

Yenne, Bill. 1991. *A History of the Burlington Northern.* New York: Bonanza Books.

Young, David, "How Do Our Commuter Lines Rate?" *Chicago Tribune Magazine,* January 11, 1981.

Zarembski, Allan M., "Effect of Material Quality on Ballast Life," *Railway Track and Structures,* March 1989.

Zarembski, Allan M., "Tracking R&D: Field Welding Rail," *Railway Track and Structures,* June 1987.

Zarembski, Allan M., "Track Replacement Needs as a Function of Traffic Densities," *Railway Track and Structures,* May 1990.

"Zestful, Zealous Don Zeiss Zooms in on Problems as Alliance Project Construction Director," *BN News,* December 1978.

Zeutschel, D. Larry, "Mountain Country Regional," *Pacific RailNews,* February 1991.

INDEX

page numbers in italic indicate illustrations